CW00747464

JESUS

According to the Earliest Witness

JAMES M.
ROBINSON

FORTRESS PRESS
MINNEAPOLIS

JESUS
According to the Earliest Witness

Copyright © 2007 Fortress Press; an imprint of Augsburg Fortress. All rights reserved. Except for brief quotations in critical articles or reviews, no part of this book may be reproduced in any manner without prior written permission from the publisher. For more information visit: www.augsburgfortress.org/copyrights or write to: Permissions, Augsburg Fortress, Box 1209, Minneapolis, MN 55440-1209.

Cover design by James Korsmo

Library of Congress Cataloging-in-Publication Data

Robinson, James McConkey, 1924-
Jesus : according to the earliest witness / James M. Robinson.
    p. cm.
    Includes bibliographical references and index.
    ISBN 978-0-8006-3862-7 (pbk. : alk. paper)
  1. Jesus Christ—History of doctrines—Early church, ca. 30-600. 2. Q hypothesis (Synoptics criticism) I. Title.

BT198.R56 2007
232.9'08—dc22   2006100705

The paper used in this publication meets the minimum requirements for American National Standard for Information Sciences—Permanence of Paper for Printed Library Materials, ANSI Z329.48–1984.

Manufactured in the U.S.A.

11   10   09   08   07   1   2   3   4   5   6   7   8   9   10

CONTENTS

ACKNOWLEDGMENTS

Chapters 1–2 and 4–11 are published with the permission and kind cooperation of Peeters Press, and drawn from *James M. Robinson, The Sayings Gospel Q,* cd. Christoph Heil and Joseph Verheyden (Leuven: Peeters, 2005). Chapter 3 first appeared in *The Princeton Seminary Bulletin,* n. s. 18/2 (1997): 135-51.

Chapter 1 first appeared in *The Sayings Source Q and the Historical Jesus,* pp. 27-52. Edited by A. Lindemann. Bibliotheca Ephemeridum Theologicarum Lovaniensium 158. Leuven: Leuven University Press and Peeters, 2001. Reprinted in *The Sayings Gospel Q: Collected Essays,* 663-88.

Chapter 2 first appeared in *Journal of Biblical Literature* 101 (1982): 5-37. Reprinted in *The Sayings Gospel Q: Collected Essays,* 131-67.

Chapter 3 first appeared in "The Real Jesus of the Sayings Gospel Q." *Princeton Seminary Bulletin,* n.s. 18 / 2 (1997): 135-51. In *The Sayings Gospel Q: Collected Essays,* 519-34, the German translation is used: "Der wahre Jesus. Der historische Jesus im Spruchevangelium Q." In *Protokolle zur Bibel* (Salzburg) 6 (1997): 1-14. Reprint with footnotes, *Zeitschrift für Neues Testament* 1 (1998): 17-26.

Chapter 4 first appeared in *Encountering Jesus: A Debate on Christology,* pp. 111-22. Edited by Stephen T. Davis. Atlanta: John Knox, 1988. Revised reprint in *Images of the Feminine in Gnosticism,* pp. 113-27. Edited by Karen King. Studies in Antiquity and Christianity. Philadelphia: Fortress, 1988. Reprinted in *The Sayings Gospel Q: Collected Essays,* 259-73.

Chapter 5 first appeared in *Tradition und Translation: Zum Problem der interkulturellen Übersetzbarkeit religiöser Phänomene—Festschrift für Casten Colpe zum 65. Geburtstag,* pp. 247-65. Edited by Christoph Elsas et al. Berlin and New York: Walter de Gruyter, 1994. Reprinted in *The Sayings Gospel Q: Collected Essays,* 405-25.

Chapter 6 first appeared in *Early Christian Voices: In Texts, Traditions and Symbols. Essays in Honor of François Bovan,* pp. 25-43. Edited by David H. Warren, Ann Graham Brock, and David W. Pao. Biblical Interpretation Series 66. Leiden and Boston: E.J. Brill, 2003. Reprinted in *The Sayings Gospel Q: Collected Essays,* 689-709.

Chapter 7 first appeared in *Profiles of Jesus,* pp. 15-17. Edited by Roy W. Hoover. Santa Rosa, Calif.: Polebridge, 2002. Reprinted in *The Sayings Gospel Q: Collected Essays,* 887-89.

Chapter 8 first appeared in *The Gospel Behind the Gospels: Current Studies on Q,* pp. 259-74. Edited by Ronald A. Piper. Supplements to *Novum Testamentum* 75. Leiden, New York, Cologne: E.J. Brill, 1995. Reprinted in *The Sayings Gospel Q: Collected Essays,* 449-63.

Chapter 9 first appeared in *Jesus Then and Now: Images of Jesus in History and Christology,* pp. 7-25. Edited by Marvin Meyer and Charles Hughes. Harrisburg, Penn.: Trinity Press International, 2001. Reprinted in *The Sayings Gospel Q: Collected Essays,* 645-62.

Chapter 10 first appeared in *The Future of Early Christianity: Essays in Honor of Helmut Koester,* pp. 173-94. Edited by Birger A. Pearson. Minneapolis: Fortress, 1991. Reprinted in *The Sayings Gospel Q: Collected Essays,* 285-307.

Chapter 11 first appeared in *The Craft of Religious Studies,* pp. 117-50. Edited by Jon R. Stone. London: Macmillan, and New York: St. Martin's, 1998. Paperback reprint: New York: Palgrave, 2000. Reprinted in *The Sayings Gospel Q: Collected Essays,* 3-34.

INTRODUCTION

The earliest witness to Jesus is not a person whose name we could name, but rather a collection of his sayings that we can reconstruct: The Sayings Gospel Q. This source contains the most important sayings that go back to Jesus himself, and hence is our primary source of information about what he was trying to say, and to do. If you really want to know about Jesus, this is the first place for you to turn.

The Sayings Gospel Q is a collection of Jesus' sayings brought together within what we might call the Jewish-Christian branch of Christianity before it disappeared from the pages of history. Fortunately for us, by that point the collection had already been incorporated into the Gentile-Christian church's New Testament, an ecumenical gesture of decisive importance. Let me explain how this happened.

Around 70 C.E., Jewish Christians were using a collection of Jesus' sayings as their "Gospel," whereas Mark had already been published among Gentile Christians as their "Gospel." Later in the first century, Matthew and Luke were composed as efforts to integrate these two "Gospels" and, in effect, the perspectives of these two Christianities, Matthew representing a more Jewish-Christian outlook, Luke that of a Gentile-Christian church at the turn of the second century.

This is how scholars have come to understand why Matthew, Mark, and Luke are, over against John, so very similar in what they present. Matthew and Luke had the same two sources, the Gentile-Christian Gospel Mark and the Jewish-Christian sayings source. Since the latter lacked a name, scholars at first referred to it simply as the second "source": in German, *Quelle*. The first letter of *Quelle,* Q, became the nickname of this source, to which we refer today as the Sayings Gospel Q in order to distinguish it from the Narrative Gospels Matthew, Mark, Luke, and John. (For further details see "The Critical Edition of Q and the Study of Jesus," chapter 1.)

A generation ago, I organized an international team of scholars to reconstruct Q as best we could, word for word.[1] My English translation is reprinted here as an appendix so that you can read it for yourself. It is the oldest collection of Jesus' sayings that we have. Indeed, most of what we know about Jesus is found in these sayings.

Since Luke usually (though not always) follows Q's order, we have adopted the habit of using Lukan chapter and verse numbers to cite Q. Hence, for example, "Q 6:22-23" refers to the Q verses used in Luke 6:22-23 (and in the parallel verses in Matthew 5:11-12).

Jesus According to the Earliest Witness contains essays that I wrote during the actual work of reconstructing Q. I sought, year after year, to move behind the glorious picture of Christ with which we are most familiar from the Narrative Gospels of the New Testament to get back to the undomesticated, down-to-earth Jesus hidden behind that halo. The results are impressive—and surprising. If you are accustomed to the New Testament Gospels, you probably don't even realize what you have been missing until you catch sight of Jesus as he really was: what we might in modern terms call a pure idealist, a fully committed radical, a very profound person. He spoke for God straight out, and called on you to hearken as if your life depended on it. To readers steeped in the traditions of the church and its New Testament, I ask: please don't retreat behind doctrines about Jesus—but do let him get to you!

Why is it that we are so ignorant about Jesus? Actually, when you think about it, the gap in our knowledge of him is made painfully clear by the Apostles' Creed, which many of us have learned by heart. It begins with what was done *for* Jesus, "conceived by the Holy Spirit, born of the Virgin Mary," and then skips to what was done *against* Jesus, "suffered under Pontius Pilate, was crucified, died, and buried." But what is skipped in the middle is what was done *by* Jesus—as if that were not important enough to include in what we believe about Jesus! Did Jesus do or say nothing worth believing between Bethlehem and Golgotha? Yes, he most surely did! And that is what I want to lay out in this book of essays.

---

1. *The Critical Edition of Q: Synopsis including the Gospels of Matthew and Luke, Mark and Thomas with English, German, and French Translations of Q and Thomas,* eds. James M. Robinson, Paul Hoffmann, and John S. Kloppenborg (Minneapolis, Minn.: Fortress, and Leuven: Peeters, 2000). See also the abbreviated edition, *The Sayings Gospel Q in Greek and English with Parallels from the Gospels of Mark and Thomas,* eds. James M. Robinson, Paul Hoffmann, and John S. Kloppenborg (Contributions to Biblical Exegesis & Theology 30; Leuven, Paris, Sterling Va.: Peeters, 2001 and Minneapolis, Minn.: Fortress, 2002). The appendix in the present volume contains only the English translation of Q, which was published separately as *The Sayings of Jesus: The Sayings Gospel Q in English* (Facets series; Minneapolis, Minn.: Fortress, 2001).

To be sure, all Jesus was trying to say and do in Galilee was cut short by his utterly horrible death in Jerusalem. The twelve disciples must with a shock have realized that his call on them to trust in an ever-loving, caring God was a hope far too good to be true. In fact, they did run for their lives when Jesus was arrested, as if it were all over.

But then they ran into Jesus again! The two witnesses to the risen Jesus who actually wrote about what they saw described his appearance as a light shining like the sun (Phil. 3:21; Rev. 1:13-16) There followed many Easter stories with which we are more familiar: a gardener outside the empty tomb; a tourist on the way to Emmaus; a stranger at dawn by the Sea of Galilee advising fishermen where to throw their nets; an apparition suddenly showing up in a locked room; a person with a wounded body pointing to the wounds in his side and hands; a teacher eating and conversing for forty days with the disciples. These stories served as the antidote for emerging Gnostic texts, where Jesus appeared as a disembodied spirit. (I explore this sequence, and what it means for us, in "Jesus from Easter to Valentinus [or to the Apostles' Creed]," chapter 2.)

But the real miracle of Easter is what Jesus resumed saying. Just consider where things had ended up, with Jesus hanging naked, dead on the cross. The disciples had every reason to be utterly disillusioned about all the wonderful things Jesus had assured them about being surrounded by a tenderly loving God: "even the hairs of your head are all numbered; do not be afraid—you are worth more than many sparrows" (Q 12:7). Put bluntly: All that Jesus had said was more than cancelled out by Jesus' anguished cry at death: "My God, my God, why have you abandoned me?" (Mark 15:34). But then the real miracle of Easter happened: What Jesus had said, impossible though it was, disproven though it had been, began to be said anew, again and again, by those utterly disillusioned disciples who had given up and gone back to fishing. Through them, Jesus continued to speak, incredible though it was. The resurrected Christ was not a ghost, not a disembodied spirit, not a myth like the dying-and-rising gods with which the ancient world was cluttered. He rose as the Word, who was with God, who was God (John 1:1).

Christianity was founded by Jesus rising into his Word, which his disciples experienced anew and launched into proclaiming in his name. (This is why their names are not mentioned in Q—the message is not what they have to say, but what Jesus has to say!) They attested Jesus' resurrection not just as witnesses to his appearances, but as auditors to his sayings. His words were experienced anew, not as melancholy recollections of the failed dream of a noble, but terribly naïve person, but rather as his still valid trust in the heavenly Father, who rules not just in heaven, but also on earth. As a result, his words, his sayings, were remembered, updated, translated, collected into smaller and larger clusters, and finally written down to become the Sayings Gospel Q, the Sermon on the Mount, and eventually the sayings material in the New Testament Gospels. That message, put into practice in Christian soup kitchens, orphanages, and safe houses throughout the ancient world, was the power of the resurrection that ultimately converted the Roman Empire. (See "The Real Jesus of the Sayings Gospel Q," chapter 3.)

The sayings of Jesus, rescued for the church in the Sayings Gospel Q, reveal the earliest stages of the effort to find for him adequate titles. We are familiar with the Christological titles that appear, already full-grown, in the Pauline letters written in the fifties: Jesus Christ the Lord, Son of God. It is easy to assume they had always been there, from the time of Jesus himself. But when one turns to the less-doctrinal Galilean followers of Jesus who reported his sayings, one finds only the beginnings of those titles. For these early followers, the issue was not which titles you might accord him, but what you do with what he told you to do. After all, the house built on bedrock consists of "everyone hearing my sayings and acting on them" (Q 6:47-48). For these early followers, Jesus' name was simply "Jesus of Nazara," the old spelling of Nazareth still attested in the Sayings Gospel (Q 4:16).

The term *Lord* occurs frequently in Q. This was used in the Old Testament to refer to God and, of course, Jesus used it in this sense to refer to God (Q 4:8, 12; 10:2, 21; 13:35). But this same Greek word is used in a purely human, secular sense, for example in parables, to mean no more than a human master, a slave owner (Q 12:42-46; 14:21; 16:13; 19:15-20). It was also used of a teacher (Q 6:40, 46; 7:6; 9:59), and as a form of address to a person one looked up to, such as "Sir" or "Master," like the archaic form of address, "Milord" (Q 13:25). Only when the Old Testament use of *Lord* for God was carried over to Jesus did *Lord* become a Christological title. This is common in Paul, but not in Q. Paul was in this sense further down the path that led to the later church's Christology than was the Sayings Gospel Q.

The term *Son of God* occurs in Q, but there it is not introduced as a Christological title but rather as a name for all the disciples of Jesus who, like God, cared even for their enemies. "Love your enemies and pray for those persecuting you, so that you may become sons of your Father, for he raises his sun on bad and good and rains on the just and unjust" (Q 6:22-23). Jesus was of course one of these children of God, but at first that term was not a Christological title reserved for him, but referred to all those in his movement. It was probably only in the subsequent effort to persuade the disciples of John the Baptist to become disciples of Jesus that the invidious point was scored: "No one knows the Son except the

Father, nor does anyone know the Father except the Son, and to whomever the Son chooses to reveal him" (Q 10:22).

A Jewish term for God acting on earth is used in Q: God's *Wisdom,* which has been sending from time immemorial prophets to the chosen people. *Wisdom,* in Greek *Sophia,* is a feminine noun in Hebrew and Greek, and so indicates the feminine dimension of God. But just as she had sent the prophets of the Old Testament (Q 11:49-51; 13:34-35), just so she not only sent Jesus, but also John the Baptist. "Wisdom was vindicated by her children" (Q 7:35). The exclusive associations we have for the Christological titles were not present at the beginning. (See "Very Goddess and Very Man," chapter 4.)

The idiom "son of man" was not originally a title either. It was just a Hebrew idiom meaning a human individual, much as "daughters of Jerusalem" simply meant female inhabitants of Jerusalem, and "son of peace" just meant someone who responded positively to Jesus knocking at the door with the greeting, "Peace," to ask for bed and breakfast. Jesus used the idiom of himself in all modesty, to contrast foxes and birds who have a place to stay with him a human, a "son of man," with no place to lay his head (Q 9:58). In the book of Daniel there is a vision of a series of beastly empires, symbolized by a series of beasts as rulers, followed then by a humane Jewish empire, symbolized by a human, a "son of man," as ruler. Only when the idea began to emerge among Jesus' followers that Jesus would return as a star witness at the day of judgment did that text from Daniel get picked up and applied to Jesus, and only then did the idiom gradually became a Christological title. (See "The Son of Man in the Sayings Gospel Q," chapter 5.)

Nowhere in the Sayings Gospel Q is Jesus referred to as Messiah, "Christ." As a matter of fact, it is a bit inappropriate to refer to the Jews who produced this Sayings Gospel as "Christians," since that name emerged not in Galilee, but in Antioch in the Gentile-Christian church of Barnabas and Paul (Acts 11:26). Similarly, other dimensions associated with later faith in Jesus as the Messiah are missing: neither is Bethlehem mentioned, where David was born and hence his successor is to be born, nor is the holy family, much less the genealogies that trace Jesus back to the patriarchs.

Other key terms that we all too automatically associate with the earliest church are also only beginning to develop. None of the twelve apostles are mentioned by name. Though the terms *apostles* and *the twelve* are missing, one can see this development beginning, just as in the case of the Christological titles. The noun *apostle* does not occur, but the participial form does occur, in referring to those "sent" (*apestalmenous*) by God (Q 13:34). And though "the twelve" are not mentioned as such, Q concludes with Jesus' followers sitting on thrones judging the twelve tribes of Israel (Q 22:30). Here it is of course only a step to the inference that there must of course have been twelve disciples, one for each tribe.

In the earliest phase, Jesus did not point toward himself (as the Gospel of John has presented him), but to God acting in him to intervening, "reigning" in human lives (too woodenly translated "the kingdom of God"). When he healed the sick, it was because God reigning had reached that house (Q 7:9). When he cast out demons, it was "by the finger of God," for "God's reign has come upon you" (Q 11:20). (See "Jesus' Theology in the Sayings Gospel Q," chapter 6.)

Jesus came to grips with the basic intentions of people. He addressed them personally, as to what kind of people they were. He called on them. He did not just teach them ideas. His message was simple, for he wanted to cut straight through to the point: trust God to look out for you by providing people who will care for you, and listen to him when he calls on you to provide for them. God is someone you can trust, so give it a try. (See "What Jesus Had to Say," chapter 7.)

Some talk today about following in the footsteps of Jesus. But we often talk the talk more than we walk the walk. At one time, I looked around among the Christian confessions and denominations for any that made a serious effort to implement in modern terms the lifestyle of Jesus in Galilee, but I was disappointed—until I discovered the liberation theologians of South America. (See "The Jesus of Q as Liberation Theologian," chapter 8.)

Throughout half a century of scholarship I have been concerned with the problem of getting back to the historical Jesus. My book of 1959, *A New Quest of the Historical Jesus,*[2] reported excitedly about the then-new trend to return to studying the historical Jesus, after the major German effort between the two World Wars to rule that question both illegitimate and impossible. (See "The Image of Jesus in Q," chapter 9.) A few years later, in an Introduction to the reprint of Albert Schweitzer's *Quest of the Historical Jesus* I showed how Schweitzer had slanted his presentation of the quest of the historical Jesus throughout the nineteenth century in an inappropriate way, so as to support his own view of Jesus as an impossible apocalypticist.[3] Then a generation of work oriented to the Nag Ham-

2. James M. Robinson, *A New Quest of the Historical Jesus* (Studies in Biblical Theology 25; London: SCM, 1959; Naperville, Ill: Allenson, 1959).
3. James M. Robinson, "Introduction" to *The Quest of the Historical Jesus* by Albert Schweitzer (New York: Macmillan, 1968), xi-xxxiii, slightly revised reprint "Albert Schweitzer's Quest of the Historical Jesus Today," in *A New Quest of the Historical Jesus and Other Essays* (Philadelphia: Fortress Press, 1983), p. 172-95.

madi Codices resulted in a focus on the most important tractate among those writings, *The Gospel of Thomas.* It is a Sayings Gospel consisting of 114 sayings ascribed to Jesus that lack any such apocalypticism.[4] This work led me to another major project, reconstructing the other Sayings Gospel, Q, where an early, pre-apocalyptic layer of Jesus traditions had also been identified. (See "The Q Trajectory: Between John and Matthew via Jesus," chapter 10.)

Although I had begun work on Q a generation earlier, my work on the Nag Hammadi Codices delayed the publication of *The Critical Edition of Q* until 2000. That publication provided the launching pad for a popularizing book on Jesus, *The Gospel of Jesus: In Search of the Original Good News,* which I published in 2005.[5] Thus, all along this rather variegated academic career, I have in one way or the other retained a focus on Jesus, as is evident in the "Theological Autobiography" I wrote a decade ago (and include here as chapter 11).

Ten of the essays that follow have been published in a much more exhaustive volume of my collected essays on Q (937 pages long!).[6] For both volumes I wish to acknowledge with appreciation the work of the Peeters volume editors, Christoph Heil and Joseph Verheyden, with whom I worked closely in editing each essay.

---

4. Stephen J. Patterson and James M. Robinson, *The Fifth Gospel: The Gospel of Thomas Comes of Age,* with a New English Translation by Hans-Gebhard Bethge et al. (Harrisburg, Pa.: Trinity Press International, 1998).

5. James M. Robinson, *The Gospel of Jesus: In Search of the Original Good News* (San Francisco: HarperSanFrancisco, 2005).

6. James M. Robinson, *The Sayings Gospel Q: Collected Essays* (Leuven: Peeters, 2005).

CHAPTER 1

The Critical Edition of Q and the Study of Jesus

The Critical Edition of Q[1] provides a written text of sayings ascribed to Jesus. At least in the more archaic collections it contains, it is generally agreed to provide the oldest surviving layer of material brought together by Jesus' disciples[2]. Hence, "Q is certainly the most important source for reconstructing the teaching of Jesus"[3].

Prior to the availability of *The Critical Edition of Q*, Q usually functioned only as a source, for individual sayings and discourses ascribed in Q to Jesus. After all, Q = *Quelle*. It was rarely treated as a text, much less a Gospel, in its own right, which, like the canonical Gospels, would inevitably have its own way of shaping the material it took over from the tradition[4]. Furthermore the Q people, that is to say, the few who still identified themselves with Jesus in Galilee[5], have largely been lost from

1. *The Critical Edition of Q. Synopsis including the Gospels of Matthew and Luke, Mark and Thomas with English, German, and French Translations of Q and Thomas*, eds. J.M. ROBINSON, P. HOFFMANN, and J.S. KLOPPENBORG, Leuven, Peeters, and Minneapolis, Fortress, 2000.
2. Skepticism has often been expressed as to there being a written Greek first edition of Q containing the six discourses identified as such a work by J.S. KLOPPENBORG, *The Formation of Q. Trajectories in Ancient Wisdom Collections* (Studies in Antiquity and Christianity), Philadelphia, Fortress, 1987, reprinted Harrisburg, PA, Trinity Press International, 2000, pp. 171-245. But it has frequently been overlooked that these discourses are in any case usually ascribed to the archaic pre-Q layer. I drew attention to this convergence of outcome in spite of quite varying points of departure in the cases of Dieter Lührmann, Siegfried Schulz, Dieter Zeller, Ronald A. Piper, and Hans Dieter Betz, in J.M. ROBINSON, *The Q Trajectory. Between John and Matthew via Jesus*, in B.A. PEARSON (ed.), *The Future of Early Christianity*. FS H. Koester, Minneapolis, Fortress Press, 1991, pp. 173-194, esp. 185-189 [in *The Sayings Gospel Q*, pp. 285-307, especially pp. 297-302], to which I then added Migaku SATO, in J.M. ROBINSON, *Die Logienquelle. Weisheit oder Prophetie? Anfragen an Migaku Sato, Q und Prophetie*, in *EvTh* 53 (1993) 367-389, p. 385 [in *The Sayings Gospel Q*, pp. 349-74, esp. 370], while Kloppenborg himself, in J.S. KLOPPENBORG, *The Sayings Gospel Q. Literary and Stratigraphic Problems*, in R. URO (ed.), *Symbols and Strata. Essays on the Sayings Gospel Q* (Publications of the Finnish Exegetical Society, 65), Helsinki and Göttingen, Finnish Exegetical Society and Vandenhoeck & Ruprecht, 1996, pp. 1-66, esp. 52, added the name of Heinz Schürmann to this list (see also the itemization of the six collections in question, p. 48).
3. G. THEIßEN and A. MERZ, *Der historische Jesus. Ein Lehrbuch*, Göttingen, Vandenhoeck & Ruprecht, 1996, p. 45: "Q ist zweifellos die wichtigste Quelle zur Rekonstruktion der Lehre Jesu". ET: *The Historical Jesus. A Comprehensive Guide*, Minneapolis, Fortress Press, 1998, p. 29.
4. A. KIRK, *The Composition of the Sayings Source. Genre, Synchrony, & Wisdom Redaction in Q* (NTSup, 91), Leiden, Boston, and Köln, E. J. Brill, 1998.
5. The location of the Q movement remains quite conjectural. The hypothesis of a Galilean location, which could have also involved a Syrian dispersion due to the war with

sight, as has always been the case since Luke almost completely bypassed Galilee in Acts, e. g. Acts 1,9: "You shall be my witnesses in Jerusalem and in all Judea and Samaria and to the end of the earth". A Galilean church is only mentioned once in passing, in a generalized statement (Acts 9,21): "So the church throughout all Judea and Galilee and Samaria had peace and was built up". Thus *The Critical Edition of Q* renders much more accessible not only the text of Q itself, but also the pre-Q collections, the *Sitz im Leben* of the Q materials, and sayings going back to Jesus.

In more practical terms, a facile offhanded dismissal of Q as a mere hypothesis is harder to carry off with *The Critical Text of Q* open on the desk. Much excitement has hence been engendered, pro and con, during the current wave of Q research working to produce the critical text. The present Colloquium Biblicum Lovaniense on "The Sayings Source Q and the Historical Jesus" brings this development to its culmination, with the actual publication of the critical text on this occasion.

1. NARRATIVE GOSPELS VS. SAYINGS GOSPELS

The canonical Gospels are all Narrative Gospels, whereas Q, in this respect more like *The Gospel of Thomas*, is largely a Sayings Gospel. One reason for preferring Narrative Gospels over Sayings Gospels might well be that one would expect Narrative Gospels to portray what actually went on during Jesus' "public ministry", in a way that a Sayings Gospel never could. But in fact that is hardly the case. The quest of the historical Jesus had indeed depended primarily on Mark to trace the outward stages of Jesus' "public ministry" and the inward stages of his emerging "Messianic self-consciousness". But in 1901 William Wrede showed that

---

Rome, is really based to a large extent on the absence from Q of traits of polity and christology associated with the Jerusalem church. See my brief comments, in J.M. ROBINSON, *Judaism, Hellenism, Christianity. Jesus' Followers in Galilee until 70 C.E.*, in V. MATHIEU (ed.), *Ebraismo Ellenismo Christianesimo* (Archivio di Filosofia, 53, 1), Padova, Cedam, 1985, pp. 241-50, esp. 244 [in *The Sayings Gospel Q*, pp. 193-202, esp. 196]:

> The Jesus movement had its center apparently in Galilee, to judge by the specific place names where this tradition says it carried on a mission, Chorazin, Bethsaida, and Capernaum (Q 10:13-15), though it should not be overlooked that this demographic information includes the point that these locations rejected the message. Q mentions neither James nor Peter (both of whom had left Galilee), nor any of the twelve, nor the concept of the twelve, nor that of apostles …, nor the names of any disciples.

For the converse hypothesis, see M. FRENSCHKOWSKI, *Galiläa oder Jerusalem? Die topographischen und politischen Hintergründe der Logienquelle*, in A. LINDEMANN (ed.), *The Sayings Source Q and the Historical Jesus* (BETL, 158), Leuven, University Press - Peeters, 2001, pp. 535-559. He advocates Jerusalem and the postulated emigration to Pella, where he locates the final redaction of Q.

Jesus' public ministry was built on Mark's theory of the "Messianic secret", rather than on recollections of Jesus' own conduct and intention[6].

To be sure, by the end of the Nineteenth Century the Synoptic Gospels, with their one-year "public ministry", had clearly won out over the Gospel of John, with its three-year "public ministry". But the last-ditch defenders of the Johannine narration took the offensive, by pointing to the problems in the Synoptic narration. This then provided the opening for Karl Ludwig Schmidt's devastating dismantling of the Synoptic narration, in his Berlin *Habilitationsschrift* of 1917:

> Thus Nagl, who holds the Gospel of John to be an authentic continuous report, formulates, in *Katholik* 1900, 494, the following judgment about the Synoptics:

> But the gaps that have been noted cannot present anything so especially noticeable, for the Evangelists pursue no purely historical interest, and on the other hand show themselves to be aware of the fragmentariness of their report. For what is the purpose of such general phrases as Lk 4,15; Mk 1,39; Lk 8,1 and 9,6, cf. Mt 4,23 and 9,35, other than to indicate gaps? Luke seems to want to structure his report precisely by means of these gap-fillers.

> Here the Catholic scholar has recognized correctly the character of the framework of the history of Jesus, to the extent it has to do with the Synoptics, in a way that has not always taken place among Protestant scholars[7].

Schmidt's own point of departure was the following:

> What is needed is a detailed literary criticism of the chronological and topographical assertions of the Gospels, which constitute the framework of the history of Jesus[8].

---

6. W. WREDE, *Das Messiasgeheimnis in den Evangelien*, Göttingen, Vandenhoeck & Ruprecht, 1901. ET: *The Messianic Secret*, Cambridge and London, T. and T. Clark, 1971.

7. K. L. SCHMIDT, *Der Rahmen der Geschichte Jesu,* Berlin, Trowitzsch, 1919, pp. 7-8: So formuliert Nagl im Katholik 1900, 494, der das Joh Ev für einen authentischen fortlaufenden Bericht hält, folgendes Urteil über die Synoptiker: "Die bemerkten Lücken aber können darum nicht so besonders Auffälliges haben, weil die Evangelisten kein rein historisches Interesse verfolgen und sich andererseits der Lückenhaftigkeit ihres Berichtes bewußt zeigen. Denn was sollen allgemeine Phrasen wie Lk 4,15, Mk 1,39, Lk 8,1 und 9,6, vgl. Mt 4,23 und 9,35 anderes als Lücken anzeigen? Lk scheint durch diese Lückenbüßer seinen Bericht geradezu gliedern zu wollen." Hier hat der katholische Forscher den Charakter des Rahmens der Geschichte Jesu, soweit es sich um die Synoptiker handelt, in einer Weise richtig erkannt, wie das unter protestantischen Gelehrten nicht immer geschehen ist.

8. SCHMIDT, *Rahmen* (n. 7), 13: Was not tut, ist eine eingehende Literarkritik der chronologischen und topographischen Angaben der Evv, die den Rahmen der Geschichte Jesu ausmachen.

The present investigation will show that Mark contains the oldest outline of the history of Jesus, but that this outline is just as much a schematism as is that of the Gospel of John, and it is to be shown wherein the
nature of this schematism consists[9].

Schmidt carried through this investigation pericope by pericope, and
concluded his epoch-making book as follows:

The oldest outline of the history of Jesus is that of the Gospel of Mark. The
unevenness of the traditions that are present in it shows how the oldest
Jesus tradition looked: No continuous report, but a mass of individual stories, which on the whole are arranged according to topical points of view.
… And since the real itinerary of Jesus, for which the Christian community
from its very beginnings had no interest, has for us become irretrievably
lost, we can, if we want to arrange the stories of Jesus, only follow
Matthew, and even go beyond him, who often still clings all too much to
Mark. … But on the whole there is no life of Jesus in the sense of a devel-
oping life story, no chronological outline of the history of Jesus, but only
individual stories, pericopes, which are put into a framework[10].

The result is that the Markan narrative sequence, which is a major reason why the Narrative Gospels are preferred to the Sayings Gospels, is
itself not historical. "This destroyed the possibility of reading a development in the personality of Jesus from the sequence of pericopes"[11].

But Matthew and Luke for their part did not improve the Markan situation. Mt 8–9 rearranged the sequence of healings so as to provide an
example of each healing mentioned in Q 7,22, prior to that verse occurring in Mt 11,5[12]: "The blind regain their sight and the lame walk

---

9. SCHMIDT, *Rahmen* (n. 7), 17:
Die vorliegende Untersuchung wird zeigen, daß Mk den ältesten Aufriß der
Geschichte Jesu enthält, daß aber dieser Aufriß ein Schema ist genau so gut wie der
des Joh Ev, und es wird klarzulegen sein, worin die Art dieses Schemas besteht.
10. SCHMIDT, *Rahmen* (n. 7), 317:
Der älteste Aufriß der Geschichte Jesu ist der des Mk Ev. Die Unausgeglichenheit
der in ihm vorliegenden Traditionen zeigt, wie die älteste Jesusüberlieferung ausge-
sehen hat: kein fortlaufender Bericht, sondern eine Fülle von Einzelgeschichten, die
im ganzen nach sachlichen Gesichtspunkten geordnet sind. … Und da uns das wirk-
liche Itinerar Jesu, für das die christliche Gemeinde von ihren Anfängen an kein
Interesse gehabt hat, rettungslos verloren gegangen ist, können wir, wenn wir die
Jesusgeschichten ordnen wollen, uns nur dem Mt anschließen und müssen ihn, der
oft noch zu sehr an Mk klebt, sogar überbieten. … Aber im ganzen gibt es kein
Leben Jesu im Sinne einer sich entwickelnden Lebensgeschichte, keinen chronologischen Aufriß der Geschichte Jesu, sondern nur Einzelgeschichten, Perikopen, die
in ein Rahmenwerk gestellt sind.
11. THEIßEN and MERZ, *Der historische Jesus* (n. 3), 25:
Damit entfiel die Möglichkeit, eine Entwicklung der Persönlichkeit Jesu aus der
Reihenfolge der Perikopen herauszulesen.
ET: *The Historical Jesus* (n. 3), 6.
12. U. LUZ, *Die Wundergeschichten von Mt 8-9*, in G.F. HAWTHORNE and O. BETZ
(eds.), *Tradition and Interpretation in the New Testament: FS E. Earle Ellis*, Grand

around, the skin-diseased are cleansed and the deaf hear, and the dead are raised, and the poor are evangelized". In order to fill out this quota, Matthew created doublets to healings from Mark and Q: The healing of blind Bartimaeus (Mk 10,46-52 par. Mt 20,29-34) is duplicated in Mt 9,27-31, and the exorcism of the mute demoniac (Q 11,14-15 par. Mt 12,22-30) is duplicated in Mt 9,32-34, in both instances with minor alterations that make the redactional repetition less noticeable. Here one sees an Evangelist creating stories to fill out a theological need, in this case to produce an instance of every kind of healing that Q, based ultimately on Isaiah[13], had listed. Then in Mt 12–28 Matthew follows rather slavishly for the rest of his narrative the unhistorical Markan sequence. Similarly in the case of Luke, it is today recognized that his intention to present an "orderly account" (Lk 1,3) so as to provide "certainty" (Lk 1,4) has in view theological rather than historiographical accuracy.

Thus the preference for Narrative Gospels rather than Sayings Gospels seems to be no more than a preference for an unhistorical itinerary – a story but not history. It might nonetheless be preferable to have a lot of individual stories, even if not in historical sequence, rather than just a scattering of sayings. For Jesus presumably not only had something to say, but also had in view something to do. Yet it is not that Q presents Jesus only as a speaker of sayings. Rather it presents him as a person who does precisely the kinds of things the Narrative Gospels report: His rôle as exorcist is clear from the exorcism initiating the Beelzebul controversy (Q 11,14-15). His rôle as faith healer is clear from the healing of the centurion's boy (Q 7,1-10). Q launched the proof that Jesus was the "One to Come" that John had predicted, by calling on John's disciples to see and hear what Jesus was doing, whereupon Q provided the list (Q 7,22) that was so extensive that Matthew had difficulty documenting it (see above). It is indeed odd that it is a Sayings

Rapids, MI, Eerdmans, and Tübingen, J.C.B. Mohr (Paul Siebeck), 1987, pp. 149-165. U. Luz, *Fiktivität und Traditionstreue im Matthäusevangelium im Lichte griechischer Literatur*, in *ZNW* 84 (1993) 153-177.

13. H.-W. KUHN, *Jesus*, in L.H. SCHIFFMAN and J.C. VANDERKAM (eds.), *Encyclopaedia of the Dead Sea Scrolls*, Oxford, Oxford University Press, vol. 1, 2000, pp. 404-08, esp. 407:

> One of the sayings of Jesus about the immediacy of the end time, *Matthew* 11.5-6 (parallels *Luke* 7.22-23), now has a parallel in 4Q521; however, this Qumran text speaks in a traditional manner only about the future. In the text from the Sayings Source (Q) that can be extrapolated from *Matthew* and *Luke*, Jesus uses words from the *Book of Isaiah* (35.5-6, 29.18-19, 26.19, 61.1) to paint a picture of the future eschatological salvation, which he understands as being already present. ... The Qumran manuscript (4Q521) ... did not necessarily originate in the Qumran community. ... Behind Jesus' saying and behind 4Q521 there may well stand a common Jewish tradition that describes the time of salvation.

Gospel that lists, as its evidence as to who Jesus is, first his healings, before listing the Sermon. Furthermore, Q 10,13 reports that "mighty works" were performed in Chorazin and Bethsaida. And the Mission Instructions call on the disciples to heal the sick (Q 10,9), making clear that Jesus' healing power continued in them. Thus Jesus' rôle as exorcist and faith healer is as clear in Q as it is in the Narrative Gospels.

It is the Jesus of Q who also explained exorcisms and faith healings: It is God reigning. "But if it is by the finger of God that I cast out demons, then there has come upon you God's reign" (Q 11,20). "If you have faith like a mustard seed, you might say to this mulberry tree: Be uprooted and planted in the sea! And it would obey you. But on being asked when the kingdom of God is coming, he answered them: The kingdom of God is not coming visibly. Nor will one say: Look, here! or: There! For, look, the kingdom of God is within you" (Q 17,6.20-21). In the house on which God's peace rests, one is to "cure the sick there, and say to them: The kingdom of God has reached unto you" (Q 10,9). The disciples had such faith in Jesus' word that God is reigning, a message still being proclaimed in the Q movement, that they told the miraculous healing stories found in the Narrative Gospels, and indeed sometimes in incredibly miraculous language. For modern people, who have trouble understanding the point of such excessive healing stories, it is not enough to say that one does not take them literally. How then is one to take them? A responsible answer would be: Take them the way the Jesus of Q says to take them! When one thus recognizes the high value of Q in understanding such things in the Gospels as exorcisms and faith healings, as God's reign taking place, the relevance of Q for understanding Jesus' "public ministry" can hardly be over-estimated.

Prominent in the Narrative Gospels are not only stories presenting Jesus as exorcist and faith healer, but also dramatic scenes presenting him as providing food for the hungry. Yet it is especially in Q that the indispensable presupposition of such feedings, their theological point, is made clear. For Jesus explicitly says again and again that one can count on God to feed the hungry: In the Lord's Prayer, the petition "Let your reign come" is followed directly by what that means in the here and now: "Our day's bread give us today" (Q 11,2-3). Jesus promises people they can trust God for food: "What person of you, whose son asks for bread, will give him a stone? Or again when he asks for a fish, will give him a snake? So if you, though evil, know how to give good gifts to your children, by how much more will the Father from heaven give good things to those who ask him!" (Q 11,11-13) Just as God feeds the ravens, just so he feeds us: "Therefore I tell you, do not be anxious about your life, what you are to eat . . . . Consider the ravens: They neither sow nor reap nor gather into barns, and yet God feeds them. Are you not much better than the birds? ... So do not be anxious, saying: What are we to eat? Or: What are we to drink?... For all these the Gentiles seek; for your Father knows that you need them all. But seek his kingdom, and all these shall be granted to you" (Q 12,22b.24.29-31). And in the Mission Instructions, the worker is assured of receiving food: "And at that house remain, eating and drinking whatever they provide, for the worker is worthy of one's reward. Do not move around from house to house. And whatever town you enter and they take you in, eat what is set before you. And cure the sick there, and say to them: The kingdom of God has reached unto you" (Q 10,7-9). Thus, according to the Jesus of Q, food, just like the healings, is again and again what happens when God reigns. Jesus does not exemplify an ascetic way of life, admired though that was in antiquity, and exemplified by his mentor John the Baptist. Rather, he is both one who eats and one who shares food with others: "The son of humanity came, eating and drinking, and you say: Look! A glutton and drunkard! A chum of tax collectors and sinners!" (Q 7,34) It is easy to see how one would imagine him – or, as he would put it, God – feeding people by the thousands.

What of course are missing in Q are the miracle stories themselves (other than the one faith healing and the one exorcism already mentioned, which, however, are not presented, in form-critical terms, as miracle stories). Especially missing are the most dramatic nature miracles, like walking on water and feeding thousands from one person's supply of bread and fish. But it is precisely these excessive miracles that are not taken literally today. Yet if such incredible stories did not come from Jesus literally doing them, where did they come from? They came from such sayings as we find in Q, which continued to be believed and proclaimed in the primitive church!

But the reason why some people play down the importance of Q may lie elsewhere. Indeed, it may be the same today as it was when the canonizing took place: The kerygmatic development, via Mark's passion narrative and then the infancy narratives and resurrection appearances of Matthew and Luke, had completely replaced the sayings of Jesus and even the "public ministry" itself, already by the time of the Apostles' Creed in the Second Century CE. For one listens in vain to hear anything about the "public ministry" and the sayings of Jesus in what we all know by heart: "... conceived by the Holy Ghost, born of the Virgin Mary, suffered under Pontius Pilate, was crucified, dead, and buried; the

third day he rose again from the dead; he ascended into heaven . . .".
It was this credal development, excluding the "public ministry" and all
sayings of Jesus, which determined what was canonized, namely
Gospels culminating in Jesus' death and resurrection, which validated
Mark and John, even though they lacked birth narratives. The mutual
acceptance of Jewish and Gentile Christianity at the "ecumenical"
Jerusalem Council had long since broken down, with the successful
Gentile Christianity rejecting the unsuccessful Jewish Christianity as
heretical, in effect no longer Christian. Thus the exclusion of its oldest
Gospel from the canon was inevitable.

As the modern secularization and commercialization of Christmas and
Easter make clear to thinking Christians, what is at issue is not the trap-
pings, but the substance. Perhaps Q does have the substance of the
kerygma, if indeed that substance is more than angels singing carols and
moving stones, more than pie in the sky by-and-by. According to Q, the
substance is that, in spite of all appearances to the contrary, God is here,
acting for our good in our lives, taking care of us, and sending us out to
care for others, thereby giving our lives ultimate meaning.

Let me clarify the point by reference to a similar point Rudolf Bultmann
made on behalf of the kerygma, but which applies more directly to Q:

> It is often said, most of the time in criticism, that according to my inter-
> pretation of the kerygma Jesus has risen in the kerygma. I accept this
> proposition. It is entirely correct, assuming it is properly understood. It pre-
> supposes that the kerygma itself is an eschatological event, and it expresses
> the fact that Jesus is really present in the kerygma, that it is *his* word that
> involves the hearer in the kerygma. If that is the case, then all speculation
> concerning the modes of being of the risen Jesus, all the narratives of the
> empty tomb and all the Easter legends, whatever elements of historical fact
> they may contain, and as true as they may be in their symbolic form, are of
> no consequence. To believe in the Christ present in the kerygma is the
> meaning of the Easter faith[14].

14. R. BULTMANN, *Das Verhältnis der urchristlichen Christusbotschaft zum his-
torischen Jesus*, in *SHAW.PH*, Jg. 1960, Abh. 3, Heidelberg, Winter, 1960, 1962³, p. 27:
Mehrfach und meist als Kritik wird gesagt, daß nach meiner Interpretation des
Kerygmas Jesus ins Kerygma auferstanden sei. Ich akzeptiere diesen Satz. Er ist
völlig richtig, vorausgesetzt daß er richtig verstanden wird. Er setzt voraus, daß das
Kerygma selbst eschatologisches Geschehen ist; und er besagt, daß Jesus im
Kerygma wirklich gegenwärtig ist, daß es *sein* Wort ist, das den Hörer im Kerygma
trifft. Ist das der Fall, so werden alle Spekulationen über die Seinsweise des Aufer-
standenen, alle Erzählungen vom leeren Grabe und alle Osterlegenden, welche
Momente an historischen Fakten sie auch enthalten mögen, und so wahr sie in ihrem
symbolischen Gehalt sein mögen, gleichgültig. An den im Kerygma präsenten
Christus glauben, ist der Sinn des Osterglaubens.
ET: *The Primitive Christian Kerygma and the Historical Jesus*, in C.E. BRAATEN and
R.A. HARRISVILLE (eds.), *The Historical Jesus and the Kerygmatic Christ*, Nashville,
Abingdon, 1964, pp. 15-42, esp. 42.

The truly amazing thing about the Q people is that, in spite of it all, namely Jesus' horrible death, which was more than enough to cancel out all his reassurances about God as a loving Father caring for his people, they turned right around and proclaimed it all over again (just as Jesus had done after the horrible death of John), as what Jesus himself was still saying, as true as ever, in their proclamation in his name.

The Q people, in their central mission of proclaiming the sayings of Jesus, were practicing their faith in his resurrection, even though resurrection language is not theirs, but ours.

> It is not the death of the sage or his subsequent vindication that interests sapiential genres, but the sage's living presence in his or her words. Hence it is a bit misleading even to evoke the notion of "resurrection" in respect to Q, at least insofar as the term implies a narratible event having to do with the overcoming of an individual's death. The notion of resurrection is absent from Q not because Q already presupposes the resurrection and exaltation of Jesus to the right hand of God as a narratible event, but because this metaphor is fundamentally inappropriate to the genre and theology of Q[15].

In Q, the followers of Jesus used Jesus' language, which Paul did not have first hand at his disposal, and so he preferred the kerygmatic language in which his Christian experience took place. We, for our part, have traditionally used Paul's language. But our real task as interpreters is to get below the level of the diverging language to what was meant. Then it becomes clear that Paul's kerygmatic language cannot be true unless Jesus' kingdom language is true.

To this position, M. Frenschkowski comments:

> This solution has an ingenious touch. With one blow the Saying Source's kind of Easter faith, its hermeneutic, and ultimately also its "usability" in our own theological present, would be explained. Yet the proposed model seems to me too enlightenment-like, or at least too near to Gnosticism. ... Robinson and Kloppenborg do not explain at all historically the position of the Q document, but rather compare [it] meta-linguistically with a modern hermeneutical Easter theology[16].

---

15. J.S. KLOPPENBORG, *'Easter Faith' and the Sayings Gospel Q*, in *The Apocryphal Jesus and Christian Origins, Semeia* 49 (1990) 71-99.

16. M. FRENSCHKOWSKI, *Welche biographischen Kenntnisse von Jesus setzt die Logienquelle voraus? Beobachtungen zur Gattung von Q im Kontext antiker Spruchsammlungen*, in J.Ma. ASGEIRSSON, K. DE TROYER and M.W. MEYER (eds.), *From Quest to Q*. FS J.M. ROBINSON (BETL, 146), Leuven, University Press – Peeters, 2000, pp. 3-42, esp. 32-33:

> Diese Lösung hat einen genialischen touch. Mit einem Schlag wären die Art des Osterglaubens der Logienquelle, ihre Hermeneutik und letzlich auch ihre "Vertretbarkeit" in unserer eigenen theologischen Gegenwart geklärt. Dennoch scheint mir das vorgeschlagene Modell zu aufklärerisch, oder allenfalls zu gnosisnah. ... Robinson

It is of course the case that we are separated from the texts by the enlightenment, and that hence a hermeneutic for today cannot be simply a repetition of theirs. For the hermeneutical task today would be to state, in terms of the modern understanding of reality ("meta-linguistically"), what (if anything) their language has to say today to people that are not simply old-fashioned. It is no more "near to Gnosticism" than is the Gospel of John, in its appeal to the Paraclete to justify restating, in subsequent language that Jesus himself had not used, what Jesus actually had in substance to say. This is still the task of theology, to the extent that it both seeks a grounding in Jesus and seeks to be "usable".

2. THE REDACTION OF Q

The renewed study of Q, as a main center of attention in the second half of the twentieth century, has built primarily on Dieter Lührmann's Heidelberg *Habilitationsschrift* of 1968, *Die Redaktion der Logien-quelle*[17]. His thesis, put very briefly, is that Q is not just a neutral "collection" of Jesus' sayings, but consists of sayings drawn together by an editor, a "redactor", who had a particular point of view, which he imposed on the text: the deuteronomistic view of Israelite history[18]. This view had been developed during the Exile, to make sense of God permitting Jerusalem to fall and the temple to be destroyed: This disaster took place not because God was unfaithful to the covenant, but because Israel, constantly rejecting prophets whom God sent, was itself unfaithful, with the fall of Jerusalem being God's inevitable punishment. This canonical view of history was then reapplied by the Q people to the fall of Jerusalem and the destruction of the temple in 70 CE. "This generation", whose rejection of God's prophets now consisted in rejecting Jesus and his message as still proclaimed by the Q people, had brought God's patience to the breaking point, and hence it was upon "this generation" that the punishment inevitably would fall.

This deuteronomistic view of history is most apparent in a section of Q where Jesus quotes God's Wisdom in person, Sophia. This text is

und Kloppenborg erklären gar nicht historisch die Position des Q-Dokumentes, sondern vergleichen metasprachlich mit einer modernen hermeneutischen Ostertheologie.

17. D. LÜHRMANN, *Die Redaktion der Logienquelle* (WMANT, 33), Neukirchen-Vluyn, Neukirchener Verlag, 1969.

18. Lührmann built on the 1965 dissertation of his Heidelberg colleague, O.H. STECK, *Israel und das gewaltsame Geschick der Propheten. Untersuchungen zur Überlieferung des deuteronomistischen Geschichtsbildes im Alten Testament, Spätjudentum und Urchristentum* (WMANT, 23), Neukirchen-Vluyn, Neukirchener Verlag, 1967.

separated into two parts in Luke (11,49-51; 13,34-35), and hence many think the two parts were separated in Q, but they are actually side by side in Matthew (23,34-39), which may well also be their position in Q[19]. This whole passage seems to be an excerpt from some lost text of Jewish Wisdom Literature. For here Jesus, explicitly quoting Sophia, has her say things that fit her, but not himself, namely that she has been sending prophets[20] from the beginning of biblical history on, from Abel through Zechariah (though, oddly enough for Q, not down to John, Jesus, and the Q people[21]), and that she has often appealed directly to Jerusalem. Indeed, this repeated appeal to Jerusalem hardly has in view the Johannine "public ministry" of Jesus himself coming repeatedly to Jerusalem, but rather reflects Sophia coming repeatedly to Jerusalem through the Israelite prophets, ending in her final withdrawal from Israel, as in the Jewish Sophia myth documented in 1 Enoch 42, only to return at the end of time as Jesus (Q 13,35b). That is to say, we have to do with a secondarily Christianized Jewish sapiential text[22]:

> Q 11,49-51: Therefore also Wisdom said: I will send them prophets and sages, and some of them they will kill and persecute, so that a settling of accounts for the blood of all the prophets poured out from the founding of the world may be required of this generation, from the blood of

19. J.M. ROBINSON, *The Sequence of Q. The Lament over Jerusalem*, in R. HOPPE and U. BUSSE (eds.), *Von Jesus zum Christus. Christologische Studien*. FS P. Hoffmann (BZNW, 93), Berlin and New York, Walter de Gruyter, 1998, pp. 225-260. [In *The Sayings Gospel Q*, pp. 554-98.]

20. This saying ascribed to Sophia is sufficient to indicate the inappropriateness of presenting wisdom and prophecy as mutually exclusive genres for Q, as does R.A. HORS-LEY, *Logoi Profētōn. Reflections on the Genre of Q*, in *The Future of Early Christianity* (n. 2), pp. 195-209. On the inappropriateness of such a mutually exclusive distinction see most recently FRENSCHKOWSKI, *Welche biographischen Kenntnisse von Jesus setzt die Logienquelle voraus?* (n. 16), pp. 5-6.

21. Both Matthew and Luke sensed this deficiency, Matt 23:34 adding "crucify," Luke 11:49 "apostles".

22. F. NEIRYNCK, *Recent Developments in the Study of Q*, in J. DELOBEL (ed.), *Logia. Les paroles de Jésus – The Sayings of Jesus* (BETL, 59), Leuven, University Press – Peeters, 1982, pp. 29-75, esp. 66-67:

> In Q the woes were most probably concluded with the saying against this generation (Lk 11,49-51) and followed by the Jerusalem saying (13,34-35). ... [T]he contrast between 13,34-35a and 35b should not be neglected and much is to be said for the hypothesis that the last sentence with the introductory λέγω ὑμῖν (Lk 13,35b δέ / Mt 23,39 γάρ) was added as an *Interpretament* to the traditional saying. Lk 11,51b is a repetition and confirmation of 11,50: ἐκζητηθήσεται (ἵνα ἐκζητηθῇ) ἀπὸ τῆς γενεᾶς ταύτης, introduced by ναὶ λέγω ὑμῖν (Mt 23,36 ἀμὴν λ. ὑ.), as the conclusion of 11,49-51 and the whole collection of the woes 11,39-51. The function of 11,51b is comparable with that of the λέγω ὑμῖν saying at the close of the mission discourse: a threat of judgment for those who rejected Jesus' envoys (compare 10,12 τῇ πόλει ἐκείνῃ with 10,10-11a, and 11,51b with 11,49-51a) followed by the condemnation of those who rejected Jesus' ministry, the towns of Galilee in 10,13-15 and Jerusalem in 13,34-35.

See also KLOPPENBORG, *The Sayings Gospel Q* (n. 2), pp. 18-24.

Abel to the blood of Zechariah, murdered between the sacrificial altar and the House. [Christianized with the gloss:] Yes, I tell you, an accounting will be required of this generation.

Q 13,34-35: O Jerusalem, Jerusalem, who kills the prophets and stones those sent to her! How often I wanted to gather your children together, as a hen gathers her nestlings under her wings, and you were not willing! [35] Look, your House is forsaken! [Christianized with the gloss:] But I tell you, you will not see me until the time comes when you say: Blessed is the one who comes in the name of the Lord!

An echo of this deuteronomistic view of history is found in a late interpolation at the end of the fourth Beatitude in the Inaugural Sermon. For here the normal reason for being blessed, the eschatological reversal, is supplemented with a second reason: "For this is how they persecuted the prophets who were before you". Jesus and his followers are presented as the heirs to this biblical tradition of Sophia's prophets being persecuted, but then being avenged by God through the destruction of the temple.

This orientation of the redactor of Q may also be detected in the frequent references to "this generation", the present generation that will have to pay the price for having martyred all the prophets from Abel to Zechariah, as the Jewish sapiential text put it, which the Q people's appropriation brought down to the present, by calling to account the generation between 30 and 70 CE. Indeed, the expression "this generation" crops up eight times in Q (7,31; 11,29 bis.30.31.32.50.51). In the first instance, "this generation" rejects the children in the market places who are trying to accommodate everyone by playing both joyfully, like Jesus, and grimly, like John. The other seven instances are clustered in the last half of Q 11: The demand of "this generation" for a sign is confronted with Jonah's message of judgment, in that the Ninevites and the Queen of the South will stand in judgment against "this generation", condemning it for having rejected Sophia's prophets (Q 11,29-32). And the saying of Sophia, as well as its Christianizing interpretation, condemn "this generation" (Q 11,50-51). Framed on each side by such judgment on "this generation", there are four Woes against the Pharisees (Q 11,42-44) and three against the exegetes of the Law (Q 11,46b.52.47-48).

This redactional layer of Q is thus quite judgmental, since it is built around God's judgment that falls on "this generation" with the fall of Jerusalem. In fact, Q's redaction into a document with an identifiable beginning and end echoes this judgmental perspective. For Q begins with the threat that God might raise up children to Abraham from the (Gentile) stones, at the expense of Israel (Q 3,8). Then, after the judgment pronounced on "this generation" in Q 11, Gentiles come from Sunrise and Sunset to the eschatological banquet with the patriarchs, while Israel wails and grinds its teeth in outer darkness (Q 13,29.28). Finally, Q ends with the followers of Jesus sitting on thrones judging the twelve tribes of Israel (Q 22,28.30).

More importantly, this judgmentalism not only seems to indicate that the Q redaction is denouncing Israel, but also that it has in fact glossed over central dimensions in the archaic collections, as to how, in Jesus' view, one should think of God and how one should act accordingly.

Such a correlation between Jesus' theology and his ethic is much more explicit than is the relation of either to his eschatology[23]:

> Jesus did not draw upon any system of teaching. It strikes one, on the contrary, that at first glance his teaching about God and his eschatology, his eschatology and ethics appear to stand alongside one another in a relatively disconnected way.

> Over against a "consistent eschatological" interpretation of the teaching of Jesus it must be emphasized that where God's governance as such is developed, the prospect of the imminent end of the world is lacking. The world appears simply as creation, the sphere of the rule and care of God.

Thus there is no explicit "interim ethic" or "death-bed repentance" in the archaic collections in Q^{24}. Rather, there is an explicit correlation between Jesus' teaching about God and Jesus' ethic (Q 6,36-38):

> Be full of pity, just as your Father is full of pity. Do not pass judgment, so you are not judged. For with what judgment you pass judgment, you will be judged. And with the measurement you use to measure out, it will be measured out to you.

Here Jesus explicitly appeals to God's pity, as the model to be followed by God's people. This he does again and again: He expected a caring heavenly Father to "cancel our debts for us, as we too have cancelled for those in debt to us" (Q 11,4). The Q people are called upon

23. H. CONZELMANN, *Jesus Christus*, in *RGG*[3], Tübingen, J.C.B. Mohr (Paul Siebeck), vol. 3, 1959, pp. 634, 637:

> J. entwirft kein System einer Lehre. Es fällt im Gegenteil auf, daß Gotteslehre und Eschatologie, Eschatologie und Ethik auf den ersten Blick relativ unverbunden nebeneinander zu stehen scheinen.
> Gegenüber einer "konsequent eschatologischen" Deutung der Lehre Jesu ist zu betonen: Wo Gottes Walten als solches entfaltet wird, da fehlt der Ausblick auf das nahe Weltende. Die Welt erscheint einfach als Schöpfung, Bereich des Regierens und der Fürsorge Gottes.

ET: *Jesus*, Philadelphia, Fortress Press, 1973, pp. 51, 58.

24. Nor was there in the view of Albert Schweitzer, at least not in the sense of something that could be disqualified by the delay of the parousia. See E. GRÄBER, *Noch einmal: "Interimsethik" Jesu?*, in *ZNW* 91 (2000) 136-42.

to forgive daily, just as they expected from God daily forgiveness. "If seven times a day [your brother] sins against you, also seven times shall you forgive him" (Q 17,4). And the central appeal of Jesus to love one's enemies is based on God's conduct (Q 6,35):

> Love your enemies, and pray for those persecuting you, so that you may become sons of your Father, for he raises his sun on bad and good and rains on the just and unjust.

To the Q people, nothing was as important as Jesus' revelation of God. It was to score this point that they present Jesus making use of the solemn Hodayot formula of Qumran, to thank God most explicitly: "I thank you, Father, Lord of heaven and earth, for you hid these things from sages and the learned, and disclosed them to children" (Q 10,21). For "no one knows the Father except the Son, and to whomever the Son chooses to reveal him" (Q 10,22).

But, apparently, the way the Son had revealed the Father, so that Jesus' followers could also be sons of God, no longer applied for the redaction of Q! God's patience seemed clearly to have run out – for he is destroying Jerusalem, punishing, rather than acting pityingly, forgivingly, lovingly, toward the "bad" and "unjust", contrary to the way Jesus had taught that God acts! Those parts of Q that have, over the years, been recognized as the archaic collections, seem to have been ignored by the redactor, where God passing judgment has replaced God taking pity on sinners! Thus the redaction-critical distinction between archaic collections and the final redaction of Q can be confirmed from a more substantive, theological perspective than that of Lührmann, namely the contrast between the two layers, with regard to one's attitude toward enemies and the correlative view of God's attitude, upon which it is based.

Already Walter Bauer had found Jesus' ideal of love of enemies both in Paul and Q, and yet had recognized the substantive tension between the emphasis on the love of enemies in Q's archaic collection, the Inaugural Sermon, and the condemnation of enemies in what we now recognize as the core of Q's deuteronomistic redaction (Q 11,49-51; 13,34-35), continued in the redaction of the Gospel of Matthew itself:

> Rather he [Paul] calls for a loving attitude toward them [one's enemies] in a form that almost permits the conjecture that not only the spirit of his Lord has touched him, but also his requirement echoes in his ear (Rom 12,14-21; 1 Thess 5,15; cf. 1 Cor 4,12). If in addition Paul at times finds sharp words for the persecutors of the congregation of God (1 Thess 2,14-16), that can surprise in no higher degree than when in the sayings source, in addition to the command of love of enemy, also sayings occur such as Mt 23,34f.37f = Lk 11,49f; 13,34f. ...

Also in the discourse source, composed during the lifetime of the apostle to the Gentiles, love of the enemy has received the evaluation it deserves. There it did not make its appearance as a virtue among others, but rather as the highest that one can ever expect from a person, as something that elevates the disciples of Jesus high above the sphere of the generally human, and makes them like God himself (Mt 5,45-48 = Lk 6,32-36). Accordingly, in the archaic form of the Sermon on the Mount the requirement of love of enemies had assumed the dominant position and, after the prelude of the Beatitudes, had come to stand at the head of the whole series of exhortations. In Matthew, who subjected that archaic form to an all-encompassing revision, that has vanished. In his Gospel, it is also limited, so to speak, to just a single communication, that Jesus has required something so great of those who were his. And the way in which, where the ἐθνικός and the τελώτης are repeated from Mt 5,46-47, these people, representing the mass of the unbaptized, are pushed to one side with indifferent coldness (18,17), the satisfaction with which Matthew reports how the king avenges, on the invited who are unwilling to come, the death of his messengers (22,6-7), do not permit one to expect such a thing as that he would have been inclined to react to expressions of hostility from non-Christians with displays of love[25].

This internal criticism of a document in terms of its substantive message, in identifying where that message is not consistently carried through, is what Rudolf Bultmann called *Sachkritik*, material criticism:

25. W. BAUER, *Das Gebot der Feindesliebe und die alten Christen*, in *ZTK* 27 (1917) 37-54, esp. 39-40:
Vielmehr verlangt er Liebesgesinnung gegen sie in einer Form, die beinahe die Vermutung zuläßt, daß ihn nicht nur der Geist seines Herrn berührt hat, sondern ihm dessen Forderung im Ohre klingt (Röm. 12 $_{14-21}$, I. Thess. 5 $_{15}$, vgl. I. Kor. 4 $_{12}$). Wenn Paulus daneben gelegentlich scharfe Worte für die Verfolger der Gemeinde Gottes findet (I. Thess. 2 $_{14-16}$), so kann das in keinem höheren Grade befremden, als wenn in der Redenquelle außer dem Gebote der Feindesliebe auch Sprüche stehen wie Mt. 23 $_{34}$ f. $_{37}$ f. = Luk. 11 $_{49}$ f., 13 $_{34}$ f. ...
Auch in der, zu Lebzeiten des Heidenapostels komponierten Redenquelle hat die Feindesliebe die ihr gebührende Wertung erfahren. Da war sie nicht als eine Tugend neben anderen erschienen, sondern als das Höchste, was man überhaupt von einem Menschen erwarten kann, als etwas, was die Jünger Jesu hoch hinaushebt über die Sphäre des allgemein Menschlichen und sie Gott selber gleich macht (Mt. 5 $_{45-48}$ = Luk. 6 $_{32-36}$). Demgemäß hatte in der Urgestalt der Bergpredigt die Forderung der Feindesliebe die beherrschende Stellung eingenommen und war nach dem Auftakt der Seligpreisungen an die Spitze der ganzen Ermahnungsreihe getreten. Bei Matthäus, der jener Urform eine umfassende Bearbeitung hat zuteil werden lassen, ist das verwischt. In seinem Evangelium bleibt es auch gewissermaßen bei der einmaligen Mitteilung, daß Jesus so Großes von den Seinen gefordert habe. Und die Art, wie dort, wo der ἐθνικός und der τελώτης aus Mt. 5 $_{46.47}$ wiederkehren, diese die Schar der Ungetauften repräsentierenden Menschen mit gleichgültiger Kälte zur Seite geschoben werden (18 $_{17}$), die Genugtuung mit der Mt. berichtet, wie der König den Tod seiner Sendboten an den widerwilligen Geladenen rächt (22 $_{6.7}$), lassen nicht gerade erwarten, daß er auf Aeußerungen der Feindschaft von nichtchristlicher Seite mit Liebeserweisen zu reagieren geneigt gewesen wäre.
See similarly D.C. SIM, *Apocalyptic Eschatology in the Gospel of Matthew* (SNTS MS, 88), Cambridge, Cambridge University Press, 1996, pp. 227-35.

Of course this concept can be used for exegesis only as a *question,* not as a recipe. As a question it provides a *critical standard* gained from Paul himself for use in interpreting separate statements. Exegesis would thus have gained the possibility of being in a real sense material criticism. How far Barth himself uses the leading theme as a guide for his interpretation must therefore be the object of investigation[26].

Unless one is to dismiss the whole problem as the normal human inconsistency regarding our highest ideals, or the inevitable but irrelevant result of the familiar biblical layering in the history of traditions, then one must take seriously the substantive – theological and ethical – tension between the two main layers in Q, that of the archaic clusters, and that of the final redaction[27]. Jesus' vision of a caring Father who is

---

26. R. BULTMANN launched the concept of *Sachkritik* in his review article, *Karl Barth, "Die Auferstehung der Toten"*, in *TBl* 5 (1926) 1-14, reprinted in BULTMANN, *Glauben und Verstehen. Gesammelte Aufsätze,* Tübingen, J.C.B. Mohr (Paul Siebeck), 1933, pp. 38-64 (quoted here). In this critical review of K. BARTH's commentary on 1 Corinthians entitled *Die Auferstehung der Toten. Eine akademische Vorlesung über 1. Kor. 15,* München, Chr. Kaiser, 1924, Bultmann pointed out again and again (pp. 39-40, 44, 52, 57; ET pp. 67, 72, 81, 86) that Barth repeatedly introduced untenable exegetical positions simply to avoid having to concede that at times Paul did not carry through consistently his own normative theological insight, e. g., pp. 39-40:

> Natürlich kann man diesen Gedanken für die Exegese nur als *Fragestellung*, nicht als Rezept benutzen; als Fragestellung, die zugleich einen aus Paulus selbst gewonnenen *kritischen Maßstab* gegenüber seinen einzelnen Äusserungen darstellt. Die Exegese hätte also zugleich die Möglichkeit gewonnen, sachkritisch im eigentlichen Sinne zu sein. Wieweit B. selbst seinen Leitgedanken als kritischen Gedanken zur Geltung kommen läßt, wird zu fragen sein.

ET: R.W. FUNK (ed.), *Faith and Understanding,* London, SCM, and New York, Harper and Row, 1969; reprinted Philadelphia, Fortress Press, 1987, pp. 66-94, esp. 67. The English translation of Barth's book, *The Resurrection of the Dead,* New York, London, and Edinburgh, Fleming H. Revell, 1933, is unfortunately so inaccurate that it can hardly be used. Barth's position is clearer from the quotations of it in Bultmann's review, where the translation is accurate.

27. It is for much the same point that P. KRISTEN, *Nachfolge leben. Drei Modelle von Kreuzesnachfolge in Q und Markus,* in S. MASER and E. SCHLARB (eds.), *Text und Geschichte. Facetten theologischen Arbeitens aus dem Freundes- und Schülerkreis. Dieter Lührmann zum 60. Geburtstag* (MTSt, 50), Marburg, N. G. Elwert, 1999, pp. 89-106, esp. 98, has criticized J. SCHRÖTER's work, *Erinnerungen an Jesu Worte. Studien zur Rezeption der Logienüberlieferung in Markus, Q und Thomas* (WMANT, 76), Neukirchen-Vluyn, Neukirchener Verlag, 1997, pp. 468-69, for rejecting out of hand pre-redactional collections such as Q 12,22b-31:

> Auch Jens Schröter akzeptiert keine literarischen Vorstufen in Q und sieht die "unterschiedlichen rhetorischen Ausrichtungen in den Redekompositionen" als "zusammengehörige Aspekte *einer* Perspektive." "Gerade das Nebeneinander von Instruktionen, Drohworten und eschatologischen Verheißungen" sei "für Q charakteristisch", eine Beschreibung, die für die Endgestalt des Spruchevangeliums zutreffend erscheint, nicht jedoch für seine erkennbare literarische Vorstufe Q[1]. Sicher stehen die Anweisungen in Q 10,2-16 und 12,22-31 "unter der Perspektive der nahen βασιλεία", wie Schröter feststellt, doch zeigen Q[1] und Q[2] gerade signifikante Unterschiede in bezug auf das, was das Gottesreich ist. Während Q[1] die βασιλεία als eine gegenwärtig mögliche alternative Lebensordnung betrachtet, wird sie in Q[2] als eine rein zukünftige, deutlich abgrenzbare Größe beschrieben, die mit dem zum Gericht kommenden Menschensohn verbunden ist.

infinitely forgiving and hence shockingly evenhanded in dealing with the bad as well as the good, may have been lost from sight a generation later, as a result of the grueling experiences of the Jewish war, understood as God's quite judgmental punishment of Israel.

It is of course the case that, for the Q redaction, the judgment on "this generation", the Pharisees, and the exegetes of the Law, is not to be carried out by the Q people themselves in the here and now, but rather by God, not only at the fall of Jerusalem, but also at the day of judgment to come. As Paul puts it in Rom 12,14.19, quoting Deut 32,35:

> Bless those who persecute you; bless and do not curse them. ... Beloved, never avenge yourselves, but give place to [God's] wrath; for it is written, "Vengeance is mine, I will repay, says the Lord".

Also Heb 10,30 quotes Deut 32,35, and comments (Heb 10,31): "It is a fearful thing to fall into the hands of the living God".

But the Q people had originally been sons of God in loving their enemies, imitating God originally understood in a quite different way, as giving sunshine and rain to the bad as well as the good. It was in this sense that they had sought to be God-like (Q 6,35-36).

The distinguished *Altertumswissenschaftler* Albrecht Dihle has laid out in detail the dramatic extent to which this transcended the common-sense justice of reward and retaliation that pervaded antiquity[28]:

> Under completely different presuppositions [from the Platonic-Neoplatonic philosophical tradition], the proclamation of Jesus of Nazareth and the early Christian theology connecting to it has eliminated that concept of retaliation as the basis for or ingredient in an ethical order.

Yet already the Q redaction had come to envisage the Q people again as God-like, but quite differently, like a judgmental God, sitting on thrones judging the twelve tribes of Israel, as Q's last word (the *explicit* of Q at Q 22,30). Jesus' basic insight into the ever-loving and forgiving nature of God would seem to have been lost from sight as the age-old view of God undergirding retaliatory justice again asserted itself. It is odd indeed that it is a non-theologian who has to draw our attention to what may be the most important theological contribution by Jesus to the history of

---

28. A. DIHLE, *Die Goldene Regel. Eine Einführung in die Geschichte der antiken und frühchristlichen Vulgärethik* (SAW, 7), Göttingen, Vandenhoeck & Ruprecht, 1962, esp. chapter V, Prinzipielle Überwindung des Vergeltungsdenkens, b) Christentum, pp. 72-79, esp. 72:

> Unter gänzlich anderen Voraussetzungen hat die Predigt Jesu von Nazareth und die an sie anknüpfende frühchristliche Theologie den Vergeltungsgedanken als Grundlage oder Bestandteil einer sittlichen Ordnung ausgeschieden.

See my review, *JHP* 4 (1966) 84-87.

ideas, matched in this regard only by the Platonic tradition. After all, it is theologians who should note this basic shift in the doctrine of God at the basis of ethical conduct, which took place between the archaic collections of Jesus' sayings incorporated into Q and the redaction of Q a generation later.

3. ARCHAIC COLLECTIONS IN Q

It is in the archaic collections imbedded in Q that one can with the most assurance speak of material that goes back to sayings of Jesus himself. The most obvious instance of such an archaic collection may be the cluster: Free from Anxiety like Ravens and Lilies (Q 12,22b-31). For an even older version of this cluster than that of Q is imbedded in Saying 36 of *The Gospel of Thomas*. To be sure, this older version is preserved not in the Fourth Century Coptic text from Nag Hammadi, for here this saying is heavily abbreviated, but rather in the much earlier and longer Greek text of P. Oxy. 655. What is striking is that this original text of *The Gospel of Thomas*, Saying 36, lacks not only a scribal error found in Matthew and Luke, and hence already present in their Q archetype reconstructed in *The Critical Edition of Q*, but also lacks other traits that, throughout the past century, have been widely recognized by scholarship as secondary accretions that already in Q intrude upon the otherwise well-structured Q collection, secondary traits that hence are striking by their absence from P. Oxy. 655. Since the scribal error in Q makes clear that the Q archetype behind Matthew and Luke is based on a written Greek text for this saying, here we surely have the oldest attestation for written sayings of Jesus, even older than the copy of Q shared by Matthew and Luke[29].

Other generally-recognized collections imbedded in Q are so strikingly similar in content to this most archaic written collection that they too must be very archaic: The Lord's Prayer (Q 11,2b-4), its commentary,

---

29. J.M. ROBINSON and C. HEIL, *Zeugnisse eines schriftlichen, griechischen vorkanonischen Textes. Mt 6,28b ℵ*, P.Oxy. 655 I,1-17 (EvTh 36) und Q 12,27*, in ZNW 89 (1998) 30-44 [in *The Sayings Gospel Q*, pp. 713-28]; J.M. ROBINSON, *The Pre-Q Text of the (Ravens and) Lilies. Q 12:22-31 and P. Oxy. 655 (Gos. Thom. 36)*, in *Text und Geschichte* (n. 27), pp. 143-180 [in *The Sayings Gospel Q*, pp. 729-75]; J.M. ROBINSON, *A Written Greek Sayings Cluster Older than Q. A Vestige*, in HTR 92 (1999) 61-78 [in *The Sayings Gospel Q*, pp. 777-94]; and J.M. ROBINSON, *Excursus on the Scribal Error in Q 12:27*, in *The Critical Edition of Q* (n. 1), pp. xcviii-c. See also the photographs of the relevant passages from Codex Sinaiticus and P. Oxy. 665 in the Endpapers of that volume. Concerning J. SCHRÖTER, *Vorsynoptische Überlieferung auf P. Oxy. 665? Kritische Bemerkungen zu einer erneuerten These*, in ZNW 90 (1999) 265-272, see the critical response of J.M. ROBINSON and C. HEIL, *Noch einmal: Der Schreibfehler in Q 12,27*, in ZNW 92 (2001) 113-122 [in *The Sayings Gospel Q*, pp. 795-808].

the Certainty of the Answer to Prayer (Q 11,9-13), and the Inaugural Sermon itself (Q 6,20-49), into which Matthew imbedded the other archaic collections. Thus one has a relatively broad basis of archaic material on which to begin determining what Jesus had to say. And it is precisely those collections that stand in tension to the judgmental deuteronomistic view of God punishing Israel with the fall of Jerusalem.

Of course Jesus said and did many other things than what is recorded in this core of Q, some of it preserved in other Gospels (or elsewhere in Q), but most lost forever. And not everything even in this core may with equal assurance go back to him, e.g. the secondary accretions in the archaic collection Free from Anxiety like Ravens and Lilies (see above). But any presentation of Jesus that lacks at *its* core these collections that comprise the oldest core of Q is to that extent deficient.

As a result of form criticism, scholarship has lost its naiveté, as if one could simply read off the biography of Jesus and his *ipsissima verba* from the text of the Gospels. Yet it is not the case that one can no longer speak of what Jesus said[30]. Rudolf Bultmann, the most skeptical of the form critics, himself emphasized this dialectic:

> By means of this critical analysis an oldest layer is determined, though it can be marked off with only relative exactness. Naturally we have no absolute assurance that the exact words of this oldest layer were really spoken by Jesus.

> Of course the doubt as to whether Jesus really existed is unfounded and not worth refutation. No sane person can doubt that Jesus stands as founder behind the historical movement whose first distinct stage is represented by the oldest Palestinian community. But how far that community preserved an objectively true picture of him and his message is another question. For those whose interest is in the personality of Jesus, this situation is depressing or destructive; for our purpose it has no particular significance. It is precisely this complex of ideas in the oldest layer of the synoptic tradition which is the object of our consideration. It meets us as a fragment of tradition coming to us from the past, and in the examination of it we seek the encounter with history. By the tradition Jesus is named as bearer of the message; according to overwhelming probability he really was. Should it prove otherwise, that does not change in any way what is said in the record. I see then no objection to naming Jesus throughout as the speaker. Whoever prefers to put the name of "Jesus" always in quotation marks and let it stand as an abbreviation for the historical phenomenon with which we are concerned, is free to do so[31].

---

30. A. JÄRVINEN, *Jesus as a Community Symbol in Q*, in LINDEMANN, *The Sayings Source Q* (n. 16), pp. 515-521, moves in this direction.

31. R. BULTMANN, *Jesus* (Die Unsterblichen. Die geistigen Heroen der Menschheit in ihrem Leben und Wirken mit zahlreichen Illustrationen, 1), Berlin, Deutsche Bibliothek, n. d. [1926], 13. bis 14. Tausend, Tübingen, J. C. B. Mohr (Paul Siebeck), 1951, p. 16:

Such critical caution must always be kept in mind, so as not to discredit its positive concomitant, which is our basic interest here[32]. To be sure, the sayings of Jesus in Q have not been kerygmatized in the narrower sense typified by Mark, where the cross and resurrection play such a prominent role that Mark seems to be only a passion narrative with a long introduction. But the imprint of the Q people on the text of Q is unmistakable, most markedly in the case of the redactor's imposing the deuteronomistic view of history on "this generation" at the time of the fall of Jerusalem. But even the older clusters come to us as structured by their use among his followers[33]. Yet, once this is acknowledged, one

Man kommt so mittels der kritischen Analyse zu einer ältesten Schicht, auch wenn man diese nur mit relativer Sicherheit abgrenzen kann. Natürlich hat man erst recht keine Sicherheit, daß die Worte dieser ältesten Schicht wirklich von Jesus gesprochen sind. Es wäre möglich, daß auch die Entstehung der ältesten Schicht schon auf einen komplizierten historischen Prozeß zurückgeht, den wir nicht mehr zu erkennen vermögen. Zwar ist der Zweifel, ob Jesus wirklich existiert hat, unbegründet und keines Wortes der Widerlegung wert. Daß er als Urheber hinter der geschichtlichen Bewegung steht, deren erstes greifbares Stadium die älteste palästinensische Gemeinde darstellt, ist völlig deutlich. Aber wie weit die Gemeinde das Bild von ihm und seiner Verkündigung objektiv treu bewahrt hat, ist eine andere Frage. Für denjenigen, dessen Interesse die Persönlichkeit Jesu ist, ist die Sachlage bedrückend oder vernichtend; für unseren Zweck ist sie nicht von wesentlicher Bedeutung. Denn der Komplex von Gedanken, der in jener ältesten Schicht der Überlieferung vorliegt, ist der Gegenstand unserer Darstellung. Er begegnet uns zunächt als ein Traditionsstück, das aus der Vergangenheit zu uns gelangt ist, und in seiner Befragung suchen wir die Begegnung mit der Geschichte. Als der Träger dieser Gedanken wird uns von der Überlieferung Jesus genannt; nach überwiegender Wahrscheinlichkeit war er es wirklich. Sollte es anders gewesen sein, so ändert sich damit das, was in dieser Überlieferung gesagt ist, in keiner Weise. So sehe ich auch keinen Anlaß, der folgenden Darstellung nicht den Titel der Verkündigung Jesu zu geben und von Jesus als dem Verkünder zu reden. Wer dieses "Jesus" für sich immer in Anführungsstriche setzen und nur als abkürzende Bezeichung für das geschichtliche Phänomen gelten lassen will, um das wir uns bemühen, dem ist es unbenommen.

ET: *Jesus and the Word*, New York, Charles Scribner's Sons, 1934, reprinted 1958, pp. 13-14.

32. I regret that in a popularizing lecture my failure to mention this dialectic, which should be obvious to us all, led H. MELZER-KELLER to a caricature of my position, *Frauen in der Logienquelle und ihrem Trägerkreis: Ist Q das Zeugnis einer patriarchatskritischen, egalitären Bewegung?*, in St. H. BRANDENBURGER / Th. HIEKE (eds.), *Wenn Drei das Gleiche sagen – Studien zu den ersten drei Evangelien. Mit einer Werkstattübersetzung des Q-Textes* (Theologie, 14), Münster, Lit, 1998, pp. 37-62, esp. 37: "… die hier pauschal vorgenommene unkritische Übertragung jeglicher Redestoffe aus Q auf den sogenannten 'historischen Jesus'". While of course rejecting this quite untenable position as "problematisch", she quite rightly continues: "… kann eines nicht zweifelhaft sein: Dass der Trägerkreis der Logienquelle Aussprüche Jesu von Nazaret in großer Zahl weitertradierte und der Jesusgruppe zeitlich und soziologisch noch sehr nahe stand. Die Logienquelle läßt also immerhin Rückschlüsse auf den 'historischen Jesus' und das Profil seiner Nachfolgegemeinschaft zu". She and I are in fact in agreement regarding both aspects of this dialectic.

33. J.S. KLOPPENBORG, "The Sayings Gospel Q and the Quest of the Historical Jesus," in *HTR* 89 (1996) 307-44, especially the section "Invention and Arrangement," pp. 326-329, whose title is defined, p. 326:

is called upon to take seriously what Bultmann called the "over-whelming probability" that this oldest layer does in fact reflect what Jesus had to say.

4. JESUS' PUBLIC MINISTRY AS SOCIAL REALITY

Perhaps the best place to realize that we can never lay claim to having reached the *ipsissima verba Christi*, and yet can with reasonable assurance feel confident that we are in fact speaking of Jesus, would be another of the archaic collections behind the final redaction of Q, namely the Mission Instructions (Q 10,2-16). No one would be so bold as to assume that Jesus ever stood before the Twelve (or the seventy-two) and made a speech to that effect. Furthermore, the Mission Instructions, if anywhere, would be where a constant updating of the tradition would take place, to keep up with the necessary changes in actual mission practice. And yet the Mission Instructions do present a rather detailed and relatively clear picture of what must actually have been the practice from very early on, a practice that Jesus himself had no doubt already exemplified.

The Mission Instructions are not only in Q, where secondary material has already been interpolated into even older Mission Instructions, but there are also in Mark quite similar, though somewhat less archaic, Mission Instructions (Mk 6,7-13). This is surely a striking instance of multiple attestation at the oldest level. Matthew has merged the two, after quite visibly introducing an intermediary updating. For he surrounded the Mission Instructions with the rejection of a Samaritan Mission (Mt 10,5b-6. 23), as well as updating it to fit the somewhat evolved practice of the Matthean community. He then finally transcended his Jewish-Christian Mission Instructions in the Great Commission (Mt 28,18-20), when the dwindling Jewish Q movement is merged into the Gentile church.

Luke in turn has Jesus finally revoke the Mission Instructions (Lk 22,35-38), right after having quoted the conclusion of Q (Lk 22,28.30), and just before turning to Mark's more liberal Mission Instructions that already permitted the taking of a stick as a weapon (Mk 6,8). Q had not permitted this most primitive weapon of self-defense (Q 10,4), but Mark had already not only permitted it, but even escalated it by the time of the

---

I use these terms not in the popular sense of "fabrication," but in the strictly rhetorical sense, denoting the intellectual process of finding and arranging materials germane to the conduct of an argument and the rendering plausible of a certain conclusion. As a deliberate composition, Q exhibits the signs of invention, both at the level of its final redaction and at the level of its smaller constituent collections.

narration of Gethsemane, where it has become a sword (Mk 14, 47). Luke for his part appropriated the sword to narrate the cutting off of an ear (Lk 22,49-50). Then, in Acts, Luke is free to presuppose the quite different mission practice of the Gentile church exemplified by Paul.

The compromise reached at the Jerusalem Council, that Paul's Gentile Mission should be accepted as legitimate, while James, Cephas and John would continue a legitimate Mission limited to the Circumcised (Gal 2,9), meant that the original Mission Instructions, as preserved in the oldest layer of Q, were initially continued in the one Mission but not in the other, and ultimately survived only as imbedded in Q.

The best that the Synoptic Gospels could do by way of recreating Jesus' Galilean ministry was to assemble disparate anecdotes that produced portrayals of Jesus wandering rather aimlessly from place to place, until they have Jesus steadfastly turn to Jerusalem to die. Only then do they become a purposeful itinerary – based on the kerygma. But it is more reasonable to assume that Jesus did in fact have something in mind for his Galilean ministry itself. Indeed, his plan of action may be relatively accurately reflected in the oldest layer of the Mission Instructions of Q. For Theißen is probably right in his view that "the earliest Christian itinerant charismatics continued the preaching and life-style of Jesus"[34]. Hence, if one uses the archaic sayings collections to interpret the oldest layer of the Mission Instructions[35], one has a relatively solid

---

34. THEIßEN and MERZ, *Der historische Jesus* (n. 3), p. 28: "Urchristliche Wandercharismatiker führten den Predigt- und Lebensstil Jesu weiter." ET: *The Historical Jesus* (n. 3), p. 10. A footnote refers to Theißen's basic essay in this regard, G. THEIßEN, *Wanderradikalismus. Literatursoziologische Aspekte der Überlieferung von Worten Jesu im Urchristentum*, in *ZTK* 70 (1973) 245-71, reprinted in G. THEIßEN, *Studien zur Soziologie des Urchristentums* (WUNT, 19), Tübingen, J.C.B. Mohr (Paul Siebeck, 1979¹, 1989³, pp. 79-105, and his monograph G. THEIßEN, *Soziologie der Jesusbewegung. Ein Beitrag zur Entstehungsgeschichte des Urchristentums* (TEH.NF, 194 = KT, 34), München, Chr. Kaiser Verlag, 1977¹, 1991⁶. An abbreviated English translation is entitled *Itinerant Radicalism. The Tradition of Jesus' Sayings from the Perspective of the Sociology of Literature*, in A. WIRE (ed.), *The Bible and Liberation. A Radical Religion Reader*, Berkeley, CA, Graduate Theological Union, 1976, pp. 84-93; an unabridged translation is entitled *The Wandering Radicals. Light Shed by the Sociology of Literature on the Early Transmission of the Jesus Sayings*, in G. THEIßEN, *Social Reality and the Early Christians. Theology, Ethics, and the World of the New Testament*, Minneapolis, Fortress Press, 1992, and Edinburgh, T. and T. Clark, 1993, pp. 33-59. See also his monograph *The First Followers of Jesus. A Sociological Analysis of the Earliest Christianity*, London, SCM Press, 1978, whose American title is *The Sociology of the Earliest Jesus Movement*, Philadelphia, Fortress Press, 1978.

35. It is the overlooking of this context in Q itself that is the basic flaw of L.E. VAAGE's book, *Galilean Upstarts. Jesus' First Followers According to Q*, Valley Forge, PA, Trinity Press International, 1994. See my critical review article, J.M. ROBINSON, *Galilean Upstarts. A Sot's Cynical Disciples?*, in W.L. PETERSEN, J.S. VOS, and H.J. DE JONGE (eds.), *Sayings of Jesus. Canonical and Non-Canonical*. FS T. Baarda (NTSup, 89), Leiden, New York, and Köln, E.J. Brill, 1997, pp. 223-49, esp. 243-49. [In *The Sayings Gospel Q*, pp. 535-57, esp. 552-57.]

basis for understanding what went on in the Galilean ministry. Thus the text of Q could in a sense be recast into the form of a Narrative Gospel:

After being baptized by John (Q 3,21-22), and resisting the temptation to resume a worldly existence (Q 4,1-13), Jesus went back to Nazara (Q 4,16), apparently only long enough to break with his past and move to Capernaum (Q 7,1). This became the base camp of a circuit that initially may have comprised Capernaum, well below sea level on the northern tip of the Sea of Galilee, Chorazin, secluded in the mountains behind it, and Bethsaida, just across the Jordan to the east, in the safer territory of Philip (Q 10,13-15).

What did he do on such a circuit? He set out without any human security. He had no backpack for provisions, no money at all – penniless –, no sandals, no stick – helpless and defenseless (Q 10,4). This hardly makes sense in terms of the history of religions. His was neither the getup of his precursor John the Baptist, nor a Cynic garb[36]. But it does make sense in terms of his message, as echoed in the other archaic Q collections: One is not anxiety-laden about food and clothing, any more than the ravens and lilies would seem to be (Q 12,22b-30). Rather one orients oneself exclusively to God reigning (Q 12,31). One prays to God to reign, and thus to provide bread (Q 11,2b-3). One trusts God as a benevolent Father to know one's needs for bread and fish and to provide them (Q 11,9-10), trusting that God will not, instead, give a stone or snake, but will in fact, in this regard as in others, reign as a benevolent Father (Q 11,11-13). That kind of message of radical trust calls for that kind of radical lack of an alternative, physical security, if it is to be validated as credible in actual reality.

In the case of the Mission Instructions, it is striking that Jesus did not advocate going to the local Synagogue (which would at the time seem to have been rather non-existent in Galilee in terms of architecture), nor address masses on a Mount or on a Plain or by the seaside. (No location is given for the Inaugural Sermon, Q 6,20-49, which in fact seems less meant as an actual scene than as the basic core collection of the sayings of Jesus[37].) Rather the Mission Instructions were oriented to houses (Q

36. J.M. ROBINSON, *Building Blocks in the Social History of Q*, in E.A. CASTELLI and H. TAUSSIG (eds.), *Reimagining Christian Origins*. FS B.L. Mack, Valley Forge, PA, Trinity Press International, 1996, pp. 87-112, esp. 87-90. [In *The Sayings Gospel Q*, pp. 493-97.]

37. It is a remarkable attestation for Matthew's familiarity with the tradition in which he obviously stood that he knew to build into the core collection of the Inaugural Sermon other archaic collections that also comprise the core of Q, so as to produce the Sermon on the Mount (with the exception of the Mission Instructions themselves, which did not fit that setting). It is thus appropriate that the Sermon on the Mount has been sensed as this core from time to time, as a surrogate for Q itself, beginning with Francis of Assisi, and re-emerging in Tolstoy, Gandhi, and Martin Luther King.

10,5.7)[38]. One walked from farm to farm, from hamlet to hamlet, from house to house, and there knocked at the door to bring attention to one's presence. To gain admission, one called out: Shalom! (Q 10,5b) If admitted by the head of the household, and thereby accorded the normal hospitality, one designated him as "son of peace" (Q 10,6a), since God's peace had been bestowed as "performative language" in the Shalom of the opening greeting. If turned away at the door, God's peace left along with Jesus or his disciple (Q 10,6b), to be offered again at the next house where one knocked. But what took place in a house that did take one in was understood as God reigning. This was in fact expressly said to the household while in their home: "The kingdom of God has reached unto you" (Q 10,9b).

God's reign involved the hospitality itself, which was accepted at face value as God's gift, and eaten as offered, without ascetic dietary restrictions such as John and other "holy men" practiced at that time. This makes it clear that the drastic absence of gear for the journey was not due to an ascetic ideology, but rather was meant as demonstrative documentation for one's trust exclusively in God for such human needs. For, as the other archaic collections make clear, the food offered and eaten in the house was in reality God already knowing one's need and providing for it, as God does for the ravens; it was the answer to prayer for God to reign by giving a day's ration of bread and not a stone.

The needs of the household itself are comparably met: The sick are healed, with the explanation that this in turn is God's reign reaching even to them (Q 10,9). For the healing is done by God's finger, which is God reigning (Q 11,20), irrespective of whether the human involved is Jesus or someone else (Q 11,19). Indeed, it was understood not as human action, but as God's action.

All of this must have been explained by means of such sayings, and by means of the Prayer itself (Q 11,2b-4). In this way "workers" were enlisted for the mission (Q 10,2), and in the process of time such "worthy" houses (Mt 10,13) might well become "safe houses", where workers knew they would be taken in. Indeed they might well develop into what Paul called "house churches" (Rom 16,5; 1 Cor 16,19; Phlm 1-2; Col 4,15). The itinerant "worker" (Q 10,2.7) and the sedentary "son of peace" (Q 10,6a) would be primitive designations for what might evolve from their functions into what we today would call church offices.

---

38. J.M. ROBINSON, *From Safe House to House Church. From Q to Matthew*, in M. BECKER and W. FENSKE (eds.), *Das Ende der Tage und die Gegenwart des Heils. Begegnungen mit dem Neuen Testament und seiner Umwelt.* FS H.-W. Kuhn (AGJU, 44), Leiden, E.J. Brill, 1999, pp. 183-199. [In *The Sayings Gospel Q,* pp. 629-44.]

This is not to say that Jesus' intent was, in effect, after all to found the church, with which his message of God reigning has all too readily been identified. But he did assume that God's peace could reign in households that would thus transcend the power of evil over their lives and become mutually supportive of other such households. This understanding does not exclude the "eschatological" dimension of God reigning, but brings to expression the concrete reality Jesus envisaged in his message about God reigning already. Thus Q makes clear that Jesus was involved in doing something in Galilee, that he did in effect have a "public ministry" there.

The decision of a member of such a household to become an itinerant worker might well not take place easily. Not only did Jesus leave home, Nazara, and in Q had no further relations with his family, but there are even sayings explicitly calling for the disruption of family ties: Jesus came to divide son against father, daughter against her mother, and daughter-in-law against her mother-in-law (Q 12,53). To become a disciple, one must hate father and mother, son and daughter (Q 14,26). What could be more drastic than to hate one's family and love one's enemies! Even if this "hating" was understood euphemistically as "loving" Jesus more than family members (Mt 10,37), in any case it meant abandoning the family and renouncing one's responsibilities at home.

Central to the way of life that Jesus envisaged was indeed to love one's enemies (Q 6,27). For this, amplified by praying for one's persecutors (Q 6,28), is accorded the supreme value of being what makes one a son of God, God-like, since God raises his sun and showers his rain on the bad as well as on the good (Q 6,35). The title "son of God" did not begin just as a christological title, borrowed from its usage as an honorific title for heroes in the Hellenistic-Roman world, but, like the title "son of peace", began as a designation for those thus committed to the Jesus movement. This was not merely a pious well-wishing sentiment, but meant in practice turning the other cheek, giving the shirt off one's back, going the second mile, lending without ever asking for anything back (Q 6,29-30).

Q was not easy at all: One must not fear those who can only kill the body (Q 12,4). Rather one must lose one's life (Q 17,33), indeed take up one's cross (Q 14,27). Enlistments must have been rare (Q 10,2), and the dropout rate must have been devastating. It is not surprising that in such a movement the salt of resolve lost its strength and had to be thrown out (Q 14,34-35). For all practical purposes, the Q movement did die out. But its remnant merged with the Gentile Christian church under the leadership of the Evangelist "Matthew", whereby its text, the Sayings

Gospel Q, was rescued, and with it the most reliable information we have about the historical Jesus.

Jesus, though not mentioned by name, must have been included among the successors to the prophets and sages sent by Wisdom (Q 11,49), but martyred by "this generation" (Q 11,50-51). For he (and John) were included among the "children" of Wisdom (Q 7,35). He, in that noble tradition, clearly gave his life for his cause[39]. Indeed, he is to reappear as Wisdom's vindication at the appointed time (Q 13,35b)[40]. But the Jesus of Q points more to the historical Jesus than to the direction in which such redactional traits already point, the kerygmatic Christ.

39. J.S. KLOPPENBORG, *The Sayings Gospel Q and the Quest of the Historical Jesus* (n. 32), pp. 331-32:

> There is no passion narrative in Q and no sayings that appear to reflect on Jesus' death in particular, yet it would be absurd to suppose that those who framed Q were unaware of Jesus' death... The key elements of trial, condemnation, assistance (by the Spirit), ordeal, vindication, acclamation, and punishment (of the opponents) are all embedded in the fabric of Q, but they are not *emplotted* as a single narrative. More importantly, the subject of these narrative functions is not Jesus himself, as in the Markan passion narrative, but the larger set of persons comprising the prophets, John, Jesus, and Jesus' followers...
>
> Thus when it is observed that Q lacks a passion narrative, this does not mean that Q has not reflected on the death of Jesus, only that it has understood it differently. While Q used elements of the "wisdom tale" to rationalize persecution and rejection, it neither used the psalms of lament nor did it privatize the interpretation of Jesus' death as an expiatory death. Q lacks explicit mention of these elements not because it presupposed them as earlier commentators assumed, but because it had a *different* rationalization of death drawn from the deuteronomistic history...
>
> Q shows that the development of a passion narrative was *not* inevitable and encourages one to look for multiple origins of early Christian attempts to render plausible and meaningful the facts of persecution and death.

See also the conjectures of FRENSCHKOWSKI about what the Q redactor may have known about Jesus' death, *Welche biographischen Kenntnisse von Jesus setzt die Logienquelle voraus?* (n. 15), pp. 25-29.

40. D. ZELLER, *Entrückung zur Ankunft als Menschensohn (Lk 13,34f.; 11,29f.)*, in R. GANTOY (ed.), *À cause de l'Évangile. Études sur les Synoptiques et les Actes offertes au P. Jacques Dupont, O.S.B. à l'occasion de son 70ᵉ anniversaire* (LD, 123), Paris, Cerf, and Brugge, Publications de Saint-André, 1985, pp. 513-30.

CHAPTER 2

Jesus from Easter to Valentinus (or to the Apostles' Creed)*

The first hundred years of Christianity – A.D. 30 to 130, more or less – is the period from Easter to Valentinus, or if you prefer, until the Apostles' Creed. That hundred years is also the time in which the NT was written. It is also the time in which oral traditions about Jesus were in circulation. It is this period, largely for these reasons, that occupies us here.

The present paper will not seek to argue for or presuppose a solution to the perennial debate between the traditional (and still largely British) view of Gnosticism as a second-century inner-Christian heresy and the *religionsgeschichtlich* (and Continental) view of Gnosticism as a broad syncretistic phenomenon surfacing at least as early as Christianity in various religions of the day, of which Christianity was only one. While the Nag Hammadi texts seem to have come out on the side of the latter alternative, in that several texts document non-Christian Gnosticism of various traditions (Jewish, Hermetic, Neo-Platonic), pre-Christian Gnosticism as such is hardly attested in a way to settle the debate once and for all. As a matter of fact the dating of the composition of most Nag Hammadi tractates, much less of their sources, has hardly begun, and so can claim nothing like the degree of relative certainty characteristic of the dating of NT books.

Yet the main reason for not approaching the issue of this paper in terms of that perennial debate is that such an approach tends to obscure rather than clarify the situation. For such a clear-cut polarized choice as that debate tends to call upon us to make could blunt our sensitivity to the actual shade of development a text may represent somewhere in the no-person's-land between those crisp options: If Gnosticism could be safely kept out of the first century A.D., then it could be ignored in interpreting Paul's opponents in Corinth, the world of Colossians and Ephesians, the Prologue of John, and the like, with the result that a traditional and misleading exegesis would result. Conversely, the presupposition of pre-Christian Gnosticism invites the anachronism of reading into the situation

---

* The Presidential Address delivered 21 December 1981, at the annual meeting of the Society of Biblical Literature, held at the San Francisco Hilton, San Francisco, CA.

behind such texts concepts of the second-century, from which our knowledge of Gnosticism primarily comes.

To assume a mediating position may thus not be the weakness of indecision and vacillation, but rather an approximation of the historical reality more useful than is either horn of the dilemma: One may assume that second-century Gnosticism did not first emerge then in the full-blown form of the Valentinian and Basilidean systems. For such historical developments call for lead-time, just as, at the next stage, Clement and Origen of Alexandria on the one hand and Irenaeus and Tertullian on the other are inconceivable apart from the century leading up to their systems. Thus even if it were true that Gnosticism as known in the second-century systems did not exist in the Pauline and Johannine schools going back to the first century, the left-wing trajectory out of which second-century Gnosticism emerged must have been contemporary with the Pauline and Johannine schools and could well be a major factor in influencing them. To erect a periodizing barrier between pre-Gnostic apostolic Christianity and second-century Gnosticism would be to falsify history by denying the existence of that trajectory until it reached its outcome in second-century Gnosticism. This would produce the exegetical error of failing to interpret those NT texts in terms of their time as the lead-time for second-century Gnosticism.

The methodological situation is similar when one envisages moving forward from A.D. 30. The apocalyptic radicalism that lead John the Baptist to lose his head, Jesus to be hung up, and Paul to become a habitué of forty lashes less one (2 Cor 11:24) could hardly have failed to have left-wing successors down through the first hundred years, as main-line Christianity, in part following the lead of Judaism at Jamnia, standardized, solidified, domesticated itself and moved, as sects are wont to do in the second and third generations, toward the mainstream of the cultural environment. Thus the lead-time for Gnosticism coincides with the follow-up time for primitive Christian radicalism. Sometimes that radicalism would have expressed itself in sufficient continuity with the original forms it had taken for the radical fringe (charismatics, martyrs, prophets) to have had the support of the more conventional mainstream. But even within such acceptable limits there occur texts such as Colossians, Ephesians and Ignatius where new thought patterns and language worlds become unmistakably audible. Ultimately at least some of apocalyptic radicalism modulated into gnostic radicalism.

The bulk of the NT, written in the second half of the first century A.D., the middle segment of the first hundred years of Christianity, is thus strung on trajectories that lead not only from the pre-Pauline confession of 1 Cor 15:3-5 to the Apostles' Creed, which developed out of the second-century baptismal liturgy of Rome, but also from Easter "enthusiasm" to second-century Gnosticism. It is on currents such as these, rather than on the traditional assumption of a straight-line development through the "apostolic age" with its unwavering faith once for all delivered to the saints, that we are to discuss the topic before us.

It is indeed in terms of such currents that the polarization of early Christianity into orthodoxy and heresy is to be understood. Heresy is so tenacious and unbending not because of the hardening of its heart, but because of its relatively valid claim to be rooted in an original Christian point. Thus the outcome of the first hundred years of Christianity in orthodoxy vs. heresy does not imply the divine protection of an original revelation from the wiles of the devil, but rather two alternative adjustments of the original position made necessary by the changing circumstances with the passage of time. Hence the theological assessment of such diverging trajectories, though it begins with the historical given that the winner in this competition has been known as orthodox, the loser heretical, has as its first task to acknowledge the historical process leading to this outcome and then to rethink critically what theological validity was gained and lost along each of the diverging trajectories, perhaps with the outcome that values from both trajectories should in fact be affirmed in some formulation for today, which would hence depart from both formulations of yesteryear.

II

The conceptualization or, more literally, the visualization of the appearances of the resurrected Christ are themselves such an instance of a bifurcating morphology. The earliest accessible documentation as a point of departure is Paul. He conceives of the resurrection as bodily, but emphasizes change within the continuity of corporeality (1 Cor 15:40, 43, 48, 54):

> There are celestial bodies and there are terrestrial bodies.
>
> It is sown in dishonor, it is raised in glory.
>
> As was the man of dust, so are those who are of the dust; and as is the man of heaven, so are those who are of heaven.
>
> When the perishable puts on the imperishable, and the mortal puts on immortality, ...

When he comes, the Lord "will change our lowly body to be like his glorious body" (Phil 3:21). Thus it is clear that Paul visualized the resurrected Christ as a heavenly body, luminous. Though the letters of Paul do not narrate the Damascus road experience with its blinding light, this visualization repeatedly narrated in Acts (9:1-19; 22:4-16; 26:9-18) does seem to reflect accurately Paul's own visualization of his experience.

Yet with regard to the significance of Paul's experience, Luke does not reflect Paul's position. Luke demotes the Damascus road experience into Paul's *conversion*, as the church, following Luke rather than Paul, tends to refer to what Paul himself would have us refer to as the resurrected Christ's *appearance* to him. In Luke's hands this event falls outside the period of forty days to which Luke restricts the normative resurrection appearances (Acts 1:3). Paul himself alluded to the appearance of the resurrected Christ to him in order to validate his claim to be an apostle "not from men nor through man, but through Jesus Christ and God the Father who raised him from the dead" (Gal 1:1). That is to say, Paul was not just a delegate, missionary or emissary from a local church, which is the common meaning of the Greek word we all too readily translate (or unthinkingly transliterate) with the very specific designation apostle. But it is the common meaning of delegate which is the only sense in which Luke concedes Paul to be an apostle. For when the church of Antioch sent Barnabas and Saul as its delegates to evangelize Cyprus (Acts 13:3): "Then after fasting and praying they laid their hands on them and *sent them off*." The latter verb is the verb whose stem is the same as that of the noun *apostolos*, though here it clearly means the church "delegated" them. It is in this sense that Acts 14:4, 14 refers to "the apostles," "the apostles Barnabas and Paul," that is to say, *delegates* of the Antioch church during the "first missionary journey." Luke goes so far as to present Paul preaching about the resurrection in such a way as to exclude himself from being a witness to the resurrection (Acts 13:30-31): "But God raised him from the dead; and for many days he appeared to those who came up with him from Galilee to Jerusalem, who are now his witnesses to the people." After that "first missionary journey" Luke reports (Acts 15:2) that "Paul and Barnabas and some of the others were appointed to go up to Jerusalem to the apostles and the elders," a usage that limits the apostles to those in Jerusalem, conformable to Luke's limitation of the appearances to the original disciples (Acts 1:22).

And yet Paul is the hero of the book of Acts! Scholars have long since recognized what Luke does to Paul, but have thus far been baffled to provide an adequate explanation. For to understand why Paul is here damned with such faint praise one must place Acts in terms of the trajectory from Easter to Valentinus.

There is relatively strong attestation to the fact that the first appearance to a male was to Peter (1 Cor 15:5; Luke 24:34). (Matthew's appending of the appearance to "Mary Magdalene and the other Mary" to the Marcan story of the empty tomb in 28:9-10 and the parallel narration of the appearance to Mary Magdalene in John 20:14-18 actually make her the first to see the risen Christ in these Gospels.) Yet, just as Luke does not narrate the tradition of the appearance to Paul within the limits he imposes on appearances (it is not narrated in Luke 24 or Acts 1), just so the story of the appearance to Peter is not among the resurrection appearances narrated in their proper place at the end of the gospels (Matt 28, Luke 24 and John 20-21).

2 Pet 1:16-17 seems to narrate that resurrection appearance, to judge by its use of a luminous story to accredit Peter in the way a resurrection appearance normally would accredit one as an apostle: "We were eye-witnesses of his majesty. For when he received honor and glory from God the Father. . . ." This seems a striking parallel to the opening words of the Great Commission by the resurrected Christ (Matt 28:18): "All authority in heaven and on earth has been given to me." 2 Peter would thus seem to describe a resurrection appearance ... were it not for the fact that what follows is similar to a Marcan narration that occurs in the middle of the public ministry, and hence known not as a resurrection appearance but as the transfiguration: "(For when he received honor and glory from God the Father) and the voice was borne to him by the Majestic Glory, 'This is my beloved Son, with whom I am well pleased,' we heard this voice borne from heaven, for we were with him on the holy mountain." It is indeed probable that Mark has "historicized" what was originally the resurrection appearance to Peter, tying it down to an unambiguous bodiliness by putting it well before the crucifixion, in spite of its luminousness (Mark 9:3): "His garments became glistening, intensely white, as no fuller on earth could bleach them." Matthew compares this luminousness with the sun: "his face shone like the sun" (17:2), language used elsewhere of the resurrected Christ, "his face was like the sun shining in full strength" (Rev 1:16, see below), "brighter than the sun" (Acts 26:13). The original association of the "transfiguration" with Easter may be betrayed in the comment appended to it (Mark 9:9): "And as they were coming down the mountain, he charged them to tell no one what they had seen, until the Son of man should have risen from the dead."

Of course in the Marcan text Peter is accompanied by James and John; but this may well be only an aspect of Marcan historicizing, in that he usually presents these three as admitted to intimate scenes (5:37; 14:33; with Andrew as well 1:29; 13:3). Furthermore Jesus is accompanied by two figures, Elijah with Moses. But far from this fact serving to distance the transfiguration from a resurrection appearance, it associates it specifically with the resurrection appearance in ... the second-century apocryphal *Gospel of Peter*:

> They saw the heavens opened and two men come down from there in a great brightness and draw nigh to the sepulchre. ... and both the young men entered in. ... They saw again three men come out from the sepulchre, and two of them sustaining the other, and a cross following them, and the heads of the two reached to heaven, but that of him who was led of them by the hand overpassing the heavens.

Of course in the Marcan version they are not such mythological heavenly "men," but rather the biblical characters Moses and Elijah, who had nonetheless according to Jewish tradition ascended to heaven. Furthermore they in their way reaffirm the association with resurrection, at least in a Valentinian interpretation of Mark (NH I, 48:6-11): "For if you remember reading in the Gospel that Elijah appeared and Moses with him, do not think the resurrection is an illusion." Thus, just as Luke transferred the luminous appearance to Paul outside the normative period by restricting normative resurrection appearances to forty days, Mark would seem to have transferred the luminous appearance to Peter outside the normative post-crucifixion period back into the public ministry. Mark in fact provides no resurrection appearances, perhaps because those available were so luminous as to seem disembodied. Thus, if Paul had tended to emphasize the difference of the resurrection body, so as to make it possible to affirm the bodiliness of a luminous appearance, the narrations of the empty tomb in the gospels tend to emphasize the continuity of the same body, lest the luminousness of the appearances suggest it was just a ghost, just religious experience.

The only resurrection appearance in the NT that is described in any detail, though it is usually overlooked due to not being placed at the end of a gospel, is in Rev 1:13-16:

> ... one like a son of man, clothed with a long robe and with a golden girdle round his breast; his head and his hair were white as white wool, white as snow; his eyes were like a flame of fire, his feet were like burnished bronze, refined as in a furnace, and his voice was like the sound of many waters; in his right hand he held seven stars, from his mouth issued a sharp two-edged sword, and his face was like the sun shining in full strength.

Although this appearance took place in the 90s (quite uninhibited by the Lucan doctrine that appearances ended with forty days), it has in common with Paul's much earlier but equally uninhibited luminous visualization of the resurrection in the 30s the fact that these are the only two resurrection appearances recorded by persons who themselves received the appearances, Paul and John of Patmos – and both these authenticated visualizations of a resurrection appearance were of the luminous kind! Thus one may conclude that the original visualizations of resurrection appearances had been luminous, the experiencing of a blinding light, a heavenly body such as Luke reports Stephen saw (Acts 7:55-56): "He, full of the Holy Spirit, gazed into heaven and saw the glory of God, and Jesus standing at the right hand of God; and he said, 'Behold, I see the heavens opened, and the Son of man standing at the right hand of God.'"

Why then would this original visualization have been deprived of its appropriate position at the conclusion of the gospels? Perhaps because these luminous appearances continued, as Stephen, Paul and John of Patmos attest, down through the first century A.D., and, as gnostic sources attest, their increasingly dubious interpretation continued down through the second. And here one can see what they came to mean.

The Letter of Peter to Philip presents a luminous resurrection appearance (NH VIII, 134:9-13)[1]: "Then a great light appeared so that the mountain shone from the sight of him who had appeared." This took place "upon the mountain which is called 'the (Mount) of Olives,' the place where they used to gather with the blessed Christ *when he was in the body*" (133:13-17). From this language it is clear that the resurrected, luminous Christ is no longer in the body; bodily existence is restricted to Jesus prior to Easter. Thus the Pauline ability to retain both bodiliness and luminousness in his doctrine of the resurrection has given way to a bifurcation: if it is luminous, it is not bodily.

From a gnostic point of view this incorporeality is all to the good. For bodily existence is deficient, stupefied with fatigue, passion, drunkenness, sleepiness, a prison from which the spirit is liberated by its ecstatic trip at conversion and the sloughing off of this mortal coil at death. Thus the gnostics had every reason to retain the original luminous visualization of resurrection appearances, not just because they thereby retained the original Christian perception, but because it was a theological asset in terms of gnostic spiritualism.

In *The Gospel of Mary* (not from Nag Hammadi but from the closely related Coptic Gnostic P. Berol. 8502), Mary not only makes no claim that such a gnostic appearance is bodily; she frankly calls it a vision (10:10-23):

---

1. Marvin W. Meyer, *The Letter of Peter to Philip: Text, Translation and Commentary* (SBLDS 53; Chico: Scholars, 1981) 105-12 interprets this text in this broader context.

> I saw the Lord in a *vision* and I said to him, "Lord, I saw you today in a *vision.*" He answered and said to me, "Blessed are you, that you did not waver at the sight of me. For where the mind is, there is the treasure." I said to him, "Lord, now does he who sees the *vision* see it through the soul or through the spirit?" The Savior answered and said, "He does not see through the soul nor through the spirit, but the mind which is between the two – that is what sees the *vision.*"

The luminous visualization of resurrection appearances may be the kind of experience that in that day would have been considered a vision. For when it is not a matter of Christ's resurrection, such a luminous appearance can readily be so classified even within the canon. The "two men ... in dazzling apparel" (Luke 24:4) can be summarized by Luke as "a *vision* of angels" (Luke 24:23). Indeed Paul himself can speak of "*visions* and revelations of the Lord" (2 Cor 12:1). This openness of the luminous visualization to such a visionary interpretation may be what made that visualization increasingly unacceptable when applied to Jesus on the trajectory from Easter to the Apostles' Creed, especially when the disembodied overtones of such visions were exploited in a Gnosticizing way on the trajectory from Easter to Valentinus.

It is just this reduction of resurrection appearances to religious experience that is the foil against which the non-luminous resurrection appearances at the ends of the gospels of Matthew, Luke and John are composed (Luke 24:37-43):

> But they were startled and frightened, and supposed that they saw a *spirit.* And he said to them, "Why are you troubled, and why do questionings rise in your hearts? See my hands and my feet, that it is I myself; handle me, and see; for a *spirit* has not *flesh and bones* as you see that I have." And when he had said this he showed them his hands and his feet. And while they still disbelieved for joy and wondered, he said to them, "Have you anything here to eat?" They gave him a piece of broiled fish, and he took it and ate before them.

This apologetic against a ghostlike experience has pushed Luke to emphasize the "flesh and bones" of the resurrection, which is clearly one step nearer "orthodoxy" than was Paul (1 Cor 15:50): "I tell you this, brethren: *flesh and blood* cannot inherit the kingdom of God, nor does the perishable inherit the imperishable." It is probably such an apologetic against this spiritualizing the resurrection away, as the orthodox would sense it, that is also intended when that conclusion of Luke is summarized at the opening of Acts (1:3-4): "To them he presented himself alive after his passion by many proofs, appearing to them during forty days, and speaking of the kingdom of God. And while staying (literally:

sharing salt, eating) with them..." Similarly Acts 10:41: "... us who were chosen by God as witnesses, who ate and drank with him after he rose from the dead." Similarly in the traditions used by John (John 20:20, 25, 27-28):

> He showed them his hands and his side.
>
> "Unless I see in his hands the print of the nails, and place my finger in the mark of the nails, and place my hands in his side, I will not believe."
>
> "Put your finger here, and see my hands; and put out your hand, and place it in my side; do not be faithless, but believing." Thomas answered him, "My Lord and my God."

This was a bit too materialistic for the "spiritual gospel" that transmitted it, and hence the Fourth Evangelist appended a corrective moving gently in the ... gnostic direction (John 20:29): "Have you believed because you have seen me? Blessed are those who have not seen and yet believe." Matthew also reports (28:17) that "some doubted." But he has a somewhat different apologetic against an accusation that the resurrection was not real (28:13, 15): "'Tell people, "His disciples came by night and stole him away while we were asleep."' ... And this story has been spread among the Jews to this day." But an apologetic for the physicality of the resurrection similar to that of Luke-Acts and the Johannine tradition may be implicit in Matthew as well (28:9): "And they came up and took hold of his feet. ..."

It may be this same apologetic that is responsible for Mark's use of the story of the empty tomb rather than of resurrection appearances. For the emptiness of the tomb makes it clear that it was the same body that was buried which rose from the dead. It must be to underline this point that one finds the otherwise irrelevant details in Luke 24:12: "he saw the linen cloths by themselves," and in John 20:5-7: "He saw the linen cloths lying there ...; he saw the linen cloths lying, and the napkin, which had been on his head, not lying with the linen cloths but rolled up in a place by itself." Thus the apologetic interest evident in each of the canonical gospels reflects a secondary stage in the transmission of resurrection appearances, a defense against a (mis)interpretation of a more original stage.

Lest it seem that such a spiritualization of the luminously resurrected Christ as is here presupposed would be limited to a specifically gnostic tendency that could hardly be called primary, one may note that the two instances where the NT contains reports by an eyewitness to the (in each case luminous) appearance of the resurrected Christ, the identification of that appearance as the Spirit seems near at hand. For Paul the resurrection body is "*spiritual*" (1 Cor 15:44), "the last Adam" "a life-giving spirit" (1 Cor 15:45). When he comes to speak of the gloriousness of Christ, he calls him the Spirit (2 Cor 3:17-18): "Now the Lord is the *Spirit*, and where the *Spirit* of the Lord is, there is freedom. And we all, with unveiled face, beholding the *glory* of the Lord, are being changed into his likeness from one degree of *glory* to another; for this comes from the Lord who is the *Spirit*." Similarly John on Patmos sees the resurrected Christ, who dictates the letters to the seven churches, as is indicated by the self-identifications (1:17-18; 2:8): "'I am the first and the last, the living one: I died, and behold I am alive for evermore. ...' The words of the first and the last, who died and came to life." Yet this takes place while John is "in the *Spirit*" (1:10), and the hermeneutical exhortation familiar at the conclusion of parables recurs at the end of each letter in the remarkable formulation (2:7, 11, 17, 29; 3:6, 13, 22): "He who has an ear, let him hear what the *Spirit* says to the churches."

This identification of the luminously resurrected Christ as the Spirit is then in substance what Luke rejects as the false assumption that they had seen a ghost. But it is in fact a way in which the luminous visualization would continue to be described in Gnosticism. In *The Sophia of Jesus Christ* the resurrected Christ appeared on a Galilean mountain (NH III, 91:10-16) "not in his first form, but in the invisible *spirit*. And his form was like a great angel of light. And his likeness I must not describe. No mortal flesh can endure it."

This gnostic spiritualization also comes to expression in a somewhat different conceptualization in an *Apocalypse of Peter*, where Jesus' death and resurrection are replaced with the idea of his bifurcation at the time of the passion into "the living Jesus" (NH VII, 81:18) that did not suffer and "his fleshly part" (81:20), "the body" (83:5) that was crucified. This "living Jesus" appeared however like the resurrected Christ (72:23-26): "I saw a new *light* greater than the *light* of day. Then it came down upon the Savior." "The body of his *radiance*" (71:32-33), "my incorporeal body" (83:7-8), is actually the Spirit (83:4-15): "So then the one susceptible to suffering shall come, since the body is the substitute. But what they released was my *incorporeal body*. But I am the intellectual *Spirit* filled with radiant *light*. He whom you saw coming to me is our intellectual Pleroma, which united the perfect *light* with my *Holy Spirit*." Luke on the other hand clearly distinguishes the appearances of the resurrected Christ, which terminate after forty days with the ascension, from the gift of the Holy Spirit at Pentecost, ten days later. The resurrected Christ is no ghost!

The primary stage of luminous appearances, in comparison with which the resurrection appearances at the ends of the canonical gospels are secondary, can be identified from vestiges in the non-luminous resurrection stories at the ends of the canonical gospels themselves, as well as from the misplaced luminous resurrection stories in the NT, the identification of the resurrected Christ with the Spirit in Paul and Revelation, and the outcome of these trajectories in second-century Gnosticism.

In the resurrection appearances at the end of the canonical gospels the luminous glory of the resurrected Christ has indeed disappeared, though vestiges of that visualization do survive: The apocryphal *Gospel of Peter*, in which the luminous visualization of the resurrected Christ had been presented, had also included "a young man sitting in the midst of the sepulchre, comely and clothed with a brightly shining robe." (This may well be intended to be one of the two men "in a great brightness" who had previously entered the sepulchre and led the resurrected Christ to heaven, since that exaltation scene is followed by the comment that "the heavens were again seen to open, and a man descended and entered into the sepulchre" – a detail that otherwise would have no function.) In the canonical gospels this luminous apparition of the attendant is all that is left of the luminous visualization of the resurrected Christ: "a young man sitting on the right side, dressed in a white robe" (Mark 16:5); "an angel of the Lord," whose "appearance was like lightning, and his raiment white as snow" (Matt 28:2-3); "two men ... in dazzling apparel" (Luke 24:4; see also Acts 1:10: "two men ... in white robes"); "two angels in white" (John 20:12).

This vacillation as to whether the apparition is human or angelic is itself revealing. Even when designated human, the apparition is not human in the ordinary sense of an early Christian witness to the resurrection, such as an apostle or the like. For example, Elaine Pagels completely overlooks this "young *man*" in the authentic ending of Mark in favor of the canonicity of the *woman* in the inauthentic long ending of Mark[2]:

> One can dispute [von] Campenhausen's claim on the basis of New Testament evidence: the gospels of Mark and John both name Mary Magdalene, not Peter, as the first witness of the resurrection. [Footnote 22: Mark 16:9; John 20:11-17.]

> This gnostic gospel [*The Gospel of Mary*] recalls traditions recorded in Mark and John, that Mary Magdalene was the first to see the risen Christ. [Footnote 40: Mark 16:9].

The church has indeed tended to classify this youth in Mark as part of the heavenly realm, not the human, in that (s)he reveals divine truth and makes a luminous appearance, as the other gospels clarify the "white

2. Elaine Pagels, *The Gnostic Gospels* (New York: Random House, 1979) 8 and 11; pp. 9 and 13 of the paperback edition, Vantage Books, 1981.

robe." Indeed the other gospels initiate the ecclesiastical exegesis to the effect that the youth is an angel, in that Matthew and John use the word angel, whereas Luke, who had spoken of two men, has a flashback in which the scene is recalled as "a vision of *angels*" (Luke 24:23). The apologetic that apparently caused the resurrected Christ's luminosity to fade into the solidity of a physical body did not affect the luminosity of the accompanying figure(s).

There are other vestiges of the luminous non-human visualization of the resurrected Christ in the otherwise very human appearances at the end of the canonical gospels. Even the *interpretatio christiana* of the OT at Easter retains the original emphasis on glory (Lk 24:26): "Was it not necessary that the Christ should suffer these things and enter into his *glory*?" In quite docetic style Jesus passes through locked doors (John 20:19, 26):

> On the evening of that day, the first day of the week, the doors being shut where the disciples were, for fear of the Jews, Jesus came and stood among them and said to them, "Peace be with you."
>
> The doors were shut, but Jesus came and stood among them, and said, "Peace be with you."

This docetic overtone may also be implicit in the abrupt entry of the resurrected Christ in Luke that leads to the thoroughly refuted assumption that they were looking at a spirit (24:36): "As they were saying this, Jesus himself stood among them, and said to them, 'Peace to you.'" The motif is more obvious in his abrupt departures (Luke 24:31, 51; Acts 1:9): "... and he vanished out of their sight." "While he blessed them, he parted from them and was carried up into heaven." "As they were looking on, he was lifted up, and a cloud took him out of their sight."

The failure to recognize the resurrected Christ may also derive ultimately from the luminous visualization. It is quite understandable that one would not recognize a blinding light (Acts 9:5; 22:8; 26:15): "Who are you, Lord?" But it is less obvious in the case of Jesus returning in the very same human body. The motif of non-recognition recurs in the story of the Emmaus road, where it is explained as divine intervention (Luke 24:16, 31): "But their eyes were kept from recognizing him." "And their eyes were opened and they recognized him." Mary Magdalene did not recognize him, but took him for a gardener (John 20:14-15): "She did not know that it was Jesus. Supposing him to be the gardener. ..." This motif also occurs in the redactional chapter added to John (21:4): "Yet the disciples did not know that it was Jesus." This motif thus retains the tradition that it is not a matter of normal vision, catching sight of a recognizable human companion, but rather that (John 21:1) "Jesus revealed himself." Yet it is no longer a matter of a completely different form, such as a blinding light, but a very human form, mistakable for a tourist on the way to Emmaus, a gardener, or a fisherman standing on the shore. But the lack of recognition and then the sudden recognition is now no longer intelligible in terms of this all-too-human visualization, as it had been and continued to be in the luminous visualization. Thus the non-recognition of Jesus, like the luminous apparition of angels and the sudden appearance and disappearance of Jesus, may be motifs originally developed in connection with luminous visualizations of the resurrected Christ.

Our prevalent view that the church was launched by Easter experiences such as we find at the end of the canonical gospels must as a result be replaced by a recognition that they are secondary to an original luminous visualization of Christ's appearances, replaced as that original Christian experience played more and more into the hands of the trajectory from Easter to Valentinus. Over against that option, emerging orthodoxy, on the trajectory from Easter to the Apostles' Creed, expressed the reality of the bodily resurrection by emphasizing, in spite of supranatural vestiges, the human-like-us appearance of the resurrected Christ: the resurrection of the *flesh*.

To be sure, just as the emerging orthodox alternative retained vestiges of the luminous visualization, the emerging gnostic alternative could on occasion make use of human categories more at home in the orthodox trajectory. For example *The Apocryphon of John* presents the luminous visualization in a kind of fluctuating trinitarian form (NH II, 1:30–2:15):

> Straightway, while I was contemplating these things, behold the heavens opened and the whole creation which is under heaven *shone*, and the world was shaken. And I was afraid, and behold I saw in the *light* a *youth* who stood by me. While I looked at him he became like an *old man*. And he changed his likeness (again), becoming like a *servant*. There was not a plurality before me, but there was a likeness with multiple forms in the *light*, and the likenesses appeared through each other, and the likeness had three forms. He said to me, "John, John, why do you doubt, or why are you afraid? You are not unfamiliar with this image, are you? – that is, do not be timid! – I am the one who is with you (pl.) always. I am the *Father*, I am the *Mother*, I am the *Son*. I am the undefiled and incorruptible one."

This threefoldness of the apparition, though described as like three human forms, does not eliminate the overarching luminosity, as may be further illustrated from a parallel text where the three forms are more explicitly luminous (*Pistis Sophia* 4):

> For he gave more *light* than in the hour that he went up to heaven, so that the men in the world were not able to speak of the *light* which was his, and it cast forth very many rays of *light*, and there was no measure to its rays. And his *light* was not equal throughout, but it was of different kinds, and it was of different types, so that some were many times superior to others, and the whole *light* together was in three forms, and the one was many times superior to the other; the second which was in the middle was superior to the first which was below; and the third which was above them all was superior to the second which was below. And the first ray which was below them all was similar to the *light* which had come down upon Jesus before he went up to heaven, and it was quite equal to it in its *light*. And the three *light*-forms were of different kinds of *light* and they were of different types. And some were many times superior to others.

But on the other hand the Valentinian *Gospel of Philip* could use the orthodox visualization for its purposes by stressing, as had Paul, the otherness of the body, but, with orthodoxy, moving beyond Paul (1 Cor 15:50) to speak of the resurrection of the flesh, though emphasizing the Pauline, and now gnostic, emphasis upon otherness (NH II, 68:31-37): "The Lord rose from the dead. He became as he used to be, but now his *body* was perfect. He did indeed possess *flesh*, but this flesh is *true flesh. Our flesh* is nothing, but we possess only an image of the true." This is as far as Gnosticism could reach out toward orthodoxy without forsaking its basic position of contrast (which it shared with Paul), expressed in *The Apocryphon of James* (NH I, 14:35-36): "From this moment on I shall strip myself that I may clothe myself." Thus although orthodoxy and heresy could on occasion accommodate themselves to language actually developed to implement the emphasis of the other alternative, by and large they divided the Pauline doctrine of luminous bodiliness between them: Orthodoxy defended the bodiliness by replacing luminousness with fleshliness, heresy exploited the luminousness by replacing bodiliness with spiritualness.

III

A still further bifurcation into heresy/orthodoxy from Easter to Valentinus or to the Apostles' Creed also has to do with the resurrection, but in this case the believer's resurrection – whether it has taken place *already*, presumably at baptism, or whether it has not yet taken place but is awaited at the end of time. Apparently this was being debated as early as the 50s in 1 Corinthians. For Paul contrasts the posture of the Corinthians with his own (4:8-9): "*Already* you are filled!

Already you have become rich! Without us you have become kings! And would that you did reign, so that we might share the rule with you! For I think that God has exhibited us apostles as last of all. ..." Apparently this is why baptism is so important to the Corinthians but is played down by Paul (1:12-17): "What I mean is that each one of you says, 'I belong to Paul,' or 'I belong to Apollos,' or 'I belong to Cephas,' or 'I belong to Christ.' Is Christ divided? Was Paul crucified for you? Or were you baptized in the name of Paul? I am thankful that I baptized none of you except Crispus and Gaius; lest any one should say that you were baptized in my name. (I did baptize also the household of Stephanas. Beyond that, I do not know whether I baptized any one else.) For Christ did not send me to baptize but to preach the gospel. ..." Apparently the experience called today (baptismal) *regeneration*, a term that is not yet attested in Paul's time, was at that time designated by some Corinthians as (baptismal) *resurrection*. Thus the ultimate outcome of personal salvation was attained at initiation and need not be reserved for the end time, whose relevance – and even its reality – would tend to disappear. This is apparently the intent of the view Paul criticizes (15:12): "Some of you say that there is no resurrection of the dead." Rather than this being the view of rationalists, who do not believe in resurrection, as used to be assumed, it has been the scholarly assumption for the past half century that this is the view of fanatics who have already attained spiritual resurrection. Paul's own divergent view is expressed in Philippians (3:10-14, 20-21):

> ... that I may know him and the power of his resurrection, and may share his sufferings, becoming like him in his death, that if possible I *may attain* the resurrection from the dead. Not that I have *already* obtained this or am *already* perfect; but I *press on* to make it my own, because Christ Jesus has made me his own. Brethren, I do not consider that I have made it my own; but one thing I do, forgetting what lies behind and *straining forward* to what lies ahead, I *press on* toward the goal for the prize of the upward call of God in Christ Jesus. ... But our commonwealth is in heaven, and from it we await a Savior, the Lord Jesus Christ, who *will* change our lowly body to be like his glorious body, by the power which enables him even to subject all things to himself.

Hardly a generation before Valentinus in the early second-century this view still was being strongly opposed in the Pauline School (2 Tim 2:16-18): "Avoid such godless chatter, for it will lead people into more and more ungodliness, and their talk will eat its way like gangrene. Among them are Hymenaeus and Philetus, who have swerved from the truth by holding that the resurrection is past *already*." Although Hymenaeus and Philetus are not mentioned by name in Gnostic sources, their view of the resurrection having taken place already is clearly attested in a Valentinian *Treatise on Resurrection* (NH I, 48:30–49:24):

> But the resurrection does not have this aforesaid character [of an illusion]; for it is the truth which stands firm. It is the revelation of what is, and the transformation of things, and a transition into newness. For imperishability descends upon the perishable; the light [!] flows down upon the darkness, swallowing it up; and the Pleroma fills up the deficiency. These are the symbols and the images of the resurrection. He (Christ) it is who makes the good. Therefore, do not think in part, O Rheginos, nor live in conformity with this flesh for the sake of unanimity, but flee from the divisions and the fetters, and *already* you have the resurrection. If he who will die knows about himself that he will die – even if he spends many years in this life, he is brought to this – why not consider yourself as risen and (already) brought to this?

But this view opposed by Paul and in the Pauline School is here presented by *appeal* to Paul, that is to say, it is a doctrine of the left wing of the bifurcated Pauline School (45:14–46:2):

> The Savior swallowed up death – (of this) you are not reckoned as being ignorant – for he put aside the world which is perishing. He transformed himself into an imperishable Aeon and raised himself up, having swallowed the visible by the invisible, and he gave us the way of our immortality. Then, indeed, as the *Apostle* said, "We suffered with him, and we *arose* with him, and we went to heaven with him." Now if we are manifest in this world wearing him, we are that one's beams, and we are embraced by him until our setting, that is to say, our death in this life. We are drawn to heaven by him, like beams by the sun, not being restrained by anything. This is the *spiritual resurrection* which swallows up the psychic in the same way as the fleshly.

Here it is made clear that a future physical resurrection has become superfluous, having been replaced by the spiritual resurrection. The doctrine of baptismal resurrection already surely deserves at least by this time the Pauline characterization that there is no [future bodily] resurrection of the dead.

Such a spiritual resurrection is also documented in another Valentinian text, *The Gospel of Philip* (NH II, 73:1-8): "Those who say they will die first and then rise are in error. If they do not *first receive the resurrection while they live*, when they die they will receive nothing. So also when speaking about baptism they say, 'Baptism is a great thing,' because if people receive it they will live."

But how could such a Gnostic view appeal to Paul as "the Apostle" *par excellence*, when in such letters as First Corinthians and Philippians Paul had opposed precisely that view? By appealing not to the historical Paul of the 50s, but rather to the "Paul" of the left wing of the Pauline

School a decade or so after Paul (Col 3:1-4): "If then you *have been raised* with Christ, seek the things that are above, where Christ is, seated at the right hand of God. Set your minds on things that are above, not on things that are on earth. For you have died, and your life is hid with Christ in God. When Christ who is our life appears, then you also will appear with him in glory." Similarly Eph 2:5-6: "(God) made us alive together with Christ (by grace you have been saved); and *raised us up* with him, and made us sit with him in the heavenly places in Christ Jesus."

A way to emphasize the basic shift in human existence taking place at baptism was developed on the trajectory moving toward orthodoxy that would not in fact jeopardize the future bodily resurrection. This solution was reached by the introduction of the concept of regeneration to describe the change at baptism, thus reserving the concept resurrection for the future (1 Pet 1:3-5): "Blessed be the God and Father of our Lord Jesus Christ! By his great mercy we have been *born anew* to a living hope through the *resurrection* of Jesus Christ from the dead, and to an inheritance which is imperishable, undefiled, and unfading, kept in heaven for you, who by God's power are guarded through faith for a salvation ready to be revealed in the last time." In substance this is almost identical with the position represented in Col 3:1-4, in that our inheritance is present already in heaven, needing only to be revealed in the future, which thus has lost most of its original eventness. But now the concept of having already risen is carefully sidestepped, so as to leave room for lip service to the apocalyptic view of future resurrection as a permanent if relatively passive ingredient in orthodoxy.

The way in which this shift from one terminology to the other could so easily be effected is evident from another Nag Hammadi text, *The Exegesis on the Soul*, in which the two terminologies occur side by side (NH II, 134:6-15):

> Now it is fitting that the soul *regenerate* herself and become again as she formerly was. The soul then moves of her own accord. And she received the divine nature from the Father for her rejuvenation, so that she might be restored to the place where originally she had been. This is the *resurrection* that is from the dead. This is the ransom from captivity. This is the upward journey of ascent to heaven. This is the way of ascent to the Father.

Actually the two conceptualizations coexist already in the Gospel of John, where the resurrection of the believer is attained spiritually in this life (5:24-25; 11:23-26):

> Truly, truly, I say to you, he who hears my word and believes him who sent me, has eternal life; he does not come into judgment, but has passed from

death to life. Truly, truly, I say to you, the hour is coming, and now is, when the dead will hear the voice of the Son of God, and those who hear will live.

Jesus said to her, "Your brother will rise again." Martha said to him, "I know that he will rise again in the resurrection at the last day." Jesus said to her, "I am the resurrection and the life; he who believes in me, though he die, yet shall he live, and whoever lives and believes in me shall never die."

But the concept of regeneration has already been introduced as an alternative conceptualization (3:3, 7): "Truly, truly, I say to you, unless one is born anew, he cannot see the kingdom of God. ... Do not marvel that I say to you, 'You must be born anew.'" And the "redactor" has apparently reintroduced as a protection against dangerous implications of eternal life now (6:40, 47, 51, 54) the resurrection "at the last day" (6:39, 40, 44, 54).

Thus some of the lead-time for Valentinus in the last part of the first century A.D. is documented in the NT itself, once the apocalyptic environment of Easter, with its reservation of much of the eschatological fulfillment until the end had fully come (an eschatological reservation shared by Paul), was replaced by spatial dimensions congenial to Gnosticism. Indeed that lead-time in this case can be traced back to Corinth early in the 50s, or, put conversely, the follow-up to Easter had already within a generation veered in a Gnostic direction.

IV

The hundred years during which the sayings of Jesus circulated orally and thus were still available for inclusion in written sources was the period of time characterized by the two trajectories from Easter to Valentinus or the Apostles' Creed sketched thus far: from the visualization of the resurrected Christ as a luminous heavenly *body* to envisioning him as a gloriously disembodied *spirit* – against which the resurrection of the same *fleshly* body emerged as an orthodox apologetic; and the trajectory from the apocalyptic expectation of a resurrection of believers in a comparably glorious body at the *end* of time to an experience of spiritual resurrection attained *already* at baptism as an ecstatic trip free of the body, needing only to be repeated at death, thereby rendering superfluous and even undesirable a future resurrection of the body – against which a *final* resurrection of the same fleshly body emerged as orthodoxy. But Easter was itself a hermeneutical event, on any account making sense of Jesus in view of his abrupt end. Hence these trajectories of Easter and resurrection experience inevitably influenced the trajectories through which Jesus' sayings and texts witnessing to them would move. The first two instances of post-Easter trajectories may in fact clarify the directionalities at work on the third.

The gloriousness of the resurrected Christ not only vindicated the ignominiously crucified Jesus; it could also, by way of contrast, put Jesus in the shade. Though Paul did not go so far as to repudiate Jesus, as some spiritualists may have done (1 Cor 12:3: "Jesus be cursed!"), nonetheless an invidious contrast is already reflected in Paul: Jesus was sent "in the likeness of sinful flesh" (Rom 8:3), but arose in "his glorious body" (Phil 3:21); "he was crucified in weakness, but lives by the power of God" (2 Cor 13:4). Thus the original disciples and Jesus' family, those who knew him when he was on earth, do not in any way outrank Paul, who never laid eyes on nor was even known to this Jesus (1 Cor 9:1-5):

> Am I not free? Am I not an apostle? Have I not seen [on the Damascus road] Jesus our Lord? Are not you my workmanship in the Lord? If to others I am not an apostle [Acts], at least I am to you; for you are the seal of my apostleship in the Lord. This is my defense to those who would examine me. Do we not have the right to our food and drink? Do we not have the right to be accompanied by a wife, as the other apostles and the brothers of the Lord and Cephas?

This de-evaluation of pre-Easter traditions about Jesus on the part of Paul could, when coordinated with the luminously glorious resurrected Christ of the first trajectory from Easter to Valentinus, ultimately replace the normative role of the sayings of Jesus for primitive Christianity with the much more current and spiritual seances and sayings of the still appearing Lord.

Although Paul would not conceptualize his conversion as already his resurrection, since as an apocalypticist he reserved the resurrection of believers for the future, his conversion was nonetheless for him a comparably dramatic transformation into the spiritual realm, granting him a completely superhuman knowledge of Jesus (2 Cor 5:16): "From now on, therefore, we regard no one from a human point of view; even though we once regarded Christ from a human point of view, we regard him thus no longer." This de-evaluation of pre-Easter interpretations of Jesus on the part of Paul could, when coordinated with the experience of resurrection already on the second trajectory from Easter to Valentinus, ultimately replace the normative role of traditional interpretations for primitive Christianity with much more current and spiritual understandings of traditional sayings of Jesus.

Over against such spiritualistic trajectories the trajectory from Easter to the Apostles' Creed would have to find some way to revalidate the traditional sayings of Jesus and reaffirm their conventional interpretation. The way that was ultimately found was the canonical Gospel *genre*, whose derivation can to a considerable extent be explained in terms of these bifurcating trajectories.

The two largest and best-known collections of Jesus' sayings, Q and *The Gospel of Thomas*, do not seem to have become involved in such an apologetic to maintain that the higher level of meaning inheres in the life of Jesus prior to Easter. In fact it is characteristic of such early sayings collections that they contain no thematic discussion of the turning point of death and resurrection about which the subsequent hermeneutical debate revolved, even though in a sense they straddle that turning point. For the authors of such collections stand within the post-Easter period, whereas much of their material goes back to the pre-Easter period. Thus they contain things said by Jesus prior to his crucifixion and also things said by the resurrected Christ; and they imply interpretations inherent in the tradition as well as interpretations recently granted to them by the resurrected Christ.

This ambivalence of the sayings tradition and hence of early sayings collections was not fully satisfactory to either side in the emerging polarization. If the orthodox manage to use and lose Q and to block the canonization of *The Gospel of Thomas*, opting for the biographical pre-Easter cast provided by the canonical Gospels, the Gnostics, while accepting *The Gospel of Thomas*, really prefer another *genre* of gospel, the dialogue of the resurrected Christ with his disciples. It is this trajectory from the sayings collection to the Gnostic dialogues, as well as its *pendant* in the orthodox trajectory from Q to the canonical Gospels, that is now to be sketched.

Q for its part had no clear bearing in terms of time and space. To be sure, the story of the temptation between the sayings of John the Baptist and the Sermon on the Mount/Plain seems to be moving toward a biographical cast such as Mark 1 offers. But the temptation is generally regarded as a late addition to Q reflecting early Christian exegetical interests; without it, there had been more nearly just a succession of John's, then Jesus' sayings, brought together as a collection of Wisdom's sayings. At the other end of Q the conclusion is so disappointing, from the more biographical point of view of a canonical Gospel, as to have been used as an argument against the existence of Q: "It 'peters out in miscellaneous oracles.'"[3] Since Q, like *The Gospel of Thomas*, refers neither to

---

3. Edward C. Hobbs, "A Quarter-Century Without 'Q'," *Perkins School of Theology Journal* 33 (1980) 13, quoting Austin M. Farrer, "On Dispensing With Q," in *Studies in the Gospels: Essays in Memory of R. H. Lightfoot* (ed. Dennis E. Nineham; Oxford: Basil Blackwell, 1955) 60.

cross nor to resurrection, it is a moot question whether the author thought of them as spoken before or after Easter.

One may illustrate the problem by comparing the empowering of the resurrected Christ at the opening of the "Great Commission" (Matt 28:18) and the empowering of the Son in the "Johannine Pericope" of Q 10:22 (Matt 11:27; Luke 10:22): "All authority in heaven and on earth has been given to me." "Everything has been entrusted to me by my Father." If in the case of Matt 28:18 this authorization presupposes the enthronement of Christ as Cosmocrator at the exaltation of Easter (Phil 2:9-11; Acts 2:36), why not in the case of Q? But such a reminiscence of the authorization of Easter in the middle of Q neither implies that Easter falls in the middle of the text, as in the case of Luke-Acts, nor that the "Easter" authorization has been transferred back into the public ministry, as would seem to be the case with the "transfiguration" in Mark, and as the position of the Q text in Matt 11 and Luke 10 might suggest. For Easter does not fall here, or at the beginning or end of Q, or anywhere in Q. Q has the timelessness of eternal truth, or at least of wisdom literature.

The perennial debate about the meaning of the term "the living Jesus" at the opening of *The Gospel of Thomas* also illustrates the problem: Does this expression mean the resurrected Christ, somewhat as, for example, the *Apocalypse of Peter* uses this term to designate the spiritual part of Jesus that ascended to observe from above the crucifixion of "His fleshly part" (NH VII, 81:18, 20)? "Living" is indeed tantamount to "resurrected" in Rev 1:17-18: "Fear not. I am the first and the last, and the *living* one; I died, and behold I am *alive* for evermore, and I have the keys of Death and Hades." Or does "the living Jesus" simply identify Jesus as part of the eternal divine realm, as would be suggested by comparison with the expressions "living Father" (Sayings 3, 50), "Living One" (Sayings 37, 59, 111), or, of the redeemed, "living spirit" (Saying 114)?

We have been accustomed to think that probably Q had in mind Jesus prior to Easter. But to what extent is such a view really objective, to what extent due to our knowing Q only within the Marcan outline of Matthew and Luke? Similarly we naturally incline to think of "the living Jesus" of *The Gospel of Thomas* as the resurrected Christ. But to what extent is this view really objective, to what extent the result of our knowing *The Gospel of Thomas* only within the context of the Coptic Gnostic codices? Since, like Q, *The Gospel of Thomas* refers neither to cross nor to resurrection, it is a moot question whether the author thought of sayings as spoken before or after Easter. This seems not to have been relevant to the author. *The Gospel of Thomas* certainly has many sayings that the canonical Gospels place prior to Easter – as do modern scholars, in regarding a good number of the sayings in *The Gospel of Thomas* as "authentic" sayings of Jesus. But such sayings are not distinguished by *The Gospel of Thomas* from those that are clearly "inauthentic."

The lack of concern in primitive Christianity and in the sayings collections as to whether the sayings were spoken by Jesus before or after Easter, that is to say, by Jesus of Nazareth or the resurrected Christ, runs parallel with Paul's considering the authority of Jesus represented by the sayings tradition as more or less interchangeable with the guidance of the Spirit given at Easter. For Paul did in fact relativize traditions of Jesus' sayings to a status hardly superior to the guidance of the Spirit (1 Cor 7:10-12, 25, 40):

> To the married I give charge, not I but the Lord, that the wife should not separate from her husband ... and that the husband should not divorce his wife. To the rest I say, not the Lord ...
>
> Now concerning the unmarried, I have no command of the Lord, but give my opinion as one who by the Lord's mercy is trustworthy ...
>
> And I think that I have the Spirit of God.

Indeed a priority of the Holy Spirit after Easter to Jesus prior to Easter may already be suggested in Q 12:10 (Matt 12:32; Luke 12:10): "And whoever says a word against the son of humanity, it will be forgiven him; but whoever speaks against the holy Spirit, it will not be forgiven him." To be sure, this usual interpretation of an otherwise obscure saying[4] does pose the problem that Jesus prior to Easter has what becomes the honorific title of the coming judge, the son of humanity, whereas the "resurrected Christ" is actually represented (replaced?) by the Holy Spirit. Mark heard this saying in a much more orthodox way, in that the Holy Spirit is the Spirit in Jesus prior to Easter (3:28-30), without any contrast to the son of humanity. But Q may even lack the Marcan (1:12) view of the Spirit entering Jesus at baptism (Q 3:22?); at best Jesus will bestow the Spirit (Q 3:16: Matt 3:11; Luke 3:16).

Rudolf Bultmann's famous *dictum*, that Jesus rose into the kerygma (with its neo-orthodox overtone: the social gospel rose into the old-fashioned gospel which leaves Q out) could perhaps be reformulated from the point of view of Q to the effect that Jesus rose, as the revalidation of his word, into the Holy Spirit. Thus, rather than narrating a resurrection story, Q demonstrates its reality by presenting Jesus' sayings in their revalidated state as the guidance of the Holy Spirit. Easter is then not a

---

4. Wolfgang Schenk, *Synopse zur Redenquelle der Evangelien: Q-Synopse und Rekonstruktion in deutscher Übersetzung mit kurzen Erläuterungen* (Düsseldorf: Patmos, 1981) 88.

point in time in Q, but rather permeates Q as the reality of Jesus' word being valid now. Or at least so it might seem especially for those who understood the resurrected Christ as Spirit. One may in this regard compare a couplet from one of the enthusiastic kerygmatic hymns (1 Tim 3:16): "He was manifested in the flesh, vindicated [or: justified] in the Spirit," with the saying in Q 7:35 that names the higher power shared by John and Jesus (Matt 11:19; Luke 7:35): "But Wisdom was vindicated by her children." It is as Spirit or Wisdom that Jesus (and John) lives on in the sayings tradition.

The Fourth Gospel brings to expression this spiritual significance of Easter within the canonical gospel *genre*. The Holy Spirit is breathed on the disciples at Easter (John 20:22) as the Counselor who will in effect continue the sayings of Jesus until the disciples reach the ultimate truth not attained prior to Easter (John 14:16; 15:26; 16:13-15):

> The Counselor, the Holy Spirit, whom the Father will send in my name, he will teach you all things, and bring to your remembrance all that I have said to you.

> But when the Counselor comes, whom I shall send to you from the Father, even the Spirit of truth, who proceeds from the Father, he will bear witness to me.

> I have yet many things to say to you, but you cannot bear them now. When the Spirit of truth comes, he will guide you into all the truth; for he will not speak on his own authority, but whatever he hears he will speak, and he will declare to you the things that are to come. He will glorify me, for he will take what is mine and declare it to you. All that the Father has is mine; therefore I said that he will take what is mine and declare it to you.

Of course the most obvious thing for which the disciples had not been adequately prepared was Jesus' death. Hence their Easter experiences primarily made up for this deficiency. Thus it is not surprising when individual sayings explicitly said to have been clarified at Easter are references to his death (John 2:22): "When therefore he was raised from the dead, his disciples remembered that he had said this ['Destroy this temple, and in three days I will raise it up,' 2:19], and they believed the scripture and the word which Jesus had spoken." But sometimes there is no such specific reference, but rather Easter has in general become the time when the light dawns (John 12:16): "His disciples did not understand this [Zech 9:9 and the triumphal entry] at first; but when Jesus was glorified, then they remembered that this had been written of him and had been done to him." Even though a specific time reference is not given in John 13:7, the same may be implied: "What I am doing [washing Peter's feet] you do not know now, but afterward you will understand."

Yet it must be said that the sayings ascribed in the Gospel of John to Jesus prior to Easter have already been so updated in terms of Easter as to leave little remaining to be done when one reaches the actual resurrection at the end of this gospel. Such a saying as John 3:13 obviously must be ascribed to the resurrected Christ: "No one *has ascended* into heaven but he who descended from heaven, the Son of Man." One need only compare a statement of the resurrected Christ in *Pistis Sophia* 6 (see below): "I *have been* to the places from whence I came forth." Thus there is an odd tension in John between the doctrine of a shift to a higher hermeneutical level first with the gift of the Spirit at Easter and the presence of that higher level actually at almost every turn prior to Easter. Jesus prior to Easter has authority in the Gospel of John precisely because of the guidance of the Spirit of truth since Easter. That is to say, the highly interpreted sayings of Jesus in the Gospel of John stand in some tension to the canonical gospel *genre* in which they occur, but might seem quite natural in a sayings collection where the question of before or after Easter does not arise.

In this Easter hermeneutic of the Gospel of John the traditions of Jesus are associated with scripture (John 2:22; 12:16, both just cited): "the scripture and the word which Jesus had spoken;" "this had been written of him and had been done to him." Here too the hermeneutical pathos at Easter is motivated by the fact that especially cross and resurrection were to be scripturally supported. But it is nonetheless significant that such hermeneutic is considered distinctive of the period after the resurrection, in that the disciples had not been prepared in advance, as was the case in the Gospel of Mark with its repeated predictions of the passion (John 20:9): "For as yet they did not know the scriptures, that he must rise from the dead."

Luke also seems aware of Easter as the distinctive time of this *interpretatio christiana* of scripture (24:25-26, 32, 44-47):

> "O foolish men, and slow of heart to believe all that the prophets have spoken! Was it not necessary that the Christ should suffer these things and enter into his glory?"
>
> "Did not our hearts burn within us while he talked to us on the road, while he opened to us the scriptures?"
>
> "Everything written about me in the law of Moses and the prophets and the psalms must be fulfilled." Then he opened their minds to understand the scriptures, and said to them, "Thus it is written, that the Christ should suffer and on the third day rise from the dead, and that repentance and forgiveness of sins should be preached in his name to all nations, beginning from Jerusalem."

Yet the emphasis on the *interpretatio christiana* of scripture at Easter is not explainable as due merely to its following immediately upon the crucifixion, whose offense could be alleviated through the reassurance that it was predicted. Luke seems to consider Easter to be a distinctive time of hermeneutical revelation. For though not called the Holy Spirit (since Luke reserves that for Pentecost), nonetheless a special divine intervention is intended in the contrasts: "foolish men and slow of heart to believe;" whereupon "he opened to us the scriptures," "he opened their minds." The idea that Easter is on principle the time of a new hermeneutic as the time of the Spirit seems to be established with regard to scripture as well as Jesus' sayings.

The apologetic view of Easter as the time for interpreting scripture as well as Jesus' sayings so as to find in them the cross and resurrection recurs in Justin Martyr (*Apology* 1.50; *Dialogue with Trypho* 106):

> Afterwards, when He had risen from the dead and appeared to them, and had taught them to read the prophecies in which all these things were foretold as coming to pass ...

> [The apostles] who repented of their flight from Him when He was crucified, after He rose from the dead, and after they were persuaded by Himself that, before His passion He had mentioned to them that He must suffer these things, and that they were announced beforehand by the prophets ...

Once the sayings of Jesus are associated with scripture in terms of authoritative texts to be interpreted, they could hardly fail to have been associated with it in terms of obscurity. For if the Jewish scriptures are not explicitly a Christian book, the sayings of Jesus are not explicitly like the Easter gospel. But the hermeneutical methods already available for providing an *interpretatio christiana* to scripture could be carried over to the sayings of Jesus as well. These hermeneutical methods for updating outmoded but authoritative texts had begun with the Alexandrian interpretation of Homer, and had been adapted within Judaism as the Platonizing interpretation by Philo, the Essene interpretation at Qumran, the gnostic interpretation by Sethians and the Christian interpretation by the early Church.

The theological presupposition of such interpretation can be illustrated from the comment to Hab 2:2 in the Qumran *Commentary on the Book of Habakkuk* (1QpHab)[5]:

> God told Habakkuk to write the things that are coming upon the last generation; but the fulness of that time He did not make known to him.

---

5. William H. Brownlee, *The Midrash Pesher of Habakkuk* (SBLMS 24; Missoula: Scholars, 1979) 107. See also his exposition, pp. 110-11: "The prophets did not know all that the messianic age would contain. According to the Babylonian Talmud (Yalk. ii, 368, Eccl. Rabbah i, 8) only part of the future glory was shown to the prophets. According to Midr. Shoher Tob to Ps. 90:1, 'With the exception of Moses and Isaiah, none of the prophets knew the content of their prophecies.' Cf. also 1 Peter 1:10-12. Philo went even further. In Special Laws 1, 65, he asserted that the prophets were so completely under the control of God that they did not even know what they were speaking."

> As for that which He said, "for the sake of him who reads it" (or, "that he who reads it may run [may divulge]"), its interpretation concerns the Righteous Teacher to whom God has made known all the mysteries of the words of His servants the prophets.

The appropriation of this hermeneutic by primitive Christianity is documented by 1 Pet 1:10-12:

> The prophets who prophesied of the grace that was to be yours searched and inquired about this salvation; they inquired what person or time was indicated by the Spirit of Christ within them when predicting the sufferings of Christ and the subsequent glory. It was revealed to them that they were serving not themselves but you, in the things which have now been announced to you by those who preached the good news to you through the Holy Spirit sent from heaven, things into which angels long to look.

That is to say, the modern heirs of scripture have a special revelation providing them with the key to its meaning. This is why average persons do not accept the sectarian interpretation – they are unenlightened. For though the text seems to mean only the superficial statement any reader sees (the literal meaning), God has revealed to the sectarians his real, esoteric meaning (the higher, deeper, fuller, spiritual meaning).

Technical terminology for such a two-level interpretation of scripture occurs, for example, in Justin's effort to convince Trypho the Jew of the validity of the *interpretatio christiana* (*Dialogue* 52.1; 68.6):

> The Holy Spirit had uttered these truths in a *parable*, and obscurely.

> There were many sayings written obscurely, or *parabolically*, or mysteriously, and symbolic actions, which the prophets who lived after the persons who said or did them expounded.

Similarly in *Pistis Sophia* (18): "Now concerning this word, my Lord, the power within the prophet Isaiah has spoken thus and has related once in a spiritual *parable*, speaking about the vision of Egypt" [Isa 19:3, 12]. The term "parable" and its synonyms really mean riddle, coded authoritative text.

But the term "parable" can also be used in *Pistis Sophia* to introduce a saying of Jesus that the canonical Gospels placed before the crucifixion, but a saying that is no more than is the Old Testament what one would normally consider a parable; the saying is designated "parable" only in the technical sense of a coded authoritative message subject to a higher interpretation (*Pistis Sophia* 50, 104, 105, 107):

> "O Lord, concerning this, thou didst once say to us in a *parable* [Luke 22:28-30]."

> "I answered, I spake to you in a *parable*, saying [Matt 18:22]."

"For concerning the souls of men such as these I spoke to you once in a *parable*, saying [Matt 18:15-17; Luke 17:3]."

"Now concerning such men, I spoke to you once in a *parable*, saying [Matt 10:12-13 parr.]."

This technical use of the term "parable" is clearly intended to set the saying or text in question off from a higher and clearer level "without parable" characteristic of the resurrected Christ's teaching in *Pistis Sophia* (88, 90, 100, 114). That higher level can be designated in its own right as Jesus teaching "openly" (*parrhēsia*: *Pistis Sophia* 17, 18, 19, 24, 25, 43, 65, 67, 69, 71, 74, 80, etc.). Thus the two technical terms come to be juxtaposed as a contrasting pair (*Pistis Sophia* 128; similarly 107, 110): "The Savior answered and said to Maria: 'Question everything which thou dost wish to question, and I will reveal them *openly* without *parable*.'"

To be sure, just as a series of synonyms can occur for the term "in parables," such as "sayings written obscurely, or parabolically, or mysteriously, and symbolic actions" quoted above from Justin, just so there are synonyms for "openly," for example in *Pistis Sophia*: "with assurance and certainty" (88, 90); "face to face" (100); "more and more, openly without parable, and with certainty" (107); "face to face without parable" (114).

Irenaeus accuses the Valentinians of this two-level interpretation of Jesus' sayings, making use of this fluid but technical terminology (1.1.5): "They tell us, however, that this knowledge has not been *openly* [*phanerōs*] divulged, because all are not capable of receiving it, but has been mystically revealed by the Savior through means of *parables* to those qualified for understanding it." Thus when Morton Smith[6] sees a "libertine" implication in an excerpt from the Valentinian Theodotus quoted by Clement of Alexandria and ascribed by Smith to a pre-Marcan Aramaic gospel, a much less exciting, indeed pedantic but methodologically more reliable interpretation would be to the effect that again one has (here divided into three progressive levels) the same contrasting hermeneutic pair expressed in a series of synonyms[7]: "The Savior taught the Apostles at first figuratively and mystically, later in parables and riddles, and thirdly clearly and *openly* [as R. P. Casey freely but accurately translates *gymnōs*, in this context meant as a synonym for *parrhēsia*, but which Smith translates literally but tendentiously as 'nakedly'] when they

6. Morton Smith, *The Secret Gospel* (San Francisco: Harper and Row, 1973) 142.
7. R. P. Casey, *The Excerpta ex Theodoto of Clement of Alexandria* (London: Christophers, 1934) 82-83.

were *alone* [also a hermeneutical cliché – see below – rather than documentation for something 'libertine'].''

The frequent use of the term "parable" to designate a coded authoritative text would readily attract to it instances in the sayings tradition of the same term "parable" occurring in the more normal meaning of a simple sermon illustration. Thus in the pre-Marcan collection of three parables imbedded in Mark 4 (vss 2-10, 13-20, 26-29, 30-34: the Parables of the Sower, of the Seed Growing Secretly, and of the Mustard Seed) the first parable is accompanied by its interpretation, introduced by the comment (vs 10): "And when he was *alone*, those who were about him ... asked him concerning the *parable(s)*." Thereupon followed the higher allegorical interpretation. The pre-Marcan collection also concluded with a specific reference to the two-level procedure (vss 33, 34b): "With many such parables he spoke the word to them, as they were able to hear it; ... but privately to his own disciples he explained everything."

The Gospel of Mark only heightens the esoteric hermeneutic of this pre-Marcan collection by interpolating a still more exclusivistic characterization of those to whom the higher meaning is granted (vss 11-12): "To you has been given the *secret (mystērion)* of the kingdom of God, but for those outside everthing is in *parables*; so that they may indeed see but not perceive, and may indeed hear but not understand; lest they should turn again, and be forgiven." This heightening of the esoteric language is also reflected in the sayings Mark adds to the collection of parables (vss 21-25, especially vss 22 and 25): "For there is nothing *hid (krypton)*, except to be made *manifest (phanerōthē)*; nor is anything *secret (apokryphon)*, except to come to *light (phaneron)*." "For to him who has will more be given; and from him who has not, even what he has will be taken away."

Much of the same esoteric concept recurs as the introductory saying in a cluster of parables imbedded in *The Gospel of Thomas* that Helmut Koester has suggested may be a source antedating that gospel (Sayings 62-65)[8]: "It is to those who are worthy of My *mysteries* that I tell My *mysteries*. Do not let your left hand know what your right hand is doing." In this context (in distinction from that of almsgiving in Matt 6:3) the latter part must mean something to the effect that common people (the "left hand") should not have access to the higher meaning of the "mysteries" known to the inner circle (the "right hand").

8. Helmut Koester, "Introduction [to the Gospel of Thomas]", in *Nag Hammadi Codex II,2-7 together with XIII,2*, Brit.Lib.Or. 4926 (1), and P.Oxy. 1, 654, 655*. Vol. 1: *Gospel According to Thomas, Gospel According to Philip, Hypostasis of the Archons, and Indexes* (with contributions by many scholars ed. Bentley Layton; The Coptic Gnostic Library; NHS 20; Leiden: Brill, 1989) 38-49: 41.

The esoteric, not to say eerie, context of a resurrection appearance would almost by definition be such a private setting for higher meaning, especially in view of the hermeneutical importance of Easter. Thus it is not surprising that the technical contrasting terms for designating the literal and spiritual levels of meaning, especially "in parables" and "openly," are used to distinguish the sayings of Jesus before and after Easter. In *The Apocryphon of James* the resurrected Christ says (NH I, 7:1-6): "At first I spoke to you *in parables* and you did not understand; now I speak to you *openly*, and you (still) do not perceive."

In gnostic perspective the resurrected Christ would also have the higher spiritual status of speaking from heaven and being free of the body. This Easter setting for the higher esoteric interpretation would also have the advantage of being able tacitly to concede to emerging orthodoxy the traditions of Jesus prior to Easter, as being only at the lower level, without those traditions being able to challenge the validity of a private séance with the resurrected Christ to which the orthodox were by definition not invited.

Indeed gnostics could shift their higher illumination from the first Easter Sunday forward down into the future beyond the limit of the physical appearances to which the orthodox had come to appeal, in that such physical transactions would in gnostic perspective be no better than the earthbound sayings prior to Easter. This may be the significance of the gnostic motif of Jesus' appearance for gnostic instruction long after the first Easter, since it is only at this later time then that he achieves the true knowledge. Irenaeus (1.28.7) reports the gnostic view: "But after his resurrection he tarried [on earth] *eighteen months*; and knowledge descending into him from above, he taught what was clear. He instructed a few of his disciples, whom he knew to be capable of understanding so great *mysteries*, in these things, and was then received up into heaven."

Similarly *Pistis Sophia* 1–6 actually deferred the normative resurrection appearance eleven years, since it is clear that only after that lapse of time does the luminous status and higher instruction emerge:

> But it happened that after Jesus had risen from the dead he spent *eleven years* speaking with his disciples. And he taught them only as far as the places of the first ordinance and as far as the places of the First Mystery which is within the veil. ... And the disciples did not know and understand that there was anything within that mystery. ... But he had only spoken to them in general, teaching them that they existed. But he had not told them the extent and the rank of their places according to how they exist. Because of this they also did not know that other places existed within that mystery. ...
>
> Now it happened when the light-power had come down upon Jesus, it gradually surrounded him completely. Then Jesus rose or ascended to the height, giving light exceedingly, with a light to which there was no measure.

And the disciples gazed after him, and not one of them spoke until he had reached heaven, but they all kept a great silence. ... As they were saying these things and were weeping to one another, on the ninth hour of the following day the heavens opened, and they saw Jesus coming down, giving light exceedingly, and there was no measure to the light in which he was.

Then Jesus, the compassionate, said to them: "Rejoice and be glad from this hour because I have been to the places from whence I came forth. From today onwards now I speak with you *openly* from the beginning of the truth until its completion. And I will speak with you face to face, without *parable*. I will not conceal from you, from this hour onwards, anything of the things of the height and of the place of the truth."

This same concept of the deferment of the gnostic teaching of the resurrected Christ is attested as 550 days in *The Apocryphon of James* itself (NH I, 2:19-20). There may have even been a reference to eighteen months, if one may take its reference to eighteen *days* as a textual corruption. Here the related concept of decoding the parabolic level is associated with the tradition of Jesus' parables in the normal sense of the term, in what seems to be a reference to a collection of such parables (NH I, 7:35–8:11):

"Since I have already been glorified in this fashion, why do you hold me back in my eagerness to go? For after the labor you have compelled me to stay with you another *eighteen days* for the sake of the *parables*. It was enough for some to listen to the teaching and understand 'The Shepherds' and 'The Seed' and 'The Building' and 'The Lamps of the Virgins' and 'The Wage of the Workmen' and 'The Didrachmae' and 'The Woman.' Become earnest about the word!"

To be sure, Gnostics could when need be take the other alternative, in claiming that Jesus even prior to Easter had taught gnostic truth, if one only had the understanding to comprehend it. For one of the things the Nag Hammadi texts are teaching us about Gnosticism is that it did not consist of the pure but largely undocumented construct that scholarship had postulated, but rather that it evolved with the changing times and thus could come to expression within Christianity not only in its own pro-Gnostic categories, and not only as an interpretation of the earliest Christian position, but also as an adaptation of later pro-orthodox positions, in this case secondary to the orthodox trajectory identifying sayings of Jesus pointedly with the period prior to Easter as they are found in the canonical gospels (see below). Thus at the luminous appearance at the opening of *The Letter of Peter to Philip* (NH VIII, 135:3-8): "Then a voice came to them out of the light, saying, 'It is you yourselves who are witnesses that *I spoke all these things to you*. But because of your unbelief I shall speak again.'" This approach of claiming the pre-Easter sayings for Gnosticism is used in the gnostic *Apocalypse of Peter*, a text that in various ways attacks orthodoxy, in order with this technique also to claim Peter for Gnosticism (NH VII, 72:9-26):

> And he said to me, "Peter, *I have told you many times* that they are blind ones who have no guide. If you want to know their blindness, put your hands upon (your) eyes – your robe – and say what you see."
>
> But when I had done it, I did not see anything. I said, "No one sees (this way)."
>
> Again he told me, "Do it again."
>
> And there came in me fear with joy, for I saw a new light greater than the light of day. Then it came down upon the Savior.

This secondary gnosticizing of the canonical tradition on the part of Valentinians is criticized by Irenaeus (1.1.6): "And it is not only from the writings of the evangelists and the apostles that they endeavour to derive proofs for their opinions by means of perverse interpretations and deceitful expositions; they deal in the same way with the law and the prophets, which contain many *parables* and allegories that can frequently be drawn into various senses, according to the kind of exegesis to which they are subjected."

The usual gnostic way of laying claim to the sayings of Jesus, by providing a higher spiritual interpretation at Easter, did not even find the sayings collection really suitable to its purposes. Rather Gnosticism found it most practical to modulate from the sayings collection to the dialogue, especially the question-and-answer version. Apart from the general proclivity for brief segments of dialogue to occur in sayings collections when needed to make a saying intelligible, the shift from the sayings collection to the dialogue may have been motivated by the greater suitability of the dialogue for the two-level interpretation constitutive of the Gnostic method. This conjecture would seem to be suggested by a survey of the use of the two-level interpretation at the opening of sayings collections.

The collection of Jesus' sayings inserted at the opening of the *Didache* begins with the format of text plus interpretation (*Did* 1:2-3):

> The Way of Life is this: "First, thou shalt love the God who made thee, secondly, thy neighbor as thyself; and whatsoever thou wouldst not have done to thyself, do not thou do another."
>
> Now, the *teaching* [*didachē*] of these words is this: "Bless those that curse you, …"

Thus the collection is presented as the "teaching" implicit in the summary of the law as love and in the (negative) Golden Rule. But much of the collection is only in a very general way such an explication, nor are the individual sayings in the "teaching" themselves subjected to such a secondary interpretation. The two-level format with which the collection is introduced is not carried through consistently and thus seems largely extraneous to the collection as such.

The Marcan apocalypse is also a sayings collection. It has at its opening a similar text-plus-interpretation format (Mark 13:1-5):

> And as he came out of the temple, one of his disciples said to him, "Look, Teacher, what wonderful stones and what wonderful buildings!"
>
> And Jesus said to him, "Do you see these great buildings? There will not be left here one stone upon another, that will not be thrown down."
>
> And as he sat on the Mount of Olives opposite the temple, Peter and James and John and Andrew asked him *privately*, "Tell us, when will this be, and what will be the sign when these things are all to be accomplished?"
>
> And Jesus began to say to them, ...

Yet here too the initial warnings against thinking the time has come (vss 5-8) are followed by exhortation (vss 9-13) that does not directly interpret the cryptic saying. Though a discussion of signs follows (vs 14ff), other apocalyptic material is freely added (through vs 37), so that the apocalyptic discourse tends to lose sight of its point of departure. Nor are the specific sayings in the body of the apocalypse themselves accompanied by interpretations. Thus the text-plus-interpretation format with which the Marcan apocalypse opens does not seem to be constitutive of the sayings collection itself.

The *Gospel of Thomas* may also have a similar opening. Saying 1 has been adapted from the tradition (see John 8:52) to provide a hermeneutical introduction to the collection calling for a two-level approach: "Whoever *finds* the interpretation [*hermēneia*] of these sayings will not experience death." Saying 2 is not just what happened to come next by way of independent saying, loosely associated by a catch-word connection ("find"), but seems to have been intentionally chosen as an interpretation of the first saying's offer of escape from death. For it provides a step-by-step *ordo salutis* of the stages between the initial seeking and finding and the ultimate salvation: "Let him who *seeks* continue seeking until he *finds*. When he finds, he will become *troubled*. When he becomes troubled, he will be *astonished*, and he will *rule* over the All." Yet such a text-plus-interpretation relationship, even if present at the opening, does not pervade the collection as such, which moves on without any discernible overall organization other than a loose catch-word kind of association and occasional smaller clusters of sayings that may have circulated together prior to *The Gospel of Thomas*. Some sayings are in a rather primitive form, needing interpretation, others are presented in highly inter-preted form, but the text-plus-interpretation format itself does not recur.

The collection of parables used by Mark also presents the two-level for-mat at its opening (the Parable of the Sower), where the text (vss 3-8) and the interpretation (vss 14-20) stand side by side, connected by a hermeneutical comment similar to that in Mark 13:3 (Mark 4:10): "And when he was *alone*, those who were about him ... asked him concerning the parable." Rather than being referred to as a *didachē* (*Did* 1:3) or a *hermēneia* (*The Gospel of Thomas*, Saying 1), the hermeneutical proce-dure in this instance would be called by a third synonym, *epilysis*, a "res-olution" or "explanation." This term occurs in its substantive form fre-quently in the *Similitudes* of *The Shepherd of Hermas*, though in the pre-Marcan collection only in its verbal form and then only at the con-clusion (Mark 4:33, 34b): "With many such parables he spoke the word to them, as they were able to hear it; ... but privately to his own disci-ples he *explained* everything." Yet in spite of the conclusion thus claim-ing the text-plus-interpretation format, that format is limited to the first of the three parables, and so would not seem to be constitutive of the col-lection as such.

It may be no coincidence that this format occurs at the beginnings of such collections. This would tend to cast upon the whole collection the aura of a higher meaning latent in the text. But the *genre* of sayings collection as such is not particularly suited to implementing that impli-cation, as these instances tend to illustrate. Nor do all sayings collections begin with that format – there is no evidence of it at the beginning of Q, and it is not characteristic of Jewish wisdom literature. The text-plus-interpretation format seems rather to be at home in the interpretation of the individual saying.

This may be illustrated by the striking parallel between the presenta-tion of the Parable of the Sower with its interpretation and the presenta-tion about ceremonial impurity in Mark 7[9]:

Mark 4		Mark 7	
3	"Listen!"	14	"Hear me, all of you, and understand:
3-8	(The Parable of the Sower)	15	There is nothing outside a man which by going into him can defile him; but the things which come out of a man are what defile him."

---

9. Willi Marxsen, "Redaktionsgeschichtliche Erklärung der sogenannten Parabeltheo-rie des Markus," *ZThK* 52 (1955) 255-71.

9	"He who has ears to hear, let him hear."	16	["If any man has ears to hear, let him hear." (This as a variant reading no longer in the critical text)]
10	And when he was *alone*, those who were about him ... asked him about the parables.	17	And when he had entered the *house*, and left the people, his disciples asked him about the parable.
13	And he said to them, "Do you not understand this parable? How then will you understand all the parables?"	18	And he said to them "Then are you also without understanding? Do you not see that ..."
14-20	(The interpretation)	18b-23	(The interpretation)

A somewhat less detailed instance of such a text-plus-interpretation format also occurs in Mark 10, where Jesus' response to the question concerning divorce (vss 5-9) and the appended interpretation (vss 11-12) are connected by a statement including the secrecy motif familiar from Mark 4:10; 7:17; 13:3 (Mark 10:10): "And in the *house* the disciples asked him again about this matter."

This text-plus-interpretation format is comparable to the Pesher method of Qumran, where a text of scripture is quoted and then an interpretation is appended with the introductory formula "its interpretation (*pesher*) is about ...," from which this kind of exegesis received its name. But such a Pesher can continue down to the end of a text, in that a verse and its interpretation are followed by the next verse and its interpretation, etc. Or in the case of longer quotations each subdivision can be recalled to introduce its specific interpretation, as in the case of the interpretation of the Parable of the Sower, or of the answers to the battery of questions posed by the apostles in *The Letter of Peter to Philip* (NH VIII, 134:18–137:13). Although a saying-by-saying commentary on a sayings collection is conceivable (and suggested by the title of Papias's five-volume *Exegesis of the Lord's Sayings*), the Gnostics did not seem ready to give up the pretense of recording an oral communication in favor of the commentary proper. They hence moved to the *genre* of dialogues of the resurrected Christ with his disciples, which thus became the distinctive gnostic *genre* of gospel. To be sure these dialogues are no longer genuine dialogues, where the discussion partners share a common innate *logos* or rationality, but rather are in the question-and-answer format of the *erotapokrisis*, where the authority figure is interrogated by the seeker[10]. Here the resurrected Christ responds to inquiries by the apostles,

---

10. Kurt Rudolph, "Der gnostische 'Dialog' als literarisches Genus," in *Probleme der koptischen Literatur* (ed. P. Nagel; Wissenschaftliche Beiträge der Martin Luther-Universität

who either inquire as to the true meaning of the preceding saying, or pose a question at times itself rooted in a saying. This format is ideally suited to dissolving the rigidity of the given tradition and providing ample opportunity for creative innovation.

The substantive outcome of this third trajectory from Easter to Valentinus, from the sayings collection to the dialogue of the resurrected Christ with his disciples, is summarized by Polycarp (*Phil* 7.1): "Whosoever perverts the oracles [*logia*] of the Lord for his own lusts, and says that there is neither resurrection nor judgment, – this man is the first-born of Satan." Here is precisely the heresy of the second trajectory from Easter to Valentinus, denying the future resurrection presumably because it has taken place spiritually in the ecstasy of baptism, that is associated with the unorthodox trajectory of Jesus' sayings.

Now the same pair of technical terms, derived from scriptural exegesis and used by Gnosticism for its invidious distinction between the gnostic higher meaning imparted by the resurrected Christ and the lower meaning of the usual sayings tradition, recurs in the canonical Gospel of John (16:25, 29) with the minor variation that for *parabolē* the Gospel of John uses *paroimia*, a synonym, as is evident from the fact that it is used at John 10:6 in the normal meaning of parable: "'I have said this to you *in figures*; the hour is coming when I shall no longer speak to you *in figures* but tell you *plainly* of the Father.' His disciples said, 'Ah, now you are speaking *plainly*, not *in* any *figure*!'" Although this takes place at the climax of John (16:32: "The hour is coming, indeed it has come."), it is not quite at Easter; rather what would be expected to be located at Easter is pushed back into the parting discourses prior to the crucifixion, leaving for the Johannine resurrection appearances not much more to be said than *Shalom*.

In Mark this turning point from coded to uncoded sayings is pushed still further back. Mark had appended to the collection of parables he had incorporated in chapter 4 the pointed comment (4:34): "He did not speak to them without a *parable*." But then this coded message is presented in uncoded form after Peter's confession at Caesarea Philippi in Mark 8, when Jesus begins to talk like a Christian. The first prediction of the passion is what the quest of the historical Jesus took uncritically to be a turning point in the life of Jesus rather than in the Marcan

Halle–Wittenberg 1968/1 [K2]; Halle [Saale] 1968) 85-107; Pheme Perkins, *The Gnostic Dialogue: The Early Church and the Crisis of Gnosticism* (Theological Inquiries: Studies in Contemporary Biblical and Theological Problems; New York/Ramsey/Toronto: Paulist Press, 1980); Stephen Emmel, "Post-Resurrection Dialogues Between Jesus Christ and His Disciples or Apostles as a Literary Genre" (1980, unpublished).

composition. Though Rudolf Otto also still attributed the shift to Jesus, he did at least recognize it as the first time Mark's frequent allusions to Jesus teaching are actually accompanied by the explicit teaching. Julius Wellhausen first recognized it as a basic shift from the time of Jesus to the time of Mark[11]. It is at this crucial juncture that Mark inserts the pointed remark (8:32): "And he said this *plainly*." Thus both Mark and John seem aware of the pair of contrasting terms, and both agree in placing the shift from one level to the other before rather than after Easter.

William Wrede overlooked this Marcan use of the pair of technical terms, understandable enough given the fact that in Mark the pair is not side by side, but widely separated. As a matter of fact the source material in which they occur side by side and thus emerge clearly as such a pair of contrasting technical terms was not yet available to Wrede. As a result Wrede in effect assimilated Mark to the view that the shift in levels took place at Easter, rather than recognizing Mark – and the canonical Gospel *genre* – to be a variant upon, indeed a corrective of, precisely that view. For the Easter timing Wrede appealed to Mark 9:9, where the resurrection is given as the time when the transfiguration is to be told. But this is more likely due to the association specifically of the transfiguration with Easter than to a general Marcan turning point at Easter. Wrede failed to recognize that Mark has, apparently intentionally, shifted that turning point back into the middle of his Gospel.

This may indeed be the key to the perennial problem of the gospel *genre*. The fact that Mark and John transfer the shift to the higher level of meaning back prior to the crucifixion may be their most explicit rationale for playing down didactic revelations at Easter and filling almost their whole books with the period prior to Easter, the period when Jesus was teaching in his physical body on earth. Luke would in his way carry this to its logical outcome in defining the qualifications of an apostle so as to include not just, *à la* Paul, the resurrection, but the whole period since John the Baptist (thus reaching the position made standard in the English language tradition through the idiom "public ministry", Acts 1:21-22): "So one of the men who have accompanied us during all the time that the Lord Jesus went in and out among us, beginning from the baptism of John until the day when he was taken from us – one of these men must become with us a witness to his resurrection."

---

11. Rudolf Otto, *The Kingdom of God and the Son of Man* (London: Lutterworth, reprint of new and revised edition, 1951) 247. Julius Wellhausen, *Einleitung in die drei ersten Evangelien* (2nd ed.; Berlin: Georg Reimer, 1911) 72.

The gospels of Matthew and Luke, by obscuring the Marcan turning point at Caesarea Philippi (they omit Mark 8:32) and by imbedding Q throughout Mark, have carried to its ultimate orthodox outcome this trend, in that the authoritative Christian sayings of Jesus are unmistakably fleshed out in the whole body of the Marcan narrative framework from the time of John the Baptist on. Rather than Easter marking a decisive shift in the truth value, authority, and quasi-canonicity of Jesus' sayings, the Evangelists' logical outcome is brought to expression in Luke 24:44: "These are my words which I spoke to you, while I was still with you." The resurrected Christ only repeats what Jesus had said prior to Easter. Or, put conversely, Jesus had always talked like a Christian.

The trajectory from Easter to the Apostles' Creed reached the somewhat paradoxical outcome in a creed omitting entirely Jesus' "public ministry" and the whole sayings tradition – or at least so it seems to us. To them it may have seemed quite the reverse: The Roman baptismal confession of the early second-century was the faith of the apostles, that is to say, the whole orthodox creed was taught them by Jesus.

If the two-level interpretation of the sayings of Jesus on the trajectory from Easter to Valentinus meant exploiting the original orientation of the shift in levels to Easter as a rationale for extrapolating from the tradition new interpretations, indeed new sayings, and in the process modulated from the sayings collection, itself poorly suited to two-level exegesis, into the dialogue *genre* whose question-and-answer format invited the engendering of higher interpretations, then conversely the trajectory from Easter to the Apostles' Creed claimed both levels of meaning increasingly for Jesus prior to Easter, creating in the process the canonical gospel *genre* as a replacement for the all too ambivalent Q.

For Jesus to rise in disembodied radiance, for the initiate to reenact this kind of resurrection in ecstasy, and for this religiosity to mystify the sayings of Jesus by means of hermeneutically loaded dialogues of the resurrected Christ with his gnostic disciples is as consistent a position as is the orthodox insistence upon the physical bodiliness of the resurrected Christ, the futurity of the believer's resurrection back into the same physical body, and the incarnation of Jesus' sayings within the pre-Easter biography of Jesus in the canonical Gospels. Neither is the original Christian position; both are serious efforts to interpret it. Neither can be literally espoused by serious critical thinkers of today; both should be hearkened to as worthy segments of the heritage of transmission and interpretation through which Jesus is mediated to the world today.

CHAPTER 3
The Real Jesus of the Sayings Gospel Q

The topic of "the real Jesus" did not even exist until the Enlightenment, unless one wanted, as a latter-day Monophysite or Arian or Adoptionist, to revive long since forgotton heresies. But with the Enlightenment, or, more precisely, with the historicism of the nineteenth century, the question of the real Jesus was posed: Who really was Jesus, as a real person in history? What can the historian say? Over the last two centuries, there gradually emerged a new access to Jesus, made available through objective historical research.

I. THE REDISCOVERY OF THE SAYINGS GOSPEL Q

Up until modern times, people could only know about Jesus through their religious experience in the church, codified in creeds and doctrines about Christ. We all know, no doubt by heart, the Jesus of the Apostles' Creed, which has turned out to be based not on a text Jesus taught his disciples but rather on the baptismal confession developed in Rome in the second century and projected back onto the beginnings. But in that familiar creed Jesus' own history, what he himself said and did during his lifetime, is fully bypassed. Not what he said and did, but only what they said about him, counted as saving information: born of the virgin Mary, suffered under Pontius Pilate. But what lies in between? Is that of no significance? Did not Jesus himself think what he said and did had saving significance? Has Paul's kerygma of cross and resurrection, which is what lies behind the Apostles' Creed, really said everything that we want to know about the significance of Jesus? In the case of other dying and rising gods of the Roman Empire, what one narrates about them, the myth, is the nub of the issue. Nothing else is known about them,—if they actually lived, nothing has survived to be reported—only the myth about their dying and rising. They are prototypes and guarantors of the afterlife, hardly more. But Jesus really lived in time and space and was significant enough that all these myths were absorbed into his significance, as the one and only dying and rising God. But what was Jesus' own significance, which gave him this predominance?

To be sure, the Evangelists themselves have already tailored their narrations of Jesus' sayings and healings to focus on the kerygma, making the gospel of cross and resurrection the quintessence of the whole ministry of Jesus. So can one then be spared the details? Yet for modern people, a person who remains historically inaccessible is somehow unreal, more fancy than fact, indeed a myth. It would boil down to a kind of modern Doceticism if, moved by awe before the exaltedness of Jesus, we were to declare his historical reality to be academically unattainable or religiously irrelevant. The result was, in the nineteenth century, the quest of the historical Jesus, of which Albert Schweitzer wrote so masterfully.

It may be no coincidence that a century and a half ago, as this rediscovery of Jesus was just getting under way, there came to light a collection of Jesus' sayings used by Matthew and Luke in composing their Gospels. Matthew and Luke updated the sayings so that they made clear what Jesus must have meant, namely, what Matthew and Luke meant, and imbedded his sayings into their copies of the Gospel of Mark, making of Matthew and Luke hybrid Gospels, partly Mark and partly the sayings collection.

Then, after Matthew and Luke used it in their enlarged, improved Gospels, that primitive collection of Jesus' sayings was itself no longer copied and transmitted by Christian scribes, since the church of course—unfortunately—preferred those more up-to-date and complete Gospels. The more primitive text was itself lost completely from sight. In fact, it ceased to exist. For since we have no first-century copies of anything Christian, no copies of Q survived. It was never heard of again, after the end of the first century, until, in 1838, a scholar in Leipzig, Germany, Christian Hermann Weisse, detected it lurking just under the surface of the Gospels of Matthew and Luke. Since after its rediscovery it was commonly referred to as a source of the canonical Gospels, scholars came to call it simply "the source," in German, *Quelle,* abbreviated Q. But since "Q" sounds rather cryptic, not to say flat, we have of late come to call it, for clarity's sake and to be able to refer to it as a text in its own right, not just a source for something else, the Sayings Gospel Q.

This old Sayings Gospel was not like the canonical Gospels, so colored over with the kerygma of cross and resurrection that the historical Jesus, though imbedded therein, was actually lost from sight by the heavy overlay of golden patina. Rather, this document was just primitive enough to contain many sayings of Jesus without kerygmatic overlay and without the Q redactor's own additions. Here the real Jesus, who actually lived in history, has his say. So what did he have to say? Such questions have again become acute in our time, at least among modern people who stand within the Christian tradition but also want to know what really happened, what Jesus was really up to.

I can of course only attempt a preliminary answer, for my work is far from complete. And I limit myself almost exclusively to this lost and rediscovered collection of Jesus' sayings. I have worked intensely on reconstructing word for word in Greek that Sayings Gospel, by undoing as best I can the improvements by Matthew and Luke, so as to listen to what Jesus himself had to say. In fact, I organized an international team of more than forty, mostly younger scholars who, during the '90s, tried to decide just how that Greek source read, before Matthew and Luke updated it, but, thank goodness, left it sufficiently intact that our efforts were not in vain.

We have assembled an enormous database of opinions expressed by scholars over the past 150 years about the original wording of Q. After sorting French, German, and English excerpts from scholarly literature in chronological order, we met up to three times a year in America and Europe to evaluate that mass of scholarly opinion and thus to work out what seems the most objective reconstruction of the sayings, one by one. We are now publishing, at Peeters Press in Leuven, our massive database under the series title Documenta Q. In view of this massive publication of scholarly opinion, I refrain here from learned-sounding discussions with the scholars, so as to keep in focus the text of the Sayings Gospel itself.

We published in 2000 a one-volume critical edition of Q in a synopsis, including the Gospels of Matthew, Luke, Mark, and Thomas, with English, German, and French translations of Q and Thomas, *The Critical Edition of Q,* at Fortress Press and Peeters Press. Just to make available a reliable copy of the oldest Gospel, lost for 1900 years, is itself worth doing. But, even more important, Q points back, in its oldest layers, to what Jesus himself had to say. What could he possibly have been thinking as he was doing what he was doing? Thanks to the Sayings Gospel, the question is really not all that impossible to answer. I do think we can catch sight of what he was up to. That is where I want to begin with you.

II. THE SAYINGS GOSPEL'S PRESENTATION OF JESUS

Since I am working from a collection of Jesus' sayings, I have to abstain from the narrative part of his biography, the stories of his birth, healings, Holy Week, and Easter, for, as we will see, they are not in the Sayings Gospel Q at all, or at most, present in a very indirect way. Yet I am happy to limit myself to the Sayings Gospel Q, to concentrate on what Jesus must have been thinking, to judge by what he was saying.

But before turning to Jesus' sayings, let me at least say what one can infer from Q about his life: He grew up in a small village of lower or southern Galilee called in Q (4:16) Nazara, but always called Nazareth elsewhere in the canonical Gospels, a hamlet perhaps too small even to have had a local synagogue in which Jesus might have learned to read the Hebrew scriptures. He must have found "sermons in stones," to judge by the local color that becomes so eloquent in his parables (the stones themselves being especially prominent in Q).

In any case, we know nothing about him until he left home to join the apocalyptic movement of John by undergoing John's initiation rite, baptism in the Jordan. John did not seem to have provided much guidance as to what to do next, other than, having straightened up, to fly right. Baptism by immersion in the Jordan must have symbolized taking off one's old worldly identity and reemerging as a new, godly person. But what does that mean? Where does one go from there?

Perhaps, it is Jesus' wrestling with this question that comes to mythical expression in Q as a debate with the devil in the three temptations of Jesus. In any case, the temptations are the only thing that occurs in Q between John's baptizing Jesus and Jesus' launching his own ministry with his inaugural sermon. For Jesus went directly to the people with the good news of a lifestyle underwritten by God himself.

Before turning to the substantive issue of where Jesus' ideas went, I would like to digress a moment to speak superficially, geographically, about where Jesus himself went: Jesus moved to Capharnaum on the northern edge of the Sea of Galilee, chosen perhaps because it was ideally suited to the lifestyle he had in mind. Capharnaum was beside the lake, which provided a God-given, year-round food supply, was well below sea level, and hence had a mild climate, and was a crossroad for land and sea travel. There were secluded villages in the forested mountains behind, to which Jesus could withdraw, one on the Galilean side of the frontier, Chorazin, and one just across the frontier, under a different ruler, Bethsaida, which seems to have been the home town of others baptized by John. He got along well with the despised custom officials (whom we probably translate inadequately as "tax collectors," not to say "publicans") and the equally unwelcome centurion of the Roman army of occupation stationed at Capharnaum, who implored Jesus to heal his boy, pointing out that Jesus could do it by just giving a command without even having to profane himself by entering a gentile house.

Let me get to the issue of what Jesus was up to. He seems to have found his own mission in speaking to the more basic question of where one goes from here rather than simply in continuing John's initiation rite. Apparently, Jesus himself did not baptize. But he must have begun by believing in the imminent day of judgment as John proclaimed, for why would he otherwise have immersed himself in John's cause? Yet he himself did not make the repetition of that rite, or John's apocalypticism, the focus of what he himself was up to.

One only needs to look at the single overlap of their vocabulary, the metaphor of the tree and its fruit. John used this metaphor to call on people to bear fruit resulting from repentance, warning that if one did not produce good fruit, one would soon be chopped down at the judgment like a diseased tree (Q 3:8-9). Jesus dropped the threat of judgment but reflected on the metaphor itself (Q 6:43): there are indeed different kinds of fruit trees, as anyone living on the land knows, and each bears its own kind of fruit. Thorn bushes do not produce figs, and bramble bushes do not produce grapes. A healthy tree produces edible fruit, but a diseased tree produces only fruit that never ripens. Now, people are like trees: If you are good, you produce good things, but if you are evil, your produce is bad. What comes out of your mouth shows what kind of heart you have, just as what fruit comes off a tree shows what kind of tree it is. What matters is being the right kind of person. Then you will automatically produce the right kind of fruit. Here Jesus' message, in distinction from that of John, was not "Be good or get chopped down!" but rather "Let me tell you what being a good person really means—I call on you to be just that!"

As this little sample illustrates, Jesus sought to come to grips with the basic intentions of people. He addressed them personally, as to what kind of people they were. He called on them—he did not teach them ideas, as would a theologian. For when we take his sayings and distill from them our doctrines, we have manipulated his sayings for our own purposes, first of all, for the purpose of avoiding his addressing us personally. We reclassify his sayings as objective teachings to which we can give intellectual assent rather than letting them strike home as the personal challenge he intended them to be. Our learned, highly technical scholarly debates about Jesus' teaching would be, from his perspective, our dodge. So he would not agree with any of it but would want to cut through it all for an honest look at our hearts.

If I then proceed to present, in as objective a way as I as a scholar can, his teachings, my very objectivity would be my dodge, by means of which I would evade his point. Therefore, in trying to talk really about what he had to say, what I say has to retain his note of direct appeal. This tone of interpersonal encounter, this person-to-person mode, is the only really objective way to talk about what Jesus was talking about, for it was that personal talk that he was talking, and walking.

III. What Did Jesus Have to Say in the Sayings Gospel?

Looking out for number one is not the way to go. One should not be concerned about one's own life. Just think of the ravens (Q 12:22-31). They neither work the fields nor store in barns, so as to have enough stored up to get through the winter. They do not need to worry about such things, for God provides their nourishment. It is similar with lilies, what we would call wildflowers, which do not need to produce their clothing on a weaver's loom, and yet the splendor of their adornment far exceeds the glorious costumes of a king like Solomon. God provides their clothing—he already knows what you need! You should count on him just as they do. Trust him without a care in the world! What one normally calls faith in God is only little faith, hardly better than what gentiles call religion. No matter how hard you work at self-preservation, you will not be able to stretch out life so as to avoid death. So it makes more sense to get involved in the actualization of God's rule, where fullness of life is to be found, than to focus on self-preservation.

What does it really mean, to seek God's rule? Here, Matthew interpreted God's reign by adding, as a kind of gloss, "God's righteousness" (Matt. 6:33). So one talks about Matthew's moralizing interpretation of the kingdom of God. But that probably is not all Jesus had in mind. For, in another place in the Sayings Gospel, almost the same as was said about the ravens and wild flowers crops up again, and so one passage can help interpret the other; that passage is the Lord's Prayer (Q 11:2-4). Here, the petition "Thy kingdom come!" is again glossed by Matthew's added interpretation, "Thy will be done on earth as it is in heaven!" But here it becomes clear that the so-called moral interest of Matthew does not come to expression as a moral appeal to the community but rather in a petition directed to God. It is he who should establish his will on earth! God's rule is what brings God's will, his own righteousness, to earth. And we can only ask him to do this for us. Of course, he will not have established his will on earth as long as people act unjustly among themselves, but that is not the actual focus of the prayer. God himself should bring to pass his just will!

The prayer in Q itself, prior to Matthew's gloss, had interpreted the first petition, "Thy kingdom come!" as having to do with God's providing food, in what had been the immediately following petition, "Give us this day our daily bread!" So God's rule has to do primarily with eating? This option, offensive not only to us but already to Matthew, motivated him both to insert "Thy will be done on earth as it is in heaven" and also, at the beginning of the Sermon on the Mount (the Beatitudes pronounced on the poor and hungry), to add that God's blessing has to do with the "poor in spirit," who "hunger and thirst after righteousness," not simply with hungry beggars, which is what the Greek word translated "poor" actually means. But Jesus himself did not take offense at talking literally about food. In this regard, liberation theologians have understood Jesus well, for they experienced the setting of his sayings as they themselves lived among the poor and oppressed of South America. It is not because the poor are better or more worthy that the Beatitudes apply to them, but simply because their plight is greater. Contrary to all outer appearances, they are fortunate, because God's rule means taking care of them.

The Lord's Prayer is followed in Q itself by its interpretation (Q 11:9-13): Even a far-from-perfect human father will not give his son a stone if he asks for bread, or a snake if he asks for fish. How much more then the heavenly Father! You only need to ask him, and he will give you good things. It is this kind of trust that Jesus meant by "faith." This time, it is Luke who spiritualized: God will give the Holy Spirit. But Jesus himself promised that the heavenly Father would give bread and fish.

One comes nearer to Jesus' lifestyle when one looks a bit more closely at his mission instructions, addressed to the most active disciples, nicknamed today "wandering radicals." They do not have a penny in their pocket. They need neither purse nor backpack, since they take with them neither money nor supplies (Q 10:4). They live like the ravens and wildflowers in the field, or like the dirt-cheap sparrows that never fall to earth without God's knowing (Q 12:7). These disciples entrust themselves, completely unprotected, to God. They do not even wear sandals (Q 10:4), perhaps as a symbol of penance, perhaps only to attest that they, even if unprotected, nevertheless get by. They are not even equipped with a club to protect against wild animals or robbers. They go like lambs among wolves (Q 10:3).

One should offer no resistance (Q 6:29-30). If someone hits you on one cheek, you should offer him the other. Even a mugger who snatches your coat should be given the shirt off your back as a gift. If someone asks you for something, give it to him, and if someone seeks a loan, do not ask for it back. We are not only to ask God to forgive us but to forgive the debts of those in debt to us (although we have accustomed ourselves not to hear that part of the Lord's Prayer).

One should love one's enemies, indeed pray for one's persecutors. Usually, one is generous to good people, one's social equals, who can return the favor. But that is being no better than customs officers and gentiles. Rather, you should imitate God, who rains, and shines his sun, on bad people as well as good. Only if you act that way, are you a child of God. Jesus was first called son of God not because he was like a Roman emperor, or like Hercules, or like other sons of God in that society, but because he was like God, loving his enemy.

With such a lifestyle, one seems not to have any chance in everyday reality. However, it has belatedly come to attention that, for example, in concentration camps, people have a better chance of survival if they band together into small groups of selfless persons who are ready to give the little they have to the most needy among them. Of course, our plight is not so desperate, and so we do not have to turn to such drastic measures. Think of the rich young ruler, who was too well off, too much like us, to be a disciple of Jesus.

We are not normally the other person's help but rather his fate, just as he is our fate. He has nothing to eat because I have stashed away extra bread. I am cold because he is hiding an extra coat in his backpack. He does not have a penny to his name because I have hoarded money in my money belt. We are all tools of evil, which is why life is ruined for us all.

In the extreme case of blood vengeance, which takes place between families or clans or villages in many "backward" parts of the world still today, we all agree that such a thing can only harm both sides and hence is to be gotten rid of by any means possible. Yet, in the less spectacular cases that take place under more normal circumstances, the equivalent selfishness, acting in one's own interest, no matter what damage is done in the process to the other, is considered somehow acceptable in our so very "civilized" culture. Everybody is normally expected to look out for number one.

But God's rule is something quite different. And it was that rule that Jesus and his circle wanted to introduce. How that took place in practice is described in some detail in the mission discourse: At the very beginning, before there were sympathizers, when there were no safe houses to which one could turn, much less house churches, the committed few disciples (and no doubt Jesus himself) walked, barefoot and without any supplies, from place to place.

One knocked on some unknown door and said, if the door was opened at all, "Shalom!" (Q 10:5-6). This greeting was not meant in a purely empty sense, the way we say "good morning" without having the least interest in what kind of day the other person will have, and as one could, then and today, say "Shalom" in a completely emptyheaded way. Rather, if one was let in, the head of the household was called "son of peace," that is to say, the blessing originally implied in the greeting "Shalom" came upon the host. But if one was turned away, the blessing returned to the one who had knocked, who then had to go farther and keep knocking until he was received and could actually give his "Shalom."

One ate what was put before one, be it simple, be it sumptuous. The Jesus people were not ascetics in the technical sense. John used for clothing and nourishment only what was, so to speak, directly offered by nature (Mark 1:6). He neither ate bread nor drank wine (Q 7:33). That is why he was thought to be crazy, demon possessed. John stood in sharp contrast to Jesus, who sat at table with such worldly people as customs officers and sinners. Of course, he was also rejected, though with the reverse justification: He was smeared as a glutton and a drunkard (Q 7:34). In any case, Jesus did not make an issue, one way or the other, out of what he got to eat.

With regard to clothing and nourishment, Jesus lived from what people, usually women, prepared for him. The interpretation of the petition

"Thy kingdom come!" in the original Prayer in Q itself, namely, "Give us this day our daily bread!" was not answered by manna falling from heaven but rather by women, who, following a recipe found in Q (13:21), hid leaven in three measures of meal until the whole was leavened then put it into the oven until it was transformed into bread.

Such wandering radicals as Jesus sent out, who went as he did from house to house, were called at that time, before there were church offices like priest or bishop, simply "workers" (Q 10:2, 7). Whatever the workers were given as food or housing, they had earned, worked for. Their work consisted in what they could offer to those who lived in the house, the "peace" they could give in return for the hospitality. It consisted in healing those who were sick, accompanied with the reassuring word "God's rule has touched you" (Q 10:9). That is to say, this is the way of life that one should seek, free of care like the ravens and wildflowers, the rule whose coming one was to ask for in the Lord's Prayer. For one only needs to ask, and it will be given; to seek, and one will find; to knock, and the door will be opened (Q 11:9). One can entrust oneself to God as heavenly Father—that is what they believed, practiced, and proclaimed.

Sickness is not the will of God, not part of his rule. It is evil. When the sickness was accompanied by odd gestures and cries, as in the case of mental illnesses and "moonstruck" epileptics, it was attributed to demons, impure spirits. So it was particularly noticeable that God intervenes in such cases. It is by his finger that demons are driven out (Q 11:20), irrespective of whether it was Jesus or "your sons" who functioned as exorcist (Q 11:21). Jesus (like other exorcists) had power over demons, not because he, like Faust, was in league with their leader Beelzebub (Q 11:15), but because God rules here and now with God's own finger (Q 11:22). It is a matter of God's intervening to provide bread, to heal the sick, that is to say, to rule. The petitions of the Lord's Prayer, no doubt used as a table prayer by Jesus when admitted to the hospitality of a home, were actually promptly answered in the house of the son of peace.

The reality of death is not denied in an illusory way. Though the sayings are reassuring, death is presupposed in a realistic way. The grass in the field, no matter how beautiful today, is tomorrow thrown into the oven (Q 12:28). The sparrows are never forgotten by God, and yet they fall to earth (Q 12:7). One is called upon not to fear physical death, so as not to lose one's very self, panicked by fear of death (Q 12:4), which is the greatest threat of evil forces, from unbearable pain to dictatorships.

The saying about taking one's cross (Q 14:27) may presuppose Jesus' own death, which is not otherwise mentioned in Q. But the two other sayings of the same cluster probably go back to Jesus himself and say much the same thing: One must even leave one's own family behind to participate in Jesus' cause (Q 14:26). Only the person who loses one's life for Jesus' cause will really save it (Q 17:33). Even if Jesus did not himself predict his death, as the predictions of his passion that recur repeatedly in Mark would have us think, one can hardly assume that Jesus did not envisage the possibility of his persecution or assassination, even though the Sayings Gospel offers no explicit predictions of his death. He was surely prepared inwardly to accept death if it came to that, as his followers should also be.

IV. HOW DOES THE SAYINGS GOSPEL HANDLE JESUS' DEATH?

Although the Sayings Gospel has no passion narrative or resurrection stories, this omission does not necessarily lead to the conclusion that the Q people know nothing of Jesus' fate or had never thought about where it left them. It is hardly probable that his death was not quickly rumored among his followers, even into the most obscure corners of Galilee. But then, after his death, was not the only sensible thing to do, to give up the whole thing as some tragic miscalculation, a terrible failure? Jesus had assured them, "the Father from heaven gives good things to those who ask him," and yet his last word according to Mark was "My God, my God, why have you left me in the lurch?" (Mark 15:34). What was there left to proclaim?

The emergence of the Sayings Gospel was, to put it quite pointedly, itself the miracle at Easter! Rudolf Bultmann formulated a famous, or infamous, saying to the effect that Jesus rose into his own word. The resurrection was attested, in substance at least, in the Q community, in that his word was again to be heard, not as a melancholy recollection of the failed dream of a noble, but terribly naïve, person, but rather as the still valid, and constantly renewed, trust in the heavenly Father, who, as in heaven, will rule also on earth.

There are a few sayings in Q that are best understood in terms of such a "resurrection" faith. "What I say to you in the darkness, speak out in the light; and what you hear whispered into your ear, preach from the rooftops" (Q 12:3/Matt. 10:27). This sounds as if Jesus had rather secretively only whispered his message and left the spreading of the good word to his disciples. We would have expected it to be just the reverse. Surely Jesus said it better, louder, and clearer than anyone! But perhaps such a saying reflects the recollection that his message was suppressed by force and thus obscured but then became all the brighter and louder as it was nevertheless revalidated and reproclaimed.

There may be the same kind of contrast between the time before Jesus' death and the time after it in the saying about the unforgiveable sin. The saying is usually thought to be telling those who had rejected Jesus himself when he was alive that afterwards they are not irretrievably lost but have a new chance through the preaching of the disciples equipped with the Spirit after his death.

In both these difficult sayings, the preaching after Jesus' death is held to be more audible, more effective, more true even, than the preaching of Jesus himself. This is an "Easter faith" of a special kind!

The Easter faith of the Sayings Gospel then has primarily to do with the authority of Jesus' sayings, which even after his death are not devalued but only then come into full power. In this high evaluation of Jesus' sayings lies the Christology of the Sayings Gospel. This is why Jesus' first disciples did not really need to use Christological titles, which seem so indispensable to us.

"Why do you call me Lord, Lord, but do not do what I tell you?" This question introduces the concluding exhortation of Jesus' inaugural sermon in Q (6:46). Thereupon follows the double parable of houses built on rock or sand (Q 6:47-49). Everyone who hears my words and does them will be acquitted in the judgment! Not the high priest in the temple in Jerusalem or the baptism of John the Baptist in the Jordan River brings the ultimate salvation, but rather keeping Jesus' words, as they are conserved in the Sayings Gospel—to be sure, on the condition that they really are kept, observed, and not just conserved!

The eschatology of the Sayings Gospel shares the view that in the general resurrection, everyone will be judged according to his or her own works, as commonly assumed in antiquity, in Judaism, and even by Paul (2 Cor. 5:10). Since all will rise at the same time, one will observe the judgment of the others and in some cases even influence it: "Your sons" who are exorcists "shall be your judges.... The queen of the south will be raised at the judgment with this generation and will condemn it, for she came from the ends of the earth to listen to the wisdom of Solomon, and behold, something greater than Solomon is here. The men of Nineveh will arise at the judgment with this generation and condemn it; for they repented at the preaching of Jonah, and behold, something greater than Jonah is here" (Q 11:19, 31-32). Q's closing word is that those who have followed Jesus "will sit on thrones judging the twelve tribes of Israel" (Q 22:30). Everyone will be there at the day of judgment, and the truth will out!

So it is not surprising that, in their own defense, people would appeal for acquittal by referring to their connection with Jesus: "The you will start saying, 'We ate and drank with you, and you taught in our streets.' And he will say to you, 'I do not know you. Away from me, evildoers!'" (Q 13:26-27). Such Q texts do not yet have in view Jesus as the Judge but rather envisage him, among the character witnesses who testify, as the crucial one in the view of the Judge. He speaks up for, or against, people who appeal to him. Another saying puts it a bit differently: "Everyone who confesses me before men, the son of man will confess before the angels." Here, too, Jesus is not Judge but a witness in court. The angels are the judges. Yet the early Christology of the Sayings Gospel can be sensed from such eschatological sayings: If Jesus' witness is decisive for one's fate, since neither God nor the angels will reject his witness, then it really does not make much difference with what title or lack of title that happens. If it's decided, it's decided! Doing what Jesus said, not what somebody else said, but really doing it, is what stands up in the day of judgment.

In the course of the Christological development, Jesus himself comes to be understood as the Judge. His witness, as after all decisive, is objectified, becoming functionally the Judge's sentence itself, and so he comes to represent or replace God or the angels. In the Sayings Gospel, this development is hardly more than suggested. The saying with which Q closes, to the effect that those who have followed Jesus will sit on thrones judging the twelve tribes of Israel (Q 22:30), has for the first time humans as judges and so surely must presuppose that Jesus himself functions as the main Judge, though this is not said explicitly. But even this concluding saying does not imply that Jesus is the exclusive judge but envisages a judging shared with his inner circle. The bare beginnings of the later Christology are only suggested but not at all developed. One thing that makes the Sayings Gospel so fascinating, not only for laypersons but even for theologians, is to see the first gingerly steps from Jesus' own, rather selfless message, oriented to God's reign, which he activated while otherwise being unaware of himself, to our focus on him as the center of our faith!

V. How Can One Get from the Sayings Gospel to Us?

If the Sayings Gospel gives us insight into the doing and thinking of Jesus, how does that connect to us? Q as a document ceased to exist after the first century. Is not its Jesus, the real Jesus, also gone? Simply detecting, a century and a half ago, a collection of his sayings imbedded in Matthew and Luke does not necessarily mean that we have any connection with him.

The real Jesus, as I have sought to portray him on the basis of the Sayings Gospel, was not only in his way otherworldly—he was worlds apart from us! Yet we may still want to understand ourselves as his disciples, his church, with him as our Lord. The efforts undertaken again and again over the past century to trace a line of continuity from the historical Jesus to Paul and from there to our church have been all too tenuous—more ingenious than convincing. It is easier to trace the path from Paul's Christ to us than to trace the path from Paul back to Jesus. Although Paul is our oldest source, dating back to around 50 C.E., Paul himself had not met the historical Jesus but only the resurrected Christ, who for Paul literally and figuratively so outshone Jesus as to leave Jesus out of sight.

Yet there was in the early Christianity another path from Jesus to the church, less dramatic than the great theologian and missionary Paul, but more pervasive in the actual life of early Christians: the Gospel of Matthew! That Gospel was by far the most widely used early Christian book, to judge by the number of copies that have surfaced in the dry sands of Egypt, or by the number of quotations in early Christian writers, or by the number of textual corruptions introduced from Matthew into other Gospels by scribal copyists obviously more familiar with Matthew. The Christianity that step-by-step won over the ancient world, until the Roman Empire became the Christian Byzantine Empire, was primarily the Matthean rather than the Pauline kind of Christianity. It was a Christianity of mercy and philanthropy, which won the allegiance of the underprivileged and suppressed, that is to say, the mass of the population, more so than the Pauline that ultimately flowed into the Neoplatonic philosophical theology of the educated minority (with literacy standing at about 15 percent). Christianity as a mass movement so powerful that Constantine finally had to yield to its pressure was more a Matthean Christianity; and that means it was, through Matthew, really connected to Jesus.

In this sense, the question of tracing the path from Matthew back to Jesus is a way to see how we effect the last step back to our roots. But here we hit upon an untilled field. The discipline of church history always traced the path of events via Paul. A conspiracy of silence has obscured what happened to the movement that Jesus launched in Galilee, ever since Luke's Acts told the story of the church's beginning with only one passing allusion to there even being a church in Galilee (Acts 9:31). Luke's view of the Christian witness skipped from "all Judea and Samaria" to "the end of the earth" without even mentioning Galilee (Acts 1:8). Paul knew very few sayings of Jesus and did not have a kind of religiosity, much less a theology, built on Jesus' sayings; he even argues that knowing Jesus according to the flesh, the earthly Jesus, is not really necessary (2 Cor. 5:16), so as to argue that he is in no regard less qualified than Jesus' own disciples.

The Book of Acts also presents such a Pauline Christianity: Jesus has ascended to heaven, and it is the Holy Spirit who since Pentecost leads the church. Sayings of Jesus are conspicuously absent from the life of the church in Acts. Luke had buried them back in his Gospel, and once he had finished copying out the end of Q (at Luke 22:30), he rather explicitly said that the idyllic, unreal world of Jesus has been put behind us, for we must now come to grips with reality, buy a sword, become the church militant, and replace the kind of mission Jesus had advocated and practiced with one like the missionary journeys of Paul. But when one turns to Matthew, the contacts with the Sayings Gospel Q are so striking that one has now come to realize that the Gospel of Matthew was written in a community that itself had been part of the Sayings Gospel's movement.

So it has become a new scholarly task to supplement the standard version of church history, based on Paul and Acts, with the church history that leads from Jesus via the Sayings Gospel to Matthew, that is to say, from Galilee directly to Antioch without the detour via the Damascus road. For the Gospel of Matthew probably comes from the region of Antioch, from a small community that had begun in Galilee and continued there for some time, since one was told not to go on the roads of the gentiles or into the towns of the Samaritans but only to the lost sheep of Israel (Matt. 10:6-7). Perhaps it was the war with Rome in the 60s, which devastated Galilee before reaching Jerusalem, that finally forced the remnants of the Q community to join the refugees fleeing north up the coast to the nearest metropolitan area, Antioch, the capital of the former Seleucid Empire.

The first steps from Galilee to Antioch, the beginning of the path from Jesus to us, can be sketched as follows:

(1) Jesus' immediate followers reproclaimed Jesus sayings, which were collected into a number of small clusters, to function as prompters or handouts for such wandering radicals.

(2) The editing of such clusters into the Jewish-Christian Sayings Gospel Q took place at about the time of the fall of Jerusalem (70 C.E.).

(3) The first major part of the body of the Gospel of Matthew, chapters 3-11, into which the text of Q is largely compressed, was composed as a kind of rationale or justification for the Q community's having held out so long in its exclusively Jewish orientation.

(4) The complete adoption of the Gospel of Mark into the Gospel of Matthew, in chapters 12-28, reflected the reorientation of the Q community, now the Matthean community, into the worldwide mission of the gentile church, legitimized through the Great Commission to convert all nations, with which the canonical Gospel of Matthew closes.

Let me in conclusion focus briefly on each of these four stages that led from the real Jesus to the Christianity of which we are heirs:

(1) The collection of sayings of Jesus that in Luke 6 is called the Sermon on the Plain and in Matthew 5–7 the Sermon on the Mount is a very old collection originally composed as a unit in and of itself, with its own introduction, the Beatitudes, and its own conclusion, the twin parables of the houses built on rock or on sand. Between, in the body of the sermon, lie the sayings most characteristic of the real Jesus: those concerning love of enemies, turning the other cheek, giving the shirt off one's back, and

forgiving debts. There was another such small collection on prayer, including the Lord's Prayer and its commentary about the father who gives to the asking son neither stones nor snakes. A third collection was about ravens and wildflowers. These three little clusters are so close to each other in meaning that the Matthean community put them all together, perhaps at a very early date, into what we know as the Sermon on the Mount. Then there was the collection of mission instructions, telling how the Q people were to carry out their Jewish-Christian mission. It is these oldest collections of sayings of Jesus that produced the picture of the real Jesus that I described at the beginning of this chapter.

(2) The final editor of Q took sayings of Jesus that were still circulating, including these small clusters, and edited them in two regards: On the one hand, he superimposed on the Q material the Deuteronomistic view of history found in the Old Testament, according to which God lets Jerusalem be destroyed not because God is unfaithful but because Israel is, having rejected God's prophets, indeed having killed them, rather than listening to them. The final editor of Q thought history had in this regard repeated itself: Jesus' offer of salvation had been by and large rejected, and so God had abandoned again his house in Jerusalem and turned it over to the Romans to destroy. So Q pronounced judgment on "this generation." For its rejecting of Jesus, God was rejecting it.

But another concern of this editor of Q was more inner-Christian, namely, to reinterpret John's talk of a "One to Come" who would hold judgment to refer not directly to God, whom John must have intended, but rather to Jesus. The editor organized the first main section of Q around a cluster of predictions from Isaiah to the effect that the One to Come will heal many sicknesses and evangelize the poor. Between John's prediction of a One to Come and the claim that Jesus, having acted as Isaiah predicted, is that One to Come, lie the inaugural sermon, beginning "Blessed are the poor, for yours is the kingdom of God," in which the evangelizing of the poor is documented, and the healing of the centurion's boy at Capharnaum, one healing representative of all in the list of healings collected from Isaiah. This is Q's "proof" that Jesus is the One to Come prophesied by John as coming to hold judgment. And so God's judgment on Jerusalem at its destruction can be interpreted as retaliation for the rejection of Jesus' message by the Judaism of that time, "this generation."

This Sayings Gospel, organized in this way, may have converted a few followers of John, but did not by any means effect the conversion of all of Israel, the impossibility of which is already writ large in the Sayings Gospel itself. The text ends with the reassurance to the disciples that they will, after all, judge the twelve tribes of Israel, even if they could not convert them. Yet this negative outcome is not the last word.

(3) The small and failing Q community knew about the much more successful gentile church. Such contacts would have emerged at the latest when the survivors of this Jewish-Christian community, which reached Antioch after the war, found there the gentile church. The community of the Sayings Gospel Q, which had intensified over the years its Jewish-Christian exclusivity, had, perhaps quite haltingly, to modulate into the community of the Gospel of Matthew, which in effect ended up repudiating that exclusivity. But Matthew, before turning to the gentiles, produced an enlarged, improved, concentrated version of the first major section of Q, in which Jesus was proven to be the One to Come predicted by John, which one can still read in chapters 3-11 of the Gospel of Matthew. But this was in effect the swan song of the Q community, as it was absorbed into the gentile-Christian church, except for holdouts who returned to the Baptist movement or to emergent normative Judaism, or became small Christian sects that we, on the winning side, call heresies: the Ebionites, meaning the "Poor," the Nazarenes, claiming Jesus of Nazara.

(4) This belated self-justification of the survivors of the Q community in Matthew 3—11 did not succeed in forestalling the inevitable. So what was left of the Q community, absorbed into what we should now call the Matthean community, took over the gentile-Christian Gospel of Mark and copied it out pretty much by rote in Matthew 12—28, with only an occasional editing out of especially offensive gentile traits, finally justifying going over to the gentile side of Christianity with the Great Commission by the resurrected Christ to evangelize all nations, thus canceling Q's Jewish-Christian basis in a Jesus who limited his mission to Israel.

So Jewish Christianity ceased, for practical purposes, to exist as an independent entity. Yet the Jewish-Christian Gospel incorporated in Matthew as the last will and testament of the Q community made its way into the growing gentile church as a major part of the most widely used Gospel of all, the Gospel according to Matthew. So the real Jesus' actual sayings remained, in spite of everything, accessible. The church today can still listen to Jesus, which, in my opinion, is precisely what we should do. He is very unsettling, as I am sure you felt as I tried to present his sayings. But his goal of a caring, selfless society may be the best future we can hope for, and work for.

CHAPTER 4

Very Goddess and Very Man: Jesus' Better Self[1]

As a hen gathers her nestlings under her wings ...
Q 13:34[2]

Masculine terminology overwhelms Christology. Jesus himself was male. The Jewish idea of the Messiah is built on the model of David and his male successors as kings of Judah. Masculine endings bind Christ*os* and Kyri*os* to the male realm. *Son* of God and *Son* of *man* do the same. Even the Word of God produced masculine overtones (log*os*). The one christological title that is an exception is also the one that failed to make it: Wisdom (Sophi*a*). The present essay seeks to investigate this aborted feminine Christology.

1. THE BEGINNINGS OF CHRISTOLOGY

Jesus apparently had no Christology. "Why do you call me good? No one is good but God alone" (Mark 10:18). Probably he would have

---

1. In lieu of more detailed notes, reference may be made to various technical articles I have written about specific dimensions of the current essay: "Basic Shifts in German Theology," *Interpretation* 16 (1962) 76-97 (on the Wisdom Christology of Q). "ΛΟΓΟΙ ΣΟΦΩΝ: On the Gattung of Q," in *Trajectories Through Early Christianity*, 71-113 (on Q as a wisdom book) [In *The Sayings Gospel Q*, pp. 37-74]. "Die Hodajot-Formel in Gebet und Hymnus des Frühchristentums," in *Apophoreta: Fetschrift für Ernst Haenchen*, 194-235 (on the christological hymns embedded in the Jewish-Christian prayers) ["The Hodayot Formula in Prayers and Hymns of Early Christianity," in *The Sayings Gospel Q*, pp. 75-118]. "On the *Gattung* of Mark (and John)," in *Jesus and Man's Hope* (ed. D.G. Buttrick and J. M. Bald), 99-129, esp. 118-26, reprinted in *The Problem of History in Mark and Other Marcan Essays*, 11-39, esp. 31-39 (on the *mythologoumenon* of the mother bird giving birth to the Savior in the *Apocalypse of Adam* and Revelation 12). "Jesus as Sophos and Sophia: Wisdom Traditions and the Gospels," in *Aspects of Wisdom in Judaism and Early Christianity* (ed. R.L. Wilken), 1-16 (on the Wisdom Christology of Q) [in *The Sayings Gospel Q*, pp. 119-30].

2. The Bible (including the Apocrypha) is quoted according to the Revised Standard Version. New Testament apocrypha are quoted according to E. Hennecke and W. Schneemelcher, eds., English edition edited by R. McL. Wilson, *New Testament Apocrypha*, vol. 1: *Gospels and Related Writings*. The Odes of Solomon are quoted according to J. H. Charlesworth, ed., *The Old Testament Pseudepigrapha*, vol. 2. Enoch is quoted according to R. H. Charles, ed., *The Apocrypha and Pseudepigrapha of the Old Testament in English*, vol. 2: *Pseudepigrapha*.

preferred that we deify the cause: the kingdom of *God*. Hence to the extent that we in our day seek to develop a Christology, as did our predecessors, we must assume responsibility for what we say and do, as did they, and not just parrot their language. If they did the best they could, given their conditions, we must do the best we can, in our often changed conditions. One is that we do not live in their mythopoeic world, another is that we live in the world of modern biblical scholarship, another is that we live in a not unchallenged patriarchal society.

First it needs to be said that all due honor was paid to leaders in the movement to which Jesus belonged without Christology. Like Jesus, John the Baptist also gave his life for the cause and was believed to have been divinely vindicated: "John the baptizer has been raised from the dead" (Mark 6:14). Jesus' own praise for John was unsurpassable: "... even more than a prophet. ... There has not arisen among women's offspring anyone who surpasses John. ... The law and the prophets were until John. From then on the kingdom of God is violated and the violent plunder it" (Q 7:26, 28; 16:16). Yet John was not deified as was Jesus. Nor did the New Testament elevate Jesus' successor, Peter, beyond the status of Rock. It is in such an unchristological environment that are to be placed factors that in retrospect might, no doubt anachronistically, be thought of as the beginnings of Christology.

Jesus was not born doing his thing, any more than was John or Peter. He only came to it near the end of his life. The early tradition, going back to Jesus himself, was quite aware of this, and indeed of its theological significance. For the inception of the time of salvation was originally not marked by the birth of Jesus but rather by the ministry of John: "from then on" (Q 16:16). This Whence of Jesus had its impact on the earliest efforts to produce a Gospel. All three of the oldest known attempts to decide where to begin the Gospel agree, independently of each other, to begin with John: Q, Mark, and John.

Luke may have respected this venerable tradition in composing his Gospel as well. For he appealed to it in defining the kind of person who would be eligible to become one of the Twelve: someone who was present "beginning from the baptism of John" (Acts 1:22). And the apostolic preaching according to Acts begins its fulfillment of the Old Testament prophecy with John. The impressive synchronized dating of the beginning of the story begins not with Jesus' birth in Luke 1–2 but with John's baptism of Jesus in Luke 3. So the Gospel of Luke may well have begun there, as the now largely discredited Proto-Lucan theory (and more recently Joseph Fitzmyer in his Anchor Bible Commentary on Luke) had it, in suggesting that after composing both Luke and Acts, Luke may have added, as a sort of belated prologue, Luke 1–2. In any case, Luke was so sophisticated that he was able to write an infancy narrative that, like the beginning of the public ministry, also began with John, thus combining the old tradition that the story begins with John with the new tradition that the story begins with Jesus' birth.

Jesus' activity could have been adequately conceptualized in the thought world of that day as a person possessed by God, in a way formally comparable to the unfortunates possessed by a demon. For according to that thought world, the human self-consciousness can be replaced either by an evil or by a holy spirit. Such a divine spirit was portrayed as having come upon Jesus at his baptism by John "like a dove" (Mark 1:10). This should not be intellectualized as some kind of Hegelian Mind, but rather was intended as the kind of animistic spirit-world force that Hermann Gunkel introduced into New Testament scholarship from the Old Testament and the ancient Near East, a history-of-religions corrective for that all too spiritual mental spirit. If Luke described the spirit as "in bodily form" (Luke 3:22), Mark described it very animistically as what "drove him out into the wilderness" (Mark 1:12).

Whereas Jesus would have more naturally understood this simply theologically, by the time of the Evangelists it is understood christologically. As the one that God chose to possess at the time of his baptism, Jesus is described with a heavenly voice: "Thou art my beloved Son" (Mark 1:11). This was not originally intended as an announcement of an inner-trinitarian relationship that has prevailed from all eternity but was meant as a Father-Son relationship that was first set up on this occasion, defining the turning point marked by John christologically in terms of Jesus. A common patristic reformulation of the Lukan parallel (Luke 3:22) reflects the event character of the voice, in adding from Ps. 2:7: "Today I have begotten you." Though this is presumably a secondary "improvement" of the Lukan text, it probably brings to the surface what was latent in this tradition, a first fumbling step toward Christology. That is to say, the early interpretation of who Jesus was, in terms of his baptism in John's public ministry, had not presupposed his antecedent or perennial divine Sonship, such as is reflected already in Paul and probably in Mark 1:1: "The beginning of the gospel of Jesus Christ, the Son of God" (if the last phrase was originally in Mark – the manuscript evidence and hence scholarly opinion are rather evenly split). This reading back of divine Sonship is carried much further, for example, by Luke at the Annunciation: "The child to be born will be called holy, the Son of God" (Luke 1:35), or in his genealogy: "the son of Adam, the son of God" (Luke 3:38). Thus the baptismal voice has already been rendered anticlimactic, and the spelling out of its original implications came to be branded the heresy of adoptionism. It is difficult for us to get out of the mind-set thereby imposed on all subsequent theology, much less to penetrate back to the prechristological level at which Jesus himself probably stood. For he probably did not associate his baptism with any kind of divine Sonship.

Perhaps a *pendant* interpretation of the end of Mark from patristic times will help one to catch sight of this primitive Christian way of thinking (heretical though it came to be regarded): "My God, my God, why hast thou forsaken me?" (Mark 15:34) reads (in the *Gospel of Peter*): "My power, O Power, thou hast forsaken me," as the moment when the possessing divine and hence immortal spirit left the Galilean mortal to die. This possession by divine spirit and the resultant transient adoptionism fit much better the functional (rather than metaphysical) context of a Jewish understanding of God's relation to the human he chooses to use (or, to put it in our more familiar, and hence bland and unoffensive language, to inspire). For this possessing spirit is originally neither the divine nature of the second person of the trinity, nor the third person of the trinity, but rather a hypostasis of the divine, a notion popular in Judaism at a time when fear of taking God's name in vain led to not taking it at all, but preferring many surrogates (such as kingdom of *heaven*), in the broader context of a polytheistic world where spirits and demons abound.

This part that God took in Jesus, in possessing him so as to become his functional self, thus did not remain within such alternatives as spirit possession and demon possession, but modulated into various male-oriented christological titles. At first, clear subordination was retained ("God" for the Father, "Lord" for Jesus; giving glory to *God* was christianized not as giving glory to *Jesus* but as giving glory to God *through* Jesus). But christological titles nonetheless headed in the direction of Chalcedon and the traditional deification of Jesus (and "subordinationism" ended as a heresy). Jesus' christological status was at times dated from the resurrection: "God has made him both Lord and Christ, this Jesus whom you crucified" (Acts 2:36); "obedient unto death. ... Therefore God has highly exalted him and bestowed on him the name ... Jesus Christ is Lord" (Phil. 2:8-9, 11). In this development the more loose, functional relation of Jesus and the divine spirit gradually sedimented into two distinct parts in a tripartite deity that blossomed under Neoplatonic tutelage into the Nicene trinity, with the Holy Spirit as the third person, and then into the Chalcedonian doctrine of the two natures of the second person.

2. THE GENDER OF GOD

The relation of this to the sex of God becomes more apparent when one recalls that the gender of nouns was often taken seriously as indicating the sex of the subject to whom the noun referred. The Hebrew word for "spirit," *ruach*, is usually feminine (though at times it is used masculinely). Thus in a Semitic world of thought the tripartite deity could reflect the core family of father, mother, and child. But the Greek word for "spirit," *pneuma*, is neuter, so that the question became relevant as to whether the third person (the Spirit's position when no longer the mother in the core family) is actually a person at all. Since the Latin word for "spirit," *spiritus*, is masculine, the personality of the Spirit was thereby assured as well as the all-male trinity. Even though a theologian-linguist such as Jerome (in commenting on Isa. 40:9-11) could point out that the three diverging genders of the noun for Spirit show that God has no sex, the metaphorical suggestiveness of the gender of the nouns dominated classical theology. We today would concede Jerome's point at the literal or metaphysical level, and yet would recognize more than he the metaphorical power of the symbols.

In the Semitic branch of early Christianity the femininity of the Spirit and her role as Jesus' mother are made explicit[3]. This is reflected in the apocryphal *Gospel of the Hebrews*, a text with the Semitic overtones that this title suggests. Here the feminine Spirit as Jesus' mother becomes explicit in a fragment quoted both by Origen and by Jerome:

> Even so did my mother, the Holy Spirit, take me by one of my hairs and carry me away to the great mountain Tabor.

Here a mythological episode about the mother of the Savior is borrowed from a tradition attested in the *Apocalypse of Adam* (NHC V,5) and Revelation 12. For in the *Gospel of the Hebrews* the parenting of Jesus as Son has nothing to do with his birth or with Mary, but takes place at his baptism, cited in Jerome to Isa. 11:2 according to a further text from this apocryphal gospel:

> But it came to pass when the Lord had come up out of the water, the whole fount of the Holy Spirit descended-upon him and rested on him and said to him: My Son, in all the prophets was I waiting for thee that thou shouldest

---

3. I am indebted to Stephen Gero for referring me to R. Murray (*Symbols of Church and Kingdom: A Study in Early Syriac Tradition*) for details of this development. See esp. "The Motherhood of the Church and of the Holy Spirit," 142-50, and "The Holy Spirit as Mother," 312-20.

come and I might rest in thee. For thou art my rest; thou art my first-begotten Son that reignest for ever.

Here he is not explicitly Son of God the Father but rather is parented by the female Holy Spirit that is an integral part of the baptism story.

In the Syriac *Odes of Solomon*, dated contemporary with the New Testament, the dove at the baptism becomes a female metaphor for the Spirit (24:1-2; 28:1-2):

The dove fluttered over the head of our Lord Messiah, because he was her Head. And she sang over him, and her voice was heard.
As the wings of doves over their nestlings, and the mouths of their nestlings towards their mouths, so also are the wings of the Spirit over my heart. My heart continually refreshes itself and leaps for joy, like the babe who leaps for joy in his mother's womb.

This female dove, the "incarnation" of the Spirit, is Jesus' mother (*Odes Sol.* 36:1-3):

(The Spirit) brought me forth before the Lord's face, and because I was the Son of Man, I was named the Light, the Son of God.

Once Jesus' divine investment was shifted from his baptism back to his conception in the womb of Mary, the femaleness of the Spirit would seem to have excluded a conception by the Spirit according to the *Gospel of Philip* (NHC II 55,23-28):

Some say, "Mary conceived by the Holy Spirit." They are in error. They do not know what they are saying. When did a woman ever conceive by a woman?

Then the Apostles' Creed, with its combination of conception by the Holy Spirit and birth from the Virgin Mary, would seem to have blocked the development of the feminine aspects of the Spirit latent in Semitic usage. The divine Mother in the trinity as a core family was replaced in feminine terms by the human mother, whose elevation toward divine status has been a concern throughout the history of dogma.

A parallel development to that which we have sketched regarding the Spirit may have been even more significant at the beginning and may be less well known today, since, unlike the Spirit, the protagonist has faded from the theological aristocracy: Wisdom. Here again the Hebrew word, *hokhmah*, is feminine, as are the Greek *sophia* and the Latin *sapientia*. Thus the survival of Wisdom in the top echelon of deity would have assured a female part at the top (which may be part of the reason that Wisdom was dropped). Wisdom was fading fast by the time the New Testament itself was written. It may be no coincidence that within the canon the strongest attestation for it (and not very strong at that) is early, two texts that are from the central third of the first century rather than from the last third, from which the bulk of the New Testament comes: 1 Corinthians 1–4 among the authentic Pauline letters dated around 50 C.E.; and Q, which is from much the same period, in that it is clearly older than Matthew and Luke which incorporate most of it.

[I made this point already in "Basic Shifts in German Theology" (see note 1 above), 82-86. But a careless mistake on my part obscured a significant point, and led a critical reviewer to correct only the careless mistake rather than to consider the point thereby obscured. See Christopher M. Tuckett, "1 Corinthians and Q," *JBL* 102 (1983) 607-19: 608, n. 13. Hence it should be corrected here. The original essay read as follows (pp. 85-86): "Q's association of Solomon's Sophia and Jonah's kerygma is not only reminiscent of Sophia as a street preacher in Proverbs 8, but also finds a very close parallel in Paul's presentation in 1 Corinthians 1–2. Only in Q and 1 Corinthians does the term kerygma occur prior to the Pastorals, and only in Q and 1 Corinthians is Sophia clearly a Christological title, and only in Q (Luke 11:29-32 and parallel) and in 1 Corinthians 1:17–2:7 are the two rare uses combined with each other and the rejection of signs required by 'this generation' (Q), 'the Jews' (1 Cor.)." The correct formulation should read: "… Only in Q and 1 Corinthians does the term kerygma occur *in conjunction with wisdom* prior to the Pastorals…" But rather than detecting and correcting this careless mistake in a later essay based on the earlier essay, the error was simply carried over: "Kerygma and History in the New Testament," in *The Bible and Modern Scholarship*, ed. J. Philip Hyatt, New York and Nashville, Abingdon, 1965, 114-50: 129, reprinted in *Trajectories through Early Christianity*, Philadelphia, Fortress, 1971, paperback edition 1979, 20-70: 42, German translation "Kerygma und Geschichte im Neuen Testament, *ZThK* 62 (1965) 294-337: 313, reprinted in *Entwicklungslinien durch die Welt des frühen Christentums*, Tübingen, Mohr, 1971, 20-66: 40. It is my hope that the correction of this repeated error will stimulate discussion of this striking similarity between Q and Paul. Actually, the point was scored, if only in passing and in a little-known publication, in my essay "Judaism, Hellenism, Christianity: Jesus' Followers in Galilee until 70 C.E.," in *Ebraismo Ellenismo Christianesimo,* edited by Vittorio Mathieu, Archivio di Filosofia, directed by Marco M. Olivetti, 53 (1985), 1, Padua, Cedam, 1985, pp. 241-50: 242: "Q is un-kerygmatic, though the term kerygma occurs in Q – in comparing Jesus' message to the kerygma of Jonah (Q 11:32) as well as in Paul, especially 1 Cor. 2:4, where Paul contrasts his kerygma to that of 'persuasive words of wisdom', much as Q presents Jonas' kerygma as parallel to Solomon's wisdom." (In *The Sayings Gospel Q,* p. 194.)]

Just *how* the female Sophia speculation was absorbed into a masculine Christology can perhaps best be approached from a form-critical observation. For Christology seems to have grown most rapidly in the exuberance (inspiration) of hymnic ecstasy, and in this ecstasy to have flown on the wings of Wisdom mythology.

The standard outline of a Jewish prayer of the day would be an opening blessing or thanksgiving to God for having done this and that (a couplet in *parallelismus membrorum*). This would then be followed by the body of the prayer, recounting typically in more detail God's mighty works, often oriented in anticipation to the third part, where a petition called upon God to do again now for us the kind of things he had just been praised for having done for others in the past. This Jewish prayer outline could be christianized by reference to Jesus in connection with the thanksgiving to God, as in Col. 1:12-13 ("giving thanks to the Father, who ... transferred us to the kingdom of his beloved Son"), whereupon the central section could be christological, in hymnic style, beginning with the masculine relative pronoun "who." This would explain this otherwise inexplicable beginning word in the christological hymns Phil. 2:6-11; Col. 1:15-20; and 1 Tim. 3:16. (In 1 Tim. 3:16 the problem is especially difficult, since the apparent antecedent of the masculine pronoun "who" is the neuter noun "mystery." This led to the misreading of "who" [ΟΣ] as "God" – ΘΕΟΣ, abbreviated to ΘΣ – as in the King James version of the Bible.) The comparable christological hymn embedded in the prologue to the Gospel of John does not begin with the masculine relative pronoun but begins in analogy to Gen. 1:1, "In the beginning." But the introduction of the masculine noun *Logos* provides the equivalent male orientation. Thus the high Christology of these hymns, upon which all subsequent high Christologies have been built, had become male-oriented, in conformity to Jesus and the masculine christological titles, though rooted in Jewish speculation about Sophia.

This high Christology, taking place within a generation of Jesus' death, was able to arise so rapidly because the intellectual apparatus it needed was preformed within Judaism. It only needed to be transferred over to Jesus (as was done in the case of other concepts such as Christ and Son of man as well), in order for this quasi-divine hypostasis of Jewish wisdom speculation to become perhaps the highest Christology within primitive Christianity. This wisdom speculation could have developed into a trinitarian formulation that might have included the male within the female context, as occurs in gnostified form in the *Trimorphic Protennoia*

(NHC XIII,1), where Sophia manifests herself successively as Father, Mother, and Son (also called Logos), thus strikingly parallel to the prologue of John. Instead, in the orthodox tradition the female context of a Logos Christology was suppressed.

3. THE INCLUSIVENESS OF WISDOM CHRISTOLOGY

One of the relevant dimensions of this Wisdom speculation is that, like the title of Prophet (which also did not prevail as a christological title), it was not sensed as exclusively applicable to Jesus. Most christological titles were in their Christian usage "divine" enough to share in the exclusivity of monotheism, in that *only* Jesus is Lord (1 Cor. 8:5-6), Son of man, Son of God (Q 10:22), Savior, and so forth (although of course Jesus having such quasi-"divine" titles alongside the Father as also God was not pure monotheism, as our Jewish colleagues like to remind us; see again 1 Cor. 8:5-6). But Wisdom has spoken down through the ages through various spokespersons whom she has inspired, according to the Jewish wisdom tradition (Wis. 7:27):

> Though she is but one, she can do all things, and while remaining in herself, she renews all things; in every generation she passes into holy souls and makes them friends of God, and prophets.

This approach continued in Jewish-Christian (that is to say, primitive Christian) Wisdom Christology. Q 7:35: "But Wisdom was vindicated by her children." This has to do with the repudiation of John and Jesus by "this generation" in the preceding context. But rather than saying "they" (or "John" and "the Son of man," as they had just been designated), the punch line speaks only of "Wisdom," as if what was at stake were not the bearers of Wisdom as human individuals but rather the divine Wisdom they bore, and as if it were *her* children, not designated as *them* or *their* disciples, who vindicate her.

The nonexclusivity of the Wisdom Christology may be suggested in another Q text, where a saying is ascribed not to Jesus but to Sophia (as Luke faithfully reports Q, though Matt. 23:34-36 shifts to the first person singular, thus making Jesus the speaker), Q 11:49-51:

> Therefore also Wisdom said: I will send them prophets and sages, and some of them they will kill and persecute, so that a settling of accounts for the blood of all the prophets poured out from the founding of the world may be required of this generation, from the blood of Abel to the blood of Zechariah, murdered between the sacrificial altar and the House. Yes, I tell you: An accounting will be required of this generation!

The saying in Q apparently continued with what follows in the Matthean context (23:37-39), although Luke has put this continuation elsewhere, Q 13:34-35:

> O Jerusalem, Jerusalem, who kills the prophets and stones those sent to her! How often I wanted to gather your children together, as a hen gathers her nestlings under her wings, and you were not willing! Look, your house is forsaken! I tell you: You will not see me until (the time) comes when you say: Blessed is the one who comes in the name of the Lord!

The extent to which this refers to Wisdom in all her manifestations and not exclusively to Jesus is apparent from the reference to her "often" appealing to the Jerusalemites.

This can be illustrated by an anecdote from the history of scholarship: One of the traditional debates in the quest of the historical Jesus had to do with the minimum amount of time that must be conjectured for Jesus' public ministry. It was assumed this could be calculated in terms of how many annual Jewish festivals Jesus is said to have attended in Jerusalem during his ministry. Such speculation led to the choice between a public ministry that need not have been more than one year in the Synoptic Gospels and a public ministry in the Gospel of John that would have had to stretch at least into a third year. Since the Synoptic Gospels became the basis of the quest of the historical Jesus, and the Gospel of John was relegated to the role of the "spiritual" Gospel and an honored top billing only in New Testament theology (and Christian theology in general), this meant that Jesus' ministry has been assumed to be one year. But advocates of the Johannine timetable have pointed to this Q passage in the Synoptic Gospels to argue in favor of the Gospel of John, in maintaining that during his public ministry Jesus had gone to Jerusalem more than once ("how often").

This Wisdom passage is formulated throughout from the point of view of the person of Wisdom, not in terms of John and Jesus as bearers of Wisdom. She has sent "prophets and sages," a stream of martyrs "from the blood of Abel to the blood of Zechariah," without any explicit reference to John and Jesus. "Kill and persecute" is Christianized in Matt. 23:34 into "kill and crucify," though "killing the prophets and stoning those who are sent to you" remains in both Gospels unaltered. Thus it is she, rather than John (who was beheaded) or Jesus (who was crucified), who has repeatedly called on the Jerusalemites to gather under her wings. Indeed, the female metaphor of the hen and her nestlings is introduced in full harmony with the feminine noun Wisdom and the resultant female hypostasis or personification Wisdom.

It may be part of the Wisdom Christology's nonexclusivity that the followers of Jesus are seen as carrying on his mission and message (just as he had carried on John's), Q 10:9: "God's reign has reached unto you" (as the message of the disciples). Q 10:16 (according to Matt. 10:40): "Whoever takes you in takes me in, and whoever takes me in takes in the one who sent me." In Q, this ongoing activity would seem to take place without the rupture of crucifixion and the subsequent reestablishment of the disciples through Easter experiences and Pentecost (just as Jesus had been able to carry on, without John's death invalidating their shared message, or John's resurrection becoming a saving event needed to relaunch the mission and its message). Of course, the disciples must have known of Jesus' terrible death. But they had not elevated it to an exclusive significance as the saving event but had seen it embedded in the suffering of all prophets as bearers of Wisdom. Similarly there would have been in the sayings tradition and its Sophia Christology something equivalent to an Easter faith, but it would seem not to have been brought to expression in the kerygmatic patterns with which we are familiar. These two tragic deaths, like that of the prophets before and since, cannot stop Wisdom, and so the mission and its message go on. To be sure, she can withdraw her presence as an anticipation of judgment (*Enoch* 42:1-2: She "found no dwelling-place" and so "returned to her place ... among the angels"), as the shaking the dust off the disciples' feet symbolizes, but she will be there at the day of judgment to be vindicated and to save (Q 13:35). And the finality of the abandonment of "this generation" to its fate seems to have taken place according to Q neither with the murder of John, nor with that of Jesus, but only with the final repudiation of the Jewish mission, at which time a gentile mission is nonetheless envisaged.

Perhaps such a Wisdom Christology, precisely because of the nonexclusivity of its beginnings, would be useful in our society today, when to leave a male deity at the top of our value structuring seems often more like the deification of the omnipotent despot of the ancient Near East than an honoring of God, more a perpetuation of patriarchalism than a liberation of women and men. If we, like Jesus, can be inspired by the feminine aspect of God, we may be able to bring good news to our still all too patriarchal society.

4. THE VISUALIZATION OF THE RESURRECTION

It may be of some relevance in this connection to speak to the question of the "Easter faith" of the Q community, which seems to have had no passion narrative or Easter story, and thus of the "Easter faith" implicit in much of the original Wisdom Christology. For modern concepts of the resurrection of Christ tend to have a monolithic cast that is quite different from that of the first generation. Probably the first resurrection appearances were not experienced like those recorded at the end of Matthew, Luke, and John, upon which our modern assumptions about the resurrection are primarily based. Rather, these texts, from the last third of the first century C.E., tend to be an apologetic tendentious corrective of dangers they perceived as latent (or perhaps already rampant) in the original perception of the resurrection a generation earlier.

Jesus' resurrection seems at the earlier time to have been experienced in a quite different visualization from that with which we are familiar, in that Jesus appeared as a blinding light rather than as a human body mistakable for a gardener or a tourist on the Emmaus road. The only New Testament texts written by persons who actually claimed to have had a resurrection experience describe it as luminosity (Paul in 1 Cor. 15:42-53 and Phil. 3:21, and the seer of Rev. 1:12-16). But such a luminous appearance could perhaps be discounted as just an apparition and become theologically suspect as the kind of appearance that gnostic sources favored. Hence the concern of emergent orthodoxy to prove the actuality and the physicality of the resurrection of Jesus, an apologetic already discernible in the resurrection stories at the end of the canonical Gospels, would readily lead to a replacement of the luminous visualization with a very human visualization.

It may be that one would have here the explanation for a series of odd and probably not unrelated facts. It was generally agreed (1 Cor. 15:5; Luke 24:34) that the first appearance was to Peter. Yet the narration of that appearance is completely missing from the ends of the canonical Gospels. The apocryphal *Gospel of Peter* does record it, though with some details that might seem to us (and them) excessive, and yet with some details that seem presupposed in some of the canonical narratives, such as a role at the resurrection itself for the two mysterious figures at the tomb in Luke 24:4. The Gospel of Mark, surprisingly enough, narrates no resurrection appearances but only the empty tomb and the promise of Galilean appearances. One may recall the bad press that Peter received in Mark (8:33: "Get behind me, Satan! For you are not on the side of God, but of men"). Mark does record a luminous appearance primarily to Peter (though also to the other two of the inner circle), but it is not at the end of the Gospel as a resurrection story but rather in the middle as a confirmation of Peter's confession. It is the story that we traditionally distinguish from resurrection appearances by calling it the transfiguration. Hence one may wonder whether Mark has not blunted the dangerous implications of the luminous resurrection story, with all its disembodied suggestiveness, by putting it prior to the crucifixion, in the middle of the public ministry, when Jesus' physicality was obvious.

This way of "handling" the story of the resurrection appearance to Peter may find its analogy in the way the story of the resurrection appearance to Paul is narrated (three times) in Acts. Luke tells the story as a luminous visualization. But he places it outside the forty-day time span of resurrection appearances. Furthermore, apostleship was, for Paul, defined by being an eyewitness of the resurrection, whereas Acts 1:22 adds to that definition being an eyewitness of the public ministry, which would exclude Paul. And Acts does not concede to Paul the kind of apostleship that Paul was so eager to maintain for himself (Gal. 1:1), but only in the temporary and rather unimportant meaning that the word *apostolos* could also have, as a "delegate" of the church of Antioch limited to the first missionary journey.

Perhaps the left wing of bifurcating primitive Christianity had been using the luminous resurrection appearances to put a prime on what Jesus said after the resurrection, when he was no longer shackled by a body of flesh and had recently been to heaven to learn firsthand the ultimate, as the Gnostics would put it. This would in effect play down the authority of what Jesus said during the public ministry. Thus it may be no mere coincidence that Mark plants this authority-bestowing (9:7: "This is my beloved Son; listen to him.") luminous appearance back into the middle of the public ministry. For it is Mark who is the first to write such a Gospel narrating the public ministry, thereby both playing down the relative importance of Jesus' ongoing sayings in comparison to his miracles, and placing back into Jesus' lifetime whatever sayings Mark does report, rather than acknowledging the validity of those people who claimed they were still hearing from the resurrected Christ. (According to Acts, God continues after the first forty days to communicate through the Holy Spirit rather than through resurrection appearances.) That is to say, Mark and Luke may be clipping the wings of the gnosticizing trajectory visible in the sayings tradition as one moves from Q to the *Gospel of Thomas*.

If thus the resurrection of Jesus during the first generation was experienced in such a luminous visualization, such appearances could well be more characterized by auditions than by actions such as eating fish or having one's wounds touched. The blinding light only talked to Paul (Acts 9:4-6). The faithful Easter witness would then be the proclamation of what the Resurrected said, not the description of how he looked and felt, or what he ate and did. The itinerant preachers who transmitted the Q tradition, prior to its being written down and then incorporated into

Matthew and Luke, kept Jesus' sayings alive by reproclaiming them, not as their words but as his or, more accurately, as Wisdom's. In the process they not only reproclaimed what he had said before his crucifixion, they also ascribed to him/her new sayings that continued to emerge throughout that generation. It was the cause for which he/she stood, his/her message, that was still valid, just as John's cause had been still valid for Jesus after John's death. That is to say, the substantive, theologically relevant aliveness of Jesus after his crucifixion was that of his cause, God's reign. Or, put in terms of Wisdom Christology, Wisdom lived on in the ongoing message, much as John's message – that is, Wisdom's message – had survived in Jesus'. And Wisdom would continue as the authority figure until the day of judgment, when her guidance would be vindicated as the criterion determining human destiny. Rudolf Bultmann's dictum that Jesus rose into the kerygma could thus be adapted to Wisdom Christology by saying that Jesus rose into the life of Wisdom's ongoing proclamation.

5. A New Lease on Life

This Sophia Christology, precisely because it did not come to fruition in Western Christianity but shared in the Western neglect of Eastern Christianity, is less a recording of a traceable strand of Christian history than a nostalgic reminiscence of what might have been. Since the mythical world in which Christianity began is for us dead, this stillborn Christology may be forever lost.

But, though we have seen through myths, in recognizing their non-literal and purely symbolic meaning – for example, in demythologization – they may as symbols have a new lease on life. If Gnosticism could engender artificially its mythology out of the myths of the ancient Near East, or Plato could create the myth of the cave to portray his idealism, or Freud could appeal to Greek mythology to interpret the Oedipus complex, it is not inconceivable that this Sophia Christology could have an appeal in our day.

In this connection we should not ignore the problem that besets the usual christological language with which we are quite familiar. Most of Christian myth is weighted down with the all too familiar, all too literal context in which we are accustomed to hearing it. It is easier for enlightened people today to free themselves of the pre-enlightenment idea that Jesus is a God, however that may have been languaged over the centuries, than to ask what that might have meant then that could still address us today. And to embrace that meaning would seem all too much like a reversion to a premodern world view to which we have no inclination to return. But to turn to Jesus-inspired-by-Wisdom could have a freshness that would make it possible to listen for meaning rather than simply fleeing from obscurantism.

The Wisdom that inspired Jesus is like God's reign he proclaimed. The metaphorical difference may be that Wisdom was portrayed as the personal Spirit that possessed him, whereas God's reign was what he, under the sway of her possession, envisioned. Thus Wisdom would be symbolized as internal, christological, while God's reign would seem external, eschatological. But if mythologically that reign was located at the end of time, one may recall that it was Wisdom that, like the Son of man, would return then for vindication. And conversely God's reign was mythologically experienced as somehow present in Jesus, as was Wisdom: Jesus' exorcisms effected by the finger of God (which Matt. 12:28 interprets as the Spirit of God) were already the coming of God's reign upon the demon-possessed (Q 11:20). But, much more important, one must come to grips with what these symbols mean unmythologically, when they were spoken, which was then in the present. It is only pseudo-theology to seek to reconcile into some harmonious doctrinal system the various *mythologoumena* by means of which their meaning came to expression.

The shared trait, that one has to do with the Wisdom *of God* and the Kingdom *of God*, may provide a relevant lead. Jesus' insight is not just the crowning achievement of some Periclean, Augustan, or Elizabethan age, any more than his vision is that of a purification of the kingdom of this world into a Christian establishment (Christendom as the Kingdom of God). What went into Jesus and came out of Jesus is not of this world. "Of God" means it is transcendent. Not of course in a literal sense: Just as Wisdom did not fly down onto Jesus like a bird, the Kingdom is not some other place, or here in some other time. God's reign is utopia, the ultimate, just as Wisdom is the purity of intention, the commitment. Jesus' whole life was caught up in the cause of humanity, which possessed him with a consuming passion and came to expression through him with radical vision. Those who are caught on fire by him are possessed by the same Wisdom and proclaim the same utopian reign.

CHAPTER 5

The Son of Man in the Sayings Gospel Q

Carsten Colpe's magisterial article on the son of man[1] (or, translated more generically, son of humanity) did not treat the Sayings Gospel Q. He ascribed the Q son of humanity sayings to "die lukanische Sonderquelle"[2]: Q 6,22; 7,34; 9,58; 11,30[3] are sayings referring to Jesus during his public ministry, although only Q 7,34; 9,58 are thought to be authentic son of humanity sayings, whereas Q 12,8.10.40; 17,24.26.30 are references to the coming Son of Humanity, of which the last three (together with five sayings not in Q) are considered authentic. In the case of Matthew[4], "die mit der lk Sonderquelle gemeinsame Spruchüberlieferung" is the source of all the Q son of humanity sayings (though in Matthew for Q 6,22; 12,8 the term son of humanity is replaced by a first personal pronoun)[5]. According to the analysis of "die Verkündigung Jesu,"[6] Jesus referred to himself in the present sayings Q 7,34; 9,58 by making use of the non-titular meaning. The question of whether Jesus identified himself with the future Son of Humanity is left open[7]. This *Festschrift* in Colpe's honor may provide an appropriate occasion for an essay intended to supplement his panoramic presentation, in terms of the Q research of the intervening generation.

---

1. Art. υἱὸς τοῦ ἀνθρώπου, ThWNT 8, 1969, 403-481. Whereas most such articles are authored by a team of experts with mutually compensating specializations, Colpe's competence covers the whole relevant area and thus made it possible for him to produce the entire article himself.

2. Colpe, op. cit., 460-461.

3. One may consult the Introduction, p. vii, for an explanation of the way in which the Lukan chapter and verse numeration is used for the numeration in Q.

4. Colpe, op. cit., 462-463.

5. Luke 17,28-29, and hence by inference 30, have to do with Lot, who is absent from Matthew. Matt 24,39, parallel to Luke 17,30 (though the latter refers to Noah), is not mentioned in Colpe's relevant footnote, 437, n. 257.

6. Colpe, op. cit., 433-444.

7. Colpe, op. cit., 442-443: "Hat sich Jesus als den apokalyptischen Menschensohn gewußt? ... Ein gedanklicher, messianologisch-dogmatischer Ausgleich zwischen sich u dem Menschensohn lag ebs jenseits seines Gesichtskreises wie ein Ausgleich zwischen dem Tag des Menschensohns u der Gottesherrschaft. ... Der apokalyptische Menschensohn ist ein Symbol für Jesu Vollendungsgewissheit. Bezieht man es von dieser Gewißheit auf ihren Träger, dann kann man diesen Sachverhalt auch als dynamische, in seiner zukünftigen Vollendung intendierte und funktionale Gleichstellung Jesu mit dem kommenden Menschensohn interpretieren."

1. Christological Titles in the Layering of Q

The layers of Q[8] may be quite useful as archaic documentation making it possible to trace the emergence of christological titles that are encountered, from Paul on, full-grown in the New Testament itself, so fully developed that they are no longer derived, explained, questioned or defended.

The earliest layer of the Sayings Gospel Q seems to have begun (at Q 6,20)[9] by identifying the main speaker not with a christological

8. The American (in distinction from the German) discussion has been dominated by John S. Kloppenborg, The Formation of Q: Trajectories in Ancient Wisdom Collections, Philadelphia 1987. For a broader context in terms of the history of the discipline see my essay: The Q Trajectory: Between John and Matthew via Jesus, in: The Future of Early Christianity. Essays in Honor of Helmut Koester, Minneapolis 1991, 173-194. [In this volume, chapter 10.]   For an analysis of the son of man sayings of Q on the basis of Kloppenborg's layering (though with some ill-advised modifications), see Leif E. Vaage, The Son of Man Sayings in Q. Stratigraphical Location and Significance, in: Early Christianity, Q and Jesus, Semeia 55, 1991 [1992], 103-129.

9. This beginning of the original draft of Q has been proposed by several scholars, perhaps first by Paul Wernle, Die synoptische Frage, Freiburg 1899, 226: "Diese zwei Stücke [the Preaching of John and the Temptation] sehen überhaupt aus wie eine geschichtliche Einleitung, die nachträglich dem Werk vorgesetzt wurde." Heinz Eduard Tödt, Der Menschensohn in der synoptischen Überlieferung, Gütersloh 1959, 216, quoted with approval Adolf von Harnack, Sprüche und Reden Jesu, 1907, 169, 170: "Q weiß es nicht anders: Jesus war der Messias, bei der Taufe zum Gottessohn eingesetzt, und alle seine Sprüche stehen daher auf diesem Hintergrund. Denkt man aber die Einleitung weg, so ergibt sich ein wesentlich anderes Bild. Man hat eine Spruchsammlung vor sich, in der ein Lehrer, ein Prophet, einer der mehr ist als ein Prophet – der letzte, entscheidende Bote Gottes spricht." "... in den in Q gesammelten Sprüchen ist die Messianität deutlich nur in der Form der Parusie gegeben, und Glauben verlangt Jesus in diesen Sprüchen nicht, weil er der gegenwärtige Messias ist – ein Ungedanke –, sondern weil er Gottestaten tut und Gottesgebot verkündet." Tödt appropriates this view (pp. 225, 243): "Daß die Abschnitte mit der 'messianischen Verkündigung des Täufers' und der Versuchungsgeschichte christologisches Interesse verraten, mag freilich noch hingenommen werden, sind sie doch, wie Harnack feststellt, einem Stoff, der ihre Tendenz nicht teilt, als Einleitung vorangestellt worden." "... da sie wohl kaum zu dem alten Hauptbestand der Spruchquelle gehören." Dieter Lührmann, Die Redaktion der Logienquelle, Neukirchen-Vluyn 1969, 31, ascribed John's Preaching to Q redaction and (p. 56) the Temptation to a non-Q tradition used independently by Matthew and Luke. Athanasius Polag, Die Christologie der Logienquelle, WMANT 45, Gütersloh 1977, 8, ascribed John's Preaching, Jesus' Baptism, and the Temptation to "eine späte Redaktion" following the "Hauptsammlung." P. 15: "Es wird nahezu allgemein angenommen, daß dieses Überlieferungsgut der Q-Sammlung vorangestellt worden ist." This view (omitting Jesus' Baptism) has received its fullest presentation in Kloppenborg, The Formation of Q, 243-262, 325-327. The original beginning at 6,20 is also accepted by Arland D. Jacobson, The First Gospel: An Introduction to Q, Sonoma, CA, 1992, 255. Christopher M. [317] Tuckett, The Temptation Narrative in Q, in: The Four Gospels 1992. Festschrift Frans Neirynck, BEThL 100, Leuven 1992, Vol. 1, 479-507, argues that the temptation narrative was part of the main redactional layer.

title comparable to Mark's "The gospel of Jesus Christ the son of God," but simply as Jesus of Nazara[10]. This spelling occurs only twice in the earliest Christian literature (and nowhere else), and both times at the same position in terms of Q: directly between the Temptation and the Sermon (Matt 4,13; Luke 4,16). This designation may have been used at the beginning of Q in the oldest layer of the Q tradition simply because fully developed christological titles were not yet current.

The title Christ, like the title Christian first introduced in the Pauline environment of Antioch (Acts 11,26), never made its way into Q. Yet the "anointing" by the Spirit (ἔχρισέ με) in Isa 61,1 LXX, a verse quite prominent in Q 7,22 (and perhaps echoed at the opening of the Sermon at Q 6,20-21 and reflected back into the Baptism at Q 3,22 / Matt 3,16), would have made intelligible the use of the term in Q, even in the absence from Q of Davidic Messianic overtones.

The considerable presence of sapiential traditions in the early layer of Q[11] stands in some contrast to the presence of Sophia only in the redactional layer: At Q 7,35 she is vindicated by her children, such as John and Jesus; and at Q 11,49, the quotation formula "therefore also (the) Wisdom (of God) said" introduces the mission of prophets and sages throughout history interpreted in a deuteronomistic way characteristic of the Q redactor. These beginnings of a christological title did not, in distinction to the others, reach full maturity[12], but such a title does show the first stages of development in Q. For "the wisdom of Solomon" is surpassed by "something more than Solomon," Q 11,31.

A similar development toward a christological title may be sensed in the term κύριος. It often refers to God, as in Old Testament quotations (Q 4,8.12; 13,35) and in other references by Jesus to God as someone other than himself (Q 10,2.21). In parabolic language it refers to the master of a servant (Q 12,42.43.45.46; 14,21; 16,13; 19,16.18.20), although a latent allegorical tendency suggests a reference to Jesus in an

10. See my essay, The Sayings Gospel Q, in: The Four Gospels 1992. Festschrift Frans Neirynck, BEThL 100, Leuven 1992, Vol. 1, 361-388, especially 373-382. [In *The Sayings Gospel Q*, pp. 319-48, especially pp. 331-40.]

11. Robinson, The Q Trajectory: Between John and Matthew via Jesus (above n. 8), 184-189. [In this volume, chap. 10.]

12. See my essay, Very Goddess and Very Man: Jesus' Better Self, in: Encountering Jesus: Live Options in Christology, ed. Stephen T. Davis, Atlanta 1988, 111-122; Images of the Feminine in Gnosticism, ed. Karen King, Studies in Antiquity and Christianity, Philadelphia 1988, 112-127. [In this volume, chap. 4.]

indeterminate number of such instances, comparable to Mark 13,35 // Matt 24,42, where "the master of the house" becomes "your Lord" (as in Rev 3,3; 16,15, where it is Jesus who comes as a thief). When used as a form of address to Jesus, κύριος is a term of respect for a person to whom one looks up as a religious leader, but need mean no more than "Sir" (Q 7,6), or "Master" (Q 9,59). But in Q 6,46 κύριε (*bis*) is a title of address directed at Jesus as authoritative teacher by those who in fact do not do what he says, followed by the parables of the house built with or without adequate foundation, leading to ultimate vindication or condemnation. In one parabolic instance of a house owner (Q 13,25; cf. Matt 25,11 of a bridegroom), the parable is applied to Jesus as teacher (Q 13,25). But only Matthew develops this saying one step further, with κύριε κύριε referring to Jesus as the definitive witness at the judgment (Matt 7,22-23; 25,11). Thus Q uses "Lord" as a designation of Jesus, but not with the full theological significance of this as a christological title, as found e.g. already in Paul.

Son of God is a christological title that seems to have been missing from the parts of Q usually ascribed to the older layering, such as the Q Sermon (6,20-49), but then emerged full-grown at the redactional level of Q. Q 6,35 / Matt 5,45 uses "sons of (your father)" to designate persons who love their enemies, in imitation of God who "raises his sun on bad and good and rains on the just and unjust." At this layer of Q one is completely unprepared for the redactional level's exclusive use of the designation son of God for Jesus, (except for Wisdom's "children," Q 7,35) pronounced on him at the Baptism (Q 3,22 / Matt 3,16). This provides the occasion for the devil to challenge and for Jesus to vindicate this designation at the Temptation (Q 4,3.9). The title is then exalted in its exclusivity in the surprisingly "high" christology of the so-called Johannine pericope of Q 10,22, where "everything has been entrusted to me by my Father, and no one knows the Son except the father and the Father except the Son, and to whomever the Son chooses to reveal him."

It is the idiom son of man, as son of humanity, an individual human, that is the most common self-designation of Jesus in Q, where the development toward a title may also be traced. In the older layer the term is infrequent, and refers to Jesus only during his public ministry (Q 6,22; 9,58), but in the redactional layer it is common, in most cases used in an apocalyptic sense, so that a directionality in the development is indicated. It is this potentiality which would seem to have emerged in scholarship since Colpe's article, and to which the present essay is hence devoted.

2. Son of Humanity Sayings Referring to Jesus' Public Ministry

Oscar Cullmann is representative of the traditional scholarly view prior to the break-through marked by Colpe's work. He especially emphasized that son of humanity is almost exclusively documented on the tongue of Jesus[13]: "Das wäre doch ganz unerklärlich, wenn erst sie [sc. the evangelists] Jesus diese Selbstbezeichnung beigelegt hätten. In Wirklichkeit haben sie das präzise Andenken daran bewahrt, daß nur Jesus selbst sich so genannt hat." Further: "Die oben festgehaltene Tatsache, daß die Synoptiker in der griechischen Übersetzung einen Unterschied zwischen 'barnascha' im christologisch-technischen Sinn (υἱὸς τοῦ ἀνθρώπου) und im gewöhnlichen Sinn von 'Menschenkind' machen (ἄνθρωπος), beweist nicht viel mehr, als daß die Evangelisten, obwohl ihnen selbst der Begriff vielleicht nicht mehr ganz durchsichtig gewesen sein mag, doch das Empfinden dafür hatten, daß Jesus mit dieser Bezeichnung bestimmte, als bekannt vorausgesetzte Vorstellungen verband."[14]

This line of reasoning became the ultimate proof of the messianic self-consciousness of Jesus. But here several arguments are fused into one, whereas they need to be distinguished and evaluated separately. The fact that the Evangelists used son of humanity only on the tongue of Jesus does indeed (as Colpe also noted) suggest Jesus used it. The alternative proposed by Protestant liberalism throughout the first half of the century (usually associated with the name of Rudolf Bultmann[15]) does not provide a fully adequate explanation for this remarkable statistical phenomenon. But to combine this insight, as Cullmann does, with the arguments that Jesus thereby referred to himself and that in the New Testament υἱὸς τοῦ ἀνθρώπου is always a title, since the translation of the non-titular Aramaic idiom would be simply ἄνθρωπος, involves a *circulus vitiosus*, or at best an over-simplification that begs the question. It is no doubt the case that the Evangelists, like other early Christians, assumed that the christological titles that were appropriate in their own time were also valid in Jesus' time, and that Jesus of course understood them correctly, as applying to himself. Thus they may have often taken the occurrence of son of humanity on the tongue of Jesus as his claiming this idiom for himself as an apocalyptic figure. But when one traces such sayings back to Jesus himself or as far back as they go, it is not necessarily

13. Oscar Cullmann, Die Christologie des Neuen Testaments, Tübingen 1957, 2. durchgesehene Aufl. 1958, 158.

14. Cullmann, op. cit., 187.

15. Rudolf Bultmann, Theologie des Neuen Testaments, Tübingen 1948, 3. durchgesehene und ergänzte Aufl. 1958, 31-32.

the case that they originally were authentic self-identifications of Jesus with an apocalyptic personage. Each instance must be examined in its own right.

Cullmann himself conceded[16]: "Es gibt vielleicht ein oder zwei Jesus-worte, wo die Bezeichnung υἱὸς τοῦ ἀνθρώπου sich jedenfalls *primär* nicht auf seine eigene Person bezieht, sondern den Menschen schlechthin in dem ganz allgemeinen Sinn von 'Menschenkind' meint." In Mark 2,27-28 ("The sabbath was made for man, not man for the sabbath; so the son of humanity is lord even of the sabbath") the logic requires that son of humanity is meant in the idiomatic sense of human, "Menschenkind."

Also in the case of Q 12,10 ("And whoever says a word against the son of humanity, it will be forgiven him, but he who blasphemes against the Holy Spirit will not be forgiven") Cullmann agreed[17] that the reference to Jesus is here difficult, but that a reference to humans generically poses no difficulty. Offense against humans, but not against God, is pardonable. He found support for this view in the parallel, Mark 3,28, where the plural, "sons of men," is used generically, though in a different syntax: "All sins will be forgiven the sons of men ...". Thus Mark provided a reminiscence of the original generic usage, but which he preserved at the cost of changing the syntax to make it refer not to the offended, but to the offender, and by putting it in the plural, lest it be misunderstood as if Jesus were the offender.

There is an instance of Matthean redaction of Mark where son of humanity has to be understood idiomatically rather than as a title, as Cullmann also conceded[18]. In Matt 16,13 the dialogue leading to Peter's confession is introduced: "Who do men say that the son of humanity is?" (Mark 8,27: "... that I am?") One should not assume this is an artificial question containing already its answer, especially since the answer Peter himself gives (Matt 16,16) would ignore the hint: "You are the Christ, the son of the living God." It is usually assumed that the reference to the son of humanity in the first prediction of the passion (Mark 8,31 // Matt 16,21) has simply been transferred out of Matt 16,21, where son of humanity is replaced by the pronoun αὐτόν, to Matt 16,13, where for Matthew τὸν υἱὸν τοῦ ἀνθρώπου has the same meaning as the αὐτόν of Matt 16,21. Thus Matthew has Jesus ask who people think "one" is; the indefinite usage of son of humanity is understood by implication to refer to Jesus. This does not however mean that the idiom was heard

16. Cullmann, op. cit., 155.
17. Cullmann, op. cit., 156-157.
18. Cullmann, op. cit., 158, n. 3.

as a title worthy to introduce the whole section, since in reality the idiom at Matt 16,13 is precisely not a title[19].

This list of instances where the term son of humanity was originally not meant christologically, but rather indefinitely, may be extended. In Mark 2,10 // Matt 9,6 ("But that you may know that the son of humanity has authority on earth to forgive sins ...") the reference is intended as a reference to Jesus. But Matt 9,8 added to the conclusion "and glorify God," the explanation "who has given such authority to men." Here, as in the preceding instances, there is a vestige of the original indefinite meaning. This is latent in the scribes' accusatory rhetorical question, "Who can forgive sins but God alone?" For it implies the dogmatic affirmation: No human can forgive sins. Matthew made it clear that forgiving could in his community be understood indefinitely, i.e. that not only Jesus as a christological exception, but that humans in general (or just Christians?) have such authority. Son of humanity is interpreted non-christologically by using the plural and the idiomatic Greek translation ἄνθρωποι. Jesus has such authority because he is human.

There are other cases of such an indefinite meaning of son of humanity in the New Testament, if one does not beg the question by reading in from elsewhere christological titular apocalyptic meaning, but simply follows the logic of the saying itself. The most obvious instance is Q 9,58 ("Foxes have holes, and birds of the sky have nests; but the son of humanity does not have anywhere he can lay his head"), which contrasts the living conditions of animals and birds with that of humans. In its Q context, where Jesus is warning off a volunteer, a reference to Jesus as such a human is implied.

This is the only son of humanity saying in the *Gospel of Thomas*[20] (Saying 86), but here there is no narrative context. It remains unclear whether the saying was originally meant simply as a sapiential proverb[21], or whether the generic usage functions in any case to imply Jesus[22]. Helmut Koester argued: "Thomas setzt ein Überlieferungsstadium der eschatologischen Sprüche voraus, in dem es die apokalyptische Erwartung des

---

19. Ragnar Leivestad, Der apokalyptische Menschensohn ein theologisches Phantom, Annual of the Swedish Theological Institute 6, 1967-68, 49-105: 67-72.

20. The only other instance of the idiom is in Saying 106, where the indefinite meaning is inherent in the use of the plural: "When you make the two one, you will become the sons of humanity."

21. So Rudolf Bultmann, Die Geschichte der synoptischen Tradition, Göttingen 1921, [3]1957, 27. Bultmann there already conjectured that the saying existed without a narrative context.

22. So Douglas R.A. Hare, The Son of Man Tradition, Minneapolis 1990, 271-273.

kommenden Menschensohnes noch nicht gab."[23] This view was not widely adopted in German scholarship, since the assumption has been either that Jesus himself had such an apocalyptic view, or, if not, then it emerged with the exuberance incited by Easter, Ernst Käsemann's "nachösterlich-judenchristlicher Enthusiasmus."[24] In either case there is no pre-apocalyptic period in the transmission of the son of humanity sayings. But in the light of Paul Hoffmann's view that "die Rezeption oder doch zumindest die literarisch-theologische Integration der MS[Menschensohn]-Vorstellung in den übrigen Q-Stoff" is due to the redaction of Q in connection with the war with Rome around 70 C.E.[25], Koester's assumption of a period of time before the apocalypticizing of the son of humanity sayings tradition is today a much more open question. This saying is ascribed by Kloppenborg to the older layer of Q.

Q 7,34 is another instance where the saying itself has no visible meaning beyond the idiomatic: "The son of humanity has come eating and drinking." Here Jesus is put antithetically parallel to John (Q 7,33): "For John came neither eating nor drinking." Both are caricatured, John as having a demon, Jesus as "a glutton and a drunkard, a friend of tax collectors and sinners." These are the responses of "this generation," which rejects both dance music and dirges (Q 7,31-32). Thus the reference is clearly to the time of Jesus' public ministry. Whereas Christian texts normally put Jesus above John, here both are put side by side (with the characterization of John actually being better than that of Jesus, given the standard admiration of asceticism). Both, as Wisdom's children, justify her (Q 7,35). Thus a title elevating Jesus above John is not in place. (The title "the Baptist" accorded to John in Luke 7,33 is a Lucan addition to Q.) Furthermore, if the passage had in fact sought to accord an

23. Ein Jesus und vier ursprüngliche Evangeliengattungen, in: Entwicklungslinien durch die Welt des frühen Christentums, Tübingen 1971, 160.

24. Ernst Käsemann, Die Anfänge christlicher Theologie, ZThK 57, 1960, 162-185, reprinted in: Exegetische Versuche und Besinnungen, Göttingen 1964, Vol. 2, 82-104, especially 91; Zum Thema der urchristlichen Apokalyptik, ZThK 59, 1962, 257-284, reprinted in: Exegetische Versuche und Besinnungen, Vol. 2, 105-131.

25. Paul Hoffmann, QR und der Menschensohn. Eine vorläufige Skizze, in: The Four Gospels 1992. Festschrift Frans Neirynck, BEThL 100, Leuven 1992, Vol. 1, 421-456, especially V. Der Menschensohn und der Fall Jerusalems, 450-456, p. 450: "Steck hat aufgrund der Nähe der Ansage [Q 13,34-35] zu den Berichten des Josephus über verschiedene Vorzeichen für das Jerusalem drohende Unheil, das Jerusalemwort in die Zeit des jüdisch-römischen Krieges datiert." Odil Hannes Steck, Israel und das gewaltsame Geschick der Propheten, Neukirchen-Vluyn 1967, 45-48, 50-58, argued on the basis of the non-Christian, Jewish content and the late date that Luke 13,34-35 par does not in fact derive from Q. Hence the impact of the identification of this *Sitz im Leben* upon the dating of the redaction of Q was delayed a generation, until the placement of Q 13,34-35 in Q had again become the standard assumption, as it is today.

honorific title to Jesus, it should have been ὁ ἐρχόμενος, the designation used in the question by John's disciples (7,19-20), in reference back to Q 3,16 / Matt 3,11, and answered by Jesus' reply (Q 7,22-23). Thus the use of the title ὁ ἐρχόμενος at the conclusion of this section of Q treating John's question would have been in this regard appropriate, whereas a title son of humanity is in no sense in place. Though not ascribed to the older layer of Q (by Kloppenborg, in preference to Vaage), it may (with Colpe) be an archaic saying.

Q 6,22, as in Luke, probably used the designation son of humanity. Matt 5,11 again understood it idiomatically (as at Matt 9,8; 16,13.21) and not as a title, and read "me" (Matt 5,11). Here too the term refers to Jesus in his public ministry. This saying is also ascribed to the older layer of Q (by Kloppenborg, in preference to Vaage).

Q 11,30 ("For as Jonah became to the Ninevites a sign, so also will the son of humanity be to this generation") has sometimes been classified as an instance of the future apocalyptic usage, to which its form tends to point (see below). But, just as the Matthean *tertium comparationis* of placing Jonah in the sea monster and Jesus in the tomb (Matt 12,40) is clearly secondary, just so an allusion to Jesus at the day of judgment seems not originally intended. This association is ascribed to the earliest commentary, already in Q, namely the association of this saying with the other Nineveh saying (Q 11,32). But in the latter case it is the Ninevites and this generation who are to be present at the day of judgment, without any reference to a presence at the judgment of Jonah and Jesus. Rather the point about Jesus in Q 11,32 has to do with Jesus' public ministry: "Something more than Jonah is here." After all, Jonah became a sign to the Ninevites not at the day of judgment, but in the past by his preaching in Nineveh, as Q 11,32 correctly says (τὸ κήρυγμα Ἰωνᾶ). Hence the *tertium comparationis* is the preaching of Jesus to "this generation." The future tense in Q 11,30 (as at Q 11,29) would seem not to be apocalyptic[26].

Philipp Vielhauer posed "die philologische Frage"[27]: "Jedoch existiert offenbar – bis jetzt – kein Beleg dafür, daß Menschensohn

---

26. Philipp Vielhauer, Gottesreich und Menschensohn in der Verkündigung Jesu, in: Festschrift fur Günther Dehn, Neukirchen 1957, 51-79, reprinted in Vielhauer, Aufsätze zum Neuen Testament, München 1965, 55-91; Jesus und der Menschensohn. Zur Diskussion mit Heinz Eduard Tödt und Eduard Schweizer, ZThK 60, 1963, 133-177, reprinted in: Aufsätze zum Neuen Testament, 92-140; Ein Weg zur neutestamentlichen Christologie? Prüfung der Thesen Ferdinand Hahns, EvTh 25, 1965, 24-72, reprinted in: Aufsätze zum Neuen Testament, 141-198. On 112 he compares the non-apocalyptic future tense in Q 11,29.

27. Vielhauer, Aufsätze (above n. 26), 118-129, here 119.

Umschreibung für Ich sein kann; und Kenner wie Dalman und Sjöberg bestreiten diese Möglichkeit ausdrücklich." The debate has been carried on subsequently by Joseph A. Fitzmyer, S.J. (agreeing with Vielhauer and the scholars he listed) and Geza Vermes, who has summarized his research as follows[28]: "I adduced ten examples of direct speech – monologue or dialogue – in which the speaker appears to refer to himself, not as 'I', but as 'the son of humanity' in the third person, in contexts implying awe, reserve or modesty. ... in none of the passages scrutinized, not even in the Jewish messianic exegesis of Daniel 7, does the expression *bar nasha* figure as a title." Vermes recognized that Fitzmyer's main argument was to the effect that such Aramaic instances are all later than the First Century C.E., to which Vermes replied[29]: "If we accept that the phrase reflected in *ho huios tou anthropou* was originally coined in Aramaic by Galileans, is it not sensible, indeed obligatory, to investigate the relics of the Galilean dialect, closest in time to the gospels, the Palestinian Talmud and similar Galilean rabbinic sources, especially when there is good reason to think that their dialectal peculiarities pre-date the period of their codification?" He is able only to report a partial *rapprochement*[30]: "He [Fitzmyer] now admits (or re-admits) that the case for the circumlocutional use of 'son of man' has been made out at least once, and that Matt. 16,13 ('Who do men say the son of man is?') compared with Mark 8,27 ('Who do men say that I am?') suggests that the substitution of "Son of Man" for "I" ... reflects current Palestinian Aramaic usage'. ... Yet at the same time, he does not flinch from the possibility that the Targumic idiom was influenced by the New Testament!"

Douglas R. A. Hare may well represent the current state of opinion of those who have followed this debate confined today largely to Aramaic specialists[31]: "In terms of form and function, it was inferred that the Aramaic expression was, as most scholars have assumed, *bar enasha* and that this phrase was capable of functioning in some contexts as a modesty idiom, whereby a speaker referred to himself exclusively. ... As many have pointed out, there is no unambiguous philological evidence in support of the proposal that *bar enasha* sometimes served as an exclusive self-reference. On the other hand, there is no philological evidence whatsoever, ambiguous or otherwise, for the opposing proposal that *bar enasha* could sometimes function as a recognizable apocalyptic

---

28. Geza Vermes, Jesus and the World of Judaism, London/Philadelphia 1983, 90.
29. Vermes, op. cit., 93-94.
30. Vermes, op. cit., 80.
31. Hare, The Son of Man Tradition (above n. 22), 256, 259.

title. ... What is being claimed here is that all the secondary sayings, however numerous they may be, are ultimately modeled on genuine sayings in which Jesus spoke about himself by means of this characteristic idiom."

There is thus a rather impressive list of instances where son of humanity refers indefinitely to a human and by implication to Jesus himself. For the ability to use the term to refer to Jesus during his public ministry would seem not to be due to the term having been used as an apocalyptic title for Jesus and then transferred back by the Q community to Jesus' public ministry, but to the term's use as an unimpressive Aramaic idiom with an implied reference to the speaker. Although not all these instances have much probability of having been said by Jesus, they do indicate a prominent presence in the tradition of sayings of Jesus, and some are indeed usually ascribed to Jesus (e.g. Q 7,34 and 9,58 by Colpe). They could well be the origin of the early Christian reminiscence that the idiom was distinctive of Jesus' language, though it originally reflected his "modesty,"[32] rather than his "messianic self-consciousness."

3. THE APOCALYPTIC SON OF HUMANITY

Colpe's survey in terms of the history-of-religions, which, after all, is his forte, led to the conclusion[33], "daß das jüdisch-apokalyptische Material keine Antwort auf die entscheidende Frage erlaubt, wie die Präformation zur neutestamentlichen Menschensohnvorstellung zwischen 50 vor u 50 nChr im Judentum aussah." Colpe may here well mark the turning point from the traditional history-of-religions derivation of the son of humanity in the sayings of Jesus that had dominated scholarship for half a century to a new assessment increasingly characteristic of scholarship today.

Only a decade earlier Hans Eduard Tödt had begun his analysis of the son of humanity sayings in the Synoptics with the presupposition: "Der intensive Zusammenhang der synoptischen mit der spätjudisch-apokalyptischen Menschensohnvorstellung kann heute nicht mehr ernstlich bestritten werden."[34] This inherited history-of-religions view functioned however as a Procrustean bed for his own analysis. He agreed with his predecessors that it is the apocalyptic sayings that are authentic,

---

32. Hare, op. cit., 256 and *passim*.
33. Colpe, υἱὸς τοῦ ἀνθρώπου (above n. 1), 431.
34. Tödt, Der Menschensohn in der synoptischen Überlieferung (above n. 9), 19.

because Jesus can have derived them from that background (though Jesus did not identify himself with that apocalyptic mythological figure, but left that for the church to do). Yet he conceded that the identifying language of that background is missing, in his opinion stripped off[35]: "Die Menschensohnworte Jesu bieten eine radikale Reduktion aller apokalyptischen Ausmalungstendenzen. Die 'vorstelligen' Züge, an deren Farbenpracht die Seher der apokalyptischen Visionen mit der Kraft ihrer Phantasie hängen, sind verschwunden. Heil und Unheil wird den Hörern zugesprochen, niemals aber ausgemalt. Erst mit zunehmender Entfernung von der Verkündigung Jesu mehren sich wieder die traditionellen Züge, die sekundär in die Menschensohnsprüche Jesu bzw. der Gemeinde eingeschleust werden." So when Tödt turns to various later inauthentic apocalyptic Son of Humanity sayings not derived from Q, the Jewish apocalyptic traditions are present on all sides. For example, with regard to Matthew's edition of the conclusion of Q at Matt 19,28[36]: "Entgegen allen bisher besprochenen Worten der Logienquelle ist Mt 19,28 also vorwiegend durch traditionell-apokalyptische Vorstellungen bestimmt; eine ähnliche Auffüllung von Menschensohnworten mit überkommenen Motiven haben wir schon in den drei Sprüchen bei Markus wahrgenommen, und wir werden sie in den redaktionellen Menschensohnsprüchen des Matthaus-Evangeliums wiederfinden. Schon diese formale Beobachtung kann uns nicht ermutigen, Mt 19,28 für ein authentisches Wort Jesu zu halten." Nothing would seem to be clearer documentation for the *Tendenz* of the synoptic gospels to merge secondarily the Jewish apocalyptic traditions to which Daniel, the Similitudes of Enoch and 4 Ezra attest with the Q tradition of apocalyptic Son of Humanity sayings where that tradition was originally lacking. The normal inference would be that the apocalyptic Son of Humanity sayings of Q were not originally derived from that Jewish apocalyptic tradition, since that tradition is secondarily added.

Tödt rejected the authenticity of the son of humanity sayings referring to the public ministry of Jesus. In his view the Easter experience of the Q community had the effect that they no longer distinguished Jesus from the apocalyptic Son of Humanity of whom he had spoken as someone other than himself but rather identified him with that future figure. They

---

35. Tödt, op. cit., 61. This summarizes previous references to "die Kargheit der Anhaltspunkte," "der Unterschied gegenüber jüdisch-apokalyptischen Texten" (both 44), "der Gegensatz zur visionären Schilderung des Menschensohnes und seines Tuns in der Apokalyptik" (47), "in äußerster Knappheit" (57), "nicht das Interesse an apokalyptisch-visionärer Ausmalung" (60), "kärglich" (61).

36. Tödt, op. cit., 57-58.

then naturally identified him already during his public ministry as the apocalyptic Son of Humanity, and hence engendered son of humanity sayings referring to him during the time of the public ministry. This then posed the insoluble problem of why, in transferring the apocalyptic title back onto the public ministry, the transcendent traits of the apocalyptic figure are deleted[37]: "Und wenn nicht Jesus, sondern die Gemeinde den danielischen Menschensohn an unserer Stelle [Q 7,34] nach Jesus gedeutet haben sollte, unter Verlust allen überkommenen Inhalts seines Namens – dann müßte gleichfalls verständlich gemacht werden, aus welchem Grunde sie das getan hat." When one then turns to the place later in the book to which Tödt refers the reader for the solution to the problem, one is merely confronted with the problem anew[38]: "Wohl stellte man das Erdenwirken jetzt auch unter den Namen Menschensohn. Aber irdisches Tun und künftiges Erfüllen blieben unterschieden. Die transzendenten Eigenschaften des kommenden Menschensohnes wurden nicht auf Jesu irdisches Tun übertragen." Yet no answer is given to the obvious initial question as to why the son of humanity sayings ascribed to Jesus as spoken during his public ministry, if inauthentic and derived from authentic apocalyptic Son of Humanity sayings, do not somewhere betray that origin. This should have raised the question, but did not, as to whether there might be another origin.

Tödt recognized this as an insurmountable *aporia* discrediting the ascription of both kinds of sayings to Jesus[39]: "Man steht vor einer unüberwindlichen Schwierigkeit, wenn man behauptet, daß Jesus in den Parusiesprüchen vom Menschensohn als einer transzendenten Gestalt gesprochen hat, während er daneben andere Worte formulierte, in denen der *Menschensohn* alle bisherigen Prädikate verlor und nach Jesu eigenem, irdischem Tun gedeutet wurde." But once Tödt conceded that the future Son of Humanity sayings do not betray the coloring of the Jewish apocalyptic tradition, and that the present son of humanity sayings do not derive their elevated status for Jesus from the apocalyptic Son of Humanity (but rather from the activity of the kingdom of God in Jesus' public ministry), then his whole thesis becomes so improbable that the converse theory is indeed suggested: Jesus used of himself the idiom son of humanity. The idiom was then put on his tongue by his disciples as characteristic of his language. Once an apocalyptic role was ascribed to him, the idiom would be used here as well. Since Jesus was understood

37. Tödt, op. cit., 108.
38. Tödt, op. cit., 249.
39. Tödt, op. cit., 116.

as the fulfillment of scripture, it would only be natural to find in Dan 7,13 a prediction fulfilled by Jesus, and therefore to embellish the portrayal of his apocalyptic role with materials available in such Jewish traditions.

The lasting contribution of Tödt's analysis resides in his recognition that the Q tradition is independent of the kerygma[40]: "... unsere These, daß traditionsgeschichtlich und sachlich zwei Traditionskreise unterschieden werden müssen: der eine ist durch das Passionskerygma bestimmt, beim anderen steht die Absicht einer erneuten Verkündigung der Botschaft Jesu im Mittelpunkt. Die Q-Stoffe gehören zum zweiten Kreis. ... Die Gedanken des Passionskerygmas blieben ausgeschlossen. So erwiesen die Stoffe der Logienquelle sich als ein selbständiges Ursprungsgebiet christologischer Erkenntnis." Hence he introduced from form criticism the thesis "von einer Gemeinde als dem Träger jener Traditionsschicht Q," which however then led to the problem[41]: "Mit Recht betont Harnack immer wieder, daß der Gedanke an die Passion Jesu, der sogenannte Paulinismus bei Markus, in Q fehlt. Wie ist das verständlich in dem Traditionsgut einer Gemeinde, die doch zweifellos von der Passion Jesu Kenntnis hatte?" Tödt's criticism of the form critics is that as a result they did not really free Q from the kerygma as its context, i.e. did not actually concede the existence of a distinct Q community[42]. Yet the basic ambivalence in Tödt's own solution was that he too presupposed that the Q community had knowledge of the cross and resurrection[43]: "Sie wollte Jesu Predigt weitergeben. Aber wie verhielt sich die Predigt zu Passion und Auferstehung? Waren diese nicht Inhalt der Verkündigung, so waren sie doch ihre Voraussetzung. ... Daher konnte eine Gemeinde, die von der Auferstehungsgewißheit erfüllt war, es dennoch unterlassen, die Auferstehung zum primären Verkündigungsinhalt zu machen; denn das Heilsgut lag nicht in Tod und Auferstehung, sondern wurde durch sie in Geltung gesetzt." Tödt's point of departure in the insistence that the apocalyptic title Son of Humanity was prerequisite to its introduction into the Jesus tradition, and hence that the son of humanity sayings about the public ministry cannot be merely idiomatic and hence cannot be authentic, but must be titular and hence inauthentic, may be the point at which he too did not fully free his analysis from the all-encompassing kerygmatic presupposition of the preceding generation of scholarship.

40. Tödt, op. cit., 244-245.

41. Tödt, op. cit., 217.

42. Tödt, op. cit., 218: "Die Meister der formgeschichtlichen Methode, Bultmann und Dibelius, fanden jeder einen besonderen Weg, die theologische Priorität des Passions-Kerygmas der Gemeinde vor den Stoffen der Logienquelle sicherzustellen."

43. Tödt, op. cit., 228-229.

Colpe himself did not contest the apocalyptic use of the son of humanity as a title by Jesus, but did maintain "daß hier [sc. in the sayings tradition] eine von Daniel, 4 Esra und Henoch unabhängige, also eine vierte Tradition sichtbar wird, welche die Variabilität der Menschensohnerwartung im Judentum anzeigt."[44] Yet the lack of documentation for this fourth apocalyptic tradition is only partially explained. The authentic sayings about the coming son of humanity "finden sich in Reden an die Jünger," and thus lead to the conclusion, "daß Jesus vor dem Bekenntnis Lk 22,69 nur in esoterischer Rede den Menschensohn ankündigte."[45] The subsequent transmission of apocalyptic Son-of-Humanity sayings ascribed to Jesus could also have been esoteric[46], though the concept of a Q community is not introduced. Colpe had been the assistant to Joachim Jeremias, who denied the existence of Q.

The conjecture of an esoteric context in which Jesus and his followers spoke of an apocalyptic Son of Humanity seems to be hardly more than an objectification of the lack of adequate documentation of a Jewish matrix, especially after the flood of contemporary Jewish apocalypticism, made available by Qumran, had been surveyed in vain[47]. Ragnar Leivestad admitted, "daß die Entdeckung, daß 'der Menschensohn' für die eschatologisch eingestellte und apokalyptisch interessierte Qumran-Gemeinde augenscheinlich vollständig unbekannt war, eine wachsende Unruhe erweckte. Es war ja eigentlich niemals eine überzeugende Antwort auf die dringende Frage gegeben: wo haben wir die Kreise zu

---

44. Colpe, op. cit., 440-441.

45. Colpe, op. cit., 443.

46. Colpe, op. cit., 441: "Diese Tradition kann auch ausschließlich in Gemeinden gepflegt worden sein; daß es charismatisch erregte Kreise gab, die nach dem Zusammenbruch auch der letzten politisch-messianischen Hoffnungen die übernational-apokaliptischen Erwartungen aktivierten, Jesus als Menschensohn erwarteten u damit von Juden zu Judenchristen wurden, ist sogar sehr wahrscheinlich."

47. Cullmann, Christologie (above n. 13), 143, introduced his discussion of the fact that "Son of Humanity" had not turned up as hoped in Qumran with the comment: "Die Erwartung eines 'Menschensohnes' scheint demnach vor allem in esoterischen Kreisen des Judentums gepflegt worden zu sein." His difficulties in finding documentation for an exalted Son of Humanity conception is evident in such comments as the following (pp. 134, 135): "So gewiß diese Lehre vom göttlichen Urmenschen in den orientalischen Religionen der jüdischen Umwelt verbreitet war, ja geradezu zu ihrem gemeinsamen Bestand gerechnet werden kann, so schwer ist sie doch in einer entwickelten Form faßbar." "Zuerst soll aber erklärt werden, weshalb zunächst im Judentum die Vorstellung vom Urmenschen und die Vorstellung vom kommenden Menschensohn sich auf zwei getrennten Geleisen entwickelt haben, so daß ihre ursprüngliche Zusammengehörigkeit nicht mehr sichtbar ist." His conclusion (p. 169) is pure speculation, a rationalization for the lack of documentation: "Wir haben gesehen, daß die Menschensohnerwartung schon im Judentum fast als Geheimlehre in gewissen esoterischen Kreisen gepflegt wurde. Jesus muß irgendwie mit diesen Kreisen Berührung gehabt haben." Similarly 186, 189.

suchen, die an den apokalyptischen Menschensohn geglaubt haben? Wo
hat Jesus diese Vorstellung kennen gelernt?" His blunt answer: "Der
apokalytische Menschensohn ist eine Erfindung der modernen
Theologie." Put positively: "Die Selbstbezeichnung, die ursprünglich
keinen titularen Inhalt hatte, konnte, weil Jesus mit dem Messias identi-
fiziert wurde, christologische Bedeutung bekommen. Es gibt späte, christliche Formulierungen, die einen gewissen titularen Sinn voraussetzen."[48]

The usual appeal to the Similitudes of Enoch has gradually had to give
ground. Vermes has summarized this development as follows[49]: "This
wind of change was greatly assisted by the absence of the Book of Parables [Similitudes], the main alleged source of the 'son of man' concept,
from the Qumran Aramaic manuscripts of Enoch, although in the late
1960s, reputable scholars admittedly queried the validity of such a deduc-
tion. In 1967 Morna Hooker still preferred to date the Parables to between
63 BC and AD 70, and declared the Qumran evidence impressive but
indecisive. A year later, J.A. Fitzmyer expressly attributed to 'sheer
chance' the silence of the scrolls. However, when it emerged from
J.T. Milik's publications that Book II, or the Parables, was not merely
lacking in the Enoch material represented by eleven fragmentary manuscripts from Cave 4, but was replaced there by the Book of Giants, the
chance theory in regard to the missing Parables became highly improbable." Leivestad commented: "In Qumran hat man Fragmente aus jedem
Kapitel des 1. Hen. gefunden – bis auf die Bilderreden. Es gibt aber m.W.
überhaupt kein einziges Zitat aus den Bilderreden in der ganzen jüdischen
und christlichen Literatur. Sie sind uns nur aus dem äthiopischen Kanon
in sehr späten Handschriften bekannt (16. Jahrhundert und später)."[50]
And in any case he denied that the use there is titular – by appeal to
Colpe: "Auch hier ist *Mensch* nicht Messiastitel, sondern umschreibt das
Aussehen des Himmelswesens."[51] Regarding 4 Ezra 13 Leivestad concluded: "Der Menschenähnliche, der hier mit deutlicher Anspielung auf
Dan. 7,13 auftritt, wird aber nicht mit dem Titel Menschensohn bezeich-
net."[52] To Dan 7,13 itself he concluded, "daß der heutige Text in Dan.
7 erstens keinen Menschensohntitel und zweitens überhaupt keine indi-
viduelle Messiasgestalt enthält. ... In dem heutigen Kontext hat der Menschenähnliche keine andere Funktion als ein Symbol des heiligen

---

48. Leivestad, Der apokalyptische Menschensohn ein theologisches Phantom (above n.
19), 49-51.
49. Geza Vermes, Jesus and the World of Judaism (above n. 28), 96.
50. Leivestad, op. cit., 53.
51. Colpe, op. cit., 425-426.
52. Leivestad, op. cit., 53.

Gottesvolkes zu sein (7,18.22.27)."[53] Furthermore neither the Similitudes of Enoch nor 4 Ezra would seem to be pre-Christian.

It was Vielhauer who broke from the standard Bultmannian solution still represented by Tödt, by arguing that even the apocalyptic Son of Humanity sayings are inauthentic[54]. He argued forcefully for the inauthenticity of Q 12,8-9, on the grounds that this saying presupposed judicial processes against Christians, which would hardly have taken place during the public ministry. Here Mark 8,38 and Luke 12,8 juxtapose the first personal pronoun with the term son of humanity in the third person, but the Q parallel in Matt 10,32-33 does not, but rather uses the first personal pronoun throughout. It is generally agreed that the Q saying, like Mark 8,38, referred to the son of humanity[55]: "Anyone who may speak out for me in public, the son of humanity will also speak out for him before the angels. But whoever may deny me in public will be denied before the angels." The absence of a reference to the son of humanity in this saying in Matthew is simply a further instance of his awareness of the idiomatic meaning (as at Matt 5,11; 9,8; 16,13.21). The son of humanity in Q 12,8-9 is not the judge of the day of judgment, nor is he anywhere so portrayed in Q. Rather he is a character witness, to the effect that his followers have kept his word (Q 6,47-49), as in the judgment scene of Matt 7,22-23.

A basic argument for the saying's authenticity has been that it distinguishes between references to Jesus in the first person and to the son of humanity in the third, who must therefore be conceived of as someone

53. Leivestad, op. cit., 54-55.
54. Vielhauer, Aufsätze (above n. 26), 73-80.
55. Tödt, Der Menschensohn in der synoptischen Überlieferung (above n. 9), 246, n. 108, suggested Matthew omitted here son of humanity, since that designation is for Matthew associated with the judge, not the witness, and because the term son of humanity had already been introduced into the context at Matt 10,23. The presence of son of humanity in the Q saying is advocated by Hare, The Son of Man Tradition (above n. 22), 267-271. Paul Hoffmann, Jesus versus Menschensohn. Mt 10,32f und die synoptische Menschensohnüberlieferung, in: Salz der Erde – Licht der Welt. Exegetische Studien zum Matthäusevangelium. Festschrift für Anton Vögtle zum 80. Geburtstag, Stuttgart 1991, 165-202, begins, 166: "Daß der Ausdruck MS [Menschensohn] nicht nur in Lk 12,8, sondern auch in Lk 12,9 ursprünglich sei, dagegen aber Mt 10,32f und Mk 8,38 sekundäre Fassungen darstellen, wird heute allenfalls von Außenseitern bestritten." The essay then proceeded to contest this consensus. Hoffmann argued that it was first Mark who introduced into the saying, under the influence of Daniel, the term son of humanity. Luke followed at the parallel position Luke 9,26, and then at the Q position recalled and repeated this updating of the saying (Luke 12,8). But whereas Mark 8,38 // Luke 9,26 are meant apocalyptically, Luke 12,8 (like Luke 12,5) refers, according to Hoffmann, to the disciple's fate at death. But in that case, why would Luke introduce an apocalyptic reference, especially since it then clashes with the same idiom used in Luke (Q) 12,10 to refer to Jesus in the public ministry?

other than Jesus. Only Jesus could have created such a saying, not the Q community, which identified Jesus with the son of humanity. Vielhauer however pointed out[56] that all the son of humanity sayings, by the very nature of the idiom, refer to Jesus only in the third person, though it is only those referring to the public ministry which by the nature of the case are clear references to Jesus. Q 12,8-9 is not the only instance where such a saying in the third person includes also a reference in the first person. Matt 19,28 has both persons, in a Matthean editing of the conclusion of Q. Yet it is precisely Matthew who feels free to read "son of humanity" as "me" in Q 6,22; 12,8-9. Cullmann's comment cited above on the Evangelists' ignorance regarding the Aramaic idiom would seem hardly fair to Matthew. Of course, as Cullmann went on, it is true that the Evangelists "doch das Empfinden dafür hatten, daß Jesus mit dieser Bezeichnung bestimmte, als bekannt vorausgesetzte Vorstellungen verband," namely their own christology. But Matthew seems nonetheless on occasion to work freely with the idiomatic meaning of son of humanity. As Leivestad argued[57], "Mt hat den ursprünglichen Gebrauch des Namens als reine Selbstbezeichnung ohne messianische Bedeutung treu übernommen und fortgesetzt." Perhaps Vermes can be forgiven for his formulation[58]: "The thesis advanced by Bultmann and his school, that the 'coming Son of humanity' alluded to by Jesus was someone other than himself, provides a nearly perfect example of how sophisticated modern scholars can be taken in by a clever Aramaic *double entendre*."

Q 12,40, "You also must be ready; for the Son of Humanity is coming at an hour you do not suspect," is an application of the preceding parable on the unpredictable arrival of the robber (Q 12,39), and as such may be secondary. It is also followed by the *locus classicus* for the "delay" (here *expressis verbis)* of the parousia in Q 12,45. Vielhauer argued[59]: "Das Faktum der Parusieverzögerung geht nicht nur aus dem Kontext hervor, sondern auch daraus, daß über die Zeit bis zum Ende überhaupt reflektiert wird; daß die Mahnung zur Wachsamkeit mit der Ungewißheit des Wann statt mit der Gewißheit der Nähe motiviert wird, weist nicht in die Verkündigung Jesu, sondern in die der Gemeinde."

In the case of Q 17,23-24, Vielhauer argued[60]: "Es geht in dem Spruch nicht um die Entgegensetzung zweier verschiedener *Gestalten,* des Messias und des Menschensohns, sondern um die Warnung vor falschen

---

56. Vielhauer, op. cit., 105.
57. Leivestad, op. cit., 69-70.
58. Geza Vermes, Jesus and the World of Judaism (above n. 28), 93.
59. Vielhauer, op. cit., 108.
60. Vielhauer, op. cit., 110.

Vorstellungen über *eine* Gestalt, religionsgeschichtlich ausgedrückt: um die Warnung, das Erscheinen des Menschensohns nach Art des 'verborgenenen Messias' zu erwarten. Daß eine solche Warnung nötig war, setzt die Identifikation von Menschensohn und Messias voraus, und diese ist erst in der Urgemeinde nachzuweisen. Tödts Argumente für die Authentizität von Lk 17,23f par sind also nicht stichhaltig." Vielhauer would seem to be correct that the saying as a Son of Humanity saying is inauthentic, though the development of this particular tradition may be further clarified by reference to the *Gospel of Thomas* and the *Gospel of Mary*[61]. The identification of Matt 24,26 with Luke 17,21 as a Q saying about the kingdom is facilitated by their occurrence in the *Gospel of Thomas* Sayings 3 (more like Matt 24,26) and 113 (more like Luke 17,21). The *Gospel of Mary* (P. Berol. 8502, 8, 15-19) shows this saying about the kingdom of God to have been secondarily made into a son of humanity saying: "Beware that no one lead you astray, saying, 'Lo, here!' or 'Lo, there!' For the son of humanity is inside you." This would document the basic transition from an authentic kingdom saying of Jesus to an inauthentic son of humanity saying of the Q community by implication, in that it was associated with the Son of Humanity saying in Q 17,24. It became a Christ saying first in Mark 13,21 // Matt 24,23.

In the case of Q 11,30 Vielhauer opposed Tödt's interpretation in analogy to the apocalyptic comparisons in Q 17,24.26-27.30[62]: "Denn 1. sind die Vergleiche ganz anders strukturiert und haben eine andere Pointe als v. 30; von der Ahnungslosigkeit der Zeitgenossen und der Plötzlichkeit der Katastrophe wie dort ist hier mit keinem Wort die Rede." Since Q 11,29-30 is a unit originally distinct from Q 11,31-32, it is not permissible to read the thought of judgment found in verse 32 into verse 30, as Tödt does. Thus Vielhauer concludes, with some uncertainty, that the saying refers to the public ministry and hence is inauthentic. Vielhauer is even less certain as to whether Q 17,26-27 is authentic, but infers that since the decision was against authenticity in the case of the other apocalyptic son of humanity sayings, this should be the assumption also in this case.

The most striking aspect of the bulk of the apocalyptic sayings about the son of humanity in Q is their form, a form almost exclusively to be found in Q within early Christian literature. It was identified as distinctive of Q and designated "eschatological correlative" by

---

61. See my essay, The Study of the Historical Jesus after Nag Hammadi, in: The Historical Jesus and the Rejected Gospels, Semeia 44, 1988, 45-55. [In *The Sayings Gospel Q,* pp. 275-84.]

62. Vielhauer, op. cit., 112.

Richard A. Edwards[63]. But, in view of LXX precedents, it was designated "prophetic correlative" by Daryl Schmidt[64]. Migaku Sato traced it from OT sapiential to prophetic contexts and designated it "heilsgeschichtlicher Vergleich."[65] He conceded that the reference in Q 11,30 is to the public ministry, since Jonah as prophet in Nineveh is the comparison, but argued that the future tense "kann kaum anders als endzeitlich-zukünftig gemeint sein." The result is to concede the "Inkongruenz" of what he accepts as "eine bewußt verfremdende Redeweise," with the resultant "Unlogik" of the saying when thus understood apocalyptically. John Dominic Crossan[66] has designated it as "apocalyptic correlative," and ascribed a late, redactional date to this apocalyptic use of Son of Humanity in Q 11,30, since it was an "explanatory gloss" to Q 11,29b added by "the *Sayings Gospel Q* itself"[67]: "Although the sign of Jonah [Q 11,29b] is older than either the *Sayings Gospel Q* or Mark, its Son of Man interpretation [Q 11,30] came in only from that former Gospel's own apocalyptic layer." This saying thus has, in terms of content, nothing pointing to an apocalyptic Son of Humanity, as discussed above, but, in form, is comparable to the apocalyptic instances of the correlative now to be discussed.

The basic apocalyptic instances of this correlative occur in the Q apocalypse: "For as the lightning streaks out from Sunrise and flashes as far as Sunset, so will the Son of Humanity be on his day." "As it took place in the days of Noah, so will it be in the day of the Son of Humanity. For as in those days they were eating and drinking, marrying and giving in marriage, until the day Noah entered the ark and the flood came and took them all, so will it also be on the day the Son of Humanity is revealed." (Q 17,24.26.27.30/Matt 24,38-39 – Luke 17,28-29 refers instead to Lot.) The striking thing about the form of these correlatives is

63. Richard A. Edwards, The Eschatological Correlative as a *Gattung* in the New Testament, ZNW 60, 1969, 9-20; The Eschatological Correlative, in: The Sign of Jonah in the Theology of the Evangelists and Q, SBT 2.18; London/Naperville, IL 1971, 47-58.

64. Daryl Schmidt, The LXX Gattung 'Prophetic Correlative', JBL 96, 1977, 517-522.

65. Migaku Sato, Q und Prophetie. Studien zur Gattungs- und Traditionsgeschichte der Quelle Q, WUNT 29, Tübingen 1988, 278-287. He treats Q 17,24 as an exception to this designation, since the comparison is with a "Naturphänomen." See my critique of Sato's dissertation, Die Logienquelle: Weisheit oder Prophetie? Anfragen an Migaku Sato, Q und Prophetie, EvTh 53, 1993, 367-389. [In *The Sayings Gospel Q,* pp. 349-74.]

66. John Dominic Crossan, The Historical Jesus. The Life of a Mediterranean Jewish Peasant, San Francisco 1991, 253. He bypassed the other instances of the correlative, since he, following Edwards, assumed they do not go back to Jesus.

67. Crossan, op. cit., 252, 253.

68. The one exception is in Matthean redaction, which is hardly surprising, since the Matthean community seems in so many ways to be in continuity with the Q community

that in the New Testament they are to be found only in Q^{68}. Thus one seems to have a form-critical focus for the apocalyptic Son of Humanity sayings in Q that Colpe considered authentic. The Q community would perhaps qualify as the otherwise unattested "fourth tradition" within Judaism as a context, a *Sitz im Leben*, for the apocalyptic Son of Humanity. Thus Q tends to indicate the initial stages of the christological development from a non-titular, non-apocalyptic idiom of a generic meaning, that by implication could have especially the speaker in mind, as used by Jesus. When the Q community then ascribed to him a decisive role at the judgment, the idiom characteristic of his speech was put on his tongue in apocalyptic sayings. This then led to the appropriation of other Jewish apocalyptic traditions where the idiom also occurred, resulting in the Danielic apocalypticism attested in the canonical Gospels, on the way to the Apostles' Creed: "... come to judge the quick and the dead."

(Matt 13,40-41): "Just as the weeds are gathered and burned with fire, so will it be at the close of the age: the son of humanity will send his angels ..."

CHAPTER 6

Jesus' Theology in the Sayings Gospel Q

The publication of *The Critical Edition of Q* [1] makes it possible not only to use individual Q sayings to talk about Jesus, as has been the custom in previous scholarship, but also, perhaps even more importantly, one can now see this Sayings Gospel in its own right. Especially, one can distinguish between the redaction of Q^2, which is now generally recognized to have superimposed a deuteronomistic, apocalyptic, judgmental slant on Q, and, on the other hand, the archaic collections imbedded in Q, much of which goes back to Jesus himself, and which are prophetic-sapiential in nature. And lest it seem that "prophetic" and "sapiential" should be set over against each other[3], one should note that it is Sophia herself who has sent both "prophets and

---

1. *The Critical Edition of Q: Synopsis including the Gospels of Matthew and Luke, Mark and Thomas with English, German, and French Translations of Q and Thomas* (ed. James M. Robinson, Paul Hoffmann, and John S. Kloppenborg; Minneapolis: Fortress, and Leuven: Peeters, 2000). An abbreviated edition, with only Greek and English on facing pages, has been published as well: *The Sayings Gospel Q in Greek and English with Parallels from the Gospels of Mark and Thomas* (Contributions to Biblical Exegesis and Theology 30; Leuven: Peeters, 2001, and Minneapolis: Fortress, 2002). There is also an even more abbreviated edition, with only the English translation of Q: *The Sayings of Jesus: The Sayings Gospel Q in English* (Facet books; Minneapolis: Fortress, 2001).

2. Dieter Lührmann, *Die Redaktion der Logienquelle* (WMANT 33; Neukirchen-Vluyn: Neukirchener Verlag, 1969).

3. The prophetic and the sapiential have all too often been put over against each other as alternatives between which one must choose, e.g. Richard Horsley, "*Logoi Prophētōn*? Reflections on the Genre of Q," in *The Future of Early Christianity: Essays in Honor of Helmut Koester* (ed. Birger A. Pearson; Minneapolis: Fortress, 1991) 195-209. But see Walter Grundmann, "Weisheit im Horizont des Reiches Gottes: Eine Studie zur Verkündigung Jesu nach der Spruchüberlieferung Q," in *Die Kirche des Anfangs: Festschrift für Heinz Schürmann zum 65. Geburtstag* (ed. R. Schnackenburg, J. Ernst, and J. Wanke; EThSt 38; Leipzig: St. Benno, 1977) 175-99: 175-76:

> Auch darin besteht in der Forschung eine weitgehende Übereinstimmung, daß die Ankündigung der genahten Himmelsherrschaft prophetische Art zeigt; darum erscheint Jesus den Leuten als Prophet und wird von ihnen als solcher beurteilt. Er gilt als der endzeitliche Prophet (nach Dtn 18,15. 18f). Aber die Eigenart dieses Jesus besteht darin, daß er zugleich wie ein Lehrer spricht, als solcher angeredet und von Freunden und Gegnern so betrachtet wird. Der Inhalt der Lehre dieses Lehrers ist Weisheit; die Leute seiner Heimatstadt fragen nach ihrem Woher (Mk 6,2). Er ist also prophetischer Weisheitslehrer und vertritt einen Typus, zu dem sich in der späteren nachexilischen Zeit, etwa vom dritten vorchristlichen Jahrhundert ab die Durchdringung von [176] Prophetie und Weisheit entwickelt hat. ...
> Wenn Jesus die Nähe der Gottesherrschaft als prophetisch-eschatologischer Weisheitslehrer verkündet, dann wäre es wohl möglich, einen wesentlichen Zug seiner

sages" (Q 11:49). In Q, the sage Solomon and the prophet Jonah stand side by side as equal foretastes of what Jesus brings (Q 11:31-32).

Jesus' Sayings about God Reigning

There are in Q really only two formulations that could be designated as distinctive theological terminology: Kingdom of God and Son of Man[4]. With regard to the term Son of Man, a major shift has taken place over the past generation, namely the "dissolution" of the "one-time consensus" that "the title had eschatological content," as Dale Allison put it, admitting that he "has changed his mind on this issue several times and now lacks all confidence about it." He goes on: "With the faltering of the apocalyptic interpretation, the idiomatic or nontitular understanding of 'the Son of Man' has come into its own."[5]

This changing position regarding the Son-of-Man sayings in Q can best be exemplified by Paul Hoffmann: "... we should take final leave from the often too "self-evident" assumption that in the SM [Son of Man] sayings we are dealing with the oldest Christian or even dominical tradition. In this respect I wish expressly to correct my own position."[6] His new

Verkündigung und seiner Lehre als Weisheit im Horizont des Reiches Gottes zu bezeichnen. Unter bewußter Beschränkung auf die Traditionen der Jesusverkündigung, wie sie in der sogenannten Spruchquelle (=Q) zusammengefaßt sind, soll an dieser Stelle dieser eben gestellten Frage nachgegangen werden.

4. The preeminence of these two terms in seeking to understand Jesus' theology was given classical expression by Rudolf Otto, *Reich Gottes und Menschensohn: Ein religionsgeschichtlicher Versuch* (Munich: Beck, 1933, [3]1954. ET: *The Kingdom of God and the Son of Man: A Study in the History of Religions* (Grand Rapids, MI: Zondervan, 1938; London: Lutterworth, 1943, 1951).

5. Dale C. Allison, Jr., in his review of Delbert Burkett, *The Son of Man Debate: A History and Evaluation* (SNTSMS 107; Cambridge: Cambridge University Press, 1999), in *JBL* 119 (2000) 766-68: 767. This would seem to be a significant shift from Allison's position in his monograph *Jesus of Nazareth: Millenarian Prophet* (Minneapolis: Fortress, 1998), "The Son of man," 115-20, where he speaks, 119, of "accept[ing] (as I do) the authenticity of one or more of the 'apocalyptic Son of man sayings.'" Burkett himself (p. 122) concludes: "I find it most plausible that the expression 'Son of Man' functions as a messianic title for Jesus throughout the tradition." But for him this alternative leaves open Jesus' own usage: "it originated as a messianic title applied to Jesus either by himself or by the early church." He thus himself remains uncertain (p. 124). See also James M. Robinson, "The Son of Man in the Sayings Gospel Q," in *Tradition und Translation: Zum Problem der interkulturellen Übersetzbarkeit religiöser Phänomene – Festschrift für Carsten Colpe zum 65. Geburtstag* (ed. Christoph Elsas et al.; Berlin and New York: Walter de Gruyter, 1994) 315-35. [In this volume, chap. 5.]

6. Paul Hoffmann, "The Redaction of Q and the Son of Man: A Preliminary Sketch," in *The Gospel Behind the Gospels: Current Studies on Q* (ed. Ronald A. Piper; NT.S 75; Leiden, New York, Cologne: E.J. Brill, 1995) 159-98: 193, n. 56.

position is: "that the SM concept gained special significance for Christian circles during this late phase in the transmission of Q, i.e. in the period around 70 C.E."[7]

The "faltering" of the apocalyptic, titular meaning of Son of Man in Jesus' usage only illustrates the truism that Jesus' focus was not on himself. If he spoke of himself as a son of man, a human, he used the expression as an idiom, not a title. It was not part of his "theology." This then suggests we should shift the focus to the other theological formulation, the kingdom of God. Though *we* want to talk about Jesus, *he* talked about the kingdom of God. Yet let us try to do justice to him at least for a moment, by investigating what *he* meant by the kingdom, not what *we* mean by Jesus.

Jesus was baptized by John[8]. Presumably he would not have undergone that rite of immersion, if he had not been immersed in John's message, which is normally thought to have been apocalyptic[9]. The problem

---

7. Paul Hoffmann, "The Redaction of Q and the Son of Man," 193:
  The Palestinian tradition from the time of the Jewish-Roman war, preserved in Mk 13, which – apart from Q – represents the earliest evidence of the Christian reception of the SM expectation of Dan 7 (though already transformed in its own way), now also sheds light on the appearance of the SM sayings in Q. ... the parallel appearance of this expectation in Mk 13 and in QR [Q Redaction] could indicate that the SM concept gained special significance for Christian circles during this late phase in the transmission of Q, i.e. in the period around 70 CE, and that it was then that its reception and theological integration into the traditional Q material that was not previously characterized by it came about.

  8. Morton S. Enslin, "John and Jesus," *ZNW* 66 (1975) 1-18: 7 argued conversely that they were completely unrelated: "their paths did not cross." Similarly Burton Mack, *The Lost Gospel: The Book of Q and Christian Origins* (San Francisco: HarperSanFrancisco, 1993) 153, 155.

  9. This standard assumption has been challenged by William Arnal, "Redactional Fabrication and Group Legitimation: The Baptist's Preaching in Q 3:7-9, 16-17," in *Conflict and Invention: Literary, Rhetorical, and Social Studies on the Sayings Gospel Q* (ed. John S. Kloppenborg; Valley Forge, PA: Trinity Press International, 1995) 165-180. His argument is that the sayings ascribed to John reflect the deuteronomistic, judgmental apocalypticism of the redaction of Q, from which they hence derive. But there is no significant shared vocabulary to document this hypothesis. John's reference to "the One to Come" (Q 3:16; 7:19) is not a creation of the Q redaction (Arnal, 171: "coheres in substance with the Son of Man figure," 173: "a redactional creation," "unique to Q"), since it recurs in John 1:27 (Arnal, 179, n. 18: "coincidental"), as well as in the familiar quotation of Ps 117:26 LXX found in Q 13:35 and Mark 11:9 parr. The deuteronomistic focus on God sending prophets who are put to death by the Israelites, leading God to let the temple be destroyed, is completely absent from Q sayings of John. The judgmental designation for the opponents of John is "snakes' litter" (Q 3:7), but for the Q redaction "this generation" (Q 7:31; 11:29,30,31,32,50,51), "Pharisees" (Q 11:42,39b,43,44), "exegetes of the Law" (Q 11:46b,52). Arnal's evidence does not get beyond the fact that both the preaching of John and the redaction of Q are apocalyptic.

is that Jesus' own message does not seem to have been apocalyptic[10]. Ernst Käsemann already put it pointedly: "Jesus obviously speaks of the coming of the *basileia* in a different sense from the Baptist and contemporary Judaism, namely, not exclusively, or even only primarily, in relation to a chronologically datable end of the world."[11]

The only overlap in language between John and Jesus in Q is the metaphor of the fruit trees, and precisely there one can see the basic difference: In the presentation of John, it is clearly apocalyptic (Q 3:9):

> And the ax already lies at the root of the trees. So every tree not bearing healthy fruit is to be chopped down and thrown on the fire.

But in Jesus' use of that same metaphor, there is no apocalypticism at all. Instead, he scored the ethical point of human integrity (Q 6:43-44a):

> No healthy tree bears rotten fruit, nor on the other hand does a decayed tree bear healthy fruit. For from the fruit the tree is known.

This striking divergence between the apocalypticism in the saying ascribed to John and the absence of apocalypticism in the saying ascribed

---

10. For this claim see Risto Uro, "John the Baptist and the Jesus Movement: What Does Q Tell Us?" in *The Gospel behind the Gospels,* 231-57. See also my critique of Uro, "Building Blocks in the Social History of Q," in *Reimagining Christian Origins: A Colloquium Honoring Burton L. Mack* (ed. Elizabeth A. Castelli and Hal Taussig; Valley Forge, PA: Trinity Press International, 1996) 87-112: 95. [In *The Sayings Gospel Q,* pp. 493-517.]

11. Ernst Käsemann, "Zum Thema der urchristlichen Apokalyptik," *ZThK* 59 (1962) 257-84: 260-61. ET: "On the Topic of Primitive Christian Apocalyptic," in *Apocalypticism: Journal for Theology and the Church* 6 (New York: Herder and Herder, 1969) 99-133: 103-4:

> Undisputed remain only the *basileia* sayings that go back to Jesus himself. That they mostly regard God's sovereignty as still outstanding cannot well be denied. It is characteristic, however, that in the reasonably certain instances this is not done in such a way that apocalyptic comes strongly to the fore, and it is precisely here that we have the constitutive difference from the preaching of the Baptist. We would do well not to forget that the baptism of Jesus by John belongs to the indubitable events of the historical life of Jesus. For this surely means that Jesus began with the glowing near expectation of the Baptist and for that reason suffered himself to be "sealed" against the threatening judgment of wrath and engrafted into the sacred remnant of the people of God. It is difficult not to feel that the path Jesus took in word and deed is a contradiction of this beginning. It is therefore no accident that the gospels draw an antithesis to the Baptist and his sect and portray Jesus as healing in the power of the Spirit, casting our demons, not practicing asceticism. ... All this leads perforce to the result that the Baptist's message of the distant God who is coming as judge recedes strangely into the background, ... Jesus obviously speaks of the coming of the *basileia* in a different sense from the Baptist and contemporary Judaism, namely, not exclusively, or even only primarily, in relation to a chronologically datable end of the world. This means, however, that the alternative so useful elsewhere between present and futurist eschatology ultimately becomes as inapplicable to the message of Jesus as the question of the messianic consciousness does if it is not permissible to lay the title "Son of man" on Jesus' lips.

to Jesus should warn against simply applying whatever one ascribes to John directly to Jesus[12].

This caution is also appropriate in view of the striking divergences in their lifestyles and practice. I have argued elsewhere: "The pervasive distinction between the lifestyles and practice of the followers of Jesus and those of John ... provides a strong working hypothesis that in the verbalization of their messages ... there would also have emerged a constitutive divergence."[13] [29]

The apocalyptic Jesus, as Albert Schweitzer portrayed him, has long since been rejected by scholarship. To quote Käsemann again:

> Hardly any New Testament scholar still shares A. Schweitzer's answer, namely, that Jesus, animated by a glowing near expectation of the end, sent his disciples out on a lightening mission through Palestine and himself proclaimed an interim ethic, and that finally, when his hopes proved illusory, he tried to compel the divine intervention by moving to Jerusalem, and perished in the attempt[14].

Of course it is usual to ascribe to Jesus the more euphemistic term "eschatology." But one carefully avoids getting tangled up *à la* Schweitzer in what that may have meant for Jesus in terms of his lifestyle. And one hardly even mentions the problem that what John predicted, and Jesus presumably believed enough to launch his "public ministry," did not happen. Even Käsemann, who in a sense re-launched apocalypticism by designating it the mother of Christian theology[15], argued that Jesus himself was not an apocalypticist. Instead, he gave Easter credit for triggering Christian apocalypticism.

But Jesus himself *was* engrossed with "the kingdom of God," God reigning, itself a rare idiom that nonetheless dominates the sayings of Jesus. So what are we to make of that?

For Paul, the kingdom of God is something purely future, itself apocalyptic, as his apocalyptic chapter made clear (1 Cor 15:24): "Then comes the end, when he [Jesus] delivers the kingdom to God the Father ...." Paul's idea was that God's reigning cannot take place in a literal

---

12. Arnal, "Redactional Fabrication and Group Legitimation," 174, presents the converse alternative, that the Q redaction composed Q 3:17: "... has recast it in an apocalyptic fashion," *"literarily dependent upon the earlier recension of Q"* (italics his).

13. James M. Robinson, "Building Blocks in the Social History of Q," 90. [In *The Sayings Gospel Q*, p. 497.]

14. Ernst Käsemann, "Zum Thema der urchristlichen Apokalyptik," 260. ET: "On the Topic of Primitive Christian Apocalyptic," 102.

15. Ernst Käsemann, "Zum Thema der urchristlichen Apokalyptik," 284. ET: "On the Topic of Primitive Christian Apocalyptic," 133: "I hope I have made clear why I call apocalyptic the mother of Christian theology."

sense so long as the hostile forces of evil continue, or, even more concretely: Only when death itself, the last enemy, is gone, will God really reign (1 Cor 15:26).

Jesus too must have realized that God is not literally and fully reigning everywhere and always now, since so much evil still prevails. Up to this point one may speak of Jesus' eschatology and know what one means. But the kingdom of God was not for Jesus just a cosmic revolution, whose imminent expectation was hence invalidated by the passage of time, indeed rendered unintelligible to us by the Enlightenment. For God reigning was something real in his world of experience[16], about which he did in fact talk, and it is that on which we need to focus our attention.

One may go one by one through the references to the kingdom of God in Q (made easily accessible by John S. Kloppenborg's "Concordance of Q" at the conclusion of *The Critical Edition of Q* and *The Sayings Gospel Q*). Though not all, yet an unusually high proportion of the Q sayings about the kingdom of God are usually ascribed to Jesus[17].

One may begin with the best-known text in Q, the Lord's Prayer: Matthew has glossed the prayer several times, to embellish it according to the more liturgical usage of his own congregation. One of these Matthean additions is the petition: "Thy will be done on earth as it is in heaven."[18] It was apparently not in Jesus' own prayer. It is not that Jesus

16. Helmut Koester, "The Sayings of Q and Their Image of Jesus," in *Sayings of Jesus: Canonical and Non-Canonical: Essays in Honour of Tjitze Baarda* (ed. William L. Petersen, Johan S. Vos, and Henk J. de Jonge; NT.S 89; Leiden, New York, Cologne: E.J. Brill, 1997) 137-54: 154:

> The earliest stage of Q's eschatology is not necessarily a direct reflection of Jesus' preaching. ... The Jesus of the earliest formation of the Sayings Gospel Q proclaims the arrival of God's kingdom as a challenge to the disciples, who are asked to realize that their own existence belongs to a new eschatological moment.

17. Helmut Merklein, *Jesu Botschaft von der Gottesherrschaft: Eine Skizze* (SBS 111; Stuttgart: Katholisches Bibelwerk, ³1989) 23:

> Zur traditionsgeschichtlich ältesten (und damit am ehesten authentischen) Sprechweise dürften die Logien beziehungsweise Texte gehören, in denen die "'basileia' Gottes" als eine *aktiv-dynamische Größe* erscheint. Dazu ist neben den Gleichnissen (Mk 4,26-29.30-32 par; Lk 13,18f.20f par Mt 13,31f.33) und der ersten Seligpreisung (Lk 6,20b par Mt 5,3) der vor allem in Q belegte Satztyp zu rechnen, der die 'basileia' als Subjekt mit einem Verbum der Bewegung verbindet (Lk 10,9 par Mt 10,7; Lk 11,2 par Mt 6,10; Lk 11,20 par Mt 12,28; Lk 16,16ba par Mt 11,12a; vgl. Mk 1,15; 9,1).

He refers, p. 23, n. 36, to H. Schürmann coming "zu einem ähnlichen Ergebnis bezüglich der ipsissima verba in der Q-Tradition."

18. *Q 11:2b-4* (ed. James M. Robinson, Paul Hoffmann, and John S. Kloppenborg; Documenta Q: Reconstructions of Q Through Two Centuries of Gospel Research Excerpted, Sorted, and Evaluated; Leuven: Peeters Press, 1996) 106-27.

would have had anything against this idea. It is just that, according to the Lukan form of the prayer, which is considered to be nearer the older form of the prayer in Q, this petition was absent. Apparently the petitions originally ran as follows (Q 11:2-4):

> Let your reign come: Our day's bread give us today; and cancel our debts for us, as we too have cancelled for those in debt to us; and do not put us to the test!

This is clearly not a prayer about the afterlife or another world, but about the here and now. Indeed, the interpretation of the Lord's Prayer, which follows directly in Q, makes this abundantly clear (Q 11:9-13): Ask, search, knock, be given, find, be opened, for a human parent will not give a stone, but bread, not a snake, but fish, so "how much more will the Father from heaven give good things to those who ask him!" This hardly means that as surely as a human parent gives bread and fish in the here and now, the heavenly Father will give pie in the sky by-and-by. No, God will see to it that you have something to eat in the here and now.

Nor does the Beatitude on the poor mean that only in the eschatological future will they prosper: "Blessed are you poor, for God's reign is for you" (Q 6:20). Surely this does not mean that the poor will get into the kingdom of God at the end of time, imminent that it is, but that between now and then the poor should be happy to continue to be hungry and cold beggars. What consolation, blessedness, is there in knowing you will be fed at the eschatological banquet (Q 13:29, 28), even if meanwhile you starve to death! No, the Beatitudes are not so cynical and cold-blooded, but give good news (Q 7:22) for the here and now.

Perhaps this present reality of the kingdom is made most clear in the case of exorcism: "But if it is by the finger of God that I cast out demons, then there has come upon you God's reign" (Q 11:20). The abnormal symptoms of a disease, which led it to be called demon possession, are in the here and now, and the exorcism, as the coming of God's reign, is also in the here and now, as the abnormal symptoms fade away.

The extent to which a day's bread, and healings, are already God reigning, is made clear in the Workers' Instructions: "And whatever town you enter and they take you in, eat what is set before you. And cure the sick there, and say to them: God's reign has reached unto you" (Q 10:8-9). Actually, the Q people thought they were already "in" the kingdom: "There has not arisen among women's offspring anyone who surpasses John. Yet the least significant in God's kingdom is more than he" (Q 7:28).

So the Woe pronounced against exegetes of the Law, who shut people out of the kingdom, does not just refer to closing access to the kingdom in the afterlife, when one might otherwise have hoped to enter it, but refers to these scribes as themselves not having entered the kingdom already now: "... for you shut the kingdom of God from people; you did not go in, nor let in those trying to get in" (Q 11:52). Q pinpointed rather precisely the point in time when the kingdom is present in history, namely just after the law and the prophets and John, since the kingdom is now violated and plundered: "From then on the kingdom of God is violated and the violent plunder it" (Q 16:16).

The parables of The Mustard Seed (Q 13:18-19) and The Yeast (Q 13:20-21) present the kingdom of God as having begun already, even if not yet fully developed. Perhaps earlier scholarship was wrong, to call them "parables of growth," with simply an evolutionary implication (belief in "progress"). The transition from seed to tree, from yeast to fermented dough, was for antiquity not really a natural process, but was more nearly imagined as a supernatural miracle. And yet they are not just"contrast parables,"[19] as others maintained, to play up the grandiose future by playing down the meager present[20]. For the parables do not limit the kingdom to the eschatological future, but describe it as something thrown now into the garden, hid now in three measures of flour. Thus the parables of the kingdom present the miracle of God, God reigning, as beginning already now. To be sure, this is not intended as a given status, like the "established church," extending over time and space, but rather as something that happens from time to time on given occasions[21].

---

19. Absent from Q, but present in the Markan doublet (Mark 4:30-32), is the contrast between the mustard seed as "the smallest of all the seeds on earth" and the full-grown mustard bush as "the greatest of all shrubs." *The Gospel of Thomas* also makes the contrast explicit, Saying 20: "the smallest of all seeds," "a large branch," and Saying 96: "a little bit of yeast," "huge loaves of bread."

20. Heinz Schürmann, "Das Zeugnis der Redenquelle für die Basileia-Verkündigung Jesu: Eine traditionsgeschichtliche Untersuchung," in *Logia: Les Paroles de Jésus – The Sayings of Jesus* (ed. Joël Delobel; BETL 59; Leuven: Peeters and Leuven University Press, 1982) 121-200: 185, n. 265:

H. Merklein, *Handlungsprinzip** [*Die Gottesherrschaft als Handlungsprinzip: Untersuchung zur Ethik Jesu* (FzB 34; Würzburg: Echter, [1]1978, [2]1981, [3]1984)], p. 166, redet von "Aus-Stand" und "Ein-Stand" der Basileia "in Jesus" und setzt sich mit Recht ab von denen, die den "Einstand" derselben nicht leugnen, aber als gegenwärtig doch nur "Zeichen" des kommenden Reiches sehen wollen ....

21. Peter Kristen, "Nachfolge leben: Drei Modelle von Kreuzesnachfolge in Q und Markus," in *Text und Geschichte: Facetten theologischen Arbeitens aus dem Freundes- und Schülerkreis. Dieter Lührmann zum 60. Geburtstag* (ed. Stefan Maser and Egbert

Jesus rejected the idea of locating any given place where the kingdom can be expected to come, since in fact it comes already "within" people (Q 17:20-21). Again, this saying should not be misunderstood, as if it had in view just a mystic inwardness. Though the rare preposition used here does seem to mean inside in contrast to outside[22], the meaning would not seem to be far from the other alternate translation, "among you" or "in your midst," since it does stand over against some apocalyptic never-never land. The point of the saying is that the kingdom is not something that will take place somewhere sometime, but is a reality in the present experience of people in the world of today.

Jesus called on people to "seek" the kingdom (Q 12:31). But this is anything but hunting for some future cosmic event, be it here, or there, which Jesus had explicitly rejected (Q 17:21). Rather this seeking is set over against the other kind of seeking (Q 12:29-30), which anxiety-laden Gentiles do, when they ask: "What are we to eat? Or: What are we to drink? Or: What are we to wear?" Hence "seeking" for the kingdom returns full circle to the petition for the kingdom to come in the Lord's Prayer: One does not need to be anxiety-laden about scrounging for such physical necessities as something to eat, because one can trust in God reigning, that is to say, answering the petitions for God's reign to come, in the form of one day's bread: "Let your reign come," specifically: "Our day's bread give us today."

Thus the kingdom of God, the one clearly recognizable theological category of Jesus' message, in a sense elevated to theological relevance much of everyday living, such as sickness, the need for food and clothing, the evil with which people are always struggling. It was in the very

---

Schlarb; MThSt 50; Marburg: N. G. Elwert, 1999) 89-106: 92, 95 speaks of what is present in the sense of taking place at individual points of time:

> Sie praktizierten diese Worte und verstanden sich, aufgrund dieser performativ wirkenden Worte und der Beauftragung durch Jesus, als Boten des in ihrer Begegnung mit den "Kindern des Friedens" und in den diese Begegnung begleitenden Heilungen punktuell gegenwärtigen Gottesreiches. ...
> Die charakteristische Vorstellung des punktuell schon präsenten Gottesreiches als einer alternativen Lebensform ist das Movens der Boten, die Sendung durch Jesus ihre Legitimation für ein Leben nach seinen Worten.

22. T. Holmén, "The Alternatives of the Kingdom: Encountering the semantic restrictions of Luke 17,20-21 (ἐντὸς ὑμῶν)," ZNW 87 (1996) 214-29. In the formulation of this saying in Saying 3.3 of *The Gospel of Thomas* in P. Oxy. 654, the preposition cannot be understood and translated any other way, since is stands over against the converse preposition, "outside": "And the kingdom [of God] is within you, [and outside]." Though the decisive word is here in a lacuna, the restoration is certain, since the Coptic text in Nag Hammadi Codex 2 is here fully extant.

real, everyday world that God reigning is very good news (Q 7:22)[23]. For it was countercultural[24], and hence gave hope to the hopeless.

JESUS' CONDUCT AND ACTION

If one thinks that the kingdom is just apocalyptic, one can in a sense be excused for not going into specific details. A "new heavens and a new earth" is so completely new that one can hardly be expected to describe it. But to talk about God reigning in the here and now does suggest it should be possible to say something about what that means in concrete reality, since we know a very great deal about present reality from our own experience. We have language, our everyday language, for talking about everyday experience, and so if God is reigning here, one ought to be able to talk about where, when, how Jesus thought God to be reigning, and how, in concrete reality, he thought one is to relate to that reigning.

To this extent Albert Schweitzer was correct, in proposing to go beyond Johannes Weiß' focus only on Jesus' sayings about the kingdom, by insisting that God reigning must have been decisive also in Jesus' "conduct and action."[25] But Schweitzer was basically misled in assuming that the Mission Instructions of Matt 10 were an eye-witness report

23. Kristen, "Nachfolge leben," 93:
Die Boten verstehen sich als legitime Nachfolgerinnen und Nachfolger Jesu und bringen denen, die sie aufgrund ihres Friedensgrußes aufnehmen, die Gegenwart des Gottesreiches (10,9), indem sie das verkündigen und tun, was Jesus (selbst getan und) ihnen aufgetragen hat. Das Gottesreich ist in ihrem Wirken angebahnt und in den ihnen aufgetragenen Heilungen und der Sphäre des Heils präsent und erfahrbar. Dieses Heil entwickelt sich als Folge der gastlichen Aufnahme in ein Haus. In ihrem ganzen Leben stellen sie die Prinzipien des Gottesreiches dar, wie sie in Q1 erkennbar werden. Gewalt- und besitzlos (10,4) leben sie die Realität der Gottesherrschaft paradigmatisch, wie es in Q 12,31 ausgedrückt ist, im Vertrauen auf die Fürsorge des Vaters.

24. Stephen J. Patterson, "Wisdom in Q and Thomas," in *In Search of Wisdom: Essays in Memory of John G. Gammie* (ed. L. G. Perdue, B. B. Scott, and W. J. Wisemann; Louisville, KY: Westminster/John Knox, 1993) 187-221, "Countercultural Wisdom," 205-207.

25. Albert Schweitzer, *Die Geschichte der Leben-Jesu-Forschung* (Tübingen: Mohr-Siebeck, [2]1913), "Vorrede zur sechsten Auflage," ([6]1951) viii, and (München: Siebenstern-Taschenbuch 77/78, 1966) 32. This preface, and hence this comment, is first available in English in *The Quest of the Historical Jesus* (First Complete Edition, ed. John Bowden; London: SCM, 2000 and Minneapolis: Fortress, 2001) xxxiii-xliii: xxxvi (SCM) and xxxv-xlv: xxxviii (Fortress). The expression is translated by Bowden less literally and more colloquially as "life and work."

of what exactly Jesus said, on a specific occasion, namely when he sent his disciples out to trigger the end of the world and bring in the millennium. But Schweitzer's basic question is nonetheless valid: What conduct and action would necessarily result from the message of the kingdom of God?

Even in our day, one has commonly used modern parables to speak of the kingdom in relation to the present. The standard instance: The kingdom is in the present only like the first drops of rain, before the clouds burst and the downpour, the kingdom itself, comes. Soon after World War II, Oscar Cullmann put it this way: It is like the Normandy landing was for us – a foothold on the Continent, assuring the final victory, even before that final victory actually came.

But such talk also just uses metaphors, modern equivalents to the parables of the Mustard Seed and the Yeast. What was Jesus actually talking about in terms of his and his followers' own life experience?

What made one as carefree as the ravens and lilies was trust in the kingdom of God, God reigning, as a caring Father (Q 12:22b-28). This in turn is what explains the radical Workers' Instructions: "Carry no purse, nor knapsack, nor shoes, nor stick, and greet no one on the road" (Q 10:4). This is then what Jesus himself actually did during his "public ministry" in Galilee. It was not an instance of the asceticism that was commonly part and parcel of the religious lifestyle at the time. For Jesus' lifestyle moved more nearly in the opposite direction, as the caricature of him as a carouser makes clear: "The son of humanity came, eating and drinking, and you say: Look! A person who is a glutton and drunkard, a chum of tax collectors and sinners!" (Q 7:34)[26].

Indeed the Workers' Instructions go on to urge Jesus' followers, the "workers," to eat what is set before them, in the house of the "son of peace" who takes them in:

> And at that house remain, eating and drinking whatever they provide, for the worker is worthy of one's reward[27]. Do not move around from house to

26. The attempt of Leif E. Vaage, *Galilean Upstarts: Jesus' First Followers According to Q* (Valley Forge, Penn.: Trinity Press International, 1994) 87-96, to present this not as a caricature but as historically accurate is based on his earlier presentations, "Q¹ and the Historical Jesus: Some Peculiar Sayings (7:33-34; 9:57-58, 59-60; 14:26-27)," *Forum* 5,2 (1989) 159-76, and, as he reports (p. 159), on an unpublished "Paper presented in the 1988 Spring meeting of the Jesus Seminar, Sonoma, CA," entitled "An Archeological Approach to the Work of the Jesus Seminar." His portrayal there of Jesus as an alcoholic is dismantled in my essay, "*Galilean Upstarts*: A Sot's Cynical Disciples?" in *Sayings of Jesus: Canonical and Non-Canonical*, 223-49: "2. The alcoholic Jesus," 228-43. [In *The Sayings Gospel Q*, pp. 535-57, especially pp. 540-52.]

27. The absence of the purse means that one neither carries nor earns money, which would provide a security less visible than food and clothing. Matt 10:9 makes this explicit:

house. And whatever town you enter and they take you in, eat what is set before you. (Q 10:7-8)

It is just here that one catches sight of the theological explanation that was intended to make sense of all this unusual conduct. For the Workers' Instructions go on: "And cure the sick there, and say to them: God's reign has reached unto you" (Q 10:9). The bestowal of "Peace" on the house with the opening "Shalom" (Q 10:5) and this retrospect of God having reigned among them, provides the theological framework for what takes place in the household: Not only is the cure of the sick, like the exorcism of Q 11:20, ascribed here to God reigning, but the provision of food is also God's kingdom coming, in the concrete sense of answering the petitions of the Lord's Prayer: "Let your reign come: Our day's bread give us today." One does not go looking for food and drink, any more than do the ravens (Q 12:24), but one seeks instead God's reign (Q 12:31), trusting that food and drink will be granted in the home of the "son of peace," where God's reigning will happen as the answer to the Lord's Prayer.

What one does not do is store up funds in a purse, or bread and clothing in a knapsack, as if one may have lucked out with God today, but tomorrow is another day, and one never knows, so be prepared for the worst! No, tomorrow, start out just as one started out today, praying: "Our day's bread give us today," and trusting that God will reign each day, just as he reigns today.

The absence of shoes would involve such debilitating deprivation, according to many exegetes, that they have hesitated to take it literally. But it must have been meant literally, just as everything else in the Workers' Instructions seems to be describing actual practice. Barefootedness is a standard symbol of penance (e.g., the Franciscans), and may have been characteristic of those baptized by John. For John is described as not worthy to take off Jesus' shoes[28], as a metaphor for not being worthy to baptize him.

"Take no gold, nor silver, nor copper in your belts." Apparently cash payment for services rendered became a temptation, leading Matt 10:10 to revise the text of Q to read: "the worker is worthy of one's food."

28. The injunction not to wear sandals fits poorly with Q 3:16 and Mark 1:7, if they are understood as John being unworthy to perform a servant's task of taking off and putting on a master's sandals. For, if applied to Jesus, this would indicate Jesus continued to wear sandals and continued in association with John. But, more probably, it referred to removing Jesus' sandals permanently prior to immersion. John's unworthiness to do this would be a stage in the subordination of John to Jesus picked up and amplified by Matt 3:14-15. Norbert Krieger, "Barfuß Busse Tun," NT 1 (1956) 227-28, referred to John 12:6; 20:13-15. He is cited with approval by Walter Bauer in Frederick William Danker, A Greek-English Lexicon of the New Testament and Other Early Christian Literature, third edition

The injunction not to carry a stick is clearly intended to prevent self-defense against humans and even wild animals. For it hardly refers to a walking stick (RSV Matt 10:10: "staff," NRSV: "stave"), but rather a club, the poor man's weapon[29]. One is not to defend oneself against attack, but to turn the other cheek (Q 6:29).

One may well wonder how Jesus, much less anyone else he might talk into it, could sustain a life of such radical deprivation. He may indeed have chosen a site for his public ministry where such literal rigors as barefootedness, giving one's shirt off one's back, taking no provisions for the trip, having no form of self-defense, were not utterly impossible. He did center his public ministry on the Sea of Galilee, perhaps a relatively mild winter climate some 700 feet below sea level, indeed the lowest point in Galilee, which hence may have been more tolerant than the hill country of such an exposed existence as that which Jesus advocated and practiced. The proximity of his base camp at Capernaum to the frontier of the territory of the less threatening Philip, with a grateful centurion stationed nearby (Q 7:1-10), and a harvest at dawn each day as the fishermen returned to shore, may all have rendered the rigorous lifestyle Jesus practiced at least possible[30].

GOD REIGNING IN JESUS' PUBLIC MINISTRY

How then is one to explain Jesus' so abnormal lifestyle? The radical list of what not to take along on the way is hard to explain in terms of the history of religions. Neither the Cynics, nor the Essenes, nor John the Baptist (Q 7:33; Mark 1:6), provides a precedent.

(Chicago and London: The University of Chicago Press, 2000), based on Walter Bauer's *Griechisch-deutsches Wörterbuch zu den Schriften des Neuen Testaments und der frühchristlichen Literatur*, sixth edition (ed. Kurt Aland and Barbara Aland, with Viktor Reichmann), s.v. βαστάζω, i.e. "remove," citing also PGM 4,1058-59 (in: K. Preisendanz et al., eds., *Papyri Graecae Magicae: Die griechischen Zauberpapyri*, Sammlung wissenschaftlicher Commentare, vol. 1 [Stuttgart: Teubner, 1928, ²1973]): βαστάξας τὸ στεφάνιον ἀπὸ τῆς κεφαλῆς.

29. The termination of Q's rigorous Workers' Instructions in Luke 22:36 indicates that one had in fact been forbidden to take what was understood as a weapon, though it is here expressed in more middle-class terms: "And let him who has no sword sell his mantle and buy one." (The requirement of a sword is here necessitated by the following Marcan story of the cutting off of an ear in Gethsemane.)

30. James M. Robinson, "Foreword: A Down-to-Earth Jesus," in Jean J. Rousseau and Rami Arav, *Jesus and His World: An Archaeological and Cultural Dictionary* (Minneapolis: Fortress. 1995) xiii-xviii: xiv.

In recent research, one has drawn the comparison especially to the Cynics, with their minimalistic, indeed intentionally offensive, lifestyle[31]. Leif E. Vaage has renewed Gerd Theissen's Cynic interpretation of the specific instances in the Q Sermon, to turn the other cheek, give the shirt off one's back, go the second mile, lend without asking for anything back (Q 6:29-30). The Cynic explanation of this core of the Sermon's ethics, as advocated by Gerd Theissen, is summarized by Vaage: "To turn the other cheek and give up both cloak and tunic were hardly expressions of 'universal love,' but just 'smart moves' under the circumstances."[32]

It was as a summary of these injunctions that the redactor created the overarching generalization to love one's enemies (Q 6:27), which hence, according to Vaage, does not go back to Jesus at all[33]. This remarkable love command is just "a strategy for handling unfriendly opposition. 'Love your enemies,' in other words, and in this way take care of the 'jerks.'"[34]

Vaage thus interprets the "itinerant radicalism" of the Q people as a shrewd strategy to evade hardship for themselves:

> The best enemies to love are those you meet only once. The best way to assure such a situation is not to stay too long in any one place[35].

31. See my review article of Vaage, *Galilean Upstarts: Jesus' First Followers According to Q*: "*Galilean Upstarts*: A Sot's Cynical Disciples?" in *Sayings of Jesus: Canonical and Non-Canonical*, 223-49. [In *The Sayings Gospel Q*, pp. 535-57.]

32. Vaage, *Galilean Upstarts*, 50.
... every material means of manipulating and imposing oneself on the ancient Cynic and first follower of Jesus in Galilee had been taken out of their enemies' hands. ...
... at stake is the procurement of the maximum available good for those who otherwise stand in danger of personal assault and battery as well as uninvited theft. The imperatives in 6:29 – and 6:30 ... – were originally prudential considerations provided for persons whose lives must wend their way through contexts of diverse insecurity. To turn the other cheek and give up both cloak and tunic were hardly expressions of "universal love," but just "smart moves" under the circumstances.

33. Vaage, *Galilean Upstarts*, 159, n. 16.

34. Vaage, *Galilean Upstarts*, 47.

35. Vaage, *Galilean Upstarts*, 44. He translates in this connection Theissen, "Gewaltverzicht und Feindesliebe (Mt 5,38-48; Lc 6,27-36) und deren sozialgeschichtlicher Hintergrund," *Studien zur Soziologie des Urchristentums* (Tübingen: Mohr-Siebeck, 1977) 191:
Der seßhafte Christ geriete durch Nachgeben gegenüber seinem Feind in immer größere Abhängigkeit. Er muß ja damit rechnen, ihm immer wieder neu zu begegnen. Nachgeben bedeutet hier oft: zur Fortsetzung von Übervorteilung und Zurücksetzung aufzufordern. Der Verzicht auf Widerstand erhöht die Wahrscheinlichkeit, daß sich Übergriffe wiederholen. Dennoch steht auch vor ihm die große Forderung, seinen Feind zu lieben. Sie kann der wandernde Charismatiker viel überzeugender verwirklichen. Er ist wirklich frei. Er kann den Ort seiner Niederlage und Demütigung verlassen. Er darf damit rechnen, daß er seinem Gegner nicht mehr begegnet. Indem er weiterzieht, kann er seine Unabhängigkeit und Freiheit wahren. Der Preis für diese Freiheit ist eine rigorose Askese: ein Leben am Rande des Existenzminimums.

The purpose of mentioning here the Cynic interpretation of Jesus is not to criticize it, which I have done elsewhere[36], in a way that F. Neirynck characterized as "devastating,"[37] but to point out how the Cynic interpretation was given an opening in our times due to a deficiency in the rest of scholarship, namely the failure to identify the real center of thought behind Jesus' conduct.

The dominant effort to place eschatology at the center of Jesus' thought has in fact not succeeded, as already Hans Conzelmann recognized: "At first glance his [Jesus'] teaching about God and his eschatology, his eschatology and ethics appear to stand alongside one another in a relatively disconnected way. ..."

> Over against a "consistent eschatological" interpretation of the teaching of Jesus it must be emphasized that where God's governance as such is developed, the prospect of the imminent end of the world is lacking. The world appears simply as creation, the sphere of the rule and care of God[38].

But though there would seem to be no clear correlation of Jesus' ethic and teaching about God to his eschatology, there is indeed an

Vaage's translation:
> The sedentary Christian falls into ever greater dependence by giving way to his enemy. Indeed, he must reckon with the fact that he will meet him repeatedly again and again. Giving way often means in this case inviting continuation of the fact that one is taken advantage of and degraded. Non-resistance heightens the probability that infringements will repeat themselves. Nevertheless, the great command to love his enemy exists for him as well. The *Wandercharismatiker* can realize the command much more convincingly. He is truly free. He can abandon the site of his defeat and humiliation. He may reckon with the fact that he will not meet his enemy again. As long as he keeps moving on, he can maintain his independence and freedom. The price of this freedom is rigorous asceticism: a life on the edge of the bare minimum for existence. But the profit is great.

36. James M. Robinson, "The History-of-Religions Taxonomy of Q: The Cynic Hypothesis," in *Gnosisforschung und Religionsgeschichte: Festschrift für Kurt Rudolph zum 65. Geburtstag* (ed. Holger Preißler and Hubert Seiwert; Marburg: diagonal-Verlag, 1994 [1995]) 247-65, "4. The Cynic Getup," 257-59. [In *The Sayings Gospel Q*, pp. 427-48, especially pp. 438-41.] See also Robinson, "Building Blocks in the Social History of Q," on "The Cynics' and the Q People's Getups," 87-90. [In *The Sayings Gospel Q*, pp. 493-97.]

37. F. Neirynck, in his review of *Sayings of Jesus: Canonical and Non-Canonical*, *EThL* 73 (1997) 456-58: 457.

38. Hans Conzelmann, *Jesus Christus*, in *RGG³* (Tübingen: Mohr-Siebeck, vol. 3, 1959) 634, 637:
> J. entwirft kein System einer Lehre. Es fällt im Gegenteil auf, daß Gotteslehre und Eschatologie, Eschatologie und Ethik auf den ersten Blick relativ unverbunden nebeneinander zu stehen scheinen. ...
> Gegenüber einer "konsequent eschatologischen" Deutung der Lehre Jesu ist zu betonen: Wo Gottes Walten als solches entfaltet wird, da fehlt der Ausblick auf das nahe Weltende. Die Welt erscheint einfach als Schöpfung, Bereich des Regierens und der Fürsorge Gottes.

ET: *Jesus* (Philadelphia: Fortress Press, 1973) 51, 58.

explicit correlation between the latter two: Jesus' teaching about God and Jesus' ethic are indeed correlated to each other. For example: "Be full of pity, just as your Father is full of pity" (Q 6:36). Here Jesus explicitly appeals to God's pity, as the model to be followed by God's people. This he does again and again: He petitioned a caring heavenly Father to "cancel our debts for us, as we too have cancelled for those in debt to us" (Q 11:4). For Jesus called upon his followers to forgive daily, just as they expect from God daily forgiveness: "If seven times a day [your brother] sins against you, also seven times shall you forgive him" (Q 17:4). And the central appeal of Jesus to love one's enemies is based on God's conduct: Love your enemies, and pray for those persecuting you, so that you may become sons of your Father, for he raises his sun on bad and good and rains on the just and unjust. (Q 6:27-28, 35).

Thus, at the core of the archaic collections behind the redaction of Q, there is a striking correlation between the actual conduct that Jesus exemplified and advocated in his sayings, and the way that he conceived of God as a forgiving Father. It is almost as if he invented Voltaire's shockingly flippant witticism of the French Enlightenment: Forgiving, that's what God is there for, it's his job! It is not surprising that Jesus' shocking view of God has been largely ignored, as has his corresponding ethic.

It took a distinguished classics scholar, Albrecht Dihle, to lay out in detail the dramatic extent to which this new ethic Jesus derived from his new understanding of God transcends the common-sense justice of reward and punishment that pervaded antiquity: "… the proclamation of Jesus of Nazareth and the early Christian theology connecting to it have eliminated that concept of retaliation as the basis for, or ingredient in, an ethical order."[39]

The love of enemies, as the highest ethic of Jesus and the Q people, was indeed very unusual. And it was rooted in an equally unusual vision of a God who gives sunshine and showers to the bad as well as to the good.

It is striking that Jesus, at this most central point, did not derive his unusual vision of God, and his highest ethic, from the Hebrew scriptures, or indeed from anywhere in the culture of the Ancient Near East. For in

---

39. Albrecht Dihle, *Die Goldene Regel: Eine Einführung in die Geschichte der antiken und frühchristlichen Vulgärethik* (SAW 7; Göttingen: Vandenhoeck & Ruprecht, 1962), "Prinzipielle Überwindung des Vergeltungsdenkens, b) Christentum," 72-79: 72:

> Unter gänzlich anderen Voraussetzungen hat die Predigt Jesu von Nazareth und die an sie anknüpfende frühchristliche Theologie den Vergeltungsgedanken als Grundlage oder Bestandteil einer sittlichen Ordnung ausgeschieden.

See my review, *JHP* 4 (1966) 84-87.

that case it could hardly have centered in God's impartiality to foe as well as friend, as the Matthean antithesis makes clear: "You have heard that it was said, You shall love your neighbor and hate your enemy. But I say to you, Love your enemies ..." (Matt 5:43-44a).

Love of enemies does indeed fly in the face of the common-sense every-day judgment that the punishment should fit the crime. It is surprising indeed that Jesus' rare view of God, and its resultant radical ethic, is derived from his experience of the world of nature around him. Presumably, in Nazareth, the climate on the wrong side of the tracks was the same as the climate on the right side of the tracks. What was unusual was for someone, Jesus, to draw such a radical ethic from this simple observation of nature. God is in charge of nature, and on all sides is showing you how he is, and how his sons should be in imitation of him – kind to all, to the bad as well as to the good.

FROM JESUS FORWARD TO THE REDACTION OF Q

To the Q people, nothing was as important as Jesus' revelation of God. It was to score this point that they portray Jesus making use of the solemn Thanksgiving formula of Qumran[40], to praise God most explicitly that Jesus had finally revealed him in such a way that, for the first time, one could truly know him: "I praise you, Father, Lord of heaven and earth, for you hid these things from sages and the learned, and disclosed them to children; ... nor does anyone know the Father except the Son, and to whomever the Son chooses to reveal him" (Q 10:21a, 22b).

This Thanksgiving in Q thanks the Father for only one thing: A vision of God higher than what had been understood before, presumably God's amazingly impartial love for the bad as well as the good.

But what happened to this shocking revelation of God? Something did change in the outlook of the Q community, as reflected in the redactional level of the text of Q. For the ethic of loving one's enemies, though based on Jesus' vision of God, was replaced by quite a different ethic. It is odd that this is not generally recognized as a major problem, deserving more attention of New Testament scholarship.

Yet it has long since been sensed to be a problem, indeed it was so sensed by Walter Bauer almost a century ago. He did find Jesus' ideal of

---

40. James M. Robinson, "Die Hodajot-Formel in Gebet und Hymnus des Frühchristentums," in *Apophoreta: Festschrift für Ernst Haenchen* (BZNW 30; Berlin: Alfred Töpelmann, 1964) 194-235. [In *The Sayings Gospel Q*, pp. 75-118.]

love of enemies both in Paul and Q. But he sensed the substantive tension between the emphasis on the love of enemies in Q's archaic collection, the Inaugural Sermon, and the condemnation of enemies in Q 11:49-51; 13:34-35, which was then continued in the redaction of the Gospel of Matthew itself[41].

41. Walter Bauer, "Das Gebot der Feindesliebe und die alten Christen," *ZThK* 27 (1917) 37-54: 39-40:

Vielmehr verlangt er [Paulus] Liebesgesinnung gegen sie [die Feinde] in einer Form, die beinahe die Vermutung zuläßt, daß ihn nicht nur der Geist seines Herrn berührt hat, sondern ihm dessen Forderung im Ohre klingt (Röm. 12 $_{14-21}$, I. Thess. 5 $_{15}$, vgl. I. Kor. 4 $_{12}$). Wenn Paulus daneben gelegentlich scharfe Worte für die Verfolger der Gemeinde Gottes findet (I. Thess. 2 $_{14-16}$), so kann das in keinem höheren Grade befremden, als wenn in der Redenquelle außer dem Gebote der Feindesliebe auch Sprüche stehen wie Mt. 23 $_{34}$ f. $_{37}$ f. = Luk. 11 $_{49}$ f., 13 $_{34}$ f. [Q 11:49-51; 13:34-35].
...
Auch in der, zu Lebzeiten des Heidenapostels komponierten Redenquelle hat die Feindesliebe die ihr gebührende Wertung erfahren. Da war sie nicht als eine Tugend neben anderen erschienen, sondern als das Höchste, was man überhaupt von einem Menschen erwarten kann, als etwas, was die Jünger Jesu hoch hinaushebt über die Sphäre des allgemein Menschlichen und sie Gott selber gleich macht (Mt. 5 $_{44-48}$ = Luk. 6 $_{32-36}$) [Q 6:32,34,35c-36]. Demgemäß hatte in der Urgestalt der Bergpredigt die Forderung der Feindesliebe die beherrschende Stellung eingenommen und war nach dem Auftakt der Seligpreisungen an die Spitze der ganzen Ermahnungsreihe getreten. Bei Matthäus, der jener Urform eine umfassende Bearbeitung hat zuteil werden lassen, ist das verwischt. In seinem Evangelium bleibt es auch gewisser-maßen bei der einmaligen Mitteilung, daß Jesus so Großes von den Seinen gefordert habe. Und die Art, wie dort, wo der ἐθνικός und der τελώνης aus Mt. 5 $_{46.47}$ wie-derkehren, diese die Schar der Ungetauften repräsentierenden Menschen mit gleich-gültiger Kälte zur Seite geschoben werden (18 $_{17}$), die Genugtuung mit der Mt. berich-tet, wie der König den Tod seiner Sendboten an den widerwilligen Geladenen rächt (22 $_{6.7}$), lassen nicht gerade erwarten, daß er auf Aeußerungen der Feindschaft von nichtchristlicher Seite mit Liebeserweisen zu reagieren geneigt gewesen wäre.

ET (unpublished):

Rather he [Paul] calls for a loving attitude toward them [one's enemies] in a form that almost permits the conjecture that not only the spirit of his Lord has touched him, but also his requirement echoes in his ear (Rom 12:14-21; 1 Thess 5:15; cf. 1 Cor 4:12). If in addition Paul at times finds sharp words for the persecutors of the congregation of God (1 Thess 2:14-16), that can surprise in no higher degree than when in the sayings source, in addition to the command of love of enemy, also say-ings occur such as Matt 23:34-35, 37-38 = Luke 11:49-50; 13:34-35 [Q 11:49-51; 13:34-35]. ...

Also in the discourse source, composed during the lifetime of the apostle to the Gen-tiles, love of the enemy has received the evaluation it deserves. There it did not make its appearance as a virtue among others, but rather as the highest that one can ever expect from a person, as something that elevates the disciples of Jesus high above the sphere of the generally human, and makes them like God himself (Matt 5:44-48 = Luke 6:32-36 [Q 6:32,34,35c-36]. Accordingly, in the archaic form of the Sermon on the Mount the requirement of love of enemies had assumed the dominant posi-tion and, after the prelude of the Beatitudes, had come to stand at the head of the whole series of exhortations. In Matthew, who subjected that archaic form to an all-encompassing revision, that has vanished. In his Gospel, it is also limited, so to

This drastic change has recently been highlighted very forcefully in a dissertation by a pupil of Graham Stanton at King's College London, David C. Sim, in an analysis of Matthew's apocalyptic eschatology. Yet his devastating analysis of Matthew's vengefulness is based largely on redactional material from Q, which was then incorporated into Matthew. Hence his analysis applies not just to Matthew, but also to the redaction of Q:

> Like most apocalyptic-eschatological schemes, Matthew's version does not merely treat the eschatological fate of the righteous; he also deals with the ultimate fate of the wicked. The evangelist depicts the fate of this group in the harshest of terms. One important function of this motif is to satisfy the desire for vengeance on the part of himself and his readers. ...
> In this section we have noted one of the evangelist's important uses of apocalyptic eschatology, particularly the abundant material relating to the horrific punishments awaiting the wicked. Matthew emphasizes this particular element and uses it to satisfy his apocalyptic community's psychological need for vengeance on those who are responsible for their suffering[42].

Love your enemies? Sim continues: "The righteous can take heart that God (or Jesus Son of Man) will balance the ledger at the eschaton and exact vengeance on their behalf."[43] He raises his sun on bad and good and rains on the just and unjust? Jesus' amazing vision of God seems to have been completely lost from sight by the redaction of Q, and hence in the Gospel of Matthew!

What is it that caused Jesus' vision of God to be replaced by its reverse? Sim himself suggests:

> Owing to the high ethical demands of Jesus' interpretation of the Torah, the *ekklesia* was prohibited from taking its own revenge upon its enemies, even if it were in a position to do so. ... These demands must have posed some problems for Matthew's community and raised doubts in their minds about the justice of God. How can God be just when he allows the righteous to

---

speak, to just a single communication, that Jesus has required something so great of those who were his. And the way in which, where the ἐθνικός and the τελώνης are repeated from Matt 5:46-47, these people, representing the mass of the unbaptized, are pushed to one side with indifferent coldness (18:17), the satisfaction with which Matthew reports how the king avenges, on the invited who are unwilling to come, the death of his messengers (22:6-7), do not permit one to expect such a thing as that he would have been inclined to react to expressions of hostility from non-Christians with displays of love.

42. David C. Sim, *Apocalyptic Eschatology in the Gospel of Matthew* (SNTSMS 88; Cambridge: Cambridge University Press, 1996), "Vengeance and consolation," 227-35: 227, 234.

43. Sim, *Apocalyptic Eschatology in the Gospel of Matthew*, 235.

suffer and the wicked to prosper and does not allow the former to take revenge on the latter?[44]

But what seems to be lacking in Sim's reflection has to do with the understanding of God. If "they were expected to be as perfect as their heavenly father," as Sim emphasizes[45], should they not love their enemies, as God exemplified with his sun and showers? How it is that "doubt in their minds about the justice of God" replaced having as much pity as God had, forgiving as often as God forgives, loving enemies the way God helps the bad and unjust? The Q people seem to have reversed their ethics! But how could they reverse their ethics, and leave Jesus' doctrine of God in place? That sublime doctrine of God must itself have given way. But how?

It may be no coincidence that the Q text cited by Bauer to document the replacement of love of enemies with vengeance (Q 11:49-51; 13:34-35) is precisely the text that Bultmann considered a quotation from an unknown sapiential text (since Q presents it as quoting Sophia)[46], which is today the main evidence for Q's deuteronomistic redaction and the late dating of the redaction of Q. For the destruction of the temple in 70 C.E. seems to be envisaged there,[47] when the text speaks of the temple, "your House," being "forsaken" by God (Q 13:35). His abandonment of the temple was thought to be theologically necessary before the temple could be destroyed again in 70 CE, as it had been in 586 BCE, since God could be otherwise expected to protect his temple. Thus God revealed himself as a vengeful God, by punishing Israel again with this second destruction of the temple. Thus the destruction of the temple in 70 CE, experienced as a new devastating punishment by God, in effect replaced Jesus' revelation of God for the Q community. Accordingly, in the redaction of Q, God no longer shines his sun and rains his showers also on the bad and unjust, but throws them "out into the outer darkness, where there will be wailing and grinding of teeth" (Q 13:28), as victims of the "impending rage," whom he will "burn on a fire that can never be put out" (Q 3:7, 17).

---

44. Sim, *Apocalyptic Eschatology in the Gospel of Matthew*, 235.

45. Sim, *Apocalyptic Eschatology in the Gospel of Matthew*, 235.

46. Rudolf Bultmann, *Die Geschichte der synoptischen Tradition* (Göttingen: Vandenhoeck und Ruprecht, ²1931) 119-21. The English translation: *The History of the Synoptic Tradition* (New York and Evanston: revised edition, 1968) 114-15, here (as elsewhere even in this revised edition) presupposes a lack of understanding of the German text, which hence has to be consulted in order to understand Bultmann's meaning.

47. Paul Hoffmann, "The Redaction of Q and the Son of Man," "The Son of Man and the Fall of Jerusalem," 190-98.

From all of this one can only conclude that it was what was left of the largely rejected Q community who produced a vision of God that replaced that of Jesus, together with an ethic of vengeance to replace his of the love of enemies, after having envisaged the destruction of the temple in 70 C.E. as an act of God. They seem to have paid only lip service to love of enemies, knowing full well that the enemies will get it in the end from a just God of vengeance: "Vengeance is mine, I will repay."[48]

If nothing else, the critical text of Q, on the basis of Lührmann's distinction between the redaction of Q and the archaic collections imbedded in it, should make it possible to catch sight again of Jesus' vision of God. And, I submit to you, that would not be an unimportant achievement.

---

48. Sim, *Apocalyptic Eschatology in the Gospel of Matthew*, 235:
It is obvious from our discussion that Matthew responds to this problem in the same manner as other apocalyptic-eschatological thinkers. He provides an eschatological solution. Since the opponents of the *ekklesia* will be punished without mercy at the judgement, the members of the community can rest assured that God is just. While Matthew does not appeal to Deuteronomy 32:35, 'Vengeance is mine, I will repay,' as do Paul in Romans 12:19 and the author of Hebrews (10:30), he is firmly in agreement with this sentiment (cf. 16:27).

CHAPTER 7

What Jesus Had to Say

We need to face up to an undomesticated Jesus, what one might call a real idealist, a committed radical, in any case a profound person who proposed a solution to the human dilemma.

What Jesus had to say centered around the ideal of God's rule ("the kingdom of God"), the main theological category Jesus created. Calling the ideal God's rule puts it in an antithetical relation both to other political and social systems, and to individual self-interest – "looking out for number one." Jesus points out that the ravens and lilies prosper without working to secure their needs. God cares about every sparrow sold a dime a dozen. God will not give a stone when asked for bread, or a snake when asked for fish, but can be counted on to give what one really needs. Indeed people should trust God to know what they need even before they ask. This Utopian vision was the core of what Jesus had to say. It was both good news – reassurance that good would happen to undo one's plight in actual experience – and the call upon people to do that good for others in actual practice.

The human dilemma is in large part that we are each other's fate. We are the tool of evil that ruins the other person, as we look out for number one, having long abandoned any youthful idealism we might once have cherished. But if I would cease and desist from pushing you down to keep myself up, and you for your part would do the same, then the vicious circle would be broken. Society would become mutually supportive, rather than self-destructive. Count on God to look out for you, to provide people that will care for you, and listen to him when he calls on you to provide for them. This radical trust in and responsiveness to God is what makes society function as God's society. This is, for Jesus, what faith and discipleship were all about. Nothing else has a right to claim any functional relationship to him.

Put in language derived from his sayings: I am hungry because you hoard food. You are cold because I hoard clothing. So we are all to get rid of our backpacks and wallets! Such "security" is to be replaced by "God's rule," which means both what we trust God to do (to tell the other person to share food with me), and what we hear God telling us to do (to share clothing with the other person). One does not carry money while passing by the poor, or a backpack full of extra clothes and food while ignoring the cold and hungry lying in the gutter. This is why the beggars, the hungry, the depressed, are fortunate: God, that is to say, those who hearken to God, those in whom God rules, will care for them. They are called upon to trust that God's rule is there for them ("... theirs is the kingdom of God"). One need not even carry a club for self-protection, but rather should return good for evil even with regard to one's enemies. One turns the other cheek. God is the kind of person who provides sunshine and rain even to those who oppose him. So God's children are those who care even for their enemies. In the original form of the Lord's Prayer, what followed directly upon and defined "Thy kingdom come" was: "Our day's bread give us today." People should ask for no more than a day's ration of food, trusting God to provide for today, and then tomorrow trusting for tomorrow.

God's rule ("the kingdom of God") was interpreted by Matthew's community to mean: "Thy will be done on earth as it is in heaven." This addition to the Lord's Prayer is, technically speaking, not a call for action, but, like "Thy kingdom come" which it interprets, an appeal to God: When one prays, one trusts in God to answer. But God answers by motivating people – to turn the other cheek; to give the shirt off one's back; to go the second mile; to lend, expecting nothing in return. The person who prays to God for help is the same person whom God motivates to help: "Forgive us our debts as we forgive our debtors!"

Part of God ruling is helping the infirm with whatever simple medical help was available. One went from door to door, and if admitted for bed and breakfast (the answer to the prayer for a day's bread), one placed God's blessing on the house, in practice by healing the sick within as best one could ("Heal the sick and say: The kingdom of God has drawn near").

Just as the sharing of food and clothing, the canceling of debts, the non-retaliation against enemies, were not seen as human virtues, but rather as God acting through those who trust him, just so healings were not attributed to a faith healer's or a magician's individual technique or skill, but to God making use not only of Jesus, but of others as well. Clearly all these were things that one could not oneself do, from renunciation of self-interest to healing disease. They took place because God was doing it, God was ruling in this unusual human society – this was in fact the "coming" of "the kingdom of God"! Jesus was a faith healer in the sense that he trusted God to thrust his finger into the human dilemma, to overcome the plight of the infirm.

But not everything had been done: Not all people lived such trust in God, not all the helpless were helped, nor all the disabled healed. Of course one trusted God to follow through to completion ("eschatology"). But Jesus' message was not intended to replace grim reality with a "pie in the sky by-and-by" Utopian ideal, but rather to focus attention on trusting God for today's ration of life, and on hearing God's call to give life now to one's neighbor.

All this is as far from today's Christian coalition and even mainline Christianity as it was from the Judaism practiced in Jesus' day. The hardest saying of Jesus is: "Why do you call me: Master, Master, and do not do what I say?" One laments the absence of a "high christology," any claim by Jesus in his sayings to be divine. But what could be higher than the belief that doing Jesus' word is what acquits in the day of judgment? Christological creeds may be no more than pious dodges to avoid this unavoidable condition of discipleship. Actually do what he said to do!

People do not do what he said, not simply because of the shift in cultural conditions, but ultimately because people do not trust God as Jesus did (in spite of claims to Christian faith). This, not the Jesus Seminar's shocking negations, is what should be unsettling about finding out what Jesus had to say.

All this of course sounds incredibly naive. Once Jesus launched himself into this lifestyle, practicing what he preached, he did not last long. A reality check is called for!

Yet the bottom line is not necessarily so cynical: In concentration camps, cells of a few who can really trust each other – due to a shared ethnic, religious, or political commitment – and who are hence willing to give an extra portion of their meager food and other necessities of life to the feeblest, have turned out to have a higher chance of survival than do individuals looking out only for themselves. Selfishness may ultimately turn out to be a luxury we can ill afford. There is a paradoxical saying to the effect that when one saves one's life one loses it, but when one loses one's life one saves it. To be sure, the point here is not longevity but integrity. What Jesus had to say is thus all the more worthy of serious consideration.

CHAPTER 8

The Jesus of Q as Liberation Theologian

I

The two-fold problematic of the title "The Jesus of Q as Liberation Theologian"[1] should be obvious to us all.

First, there is the problem of speaking of Jesus, when all we have is a secondary text. The very process of discussing what may and may not be ascribed to Jesus, and the divergence of opinions among respected colleagues, serve to keep us painfully aware of the problematic of this whole undertaking.

But there is an alternative to this never ending and ultimately rather frustrating process of trying to recover genuine mosaic stones and then to fit them into the same coherent picture from which they originally came. For there is an overriding *directionality* to the earliest stages of the tradition, which shows the flow, the *Tendenz* of the transmitting process, the main direction in which revisionism was moving. Thus, when analysed in reversed chronological sequence, the trajectory points toward the originative point, the approximate position where Jesus would have to be located. To this extent one can at least mock up a silhouette of the historical Jesus – the black box gains contours and directionality.

This does not in concrete factual biographical terms bring Jesus out of obscurity, but does point to his relative position: He was more this than the ensuing tradition; he was less that than, for example, the canonical Gospels. Thus the way he cuts, as a role model, as an authority, as a precedent, a pointer, may be clearer than are the actual biographical facts. Back to Jesus, *ad fontes*, means going this way, not that way. Hence his relevance for us may not ultimately be dissolved by the obscurity in which his biography lies. Indeed the direction he points may be ascertained with sufficient clarity to be uncomfortable.

Second, there is the problem of the often latent apologetic inherent in the association of Jesus, as an authority figure of the past, with a movement one seeks to support in the present, such as the dominant

---

1. This paper was presented at the Jesus Seminar of the Westar Institute in Edmonton, Canada at its semi-annual meeting of 25-27 October 1991.

theological movement that the third world has contributed to ecumenical discussion, liberation theology.

Of course, Jesus cannot be simply identified with any modern alternative. But since all Christian theologies claim him as their own, it is relevant to pose the question of the relative legitimacy of such claims.

It is more customary to adjust Jesus to one's theology than to adjust one's theology to Jesus. Hence it may be of some relevance toward transcending such drastic relativity to detect the main direction the interpretation was taking in the middle third of the first century, as one moved away from Jesus and toward the canonical gospels.

The redaction criticism of Matthew and Luke, based upon their editing of Mark, may have disappointingly few implications concerning Jesus. For Mark had already superimposed on the traditions about Jesus the overlay of the Messianic Secret, which Matthew and Luke in turn water down. Thus they are often moving more directly away from Mark than from Jesus[2]. But, on the other hand, their editing of Q, once the reconstruction of a critical text of Q makes this kind of redaction criticism possible[3], has to do directly with some very old Jesus traditions, affecting the transmission of what Jesus had to say, in spite of there also being later traditions in Q, which do not necessarily conform to the layering of Q[4], although by and large this would seem to be the situation[5].

---

2. William Wrede, *Das Messiasgeheimnis in den Evangelien* (Göttingen: 1901); ET *The Messianic Secret* (Cambridge: 1971). An analogous modern analysis of Mark is Burton L. Mack, *A Myth of Innocence* (Philadelphia: 1988).

3. "The International Q Project Work Session 17 November 1989," *JBL* 109 (1990) 499-501. "The International Q Project Work Session 16 November 1990," *JBL* 110 (1991) 494-498. "The International Q Project Work Sessions 12-14 July, 22 November 1991," *JBL* 111 (1992) 500-508. "A Critical Text of the Sayings Gospel Q," *Revue d'Histoire et de Philosophie Religieuses* 72 (1992) 15-22. [In *The Sayings Gospel Q,* pp. 309-317.] "The International Q Project Work Sessions 31 July–2 August, 20 November 1992," *JBL* 112 (1993) 500-506. [*The Critical Edition of Q. Synopsis including the Gospels of Matthew and Luke, Mark and Thomas with English, German, and French Translations of Q and Thomas,* ed. J.M. Robinson et al. (Minneapolis/Leuven: 2000).]

4. The current status of the discussion of the layering of Q has its centre in John S. Kloppenborg, *The Formation of Q* (Studies in Antiquity and Christianity; Philadelphia: 1987): The formative layer (Q[1]) contains six discourses, (1) Q 6:20b-23b, 27-49; (2) Q 9:57-62; 10:2-11, 16; (3) Q 11:2-4, 9-13; (4) Q 12:2-7, 11-12; (5) Q 12:22b-31, 33-34; (6) Q 13:24; 14:26-27, 34-35; 17:33 and perhaps Q 15:4-7, (8-10); 16:13; 17:1-2, 3b-6. This listing is very [261] similar to and no doubt suggested by that in Dieter Zeller, *Die weisheitlichen Mahnsprüche bei den Synoptikern* (FzB 47; Würzburg: 1977) 191. A redactional layer (Q[2]) interpolated five blocks of material, (1) Q 3:7-9, 16-17; (2) Q 7:1-10, 18-28, 31-35; 16:16; (3) Q 11:14-26, (27-28?), 29-36, 39b-44, 46-52; (4) Q 12:39-40, 42-46, 49, 51-59; (5) Q 17:23-24, 26-30, 34-35; 19:12-27; 22:28-30. The redaction of Q[2] also involved interpolations into Q[1] (which is an argument for the sequence of the layers): Q 6:23d; 10:12-15; 12:8-10; 13:25-27; 19:18-20; 13:34-35; 14:16-24. This second layer corresponds to Dieter Lührmann, *Die Redaktion der Logienquelle* (WMANT 33;

To anticipate the outcome of such an investigation directed backward toward Jesus, which the discussion that follows is intended to begin[6]: In terms of modern theological alternatives, Jesus was more nearly a liberation theologian, if one may refer to such an untrained leader as a theologian at all, than a Prefect of the Congregation for the Doctrine of the Faith (Magisterium), not to speak of Protestant theologians of various kinds. Thus a redaction-critical investigation of the move from Jesus via Q to the canon provides a much-needed canonical precedent for the church's efforts to play down and control liberation theology, as well as pointing up liberation theology's relatively higher claim to the historical Jesus.

The two-fold problematic of, on the one hand, discussing the Jesus of Q and, on the other, discussing him as liberation theologian, should stay in our awareness throughout the discussion, even if not repeatedly mentioned.

II

When thinking of Q's leading theological categories, one normally focusses upon the kingdom of God and the son of man. But, for Q, important though usually overlooked theological categories are also such mundane matters as bread and rock.

To catch sight of these metaphors, one should visualise a small loaf of bread, or roll (since bread came not in slices but in loaves), and a

Neukirchen-Vluyn: 1969), and the most significant interpolation reflects Odil Hannes Steck, *Israel und das gewaltsame Geschick der Propheten: Untersuchungen zur Überlieferung des deuteronomistischen Geschichtsbildes im Alten Testament, Spätjudentum und Urchristentum* (WMANT 23; Neukirchen-Vluyn: 1967). Of course this analysis may not ultimately be definitive, and has indeed undergone minor revision of the extent of Q by the International Q Project, as well as fluctuations in detail as to what belongs in which layer by supporters of the basic approach; but it does, in addition to its own cogently argued presentation, tend to represent a convergence of quite different kinds of analysis leading to much the same structuring of priority to the sapiential strand. See my essay "The Q Trajectory: Between John and Matthew via Jesus," in *The Future of Early Christianity: Essays in Honor of Helmut Koester*, ed. Birger A. Pearson (Minneapolis: 1991) 173-194. [In this volume, chap. 10.]

5. It is remarkable how much congruence there is between the layering of older and younger traditions in Siegfried Schulz, *Q. Die Spruchquelle der Evangelisten* (Zürich: 1972), and the two main literary layers that Kloppenborg has disengaged. It would of course weaken considerably Kloppenborg's position if what he identified as the younger literary layer contained primarily traditions older than the older literary layer. Conversely the congruence with the analysis of layers of tradition by Schulz is one reason that Kloppenborg's analysis has much to commend it.

6. The discussion of Q and the historical Jesus in general dependence on this layering has hardly begun. Leif E. Vaage, "Q[1] and the Historical Jesus: Some Peculiar Sayings (7:33-34; 9:57-58, 59-60; 14:26-27)," *Forum* 5.2 (1989) 159-176, reaches a Cynic conclusion more provocative than convincing; see note 61 below.

fist-size stone, the Palestinian dimension with which we are familiar from David-and-Goliath to the Intifada.

The Jesus of Q thought of loaves roughly resembling stones[7], much as a fish resembles a snake[8]. His trust in God was to the effect that God, like a human father, would not replace the daily loaf for which one prayed with an inedible stone. In the next layer of Q (Q^2), traditions associated with John saw such common field stones as God's universal source of children of Abraham[9]. But in a still further stage of the Q trajectory (Q^3), Jesus, as exclusive son of God, becomes the role model for those who do not force God's hand in expecting stones to become loaves from God, but let stones stay stones. By now asking for bread from stones amounts to an inappropriate temptation[10]. The painful human awareness that one needs to be able to count on bread, not stone, from God, is overridden by the religious concern not to permit such trust, when it falters, to test God by asking for bread from stones. The issue is no longer food, but trust.

To return to the painful human point of departure: The Q Prayer has at its centre a loaf of bread: "Our day's bread give us today."[11] One may recognize the petition "thy will be done"[12] as a secondary Matthean interpretation of "let your reign come", comparable to other Matthean moralizing additions such as seeking the kingdom of God *and his righteousness*[13], hungering *and thirsting after righteousness*[14]. Conversely one may suspect that in Q it was the loaf of bread[15] that was intended to give the interpretative clarity to the immediately preceding petition for God's reign to come[16], by making God's reigning as specific as a day's ration.

The petition for bread is meant literally. For in Q's commentary on the prayer, which stands in sharp contrast to the Matthean religious interpretation oriented to forgiveness by humans and hence by God[17], one finds the reassurance that if one asks, searches, knocks, one will be provided, as with bread and fish by humans, with good things by God[18].

7. Q 11:11 // Mt 7:9.
8. Q 11:12.
9. Q 3:8.
10. Q 4:3-4.
11. Q 11:3.
12. Mt 6:10 at Q 11:2.
13. Mt 6:33 at Q 12:31.
14. Mt 5:6 at Q 6:21.
15. Q 11:3.
16. Q 11:2.
17. Mt 6:14-15 at Q 11:4 // Mt 6:12.
18. Q 11:9-13.

Luke also first interprets the petition for bread literally, in that he interpolates between the prayer and its Q interpretation an illustration of a person who asks for three loaves for a late-arriving guest and finally gets what he needs[19].

Yet the Q interpretation does have a dimension *a minore ad majorem* in that God's giving moves beyond the specifics, to good things more broadly[20]. And yet to persons who do not have to worry about where their next meal is coming from (for example, non-liberation theologians), this may still seem to be something of a let-down. For it could suggest a crass materialism to the Q folk: a real feast. So Luke appends a corrective spiritualizing reformulation of the Q interpretation[21]: To those who ask, God will give the Holy Spirit – with which however the prayer itself was not at all concerned[22]. But one need only recall Paul's spiritualizing exegesis[23]: "The kingdom of God is not food and drink but righteousness and peace and joy in the Holy Spirit." Paul thus stopped the "rice Christians"

19. Lk 11:5-8.

20. Q 11:13.

21. Lk 11:13 at Q 11:13.

22. This came to expression in a spiritualizing corruption of the Lucan text as early as Marcion. See B. H. Streeter, *The Four Gospels: A Study of Origins* (New York: 1925) 277, who advocated this reading as the Lucan text of the prayer itself, which led to the conclusion that the Prayer was not in Q:

> Here we find that **B**, as usual, has been less affected by assimilation than most other MSS.; but here also there is evidence that **B** has not entirely escaped. For **700**, **162**, instead of "Thy kingdom come," read "thy holy spirit come upon us and cleanse us" (ἐλθέτω τὸ πνεῦμα ... ἐφ' ἡμᾶς) And **D** has ἐλθέτω ἡ βασιλεία ἐφ' ἡμᾶς, where Rendel Harris pointed out, ἐφ' ἡμᾶς is only explicable as a remainder of the other reading which a corrector of some ancestor of **D** omitted to strike out, and this reading was in the text of Luke used by Gregory of Nyssa in Cappadocia in 395; he says so plainly twice, and moreover gives no hint that he had even heard of any other reading. It is also quoted by Maximus of Turin, *c*. 450. So the reading was current both in the East and in the West to quite a late period. But it also stood in the text of Marcion (AD 140), and from Tertullian's comment on this it is not at all clear that his own text was in this respect different from Marcion's. Now in view of the immense pressure of the tendency to assimilate the two versions of this specifically familiar prayer, and of the improbability that various orthodox Fathers should have adopted (without knowing it) the text of Marcion, the probability is high that the reading of **700**, **162**, which makes the Gospels differ most, is what Luke wrote. Matthew's version is here the more original.

> Now, even if we accept the reading of **B**, the difference between the two versions of the Lord's Prayer, Lk. xi. 1-4 and Mt. vi. 9-13, is so great as to put a considerable strain on the theory that they were both derived from the same written source. But, if we accept the reading of **700** and its supporters, that theory becomes quite impossible.

23. Rom 14:17. cf. also Jas 1:5: "But if someone among you lacks wisdom, let him ask from God – who gives to all without hesitation and without grumbling – and it will be given to him."

of his day – the Q people – in their tracks. The Q people had been led to expect that trust in the coming of the kingdom would involve daily bread, a hope which was ultimately reduced to the eschatology of the Messianic banquet[24].

It is as if Christian charitable organizations should in our world air-lift in to the Kurdish refugees on the Turkish border or to the famine areas of Somalia or besieged cities of Yugoslavia not bread and blankets so much as – a stack of Bibles.

To be sure, the triple formulation: ask, search, knock[25], can not only be interpreted as rough synonyms all exhorting to prayer, but also as distinct metaphors pointing to distinct facets of the Q stance.

One not only "asks" for the kingdom and bread in the Prayer[26]; one "seeks" the kingdom, rather than scrounging food and clothing by human means[27]. For the Father, who knows our needs[28], will just as surely provide for us without our lifting our hands as he does for ravens and lilies[29]. This way the food and clothing will be ours as well[30]. Thus there is no contradiction between asking God for bread and not seeking from human resources food and clothing, even though God answers through human action.

One also "knocks", of course on a door, which in Q is thought of as having food and lodging on the other side[31]. If one's greeting of Shalom is reciprocated, and one is admitted, then the host is by definition a "son of peace"[32]. This was not originally meant as the selection of an already-identified "safe-house", an incipient house church[33], but rather involved knocking at an unknown address, where God, not a sympathizer, is counted on for food and lodging. Nor does one drop in on relatives or

---

24. Q 13:28-29.
25. Q 11:9.
26. Q 11:2-4.
27. Q 12:31.
28. Q 12:30.
29. Q 12:22-31.
30. Q 12:31.
31. Q 13:25-27.
32. Q 10:6.
33. This may be the meaning in Mt 10:11, reflecting the situation a generation later when circuits of "safe houses" were being developed, such as the Essenes used. This may explain Matthew's rearranging of the order of his Mission Instruction so as to list first not a house but a city or village, where there is a choice of houses. One searches out someone who is worthy, by which Matthew means someone who is a disciple, Mt 10:37-38. This practice is documented in Acts 21:7. Perhaps Q 13:26 has its place in this development.

friends for a break from the rigors of the mission[34]. There were no "rest and recreation" centers free of the call of duty.

Thus the injunction to ask, search, knock was not a program such as a Protestant work ethic, Gandhian cottage industries, agricultural missions, or the Peace Corps, and to this extent not as developed in practical terms as is modern liberation theology. The emphasis is on sustenance as a gift of God, even if in practice this meant being dependent on a son of peace providing room and board.

Yet the loaves are not spiritualized away in Johannine style, as manna from heaven that points christologically toward the Son whom the Father sent from heaven, or sacramentally as the tidbits that only whet one's appetite for the word of God. Rather they are a square meal, a real loaf of bread. The Johannine Jesus "tempted" Philip[35] with the idea of buying loaves to feed the hungry[36]. Once they are miraculously fed, they recognize Jesus as the Prophet, the one to come[37], and are ready to make him

---

34. This may be the meaning of the very obscure injunction, Q 10:4, "Salute no one on the road" (RSV). Bernhard Lang, "Grussverbot oder Besuchsverbot? Eine sozialgeschichtliche Deutung von Lukas 10,4b," *BZ* N.F. 26 (1982) 75-79, ascribes the statement to Q (p. 78). He develops a suggestion made in the Lukan commentary of G. L. Hahn in 1894, to the effect that one should translate "Visit no one during the trip". For ἀσπάζεσθαι can mean not just to greet, but also to visit someone for a period of time (Acts 18:22; 21:7; 25:13). It was the normal custom in that society that one could drop in unannounced at friends or relatives, and count on food and lodging (Lk 11:6). Risto Uro, *Sheep among the Wolves: A Study on the Mission Instructions of Q* (AASF. Dissertationes Humanarum Litterarum 47; Helsinki: 1987) 136 n. 80, rejects this interpretation, since he understands by "son of peace", in analogy to "sons of light", as "one who has a share in the new faith or at least sympathizes with it", "a sectarian designation" (140-141). But this is not attested anywhere as a Christian self-designation. Uro seems to put more theological meaning than is intended in the common, everyday exchange of greetings: "The 'peace' probably had a specifically Christian connotation and in the mouth of a wandering charismatic functioned as an effective blessing providing magical protection to the household" (141). Mt 10:12 interprets "Peace" as just a normal greeting: "As you enter a house, salute it." The statement that the peace would rest upon the son of peace or return to the speaker if no such welcoming host opens the door does in fact suggest a potential meaning in the common greeting, which would be unpacked, if one were admitted, in terms of the kingdom of God (Q 10:9), or, as Lk 10:11 interprets wiping the dust of one's feet off on leaving an unreceptive town, "nevertheless know this, that the kingdom of God has come near." But it could hardly function as a "password" (141 n. 100), since it was the standard greeting with no more distinctive connotation than our well-worn greetings of today. Its use may have been mentioned to clarify just how indeterminate the reception was, i.e. whether one would be heard only in a superficial "secular" way or whether one would be received as a bearer of the kingdom. The householder who responds positively to such an opening greeting by replying Shalom and opening the door is all that needs to be ascribed to the designation "son of peace".

35. Jn 6:6.

36. Jn 6:5.

37. Jn 6:14.

King[38], much as in Q John's disciples are referred to Jesus's healings and his evangelizing the poor to prove he is the One to Come[39].

The Q people are hence characterized not fully inappropriately by the Johannine Jesus[40]: "You seek me not because you saw signs, but because you ate of the loaves and were filled." Of course there was for the Q people no such dichotomy – the very experience of being filled was a reality of the kingdom, not an overlooking of the kingdom, and hence indeed a sign of the kingdom, though not just a sign. But in John, one should rather seek the nourishment that lasts to eternal life[41], not even manna from heaven[42], but Jesus the true bread from heaven[43], whose believers will metaphorically never hunger and thirst[44], for he is the bread of life[45].

Of course the disciples found this word to be difficult[46], and a schism resulted[47]: "After this many of his disciples drew back and no longer circulated with him." Yet the twelve (including Judas son of Simon Iscariot[48]) stuck by him, led by Simon Peter, all of whom are missing in Q. The twelve apostles thereupon moved with Jesus not only toward Jerusalem and away from Galilee[49], but also moved toward the canon – and away from the oldest layer of Q. Those that "no longer circulated with him" are those "that did not believe"[50], that is to say, those who would have enthroned him on the grounds of the unspiritualized loaves[51], with which the oldest layer of Q was in fact concerned.

To be sure, this Johannine text is a spiritualizing not of Q, but of the Signs Source, specifically its Feeding of the Five Thousand[52]. But these two most firmly established pre-canonical sources, though quite different, in that one is a collection of sayings (Q), the other of miracle stories (the Signs Source), do have much in common, perhaps due to the early period in which they share, that is to say, their relative proximity to Jesus. Indeed

---

38. Jn 6:15.
39. Q 7:22.
40. Jn 6:26.
41. Jn 6:27.
42. Jn 6:31.
43. Jn 6:32-35a.
44. Jn 6:35b.
45. Jn 6:48-58.
46. Jn 6:60.
47. Jn 6:66.
48. Jn 6:67-71.
49. Jn 5:1, if John 6 originally followed John 4, or in 7:10b, after shaking off his brothers (Jn 7:1-10a), if one prefers the present canonical order.
50. Jn 6:64.
51. Jn 6:15.
52. Jn 6:1-13.

the one miracle story of Q is shared with the Signs Source, the Capernaum Healing of the Centurion's Boy[53].

The Capernaum connection goes even further. For the Signs Source and Q share the questionability of Capernaum. Just as John locates the schism over heavenly bread at Capernaum[54], just so Q pronounces condemnation on Capernaum for exalting itself to heaven[55]. If there was actually a schism among Jesus' followers at Capernaum, it may well be that the Signs Source and Q would have been on the same side, in that both focussed on the down-to-earth dimension of what Jesus had to offer. The role of the Fourth Gospel as spiritualizing the Signs Source may provide a model for understanding the relation of Matthew and Luke to Q.

The Q people were thus originally somewhat reminiscent of a grazing-and-gathering (but not storing) prehistoric ecological system still witnessed to, as God's way, by the flourishing birds and flowers. For the outcome of not seeking food and clothing, but instead the reign of God, is that these things, the necessities of life[56], are supplied to them. Q does not really favor privation, any more than the really poor appreciate the romance of poverty. Liberation theology recognizes such romantic illusion as just a ploy of the suppressors. The Q people just have a different, God-given route to a square meal: Get through the door! Knock![57] Don't knock it down, but with a smile on your face, say Shalom![58] Eat anything they will give you![59] Don't demand it be Kosher. Or: Don't be uptight about killing vegetables by plucking them to make food, as reflected in the debates between Mani and the Jewish Christian Elkesaites among whom Mani grew up. Or: Don't insist that it be locusts and wild honey[60]. Or: Don't be abstemious in what one eats and drinks, as befits an ascetic. In one way or the other, eat whatever God provides.

The Q movement then was not ascetic, in the sense of physical privation being an end or goal in itself. Dig in! Eat what is set before you! Be like Jesus, eating and drinking, or, in caricature, a glutton and drunkard, carousing with tax collectors and sinners[61], but quite unlike John

---

53. Q 7:1-9; Jn 4:46b-54.
54. Jn 6:24.
55. Q 10:15.
56. Q 12:31.
57. Q 11:9-10.
58. Q 10:5.
59. Q 10:7-8.
60. John's menu according to Mk 1:6.
61. Q 7:34. Leif A. Vaage, "Q¹ and the Historical Jesus," does not distinguish between what is presented as descriptive (ἦλθεν) and what is presented as hostile caricature (λέγετε). This facilitates his characterization of Jesus as "a bit of a hellion and wanderer

the ascetic who neither ate bread nor drank wine, or in caricature, was demon-possessed[62]. John's diet was apparently what he was able to scrounge from nature[63], and he may have made a virtue of fasting[64], as did Jesus' disciples at a later time[65]. But in the case of Jesus' disciples this is set over against an earlier time when they did not fast[66]. The practice reflected in the Mission Instructions would tend to indicate that when a host provided a banquet, there was no reason not to accept it. If what could be offered was much more modest, one would accept that too. To judge by the success Jesus may well have had (in contrast to the probable failure of the ongoing Mission of his disciples), he might well have ended up looking like Buddha, had he not headed for Jerusalem, but rather stayed in the Galilee that heard (and fed) him gladly[67]. There is no justification in the Jesus of Q for asceticism in its own right, or for poverty as an ideal to be imposed (by the well-to-do) on the poor.

If Shalom works, one exchanges gifts of healings and food, under the auspices of the kingdom of God[68]. This content of the Mission is presented by Mark in narrative form[69], when Jesus goes home with Peter to heal his sick mother-in-law and eat the food she serves. He may well not have gone from house to house, but stayed there and made it his base camp, which the Franciscan brothers, who now own and have excavated "Peter's House" in Capernaum, will be glad to show you. In fact when Jesus was invited by a centurion to another Capernaum home for a healing, he declined the implicit offer of hospitality, while providing from a distance the healing[70].

If the Q folk were not ascetics in a doctrinaire sense, they were of course also not merely *bon vivants*. The usual understanding of the policy not to go from house to house, but to stay where one was first

on the wild (or, at least, illicit) side of things" (166), "an imp, in Socrates' terms a social gad-fly, an irritant on the skin of conventional mores and values, a marginal figure in the provincial context of Galilee and Judea" (175). However the use of the caricature as objective description would, in the adjoining and structurally parallel case of John (Q 7:33), make of him a demoniac, which is hardly true of the historical John. The point of the text is to indicate that Jesus coming eating and drinking is distorted by hostile caricature, just as John coming not eating bread and drinking wine is distorted by hostile caricature. The caricatures, to the extent they go beyond the descriptions, are historical evidence only to there having been efforts at hostile caricatures of the diverging lifestyles.

62. Q 7:33.
63. Mk 1:6.
64. Mk 2:18.
65. Mk 2:20; Mt 6:16-18.
66. Mk 2:18.
67. Mk 12:37 uses this familiar phrase of the Jerusalem crowd.
68. Q 10:6-9.
69. Mk 1:29-31.
70. Q 7:1-10.

received[71], is that one stays even after the fatted calf there has been consumed. Nor does one stash away supplies from the pantry in one's knapsack for the next day's road, much less for a rainy day, for again and again one sets out in the morning empty-handed[72].

Why the deprivation, if not derived from ascetic ideology? Perhaps as a show, to attract attention, a visual advertisement for the illiterate masses, like the chimney-sweep's blackened face, top hat and ladder, or other *sigla* or sounds of Medieval trades people hawking their wares on the streets, or like the contemporary Cynics, whose disdain for respectable society's values was visible in their distinct primitive garb as far as the eye could see. Though this may not be the point of the injunction not to greet anyone on the road[73], since this may indeed refer more nearly to an injunction against dropping in on friends for rest and recreation, other traits which seem to us to have served no earthly good other than to dramatize their message, such as barefootedness, may have to be thus explained, at least until we have a better explanation – a sign of penance?[74]

71. Q 10:7.

72. Q 10:4. The policy of not accepting provisions for the continuation of the trip seems to have been violated by the Maltese, who provided Paul with provisions for the journey in return for his healings (Acts 28:10), consistent with the Lucan revocation of carrying purse and bag (Q 10:4) as the passion narrative begins (Lk 22:35-38).

73. I. Bosold, *Pazifismus und prophetische Provokation. Das Grussverbot Lk 10,4b und sein historischer Kontext* (SBS 90; Stuttgart: 1978), interpreted this statement as intentionally provocative, to draw attention and thus to serve as propaganda. It would seem counter-productive to seek to attract attention, in order to provide an opportunity for the message, by means of refusing a greeting that usually opens a conversation. Lang's argument (see note 34) is presented as a corrective of that view. Bosold, 43-51, ascribes the statement to Q. "The International Q Project: Work Session 16 November 1990," *JBL* 110 (1991) 496, followed Bosold's interpretation, but expressed considerable doubt about the reading in Q, omitting completely κατὰ τὴν ὁδόν. Lang's interpretation might make the ascription of the saying to Q more certain. [*The Critical Edition of Q* includes κατὰ τὴν ὁδόν in Q.]

74. Norbert Krieger, "Barfuss Busse Tun," *NT* 1 (1956) 227-228, especially 227:
Busse aber wurde und wird unter Juden seit jeher ohne Schuhe begangen.
2 Sam xv 30; Ez xxiv 17, 23; Mi i 8 ...
Bedeutung des Wegnehmens wie Jo xii 6; xx 13-15.
Doch geht es Mt iii 11, meiner Meinung nach, nicht um ein Abnehmen zu gelegentlicher Bequemlichkeit; es ging dort vielmehr um ein Wegnehmen zu ständiger Unbequemlichkeit, so dass ein Barfüsserorden der Johannesjünger denkbar wäre.
Krieger is followed by Walter Bauer, *A Greek-English Lexicon of the New Testament and Other Early Christian Literature*, ET by William F. Arndt and F. Wilbur Gingrich, 2nd edition revised and augmented by F. Wilbur Gingrich and Frederick W. Danker from Walter Bauer's 5th edition, 1958 (Chicago / London: 1979), s.v. βαστάζω, 3.a, "remove", citing also *PGM* 4,1058: βαστάξας τὸ στεφάνιον ἀπὸ τῆς κεφαλῆς.

The Love-Your-Enemies composition at the heart of the Sermon[75] would seem to provide a more specific explanation for the weird lifestyle. For one is not merely to love an occasional enemy, but even to act lovingly toward the pervasive sponger. Give the shirt off one's back! Even give away one's money! Lending to those who can never repay can only for politeness' sake be called lending – it's a bald hand out! The traveller's usual equipment of purse and pack is rejected in the Mission Instructions, no doubt since they can be there only for one reason – to hold on for oneself to what the beggar on the street calls out for, an appeal which, if always acceded to, would soon leave one empty-handed, oneself in the same fix as the beggar. This, rather than baptism, may have been the *rite de passage* into the Q movement. Barnabas may illustrate the way a sympathizer's sale of property for charitable purposes leads to itinerancy[76].

---

75. Walter Bauer, "Das Gebot der Feindesliebe und die alten Christen," *ZThK* 24 (1913) 37-54 (Wilhelm Herrmann *Festschrift*), wrote the history of the injunction to love one's enemy in the early church, to the effect that, though the apologists often refer to the Christian practice of loving one's enemy for its apologetic value, this ideal was not nearly so well implemented as this boastful claim might suggest. Matthew (pp. 39-40) has removed it from the central role it had in the Q sermon just after the Beatitudes, and states it only once (Mt 5:44), rather than twice (Lk 6:27, 35). The way in which the tax collectors and Gentiles, types of those to whose conduct one does not want to condescend (Q 6:32, 34 // Mt 5:46-47), "who represent the crowd of the unbaptised, are pushed to one side with indifferent coolness," as the model for the way in which an excommunicated person is treated (Mt 18:17), or "the satisfaction with which Matthew reports how the king avenged the death of his emissaries on the unwilling invitees" (Mt 22:6-7) "do not particularly lead one to expect that he would have been inclined to react to expressions of animosity from non-Christians with expressions of love." Luke (p. 40) seems more sympathetic with the love of enemies, in refraining from destroying the Samaritan village (Lk 9:51-56) and in presenting Jesus (Lk 23:34) and, in imitation, Stephen (Acts 7:60), as dying with a prayer for their tormentors. But the widow's plea for justice (Lk 18:6-8) is already reminiscent of the hateful demand for justice of Rev 6:9-11. Mark (p. 48) is completely silent about love to enemies; nor does John, who has a very different view, call for a love of enemies (p. 48). Paul, the only contemporary of the Q Sermon, seems more influenced by the original view (p. 39):

> He did not at all only praise love in general in lofty tones. He called for love to one's fellow human, and in fact not only to such as belonged to the same community of faith, even though he often called for brotherly love, but rather to people in general (Rom 13:8-10; 1 Thess 3:12; Gal 6:10). The opponents and oppressors of the Christian he does not want to consider excluded. Rather he calls for the attitude of love toward them in a way that almost permits the conjecture not only that the spirit of his Lord has touched him, but that his requirements echo in his ear (Rom 12:14-21; 1 Thess 5:15; cf. 1 Cor 4:12).

Occasional sharp words (1 Thess 2:14-16) are compared to Q 11:49-50; 13:34-35, precisely the two Q passages that were later (from O. H. Steck on) recognized as most distinctive of the Deuteronomistic redaction of Q.

76. Acts 4:32-37; 11:22.

This correlation between the composition Love-Your-Enemies and the Mission Instructions would also suggest that turning the other cheek[77] may have meant in practice not carrying a weapon[78]. A graduate student from Kenya first made me aware that it was of course obvious that the "staff" one was not to take was thought of as a weapon, a "club". I then recalled that, the first time I had an interview with the *fellah* who discovered the Nag Hammadi codices in Upper Egypt, he carried a thick, solid, heavy, polished, two-meter-long club which I hardly noticed at the time. I did not see it again until, a couple of years later, I had a first interview with his brother. In retrospect, wised up by the student from nearby Kenya, I realise that these interviews apparently had been entered into with apprehension, but had a disarming effect. The *Los Angeles Times* of 17 December 1992, reporting on the new sense of security provided by the arrival of U.S. military forces in the famine-ridden town of Baidoa in Somalia, provides the anecdote:

> Wednesday, the feeding centre was filled with optimism and a new sense of security; commodities as rare as grain in this parched land. 'Where's your gun?' Rice teased Abduhakim, 19, one of the centre's security guards. Only a day before, he had been carrying an automatic weapon. Wednesday, he was carrying a walking stick.

The stick was obviously not due to a sudden lameness, but rather was a weapon permissible in the presence of U.S. forces in a way that a gun would not be. On 14 March 1993 another *Los Angeles Times* article included a photograph bearing the caption:

> Two Somali men walk through the ruins of what was once the Hotel Aruba in the capital, Mogadishu. They carry sticks for protection.

Luke may also have understood the staff as a weapon. For when he undoes the Mission Instructions to introduce the Church Militant, he points out that swords have now become part of the approved equipment[79]. A sword is a middle-class equivalent to a poor person's club, just as in the Holy Land today an automatic rifle is a prosperous equivalent to throwing stones. The Q movement was originally defenceless. It had no alternative to loving one's enemy[80]. One may recall the injunction to make peace with one's accuser on the way to court, where one was sure

77. Q 6:29.

78. Q 10:4 / Mt 10:10. Since the staff is in Lk 9:3, but not in Lk 10:4, it is not a certain reading, but has been graded C by the International Q Project; see "The International Q Project Work Session 16 November 1990," *JBL* (1991) 496. [*The Critical Edition of Q* includes the staff.]

79. Lk 22:36, 38.

80. Q 6:27, 35.

to lose, i.e. was guilty of unpaid debts[81]. The system kept the poor guilty – as liberation theologians know all too well.

The spiritualizing trajectory of the Q movement that we have already observed is also quite apparent in the Beatitudes. Apparently there was an initial triad of blessing the poor, hungry, mourning[82], perhaps brought together on the basis of a random practice of blessing any and every victim of fate that one came across. The triad became a representative cluster standing for all such victims, with the *primus inter pares* awarded to what may have become a self-designation of the Q movement, the Poor, the Proto-Ebionites[83]. Thus this triad may already by implication have shifted the blessing away from any-and-every victim of fate to Jesus' disciples, thus marking a decisive if only gradually perceptible social formation. This becomes explicit with the secondary appending of a fourth Beatitude, where it is not a matter of victims of fate in general, but rather people of Q who are victimized because of their identification with Jesus[84]. Q later adds blessings explicitly on those who take no offence in him[85], but see what he does[86], that is to say, on the Q people themselves.

This christianizing trend is then expanded in the Matthean community by adding Beatitudes created to designate the virtues of the Q / Matthean folk: the meek, the merciful, the pure in heart, the peacemakers[87]. And the Beatitudes that had originally been formulated prior to or apart from this social formation are recast or updated to reflect this trend, as poor *in spirit*[88], hungering *and thirsting after righteousness*[89]. The Matthean, or pre-Matthean emphasis on righteousness may explain an additional beatitude for those persecuted for righteousness sake[90].

---

81. Q 12:58-59.
82. Q 6:20-21.
83. Cf. my essay, "The Sayings Gospel Q," in *The Four Gospels 1992: Festschrift F. Neirynck*, ed. F. Van Segbroeck et al. (BETL 100; Leuven: 1992) 1.361-388. [In *The Sayings Gospel Q*, pp. 319-48.]
84. Q 6:22-23.
85. Q 7:23.
86. Q 10:23. The Beatitude on those who keep God's word in Lk 11:28 may also be in Q. [In 1994 the International Q Project voted that it is indeterminate whether it is in Q, as does *The Critical Edition of Q*; John S. Kloppenborg voted with the grade of C that it is in Q.]
87. Mt 5:5, 7-9.
88. Mt 5:3 at Q 6:20.
89. Mt 5:6 at Q 6:21.
90. Mt 5:10. The usual assumption that this is Matthean redaction is challenged by Helmut Koester, *Ancient Christian Gospels: Their History and Development* (London and Philadelphia: 1990) 65, who on the basis of 1 Pet 3:14 postulates "a Jewish-Christian document that Matthew used in chapters 5–7".

Thus a movement that had its original focus on re-evaluating the status of all victims of fate, in view of the radical nature of the kingdom of God, came to identify itself as the *beati possidentes*. The Church had become aware of itself as the distinct people of God. An original liberation theology was transmuted into the social concerns of the Church.

To be sure, in quite obvious senses Jesus was not a modern liberation theologian. He was not guilty of covertly presupposing Karl Marx's system; it is more nearly the reverse. Nor did Jesus engender an effective program to counter the abysmal plight of the masses. His movement died out in Galilee with hardly a trace[91]. One hopes for a better outcome in the case of liberation theology. But Jesus did recognize the plight of the masses living without the bare necessities of life as systemic – that in any case is inherent in his otherwise obscure talk of the kingdom of God. Jesus elevated that plight to the central theme of theology, as has been rediscovered by the liberation theologians of today. And, like them, he went about doing something about it. His implementation was not successful, and in any case is not suited to meet our needs. But that we should implement his message is itself central to that message, as liberation theologians have put at the center of their message.

91. Acts 9:31.

CHAPTER 9

The Image of Jesus in Q

The twentieth century began with the quest of the historical Jesus at its peak. But the first half of the century was largely devoted to dismantling that "assured result of critical scholarship," and only in the last half of the century has there been a series of efforts to return to the study of the historical Jesus. It is the contours of these developments leading to the present status of the scholarly study of Jesus that I would like to summarize in this essay, as the context for the use of *The Critical Edition of Q*[1] for the study of Jesus today.

THE TEACHINGS OF JESUS

At the opening of the twentieth century, it was Q to which critical scholarship had naturally turned in its quest of the historical Jesus. For it was upon the sayings of Jesus that Adolf Harnack had built his "essence of Christianity":

> If, however, we take a general view of Jesus' teaching, we shall see that it may be grouped under three heads. They are each of such a nature as to contain the whole, and hence it can be exhibited in its entirety under any one of them.
> *Firstly, the kingdom of God and its coming.*
> *Secondly, God the Father and the infinite value of the human soul.*
> *Thirdly, the higher righteousness and the commandment of love*[2].

---

1. James M. Robinson, Paul Hoffmann, and John S. Kloppenborg, eds., *The Critical Edition of Q: Synopsis including the Gospels of Matthew and Luke, Mark and Thomas with English, German, and French Translations of Q and Thomas* (Leuven: Peeters and Minneapolis: Fortress, 2000). The present essay is based on this publication.

2. Adolf Harnack, *Das Wesen des Christentums: 16 Vorlesungen vor Studierenden aller Fakultäten im Wintersemester 1899/1900 an der Universität Berlin* (Leipzig: Hinrichs'sche Buchhandlung, 1900) 33. A student, Walther Becker, took down the lectures in shorthand, which Harnack edited for publication. It was an immediate best-seller: 1900, 3d ed. (11 to 15 thousand [quoted here]), 45 to 50 thousand 1903, 56 to 60 thousand 1908, 70 thousand 1925; more recent reprints: Adolf von Harnack, *Das Wesen des Christentums*: Neuauflage zum fünfzigsten Jahrestag des ersten Erscheinens mit einem Geleitwort von Rudolf Bultmann (Stuttgart: Klotz, 1950); Adolf von Harnack, *Das Wesen des Christentums*: Mit einem Geleitwort von Wolfgang Trillhaas, Gütersloher Taschenbücher/Siebenstern 227 (Gütersloh: Gütersloher Verlagshaus Mohn, 1985); Adolf von Harnack, *Das Wesen des Christentums*: Herausgegeben und kommentiert von Trutz Rendtorff (Gütersloh: Chr. Kaiser/Gütersloher Verlagshaus, 1999) 33 (1900), 40 (1985), and 87 (1999):

> But the fact that the whole of Jesus' message may be reduced to these two heads – God as the Father, and the human soul so ennobled that it can and does unite with Him – shows us that the Gospel is in no wise a positive religion like the rest; that it contains no statutory or particularistic elements; *that it is, therefore, religion itself*[3].

This sublime picture of Jesus' teaching is no doubt responsible for the emphasis in American Protestantism throughout most of the twentieth century on "the teachings of Jesus." But one should not uncritically idealize Q as a definitive ethical code. Jesus was not a theoretician in the field of ethics. Hence the sayings of Jesus in Q do not derive from reflection in the abstract, but from concrete situations. Jesus, as a person of his time, did not speak to all issues important in our time, nor did his conduct conform to all our ideals of today. "The peril of modernizing Jesus,"[4] inherent in ethical idealism's definition of the quintessence of religion, only aggravates the historian's recognition, for example, that the ideals of the Pauline church, "There is no longer Jew or Greek, there is no longer slave or free, there is no longer male and female ..." (Gal. 3:28), are topics that for Q, and to this extent apparently for Jesus, were quiescent.

This first became apparent with regard to Gentiles. Q presents Jesus caring for the Centurion's sick boy (Q 7:1-10), but without risking defilement by coming under his gentile roof (Q 7:6), even though his faith exceeded any Jesus had found in Israel (Q 7:9). The Cornelius story of Acts 10–11 makes clear what was involved in such a major step, a step apparently taken only after Jesus' death. Jesus' first disciples, as documented in Q, consisted of a Jewish community, to which the gentile mission, led by Barnabas and Paul, was added rather independently, as an

---

Überschauen wir aber die Predigt Jesu, so können wir drei Kreise aus ihr gestalten. Jeder Kreis ist so geartet, dass er die *ganze* Verkündigung enthält; in jedem kann sie daher vollständig zur Darstellung gebracht werden:
Erstlich, das Reich Gottes und sein Kommen,
Zweitens, Gott der Vater und der unendliche Wert der Menschenseele,
Drittens, die bessere Gerechtigkeit und das Gebot der Liebe.
English Translation: *What Is Christianity* (London, Edinburgh, Oxford: Williams and Norgate, and New York: Putnam, 1901, 3d revised edition [quoted here] 1904) 52.

3. Harnack, *Das Wesen des Christentums*, 41 (1900), 47 (1985), and 96 (1999):
Indem man aber die ganze Verkündigung Jesu auf diese beiden Stücke zurückführen kann – Gott als der Vater, und die menschliche Seele so geadelt, dass sie sich mit ihm zusammenzuschließen vermag und zusammenschließt –, zeigt es sich, dass das Evangelium überhaupt keine positive Religion ist wie die anderen, dass es nichts Statuarisches und Partikularistisches hat, *dass es also die Religion selbst ist.*
English Translation: *What Is Christianity*, 65.

4. Henry J. Cadbury, *The Peril of Modernizing Jesus* (New York: Macmillan, 1937).

afterthought. At the Jerusalem Council, a mutually tolerant double mission was agreed on, which at times, such as the crisis in Antioch reflected in Gal. 2:11-14, tended to break down.

The *explicit* of Q (22:30) presents Jesus' followers as judging the twelve tribes of Israel[5]. This again recognizes the focus of Jesus on Israel, yet with the judgmental recognition that Israel did not produce the needed kind of faith (Q 7:9). Hence God would, as John said (Q 3:8), have to produce children to Abraham from the (gentile) stones. Gentiles will replace Abraham, Isaac, and Jacob's lineal descendents at the eschatological banquet (Q 13:29, 28). There are invidiously favorable sayings about biblical Gentiles (but not Jesus' Gentile contemporaries): Sodom (Q 10:12), Tyre and Sidon (Q 10:14), the Queen of the South (Q 11:31), the Ninevites (Q 11:32). But they function in Q primarily as a foil to put to shame "this generation" (Q 7:31; 11:29 *bis,* 30, 31, 32, 50, 51), made up of the chosen people, Israel. There is no indication that uncircumcised Gentiles were part of the Q community.

Nor had "there is no longer slave or free" been adequately implemented. Q refers to slaves as part of the real world presupposed in parables (Q 7:8; 12:43-46; 14:21; 19:15-22), without using the occasion to condemn the inhumanity of slavery. Paul's Letter to Philemon shows that "no longer slave or free" had not been adequately addressed. The American experience in the "Bible Belt" surely shows how slavery remained unfinished business for the church down to modern times.

In a somewhat similar way the text of Q does not do justice to our modern feminist sensitivity as to the full equality of women. The most that one can say is that male-female pairs are present in Q, with which both men and women can hence identify. The male Ninevites are paired with the Queen of the South standing in judgment against Israel (Q 11:31-32); a man sowing a field with mustard seed (Q 13:18-19) is paired with a woman making bread out of yeast (Q 13:20-21); the shepherd hunting for a lost sheep (Q 15:4-5a, 7) is paired with the woman seeking a lost coin (Q 15:8-10); two males in a field (Q 17:34) are paired with two females grinding at a mill (Q 17:35). Pairings may be implicit, even

---

5. Richard A. Horsley's repeated argument, most recently in Richard A. Horsley with Jonathan A. Draper, *Whoever Hears You Hears Me: Prophets, Performance, and Tradition in Q* (Harrisburg, Pa.: Trinity Press International, 1999) 261-63: 263, understanding Q's *explicit* to have "the highly positive sense of liberating/delivering/saving/effecting justice for," as the basis for the thesis "that the context of those discourses and of Q as a whole was the renewal of Israel (movement) underway," has been already adequately refuted by John S. Kloppenborg, "The Sayings Gospel Q and the Quest of the Historical Jesus," *HTR* 89 (1996) 307-44: 327-28.

if less visible, in such formulations as bread (baked by women) and fish (caught by fishermen) in Q 11:11-12, and ravens (in contrast to men working in the fields) and lilies (in contrast to women making cloth) in Q 12:24, 27-28. The Q movement's disruption of family ties between generations involves the women as well as the men (Q 12:53; 14:26). Though such pairings thus recognize women as well as men, no inclusive point is explicitly scored. The patriarchal culture is tacitly presupposed, in such formulations as "marrying and giving in marriage" (Q 17:27), and in addressing God as "Father" (Q 10:21 *bis;* 11:2; cf. 6:36; 10:22 *bis;* 11:13; 12:30)[6].

In sum, there are major ethical problems of society that Q, and hence presumably Jesus, did not adequately address. It is clear that the "teachings of Jesus" as reflected in Q do not present the "political correctness" of an ethical idealism for today.

JESUS THE APOCALYPTICIST

The central position that Q had attained in terms of ethical idealism a century ago did not go unchallenged at the time. It was Albert Schweitzer who carried to its ultimate consequences a dramatic renunciation of that quest of the historical Jesus, as a modernization of Jesus effected by projecting Protestant liberalism's ideology back on him.

Central to Schweitzer's own solution was his assumption that Q did not exist. For he preferred Ferdinand Christian Baur's prioritizing of Matthew rather than the development of the Q hypothesis from its discovery in 1838 by Christian Hermann Weisse to its definitive demonstration in 1863 by Heinrich Julius Holtzmann.

> Research was initially spared having to experience the problem in its whole weight, in that it, under the influence of Christian Hermann Weiße, *Die Evangelienfrage* (1856), and Heinrich Julius Holtzmann, *Die synoptischen*

6. Luise Schottroff, *Itinerant Prophetesses: A Feminist Analysis of the Sayings Source Q*, Occasional Papers 21 (Claremont, Calif.: Institute for Antiquity and Christianity, 1991); Schottroff, "Wanderprophetinnen: Eine feministische Analyse der Logienquelle," *EvT* 51 (1991) 332-44. Very critical of the Jesus of Q: Helga Melzer-Keller, *Jesus und die Frauen: Eine Verhältnisbestimmung nach den synoptischen Überlieferungen*, Herders biblische Studien 14 (Freiburg: Herder, 1997), Teil IV: "Jesus und die Frauen in der Logienquelle," 330-53; Melzer-Keller, "Frauen in der Logienquelle und ihrem Trägerkreis: Ist Q das Zeugnis einer patriarchatskritischen, egalitären Bewegung?" in *Wenn Drei das Gleiche sagen ... Studien zu den ersten drei Evangelien,* ed. Stefan H. Brandenburger and Thomas Hieke, Theologie 14 (Münster: Lit, 1998) 37-62; Melzer-Keller, "Wie frauenfreundlich ist die Logienquelle?" *BiKi* 54 (1999) 89-92.

Evangelien (1863), gives up the view advocated by Ferdinand Christian Baur (1792–1860) and the Tübingen School, to the effect that the Gospel of Matthew is the oldest and most original, and regards the Gospel of Mark to be this. The preference for the shorter Gospel made it possible for it to evaluate the significant material that Matthew offers over and beyond that of Mark as not fully valid. And it is precisely this that contains the discourses and reports in which Jesus' thought world is shown to belong to that of late Jewish eschatology. It is especially the Sermon on the Mount (Matthew 5–7), the great discourse at the sending forth of the disciples (Matthew 10), the inquiry of the Baptist and the statements of Jesus it called forth (Matthew 11), the discourse on the coming of the Son of Man and the judgment he will hold (Matthew 25) ....

For the quest of the historical Jesus, the point is not which of the two oldest Gospels could be a little bit older than the other. Incidentally, this literary question will hardly ever be solved. With the fragmentary report of Mark, the historical problem of the life of Jesus could not be resolved, indeed would not even come in view. The reports of the two oldest Gospels are in their way of equal value. That of Matthew is, however, as the more complete, of more value. In substance, Ferdinand Christian Baur and his school, in preferring it, are still right[7].

7. Albert Schweitzer, *Von Reimarus zu Wrede: Die Geschichte der Leben-Jesu-Forschung* (Tübingen: Mohr-Siebeck, 1906). The second edition, entitled only *Die Geschichte der Leben-Jesu-Forschung* (Tübingen: Mohr-Siebeck, 1913), is considerably revised, especially in the concluding sections under discussion here. The quotations are from the first edition, with the pagination in the second edition, when parallel (though, even then, copyedited to produce a smoother text), given in parentheses, both according to the 6th ed. of 1951, and the republication (for which I wrote the Einführung) as Siebenstern-Taschenbuch 77/78, Munich, 1966. A retrospective "Vorrede" dated 1950, included only in the German editions, beginning with the 6th edition of 1951, is quoted here, vi, xii (1951) and 30, 36 (1966):

Das Problem in seiner ganzen Schwere erfahren zu müssen bleibt der Forschung vorerst dadurch erspart, daß sie unter dem Einfluß von Christian Hermann Weißes "Die Evangelienfrage" (1856) und Heinrich Julius Holtzmanns "Die synoptischen Evangelien" (1863) die von Ferdinand Christian Baur (1792–1860) und der Tübinger-schule vertretene Ansicht, daß das Matthäusevangelium das älteste und ursprünglichste sei, aufgibt und als solches das Markusevangelium ansieht. Die Bevorzugung dieses kürzeren Evangeliums erlaubt es ihr, das bedeutende Material, das Matthäus über das des Markus hinaus bietet, nicht als ganz vollgültig zu bewerten. Und gerade dieses enthält die Reden und Berichte, in denen sich die Zugehörigkeit der Gedankenwelt Jesu zu der spatjüdischen Eschatologie bekundet. Vornehmlich sind dies die Bergpredigt (Mt 5–7), die große Rede bei der Aussendung der Jünger (Mt 10), die Anfrage des Täufers und die durch sie veranlaßten Äußerungen Jesu (Mt 11), die Rede vom Kommen des Menschensohnes und des von ihm abzuhaltenden Gerichts (Mt 25) ....

Für die Leben-Jesu-Forschung kommt es nicht darauf an, welches der beiden ältesten Evangelien ein klein wenig älter sein konnte als das andere. Diese literarische Frage wird sich überdies kaum je entscheiden lassen. Mit dem lückenhaften Bericht des Markus wäre das historische Problem des Lebens Jesu nicht zu lösen, ja nicht einmal zu erkennen gewesen. Die Berichte der beiden ältesten Evangelien sind ihrer Art nach gleichwertig. Das des Matthäus ist aber als das vollständigere das

Though Schweitzer was guarded in his statements (Holtzmann had, after all, been his professor in Strassburg), the position that he took on the sources only makes sense if he considered the canonical Gospel of Matthew to be the product of an eyewitness, which amounts to treating it as a definitive work of the apostle Matthew, the prevalent precritical view ever since Papias. He simply dismissed, as absurd, efforts to dismantle into its sources Matthew's Mission Instructions, whose detailed historicity was decisive for his own interpretation of Jesus' public ministry. Whereas one maintained, then and now, that material from the Markan apocalypse was interpolated by Matthew into the Mission Instructions of Mark and Q, which were conflated both with each other and with other Q and special Matthean material, Schweitzer maintained:

> Thus this discourse [Matt. 10] is historical as a whole and down to the smallest detail precisely because, according to the view of modern theology, it must be judged unhistorical ....
>
> That being so, we may judge with what right the modern psychological theology dismisses the great Matthean discourses off-hand as mere "composite structures." Just let any one try to show how the Evangelist when he was racking his brains over the task of making a "discourse at the sending forth of the disciples," half by the method of piecing it together out of traditional sayings and "primitive theology," and half by inventing it, lighted on the curious idea of making Jesus speak entirely of inopportune and unpractical matters; and of then going on to provide the evidence that they never happened[8].

---

wertvollere. Sachlich haben Ferdinand Christian Baur und seine Schüler mit ihrer Bevorzugung desselben Recht behalten.

(In the 1951 edition Baur's last name is omitted, but is added in the 1966 edition.) ET: *The Quest of the Historical Jesus: A Critical Study of Its Progress from Reimarus to Wrede* (New York: Macmillan, 1910). Even the paperback edition of 1961 (for which I wrote the Introduction) and its reprints – ninth printing 1975 – lack this "Vorrede" of 1950. Christian Hermann Weisse's 2-volume basic work of 1838, *Die evangelische Geschichte kritisch und philosophisch bearbeitet* (Leipzig: Breitkopf und Härtel), is not mentioned in this retrospective summary.

8. Schweitzer, *Von Reimarus zu Wrede*, 360 (*Die Geschichte der Leben-Jesu-Forschung*, 410 [1951] and 420 [1966]):

So ist die Aussendungsrede als Ganzes und bis in das kleinste Detail geschichtlich, gerade weil sie nach der Auffassung der modernen Theologie als ungeschichtlich erfunden werden muß....

Danach beurteile man, mit welchem Recht die modern-psychologische Theologie die großen matthäischen Reden kurzerhand als "Redekompositionen" hinstellt. Man beweise doch einmal, wie der Evangelist, der an seiner Feder saugte, um eine Aussendungsrede aus überlieferten Sprüchen und aus der "Gemeindetheologie" halb zusammenzustellen, halb zu erfinden, auf den seltsamen Gedanken kommen konnte, Jesum von lauter unzeitgemäßen und unsachlichen Dingen reden zu lassen und nachher selber zu konstatieren, daß sie nicht in Erfüllung gingen.

ET: *The Quest of the Historical Jesus*, 363.

He remained completely unaware of how form and redaction criticism would show the Gospels to be mirrors of the intervening time of the church in their portrayal of Jesus' time. Hence he could hang his whole thesis on Matt. 10:23, "... you will not have gone through all the towns of Israel before the Son of Man comes," which is a bit of special Matthean material absent both from the Mission Discourse of Q and from the Mission Discourse of Mark, reflecting no doubt only the history of the Matthean community.

The result was Schweitzer's own bizarre "life of Jesus," with which his *Quest of the Historical Jesus* concluded. His point of departure was Jesus' fascination with parables of harvest:

> If this genuinely "historical" interpretation of the mystery of the Kingdom of God is correct, Jesus must have expected the coming of the Kingdom at harvest time. And that is just what He did expect. It is for that reason that He sends out His disciples to make known in Israel, as speedily as may be, what is about to happen[9].

The Mission of the Twelve was to be Jesus' final act before the end:

> He tells them in plain words (Matt. x. 23), that He does not expect to see them back in the present age. The Parousia of the Son of Man, [359] which is logically and temporally identical with the dawn of the kingdom, will take place before they shall have completed a hasty journey through the cities of Israel to announce it[10].

Schweitzer described "the significance of the sending forth of the disciples and the discourse which Jesus uttered upon that occasion" as follows:

> Jesus' purpose is to set in motion the eschatological development of history, to let loose the final woes, the confusion and strife, from which shall issue

---

9. Schweitzer, *Von Reimarus zu Wrede*, 355 (*Die Geschichte der Leben-Jesu-Forschung*, 405 [1951] and 415 [1966]):
   Ist diese in Wahrheit "historische" Deutung des Geheimnisses des Reiches Gottes richtig, so muß Jesus zur Erntezeit den Anbruch des Reiches Gottes erwartet haben. Das hat er wirklich getan. Darum sendet er ja die Jünger aus, damit sie eilend in Israel verkünden, was kommen soll.
   ET: *The Quest of the Historical Jesus*, 358.

10. Schweitzer, *Von Reimarus zu Wrede*, 355 (*Die Geschichte der Leben-Jesu-Forschung*, 405 [1951] and 416 [1966]):
   Jesus sagt den Jüngern in dürren Worten, Mt 10 23, daß er sie in diesem Äon nicht mehr zurückerwartet. Die Parusie des Menschensohnes, die mit dem Einbruch des Reiches logisch und zeitlich identisch ist, wird stattfinden, ehe sie mit ihrer Verkündigung die Städte Israels durcheilt haben.
   ET: *The Quest of the Historical Jesus*, 358-59.

the Parousia, and so to introduce the supra-mundane phase of the eschatological drama[11].

He was convinced that "at the time of their mission," Jesus "did not expect them to return before the Parousia."[12] But that is in fact just what happened:

There followed neither the sufferings, nor the outpouring of the Spirit, nor the Parousia of the Son of Man. The disciples returned safe and sound and full of a proud satisfaction; for one promise had been realized – the power which had been given them over the demons[13].

Schweitzer drew the inevitable consequence:

It is equally clear, and here the dogmatic considerations which guided the resolutions of Jesus become still more prominent, that this prediction was not fulfilled. The disciples returned to Him; and the appearing of the Son of Man had not taken place. The actual history disavowed the dogmatic history on which the action of Jesus had been based. An event of supernatural history which must take place, and must take place at that particular point of time, failed to come about. That was for Jesus, who lived wholly in the dogmatic history, the first "historical" occurrence, the central event which closed the former period of His activity and gave the coming period a new character[14].

---

11. Schweitzer, *Von Reimarus zu Wrede*, 367:
Diese Erwägungen über den besonderen Charakter der synoptischen Eschatologie waren notwendig, um die Bedeutung der Aussendung und der sie begleitenden Rede zu verstehen. Jesus will die eschatologische Geschichte in Gang bringen, die Enddrangsal, die Verwirrung und den Aufruhr, aus denen die Parusie hervorgehen soll, entfesseln und die überirdische Phase des eschatologischen Dramas einleiten.
ET: *The Quest of the Historical Jesus*, 371.
12. Schweitzer, *Von Reimarus zu Wrede*, 383: "... zur Zeit der Aussendung, als er sie vor der Parusie nicht mehr zurückerwartete ...." ET: *The Quest of the Historical Jesus*, 386.
13. Schweitzer, *Von Reimarus zu Wrede*, 360 (*Die Geschichte der Leben-Jesu-Forschung*, 411 [1951] and 421 [1966]):
Es traf aber weder das Leiden, noch die Geistesausgießung, noch die Parusie des Menschensohnes ein, sondern gesund und frisch, voll stolzer Genugtuung kehrten die Jünger zum Herrn zurück. Eine Verheißung war real geworden: die Vollmacht, die er ihnen über die Dämonen gegeben.
ET: *The Quest of the Historical Jesus*, 364. Schweitzer did not point out that this anticlimactic return of the disciples from their mission is not mentioned in Matthew 10, but only in Mark 6:30 and Luke 10:17-20. Indeed the "proud satisfaction" in "the power which had been given them over the demons" is only in Luke, although Schweitzer had confidence primarily in Matthew, and to a lesser extent in Mark, and even less in Luke.
14. Schweitzer, *Von Reimarus zu Wrede*, 355 (*Die Geschichte der Leben-Jesu-Forschung*, 406 [1951] and 416 [1966]):
Ebenso klar ist aber, und hier tritt das Dogmatische der Entschließungen Jesu noch stärker hervor, daß diese Weissagung nicht in Erfüllung ging. Die Jünger kehrten zu ihm zurück und die Erscheinung des Menschensohnes fand nicht statt. Die natürliche Geschichte desavouierte die dogmatische, nach welcher Jesus gehandelt hatte.

The failure of the apocalyptic end to come before the end of the mission must have been a terrible letdown for Jesus, to such an extent that he felt compelled to change his strategy:

> This change was due to the non-fulfillment of the promises made in the discourse at the sending forth of the Twelve. He had thought then to let loose the final tribulation and so compel the coming of the Kingdom. And the cataclysm had not occurred. He had expected it also after the return of the disciples ....
>
> In leaving Galilee He abandoned the hope that the final tribulation would begin of itself. If it delays, that means that there is still something to be done, and yet another of the violent must lay violent hands upon the Kingdom of God. The movement of repentance had not been sufficient. When, in accordance with His commission, by sending forth the disciples with their message, he hurled the fire-brand which should kindle the fiery trials of the Last Time, the flame went out[15].

So Jesus determined to go to Jerusalem for Passover, in order to provoke there his own martyrdom as an alternate way to compel God to bring in the end:

> ... His death must at last compel the Coming of the Kingdom ....
>
> The new thought of His own passion has its basis therefore in the authority with which Jesus was armed to bring about the beginning of the final tribulation .... For now He identifies his condemnation and execution, which are to take place on natural lines, with the predicted pre-Messianic tribulations. This imperious forcing of eschatology into history is also its destruction; its assertion and abandonment at the same time[16].

Ein Ereignis der übernatürlichen Geschichte, welches stattfinden mußte, in jenem Zeitpunkte stattfinden mußte, blieb aus. Das war für Jesus, der einzig in der dogmatischen Geschichte lebte, das erste "geschichtliche" Ereignis, das Zentralereignis, welches seine öffentliche Tätigkeit nach rückwärts abschließt, nach vorn neu orientiert.
ET: *The Quest of the Historical Jesus*, 359.
15. Schweitzer, *Von Reimarus zu Wrede*, 385-86:
   Die Wandlung beruht auf dem Nichteintreten der Verheißungen der Aussendungsrede. Er hatte damals die Enddrangsal zu entfachen gemeint, um damit das Reich herbeizuzwingen. Und der Aufruhr war ausgeblieben. Er hatte ihn auch nach der Rückkehr der Jünger noch erwartet ....
   Mit dem Verlassen des Bodens Galiläas gibt er die Hoffnung auf, daß sich die Drangsal von sich aus einstellen werde. Wenn sie ausbleibt, will dies besagen, daß noch eine Leistung fehlt und noch ein Gewalttätiger zu den Vergewaltigern des Reiches Gottes hinzutreten müsse. Die Bußbewegung hatte nicht ausgereicht. Als er seiner Vollmacht gemäß bei der Aussendung den Feuerbrand, der die Drangsal zum Auslodern bringen sollte, in die Welt schleuderte, erlosch er.
ET: *The Quest of the Historical Jesus*, 389.
16. Schweitzer, *Von Reimarus zu Wrede*, 387, 388:
   ... sein Tod – endlich – das Reich herbeizwingt ...
   Der neue Leidensgedanke ist also seinem Wesen nach begründet in der auf das Heraufführen der Drangsal gehenden Vollmacht, mit welcher Jesus in der Welt auftritt

This heroic resolve ended in a second, even more painful encounter with actual history, leading to his last anguished cry: "My God, my God, why have you abandoned me?" In summary:

> The Baptist appears, and cries: "Repent, for the Kingdom of Heaven is at hand." Soon after that comes Jesus, and in the knowledge that He is the coming Son of Man lays hold of the wheel of the world to set it moving on that last revolution which is to bring all ordinary history to a close. It refuses to turn, and He throws Himself upon it. Then it does turn; and crushes Him. Instead of bringing in the eschatological conditions, He has destroyed them. The wheel rolls onward, and the mangled body of the one immeasurably great Man, who was strong enough to think of Himself as the spiritual ruler of mankind and to bend history to His purpose, is hanging upon it still. That is His victory and His reign[17].

Q OR THE KERYGMA

Between the two world wars, the focus of attention moved to the oral transmission of traditions under the influence of their social settings, thus shifting away from the social setting in the public ministry of Jesus to social settings in the primitive church, and shifting away from written sources embedded in the Gospels to oral material the Evangelists collected.

Though the form critics Rudolf Bultmann and Martin Dibelius both assumed the existence of Q, their point of departure was more nearly the Q of Julius Wellhausen[18] than that of Adolf Harnack. For it was Wellhausen who had anticipated the new kerygmatic orientation[19].

> .... Denn jetzt identifiziert er seine natürliche Verurteilung und Hinrichtung mit der geweissagten vormessianischcn Drangsal. Dieses gewaltsame Hineinzerren der Eschatologie in die Geschichte ist zugleich ihre Aufhebung; ein Bejahen und Preisgeben zugleich.

ET: *The Quest of the Historical Jesus*, 390-91.

17. Schweitzer, *Von Reimarus zu Wrede*, 367:

> Da erscheint der Täufer und ruft: Tuet Buße! das Reich Gottes ist nahe herbeigekommen! Kurz darauf greift Jesus, als der, welcher sich als den kommenden Menschensohn weiß, in die Speichen des Weltrades, daß es in Bewegung komme, die letzte Drehung mache und die natürliche Geschichte der Welt zu Ende bringe. Da es nicht geht, hängt er sich dran. Es dreht sich und zermalmt ihn. Statt die Eschatologie zu bringen, hat er sie vernichtet. Das Weltrad dreht sich weiter und die Fetzen des Leichnams des einzig unermeßlich großen Menschen, der gewaltig genug war, um sich als den geistigen Herrscher der Menschheit zu erfassen und die Geschichte zu vergewaltigen, hängen noch immer daran. Das ist sein Siegen und Herrschen.

ET: *The Quest of the Historical Jesus*, 370-71.

18. Bultmann's only essay on Q, written before World War I, came only two years after Wellhausen's second edition, and built explicitly on him rather than on Harnack: "Was läßt die Spruchquelle über die Urgemeinde erkennen?" *Oldenburgisches Kirchenblatt* 19 (1913) 35-37, 41-44: 35:

It is as the crucified, resurrected and returning one that Jesus is the Christian Messiah, not as religious teacher. The apostolic gospel, which preaches faith in the Christ, is the real one, and not the gospel of Jesus which prescribes to the church its moral.... And the expression purportedly committed by Harnack, "not the Son, but only the Father belongs in the Gospel," is basically false, if it is intended to claim a fact and not merely to express a postulate[20].

Harnack had indeed said: *"The Gospel, as Jesus proclaimed it, has to do with the Father only and not with the Son."*[21] Wellhausen, apparently

Den folgenden Ausführungen liegt also eine bestimmte Auffassung der synoptischen Frage zu Grunde, die ich natürlich hier nicht näher entwickeln kann. Ich verweise auf B. Weiß, A. Jülicher und J. Wellhausen.
ET: "What the Sayings Source Reveals about the Early Church," *The Shape of Q: Signal Essays on the Sayings Gospel*, ed. John S. Kloppenborg (Minneapolis: Fortress, 1994) 23-34: 23, n. 1:
    The following explication presupposes a definite solution to the Synoptic problem, which obviously I cannot pursue in more detail here. I refer the reader to B. Weiss 1908; Jülicher 1904; and Wellhausen 1905, 1911.
    Rudolf Bultmann, *Jesus*, 1926, 18 (reprint Tübingen: Mohr-Siebeck, 1951, 16): "Die Übersetzung der evangelischen Texte schließt sich oft an die von J. Wellhausen an." ET: "The translation of the Gospel texts often makes use of that of J. Wellhausen." Martin Dibelius, *Die Formgeschichte des Evangeliums* (Tübingen: Mohr-Siebeck, 1919, revised 1933, 2d ed., 1966, 5th ed., ed. Günther Bornkamm [quoted here]) 236, n. 1. ET: *From Tradition to Gospel*, trans. Bertram Lee Woolf (New York: Scribners, n.d.) 235, n. 1, appeals to the first edition of Julius Wellhausen, *Einleitung in die drei ersten Evangelien* (Berlin: Reimer, 1905, 1st ed., 1911, 2d ed.) 66-67, for his own skepticism (quoted below) regarding Q.
    19. The second revised edition of Julius Wellhausen, *Einleitung in die drei ersten Evangelien*, was reprinted with the same pagination in Wellhausen's *Evangelienkommentare* (Berlin and New York: de Gruyter, 1987), with an "Einleitung" by Martin Hengel, who commented, vi-vii: "Er endet mit einer harschen Kritik der Leben-Jesu-Forschung des 19. Jh.s, die wesentlich über die A. Schweitzers, mit dem er sich kritisch auseinandersetzt, hinausgeht und die sich in manchen Punkten mit Martin Kähler und der frühen dialektischen Theologie K. [vii] Barths und R. Bultmanns berührt. In der dadurch befruchteten kritischen Evangelienforschung zwischen den beiden Weltkriegen wird die Wirkung des Neutestamentlers Wellhausen am ehesten sichtbar."
    20. Wellhausen, *Evangelienkommentare*, 153, also quoted by Hengel, "Einleitung," vii:
        Als der Gekreuzigte, Auferstandene und Wiederkommende ist Jesus der christliche Messias, nicht als Religionslehrer. Das apostolische Evangelium, welches den Glauben an den Christus predigt, ist das eigentliche, und nicht das Evangelium Jesu, welches der Kirche ihre Moral vorschreibt .... Und der angeblich von Harnack getane Ausspruch: "nicht der Sohn, sondern nur der Vater gehört ins Evangelium" ist grundfalsch, wenn damit ein Faktum behauptet und nicht nur ein Postulat ausgesprochen werden soll.
    Hengel, vi, inaccurately states that chapter 17 of the second edition ("Das Evangelium und das Christentum," 147-53) corresponds to chapter 12 of the first edition, which, however, in fact corresponds to chapter 10 of the second ("Das Evangelium und Jesus von Nazareth," 98-104). There is in the first edition no chapter equivalent to chapter 17 of the second edition. Hence the quotation is not in the first edition at all.
    21. Harnack, *Das Wesen des Christentums*, 91 (1900) and 90 (1985): *"Nicht der Sohn, sondern allein der Vater gehört in das Evangelium, wie es Jesus verkündigt hat, hinein."* ET: *What Is Christianity*, 147.

quoting from hearsay, left out the decisive *"as Jesus proclaimed it."*[22] The "Gospel" that Wellhausen has in view is of course that of the church, i.e., the kerygma, which became more nearly what one could refer to as "the essence of Christianity" down through the history of the church, e.g., in the form of the *Apostolicum* and subsequent creeds, whereas Jesus' message was largely overlooked, though occasionally rediscovered, as by Francis of Assisi.

This debate between Wellhausen and Harnack was to a remarkable extent repeated in 1923 in a debate between Karl Barth and Harnack. Here it is quite clear that dialectic theology created a theological climate in which Wellhausen's position regarding the relative unimportance, not to say illegitimacy, of Q would have the ascendancy[23].

Harnack spoke of "the close connection, even equating, of love for God and love for one's neighbor which constitutes the heart of the gospel,"[24] to which Barth replied:

> Does anything show more clearly than this "heart" (not of the gospel, but of the law), that God does not make alive unless he first slays?[25]

---

22. Harnack, *Das Wesen des Christentums*, in the endnotes added to the 1908 edition (56th to 60th thousand), drew attention to this omission as distorting his position (on p. 183 of the 1950 edition and pp. 154-55, n. 22, of the 1999 edition):
Dieses Wort ist von vielen Seiten aufs schärfste bekämpft, aber nicht widerlegt worden. Ich habe nichts an ihm zu ändern. Nur sind die Worte: "Wie es Jesus verkündigt hat," hier kursiv gesetzt worden, weil sie von vielen Gegnern übersehen worden sind. Dass Jesus in das Evangelium, wie es Paulus und die Evangelisten verkündigt haben, nicht nur hineingehört, sondern den eigentlichen Inhalt dieses Evangeliums bildet, braucht nicht erst gesagt zu werden.
23. This exchange was published in *Die christliche Welt*, 1923, as follows: Harnack: "Fünfzehn Fragen an die Verächter der wissenschaftlichen Theologie unter den Theologen," 6-8; Barth: "Fünfzehn Antworten an Herrn Professor von Harnack," 89-91; Harnack: "Offener Brief an Herrn Professor K. Barth," 142-44; Barth: "Antwort auf Herrn Professor von Harnacks offenen Brief," 244-52; and Harnack: "Nachwort zu meinem offenen Brief an Herrn Professor Karl Barth," 305-6. This debate has been republished in Barth's *Gesammelte Vorträge*, vol. 3: *Theologische Fragen und Antworten* (Zollikon: Evangelischer Verlag, 1957) 7-31: 7-9, 9-13, 13-17, 18-30, 30-31 (quoted here). ET in *The Beginnings of Dialectic Theology*, vol. 1, ed. James M. Robinson (Richmond, Va.: John Knox, 1968); Harnack: "Fifteen Questions to Those Among the Theologians Who Are Contemptuous of the Scientific Theology," 165-66; Barth: "Fifteen Answers to Professor von Harnack," 167-70; Harnack: "An Open Letter to Professor Karl Barth," 171-74; Barth: "An Answer to Professor von Harnack's Open Letter," 175-85; and Harnack: "Postscript to My Open Letter to Professor Karl Barth," 186-87.
24. Harnack, "Fünfzehn Fragen," 8: "... die enge Verbindung, ja Gleichsetzung der Gottes- und Nächstenliebe, welche den Kern des Evangeliums bildet, ..." ET: "Fifteen Questions," 165.
25. Barth, "Fünfzehn Antworten," 11: "Was zeigt deutlicher als dieser 'Kern' (nicht des Evangeliums, aber des Gesetzes), daß Gott nicht lebendig macht, er töte denn zuvor?" ET: "Fifteen Answers," 168.

Thus the central sayings of Jesus (Mark 12:28-34; Matt. 22:34-40; Luke 10:25-28) that Harnack hailed as "gospel" were for Barth "law," over against which he appealed to the "gospel" of God granting life only in death.

It was primarily in terms of the history of religions that Wellhausen had made it clear that "Jesus was no Christian, but rather a Jew."[26] This was echoed by Bultmann:

> I am further attacked because in my book *Primitive Christianity* I have not described Jesus' preaching in the chapter on "Primitive Christianity," but rather in the chapter on "Judaism," and hence have conceived of Jesus as a Jew. Similarly, the objection has been raised that in my *Theology of the New Testament* I have stated that Jesus' preaching belongs to the presuppositions of New Testament theology. Over against the reproach that I conceive of Jesus as a Jew and assign him to the sphere of Judaism I must first of all simply ask: Was Jesus – the historical Jesus! – a Christian? Certainly not, if Christian faith is faith in him as the Christ. And even if he should have known that he was the Christ ("Messiah") and should actually have demanded faith in himself as the Christ, then he would still not have been a Christian and ought not to be described as the subject of Christian faith, though he is nevertheless its object[27].

Yet the implication of this history-of-religions classification of Jesus as Jew by Wellhausen and Bultmann was heard theologically by Barth as the dialectic of law and gospel, in which sense Q is by definition not gospel, but law.

---

26. Wellhausen, *Einleitung in die drei ersten Evangelien* (Berlin: Georg Reimer, 1905, 1st ed., 1911, 2d ed., *Nachdruck* of the second edition, *Evangelienkommentare*; Berlin: Walter de Gruyter, 1987) 1905, 1st ed., 113; 1911, 2d ed., 102: "Jesus war kein Christ, sondern Jude."

27. Rudolf Bultmann, "Das Verhältnis der urchristlichen Christusbotschaft zum historischen Jesus," SHAW.PH, Jg. 1960, Abh. 3 (Heidelberg: Winter, 1960, 1st ed., 1962, 3d ed.) 8:

> Nun werde ich ferner angegriffen, weil ich in meinem Buch "Das Urchristentum im Rahmen der antiken Religionen" die Verkündigung Jesu nicht in dem Kap. "Das Urchristentum," sondern im Kapitel "Das Judentum" dargestellt, Jesus also als Juden aufgefaßt habe. Im gleichen Sinne hat man beanstandet, daß ich in meiner "Theologie des Neuen Testaments" gesagt habe, die Verkündigung Jesu gehöre zu den *Voraussetzungen* der Neutestamentlichen Theologie. Gegenüber dem Vorwurf, daß ich Jesus als Juden verstehe und ihn in den Bereich des Judentums rechne, habe ich zunächst einfach zu fragen: war Jesus – der historische Jesus! – denn ein Christ? Nun, wenn christlicher Glaube der Glaube an ihn als den Christus ist, doch gewiß nicht, und selbst wenn er sich als den Christus ('Messias') gewußt haben und gar den Glauben an sich als den Christus gefordert haben sollte, so wäre er immer noch kein Christ und nicht als Subjekt des christlichen Glaubens, dessen Objekt er doch ist, zu bezeichnen.

ET: "The Primitive Christian Kerygma and the Historical Jesus," in *The Historical Jesus and the Kerygmatic Christ*, ed. Carl E. Braaten and Roy A. Harrisville (Nashville: Abingdon, 1964) 15-42: 19.

Whereas Q uses the verb that etymologically corresponds to the noun "gospel" to refer to its sayings as "evangelizing the poor" (Q 7:22), Paul makes clear that any other "gospel" than his kerygma, even if it were to come from an angel, is anathema (Gal. 1:8-9). This tension persists down to the present, as the theological background of the discussion as to whether Sayings Gospels such as Q and the Gospel of Thomas should be called Gospels at all[28].

There were many Gospels circulating in early Christianity. Even those that the early church did not canonize were nonetheless called Gospels, and so they are still called Gospels. But they were declassified in the nineteenth century, by inserting the pejorative adjective "apocryphal" ("hidden"), and by assigning them to the postapostolic age. Yet this reasoning does not function in the case of Q, which is older than the canonical Gospels, and is no longer hidden, but rather has resurfaced, visible in Matthew and Luke, and thus indirectly in the canon. And Q texts have, down through the ages, in their Matthean and Lukan form, been the basis for preaching, which was originally the function the designation *canonical* had in view. Furthermore, since Q consists of sayings ascribed to Jesus, it is ultimately based on his Galilean disciples – their memory, reformulation, and reuse of what Jesus had said. On the other hand, none of the canonical Gospels was written by an apostle or eyewitness. Hence the relative appropriateness of calling Q also a Gospel should not be underestimated.

THE IMAGE OF JESUS IN Q

Albert Schweitzer resolved to move beyond Johannes Weiß's limitation to the eschatological sayings of Jesus[29], in order to present the resultant eschatological "conduct and action" of Jesus:

> Johannes Weiß demonstrates the thoroughly eschatological character of Jesus' proclamation of the kingdom of God. My contribution consists primarily in that I proceed to make comprehensible not only his proclamation but also his conduct and action as conditioned by the eschatological expectation[30].

---

28. For the resultant discussion about the legitimacy of calling Q a "Sayings Gospel," see Frans Neirynck, "Q: From Source to Gospel," *ETL* 71 (1995) 421-34.

29. Johannes Weiß, *Die Predigt Jesu vom Reiche Gottes* (Göttingen: Vandenhoeck & Ruprecht, 1892). ET: *Jesus' Proclamation of the Kingdom of God* (Philadelphia: Fortress, 1971).

30. Schweitzer, *Die Geschichte der Leben-Jesu-Forschung*, "Vorrede zur sechsten Auflage," viii [1951] and 32 [1966]:

> Johannes Weiß weist den durchaus eschatologischen Charakter der Verkündigung Jesu vom Reiche Gottes nach. Mein Beitrag besteht hauptsächlich darin, daß

But Schweitzer's presentation of Jesus as a deluded fanatic had such disastrous results that subsequent scholarship has in all timidity retreated to Weiß's limitation to the sayings of Jesus. This is exemplified perhaps most clearly in Bultmann's *Jesus and the Word*[31]. Yet Schweitzer was in a sense correct, that Jesus' message must have meant something in Jesus' actual practice. If Schweitzer found the key in Matthew's redactional Mission Instructions, which he took to be historically factual down to the last detail, and as a result depicted a "public ministry" that in fact never took place, perhaps the archaic Mission Instructions of Q can provide a more solid foundation for what actually went on during Jesus' Galilean ministry.

The best that the Synoptic Gospels could do by way of presenting Jesus' Galilean ministry was to assemble disparate anecdotes that produced portrayals of Jesus wandering rather aimlessly from place to place, until they have Jesus steadfastly turn to Jerusalem to die, with a bee-line, purposeful itinerary based on the kerygma. But it is more reasonable to assume that Jesus did in fact have something in mind for his Galilean ministry. His plan of action may be relatively accurately reflected in the Mission Instructions of Q. For Gerd Theissen is probably right that "the earliest Christian itinerant charismatics continued the preaching and life-style of Jesus."[32] Hence, if one uses the archaic sayings collections to

ich dazu fortschreite, nicht nur seine Verkündigung sondern auch sein Verhalten und Handeln als durch die eschatologische Erwartung bedingt begreiflich zu machen.

31. Rudolf Bultmann, *Jesus*, Die Unsterblichen: Die geistigen Heroen der Menschheit in ihrem Leben und Wirken mit zahlreichen Illustrationen 1 (Berlin: Deutsche Bibliothek, n.d. [1926]). ET: *Jesus and the Word* (New York: Scribner's Sons, 1934). In the "Translators' Preface to the New Edition" of 1958, Louise Pettibone Smith and Erminie Huntress Latero explain the enlarged title: "It was felt by both publishers and translators that the title, *Jesus and the Word*, would convey a more definite idea of the content and viewpoint of the book than the original title, *Jesus*. This change was made with the approval of the author."

32. Theissen and Merz, *Der historische Jesus*, 28: "Urchristliche Wandercharismatiker führten den Predigt- und Lebensstil Jesu weiter." ET: *The Historical Jesus*, 10. The footnote refers to Theissen's basic essay in this regard, "Wanderradikalismus: Literatursoziologische Aspekte der Überlieferung von Worten Jesu im Urchristentum," *ZTK* 70 (1973) 245-71, reprinted in: Theissen, *Studien zur Soziologie des Urchristentums*, WUNT 19 (Tübingen: Mohr-Siebeck, 1979, 1st ed., 1989, 3d ed.) 79-105, and his monograph *Soziologie der Jesusbewegung: Ein Beitrag zur Entstehungsgeschichte des Urchristentums* (Munich: Kaiser, 1977, 1st ed., 1991, 6th ed.). ET: "Itinerant Radicalism. The Tradition of Jesus' Sayings from the Perspective of the Sociology of Literature," an abbreviation in *The Bible and Liberation: A Radical Religion Reader*, ed. Antoinette Wire (Berkeley, Calif.: Graduate Theological Union, 1976) 84-93; "The Wandering Radicals: Light Shed by the Sociology of Literature on the Early Transmission of the Jesus Sayings," in Theissen, *Social Reality and the Early Christians: Theology, Ethics, and the World of the New Testament* (Minneapolis: Fortress, 1992; Edinburgh: T. & T. Clark, 1993) 33-59, and abbreviated as "The Role of the Wandering Charismatics," 3-16, in his monograph *The*

interpret the oldest layer of the Mission Instructions, one has a relatively solid basis for understanding what went on in Jesus' Galilean ministry.

After being baptized by John (Q 3:21-22), Jesus apparently went back to Nazara (Q 4:16) only long enough to break with his past and to move to Capernaum (Q 7:1), as the base camp of a circuit that initially may have comprised Capernaum well below sea level on the northern tip of the Sea of Galilee, Chorazin in the mountains behind it, and Bethsaida just across the Jordan to the east, in the safer territory of Philip (Q 10:13-15).

What did he do on such a circuit? He set out without any human security. He had no backpack for provisions, no money at all, no sandals, no stick – helpless and defenseless (Q 10:4). This hardly makes sense in terms of the history of religions. His was neither the getup of his precursor John the Baptist, nor a Cynic garb[33]. But it does make sense in terms of his message, as echoed in the other archaic Q collections[34]: One is not anxiety-laden about food and clothing, any more than the ravens and lilies would seem to be (Q 12:22b-30). Rather, one orients oneself exclusively to God reigning (Q 12:31). One prays to God to reign, and thus to provide bread (Q 11:2b-3). One trusts God to know one's needs for bread and fish and to provide them (Q 11:9-10), trusting that God as a benevolent Father will not instead give a stone or snake, but will in fact, in this regard as in others, reign as a benevolent Father (Q 11:11-13). That kind of message of radical trust calls for that kind of radical lack of physical security, if it is to be validated as credible in actual reality.

In the case of the Mission Instructions, it is striking that Jesus did not advocate going to the local synagogue, which would at the time seem to have been rather nonexistent in Galilee in terms of architecture, nor address masses on a Mount or on a Plain or by the seaside. No location is given for the Inaugural Sermon (Q 6:20-49) which in fact seems less meant as an actual scene than as the basic core collection of the sayings of Jesus[35]. Rather, the Mission Instructions were oriented to houses

First Followers of Jesus: A Sociological Analysis of the Earliest Christianity (London: SCM, 1978), American title The Sociology of the Earliest Jesus Movement (Philadelphia: Fortress, 1978).

33. James M. Robinson, "Building Blocks in the Social History of Q," in Reimagining Christian Origins: A Colloquium Honoring Burton L. Mack, ed. Elizabeth A. Castelli and Hal Taussig (Valley Forge, Pa.: Trinity Press International, 1996) 87-112: 87-90. [In The Sayings Gospel Q, pp. 493-517, especially pp. 493-97.]

34. James M. Robinson, "Galilean Upstarts: A Sot's Cynical Disciples?" in Sayings of Jesus: Canonical and Non-Canonical: Essays in Honour of Tjitze Baarda, ed. William L. Petersen, Johan S. Vos, and Henk J. de Jonge, NovTSup 89 (Leiden, New York, Cologne: Brill, 1997) 223-49: 243-49. [In The Sayings Gospel Q, pp. 535-57, esp. pp. 552-57.]

35. It is a remarkable attestation for Matthew's familiarity with the tradition in which he obviously stood that he knew to build into the core collection of the Inaugural Sermon

(Q 10:5, 7)[36]. One walked from farm to farm, from hamlet to hamlet, from house to house, and there knocked at the door to bring attention to one's presence. To gain admission, one called out: Shalom! (Q 10:5b) If admitted by the head of the household, and thereby accorded the normal hospitality, one designated him as "son of peace" (Q 10:6a), since God's peace had been bestowed as "performative language" in the shalom of the opening greeting. If turned away at the door, God's peace left along with Jesus or his disciple (Q 10:6b), to be offered again at the next house where one knocked. But what took place in a house that did take one in was understood as God reigning. This was in fact expressly said to the household while in their home: "God's reign has reached unto you" (Q 10:9b).

God's reign involved the hospitality itself. Food was accepted at face value as God's gift, and eaten as offered, without ascetic dietary restrictions such as John and other "holy men" practiced at that time. This makes it clear that the drastic absence of gear for the journey was not due to an ascetic ideology, but rather was meant as demonstrative documentation for one's trust exclusively in God for such human needs. For, as the other archaic collections make clear, the food offered and eaten in the house was in reality God already knowing one's need and providing for it, as God does for the ravens; it was the answer to prayer for God to reign by giving a day's ration of bread and not a stone.

The needs of the household itself are comparably met. The sick are healed, with the explanation that this is in turn God's reign reaching even to them (Q 10:9). For the healing is done by God's finger, which is God reigning (Q 11:20), irrespective of whether the human involved is Jesus or someone else (Q 11:19). For it was understood not as human action, but as God's action.

All of this must have been explained by means of such sayings, and by means of the Prayer itself (Q 11:2b-4). In this way "workers" were enlisted for the mission (Q 10:2), and in the process of time such "worthy" houses (Matt. 10:13) might well become "safe houses," where

other archaic collections that comprise the core of Q, so as to produce the Sermon on the Mount, with the exception of the Mission Instructions themselves, which did not fit the setting of the Sermon on the Mount. It is thus appropriate that the Sermon on the Mount has been sensed as this core from time to time, beginning with Francis of Assisi, and re-emerging in Tolstoy, Gandhi, and Martin Luther King.

36. James M. Robinson, "From Safe House to House Church: From Q to Matthew," in *Das Ende der Tage und die Gegenwart des Heils. Begegnungen mit dem Neuen Testament und seiner Umwelt: Festschrift für Heinz-Wolfgang Kuhn zum 65. Geburtstag*, ed. Michael Becker and Wolfgang Fenske, AGJU 44 (Leiden: Brill, 1999) 183-99. [In *The Sayings Gospel Q*, pp. 629-44.]

workers knew they would be taken in. Indeed they might well develop into what Paul called "house churches" (Rom. 16:5; 1 Cor. 16:19; Philem. 1-2; Col. 4:15). The itinerant "worker" (Q 10:2, 7) and the sedentary "son of peace" (Q 10:6a) would be primitive designations for what might evolve from their functions into what we today would call church offices.

The decision of a member of such a household to become an itinerant worker might well not take place easily. Not only did Jesus leave home, Nazara, and in Q had no further relations with his family. There are even sayings explicitly calling for the disruption of family ties: Jesus came "to divide son against father, daughter against her mother, and daughter-in-law against her mother-in-law" (Q 12:53). To become a disciple, one must "hate father and mother,... son and daughter" (Q 14:26).

What could be more drastic than to hate one's family and love one's enemies? Even if this "hating" was understood euphemistically as "loving" Jesus more than family members (Matt. 10:37), in any case it meant abandoning the family and one's responsibilities at home. Central to the way of life that Jesus envisaged was indeed to love one's enemies (Q 6:27). For this, amplified by praying for one's persecutors (Q 6:28), is accorded the supreme value of being what makes one a child of God (literally "sons of your Father"), God-like, since God raises his sun and showers his rain on the bad as well as on the good (Q 6:35). The title "son of God" did not begin just as a christological title but, like the title "son of peace," began as a designation for those involved in the Jesus movement. This was not just a pious well-wishing sentiment, but meant in practice turning the other cheek, giving the shirt off one's back, going the second mile, lending without ever asking for it back (Q 6:29-30). It was living the Golden Rule even though faced with opposition (Q 6:31).

Jesus was not easy at all; one must lose one's life (Q 17:33), take up one's cross (Q 14:27). It is not surprising that in such a movement the salt of resolve lost its strength and had to be thrown out (Q 14:34-35). Enlistments must have been rare, and the dropout rate must have been devastating. For all practical purposes, the Q movement did die out. But its remnant merged with the gentile Christian church under the leadership of the Evangelist "Matthew," whereby its text, the Sayings Gospel Q, was rescued, and with it the most reliable information we have about the image of Jesus, who clearly gave his life for his cause (Q 11:47-51; 12:4-5; 13:34-35).

CHAPTER 10

The Q Trajectory: Between John and Matthew via Jesus

... the problem of the *continuity* between Jesus and the community, i.e. the basic problem of New Testament theology as a whole ...[1]

Helmut Koester is clearly the most creative of the younger generation of pupils of Rudolf Bultmann, those who completed their doctorates under him in Marburg after World War II, in distinction from the older generation between the wars. Koester began his academic career in Heidelberg, as Dozent under the patronage of one of the older Bultmannians, Günther Bornkamm, who with his numerous students formed what one might call the central strand of the Bultmannian school. But Koester soon moved from Heidelberg to Harvard University and subsequently resisted the temptation to return to Heidelberg as Bornkamm's successor. Koester has thus combined the German *Gründlichheit* of the Marburg and Heidelberg contexts in which he was formed with the openness and creativeness of the Harvard and American context in which he has flourished. The Bultmannian impetus, though it has largely died out in Germany, has continued in America – and, of course, first of all in the steady stream of highly gifted and thoroughly trained Harvard graduates who by now dominate the American scene in New Testament studies. Yet the impact of Koester's work has extended far beyond the circle of his actual students. For one of the growing edges of American New Testament scholarship, most visible in the Jesus Seminar of the Westar Institute and the Q Seminar of the Society of Biblical Literature, has built on creative insights he developed on the basis of his Bultmannian heritage.

Such a sweeping panorama, painted with too broad a brush, needs of course to be nuanced and made specific, in order to clarify precisely where it is and is not fully valid. The present essay is intended to trace only a single strand, which is nonetheless central and of major importance.

---

1. Hans Conzelmann, "Gegenwart und Zukunft in der synoptischen Tradition," *ZTK* 54 (1957) 279.

ALBERT SCHWEITZER'S APOCALYPTIC PARADIGM

Albert Schweitzer championed apocalyptic as a new paradigm in terms of which Jesus and primitive Christianity became more intelligible than they were on the previous model of ethical idealism implemented as the social gospel. The power of Schweitzer's position lay largely in his posture as the inevitable outcome of the preceding century of critical scholarship ("from Reimarus to Wrede"). Actually, it was only after publishing his own solution to the problem of the historical Jesus that Schweitzer turned to studying the history of the problem, which then, not by coincidence but of necessity, vindicated his solution. That this thesis was foisted upon the evidence has gone largely unnoticed, since no one has controlled the literature to the extent Schweitzer did.

Schweitzer's schematization of the quest of the historical Jesus was in terms of three decisive either-or decisions reached in the 1830s, 1860s, and 1890s:

> [David Friedrich] Strauss posed the first: Either purely historical or purely supernatural. The Tübingen School and [Heinrich Julius] Holtzmann worked out the second: Either Synoptic or Johannine. Now we have the third: Either eschatological [Johannes Weiss and Albert Schweitzer] or uneschatological[2].

Schweitzer's tendentiousness is evident already in the way he posed the first either-or alternative. Actually Strauss had transcended a standoff between the "historical" interpretation of the rationalists and the "supernatural" interpretation of the conservatives, by advocating the "mythical" interpretation. On occasion Schweitzer did formulate Strauss's alternative correctly: "Myth or history."[3] But, since neither alternative fitted Schweitzer's own, he actually modulated out of this either-or dilemma to the Hegelian both-and model, with Strauss becoming the "synthesis" of the supernatural and the historical[4].

Strauss's position can be described as the "synthesis" only as a combination of supernaturalism's insistence that the point of the text is to affirm the supernatural and rationalism's insistence that this supernatural

---

2. Albert Schweitzer, *Geschichte der Leben-Jesu-Forschung* (Tübingen: Mohr, 1913), second revised edition of *Von Reimarus zu Wrede: Eine Geschichte der Leben-Jesu-Forschung* (Tübingen: Mohr, 1906). The sixth edition of 1951 is cited here (p. 232). A seventh, two-volume paperback edition appeared in 1966. Eng. trans. of the first German edition: *The Quest of the Historical Jesus: A Critical Study of Its Progress from Reimarus to Wrede* (London: Macmillan, 1910), first Macmillan Paperback Edition (New York: Macmillan, 1961; fifth printing 1968) cited here (p. 238).

3. *Geschichte*, 115; *Quest*, 113.

4. *Geschichte*, 82; *Quest*, 80.

point is non-historical, from which Strauss's mythical position results. But Schweitzer's own solution was a converse synthesis, a combination of supernaturalism's insistence on abnormal conduct being historical, and rationalism's insistence that the historical is not miraculous, from which Schweitzer's apocalyptic history resulted. Schweitzer derived Jesus' abnormal conduct not from any miraculous powers but from Jesus' apocalyptic ideology. Thus he was able to rescue the narrative's historicity without recourse to some modern, often-ridiculous rationalization, as did the rationalists, but rather by making the events intelligible as the conscious planning of a somewhat ridiculous apocalypticist.

Schweitzer conceded that he made of Strauss's position "something different from what it was for his contemporaries," in that Strauss was "the prophet of a scholarship to come" that would discover "a Jewish Messianic pretender who lived in a purely eschatological world of thought."[5] It is this "something different" that leads directly to Schweitzer's position, since it is simply his position projected back onto Strauss.

By turning Strauss on his head Schweitzer could claim him as his own: "Thus the terrain was prepared on which research today operates."[6] Actually, Strauss's mythical interpretation points not to Schweitzer's apocalyptic historical Jesus but rather to Rudolf Bultmann's abandoning of the quest of the historical Jesus in favor of the demythologization of the kerygmatic text, whose existential meaning, rather than the historical Jesus, was to become the essence of Christianity.

Strauss's mythical interpretation laid the groundwork for twentieth-century form criticism's skepticism about the historicity of most Jesus traditions, a skepticism Schweitzer himself recognized in his own day as unfavorable to his own apocalyptic solution. Schweitzer is in fact the last stage in the reaction against Strauss, an effort to rescue the historicity of the narrative to an almost gullible extent.

The second either-or decision, "either Synoptic or Johannine," had been decided in favor of the Synoptics, in view of the theory that the Synoptics are historically more reliable because they rest upon two early sources, Mark and Q.

Schweitzer could only endorse this decision, since the Gospel of John is the least apocalyptic of the canonical Gospels. But he could not accept the justification for this decision, namely, that Matthew and Luke are secondary conflations of Mark and Q. For neither Mark nor Q provides an adequate basis for his solution, which depends primarily on the

5. *Geschichte*, 97; *Quest*, 95.
6. *Geschichte*, 85; *Quest*, 84.

Gospel of Matthew, seen not as a secondary conflation but as a primary and historically reliable source in its own right.

Schweitzer's own innovation had been to move beyond Johannes Weiss's apocalyptic interpretation of Jesus' sayings, in order to show how the apocalyptic sayings explain the narrative in which they are imbedded: Jesus' action was motivated by the same apocalypticism that came to expression in his sayings. But Q, like Weiss, was limited to the sayings, and Mark had too little by way of sayings to justify the apocalyptic interpretation of the action (especially since Schweitzer recognized that the Markan apocalypse did not go back to Jesus). Protestant liberalism had hence succeeded in reading a modern psychology rather than a Jewish apocalypticism into the Markan narratives[7].

The most important instance of the intertwining of Jesus' sayings and actions is put together by Schweitzer as follows: Jesus' identification of himself as the apocalyptic Son of man is "for us the great fact of His self-consciousness."[8] The most important saying is Matt 10:23, "... you will not have gone through all the towns of Israel before the Son of man comes."[9] But this is not in Mark, and perhaps not even in Q (since it is not in Luke). Yet it is Schweitzer's key to the mission discourse, with its message: "The kingdom of heaven is at hand" (Matt 10:7, derived from Q 10:9). After sending the disciples out, Jesus actually never expected to see them again until after the parousia[10]. The return of the disciples (Mark 6:30) was the first time Jesus was forced out of his dogmatic obsession and made to face up to reality. Thus Schweitzer pulled together a mosaic from various Synoptic sources and elevated this secondary mosaic to a primary causal connection that should explain historically Jesus' odd behavior.

Yet Schweitzer could not argue the historicity of this causal nexus in terms of its disparate pre-Synoptic sources, but had to maintain the historicity of Matthew's own mosaic: "Without Matt. 10 and 11 everything remains enigmatic."[11] But even Matthew left out Mark's return of the disciples that triggered the encounter with reality and hence the march on Jerusalem. "The Life of Jesus cannot be arrived at by following the arrangement of a single Gospel, but only on the basis of the tradition which is preserved more or less faithfully in the earliest pair of Synoptic Gospels."[12] That is to say, Schweitzer built his apocalyptic life

7. *Geschichte*, 407; *Quest*, 360.
8. *Geschichte*, replaced after the first edition (p. 363) by an expanded text; *Quest*, 367.
9. *Geschichte*, 407; *Quest*, 359-60.
10. *Geschichte*, 431; *Quest*, 386.
11. *Geschichte*, 407; *Quest*, 360.
12. *Geschichte*, 441; *Quest*, 394.

of Jesus on Matthew and Mark, but only by disregarding the classical solution to the Synoptic problem that gave to the Synoptics their priority as historical sources. Thus he had no moral claim to the advance marked by the second either-or decision, even though he was a pupil of Heinrich Julius Holtzmann in Strassburg.

The third either-or decision was this: "either eschatological or uneschatological." But alongside of this either-or alternative Schweitzer put another:

> One must either be quite sceptical, as was Bruno Bauer, and contest equally all reported facts and connections in Mark; or, if one proposes to build a historical Life of Jesus on Mark, one must recognize the Gospel as a whole as historical, in view of its connections running through the whole material[13].

Schweitzer considered the renewed skepticism of his day to be merely a desperate effort to avoid the inescapable eschatological conclusion: "But what survives as historical in the Gospels for the main stream of theology, if it considers itself obliged to sacrifice hand and foot and eye because of the offense of pure eschatology?"[14] Thus Schweitzer merged the two decisions into one:

> There is either the eschatological solution, which then at one stroke elevates the unsoftened, disconnected and contradictory Marcan presentation as such to the status of history; or there is the literary solution, which regards the dogmatic and foreign element as the earliest evangelist's interpolation into the tradition about Jesus and thus eliminates from the historical life of Jesus his Messianic claim as well. *Tertium non datur*[15].

Rather than being scared off by such a heretical-sounding outcome as the denial that Jesus claimed to be the Messiah, critical scholarship of the twentieth century has in fact built upon the three either-or decisions reached by the nineteenth century: The canonical Gospels are in their primary intent mythical (we have become accustomed to saying "kerygmatic") rather than historical. What can be known about the historical Jesus lies behind the Synoptics, in Mark and Q, more than behind John. But one must be skeptical as to the historicity even of the Synoptic Gospels, since, as form criticism insisted, they are primarily witnesses to the life of the primitive church and only secondarily witnesses to the life of Jesus.

Yet with regard to the other either-or decision that Schweitzer merged with the decision concerning historical versus skeptical – namely, eschatological versus uneschatological – the twentieth century has in fact

---

13. *Geschichte*, 338; *Quest*, 307-8.
14. *Geschichte*, 256 (cf. 597); *Quest*, 265.
15. *Geschichte*, 375; *Quest*, 337.

followed a sort of *tertium*, even though Schweitzer had warned: *non datur:* Although a messianic self-consciousness is often no longer ascribed to Jesus, his emphatic reference to an apocalyptic Son of Man other than himself and hence his basically apocalyptic orientation, has been maintained throughout the first half of the century. Schweitzer's thesis that the more skeptical the less apocalyptic has been ignored.

But then, when Jesus' expectation of an apocalyptic Son of Man other than himself also came to be questioned in the last half of the century, Matt 10:23 and all, the apocalyptic organizing principle for understanding Jesus was decisively undermined. A new paradigm is needed.

PHILIPP VIELHAUER'S ELIMINATION OF THE SON OF MAN

Rudolf Bultmann followed the dominant liberal Protestant view of his day in maintaining that Jesus spoke of a future apocalyptic Son of Man, though not identifying himself with that figure. Yet, by the end of Bultmann's career, a shift away from this apocalypticism, the temporal nearness of the kingdom, was well under way, even within his own school. Werner Georg Kümmel noted this anomaly as follows:

> Rudolf Bultmann introduces the description of Jesus' proclamation at the beginning of his *Theology of the New Testament* with the following statements: "The dominant concept of Jesus' message is the *Reign of God* (βασιλεία τοῦ θεοῦ). Jesus proclaims its immediately impending irruption now already making itself felt. Reign of God is an eschatological concept. It means the regime of God which will destroy the present course of the world ..." This basically futuristic-eschatological understanding of Jesus' message for which J. Weiss and A. Schweitzer had laid the groundwork seems to Bultmann so self-evident that he adduces no proof of it and mentions no contrary opinions. And yet this view, according to which Jesus proclaimed the temporal nearness of the coming of the Reign of God, has always met with serious opposition and in the last few years has again been energetically disputed[16].

Kümmel himself could hardly understand this departure from standard procedure and proceeded to refute it by presenting proof for the authenticity of sayings containing the imminent expectation: Q 10:9 (in the

16. W. G. Kümmel, "Die Naherwartung in der Verkündigung Jesu," in *Zeit und Geschichte: Dankesgabe an Rudolf Bultmann zum 80. Geburtstag,* ed. E. Dinkler (Tübingen: Mohr-Siebeck, 1964) 31-46; reprinted in *Heilsgeschehen und Geschichte* (Marburger Theologische Studien 3; Marburg: Elwert, 1965) 351-63; Eng. trans., "Eschatological Expectation in the Proclamation of Jesus," in *The Future of Our Religious Past: Essays in Honour of Rudolf Bultmann,* ed. J. M. Robinson (London: SCM; New York/Evanston/San Francisco/London: Harper & Row, 1971) 29-48 (here 29).

wording of Matt 10:7; Mark 1:15 is at least partially edited by the church); Mark 9:1; 13:28-29, 30; Luke 18:2-8a; Matt 10:23b.

The fact that this departure from the established critical view took place even within the Bultmannian movement may nonetheless be due to Bultmann himself. His existentialistic interpretation assumed a futuristic eschatological meaning of Jesus' preaching only on the surface level of the mythological language, for the demythologized existential meaning applies to the present. Even eschatological existence refers to the present, though this present is called eschatological because it is lived out of the future. Yet this future out of which the present is lived is not a duration of time that will fill a segment of time sometime in the future, but rather refers to the futures or options that one may actualize right now through an act of existential decision. Thus Bultmann recognized that though Jesus talked about the future and in this sense was eschatological or even an apocalypticist, the meaning of that futuristic talk had to do with the openness of every present moment to free decision, to choose a future to constitute one's being in the present. This focusing of the meaning of Jesus' message on the present, though at the hermeneutical level rather than on the usual exegetical level, may nonetheless have made possible the exegetical advances that did take place in the left wing of his school.

Philipp Vielhauer had taken the first major step within the Bultmannian movement toward reducing the centrality of eschatology, in that he argued that traditions in Judaism and early Christianity concerning the Son of Man represent a separate strand of eschatology from that represented by the kingdom of God. Since the kingdom of God is central in the authentic sayings of Jesus, all eschatological Son of Man sayings are to be excluded from those ascribed to Jesus and are to be ascribed first to the primitive church[17].

---

17. Philipp Vielhauer, "Gottesreich und Menschensohn in der Verkündigung Jesu," in *Festschrift für Günther Dehn* (Neukirchen: Buchhandlung des Erziehungsvereins, 1957) 51-79; "Jesus und der Menschensohn. Zur Diskussion mit Heinz Eduard Tödt und Eduard Schweizer," *ZTK* 60 (1963) 133-77; "Ein Weg zur neutestamentlichen Christologie? Prüfung der Thesen Ferdinand Hahns," *EvT* 25 (1965) 24-72. All three are reprinted in Philipp Vielhauer, *Aufsätze zum Neuen Testament* (TBü 31; München: Kaiser, 1965) 55-91, 92-140, 141-98 respectively, to which reference is here made. Vielhauer pointed out (pp. 82-83) that the use of Son of Man in Daniel 7 was not yet titular, but referred generically to a human. Hence, though Daniel 7 also refers to kingdoms (though without literal use of the expression "kingdom of God"), Daniel for him did not present an exception to the generalization: "Where the Son of Man is an individual figure and plays an active role, there is no mention of the kingdom of God. The Son of Man is not an integral part of the hope in the eschatological kingdom of God" (p. 86).

Vielhauer's position was not simply based on the distinction of two separate strands of tradition, but also substantively on the incompatibility of Jesus' "strict orientation to God being king," an "object of lively hope," with any apocalyptic expectation:

> In such an eschatology the figures of the Son of Man and the Messiah have as little place as do speculations about the date of the end or fantasies about the future world. On the basis of the strict concept of God's reign it is impossible that Jesus awaited the coming Son of Man or even more that he identified himself with him[18].

Hans Conzelmann presented on 22 October 1957 at the annual Bultmannian meeting of "Old Marburgers" a first endorsement of Vielhauer's position:

> The question is whether Jesus' expectation of the kingdom of God is accurately interpreted when it is presented as combined *in any way* with the expectation of a personal eschatological Fulfiller, i.e., whether the *structure* of his thought tolerates a synthesis of kingdom of God and Son of Man. What one finds in the texts seems to me to lead to denying this question. ... Jesus' person is taken up into the procedure in a way that no room remains for a further intervening person[19].

Conzelmann focused attention on the way in which the removal of the futuristic Son of Man from the teaching of Jesus fits with collapsing the time between Jesus' present and the imminently expected kingdom of God, a mythologoumenon that in effect should not be taken literally and in that sense not seriously. The eschatology of the kingdom functioned only existentially, not temporally and hence not futuristically[20]. This non-temporal eschatology is what Koester would come to call "Jesus' radicalized eschatology."

Vielhauer was soon able to appeal to most of the important representatives of the Bultmannian school in his support: Ernst Haenchen, Ernst Käsemann, Hans Conzelmann, and even Eduard Schweizer, though more a Barthian than a Bultmannian[21].

---

18. Vielhauer, "Gottesreich und Menschensohn in der Verkündigung Jesu," 88.

19. Conzelmann, "Gegenwart und Zukunft," 281.

20. Ibid., 286-88.

21. Vielhauer ("Ein Weg," 146) cited Haenchen, "Die Komposition von Mk viii,27–ix,1 und Par.," *NovT* 6 (1963) 81-109. Haenchen ascribed Mark 8:38 // Q 12:8-9 to the community, which at first distinguished terminologically between the past Jesus on earth and the future Jesus coming as the Son of Man on the clouds (pp. 93-96).

Vielhauer ("Jesus und der Menschensohn," 93 n. 4) cited Käsemann, *VF*, 1958-59 [1960-62] 99-102, esp. 101. Käsemann's emphasis on apocalyptic as the matrix of Christian theology presupposes that apocalypticism was ignited by the Easter experience and that Jesus himself was not an apocalypticist. See the following works by Käsemann: "Die

Günther Bornkamm was already committed in print to Bultmann's view of the Son of Man, to the effect that Jesus expected an apocalyptic Son of Man other than himself[22]. Bornkamm became in effect the leader of that strand of the Bultmannian movement that retained this classical position[23].

Anfänge christlicher Theologie," *ZTK* 57 (1960) 161-85, esp. 179; reprinted in *Exegetische Versuche und Besinnungen* (Göttingen: Vandenhoeck & Ruprecht, 1960-64) 2:82-104, esp. 99; Eng. trans., "The Beginnings of Christian Theology," *JTC* 6: *Apocalypticism* (New York: Herder & Herder, 1969) 17-46, esp. 39; and in Käsemann, *New Testament Questions of Today* (London: SCM; Philadelphia: Fortress Press, 1969) 82-107, especially 101-2. "Zum Thema der urchristlichen Apokalyptik," *ZTK* 59 (1962) 257-84; reprinted in *Exegetische Veersuche und Besinnungen,* 2:105-31; English translation, "On the Topic of Primitive Christian Apocalyptic," *JTC* 6: *Apocalypticism,* 99-133, esp. 104; "On the Subject of Primitive Christian Apocalyptic," in Käsemann, *New Testament Questions of Today,* 108-37.

Vielhauer ("Ein Weg," 146) cited Conzelmann without specific reference. See Conzelmann, "Jesus Christus," *RGG³* 3 (1959) 631; Eng. trans., Conzelmann, *Jesus* (Philadelphia: Fortress Press, 1973) 44-45: "The firming up of the language there [Dan 7:13] of 'a' figure like a human to 'the' Son of Man" is "not thinkable apart from the Christian (community) exegesis of Dan 7 and its application to the person of Jesus."

Eduard Schweizer ("Der Menschensohn [Zur eschatologischen Erwartung Jesu]," *ZNW* 50 [1959] 185-209, esp. 192) agrees with Vielhauer "that Jesus apparently did *not* await the coming of the Son of Man," and that *Q* sayings referring to the Jesus of the public ministry as Son of Man are held to be authentic (Q 7:34; 9:58; 11:30) (pp. 199-200), and that the term is not a generic designation ("human") but presupposes a latent Christology ("this circumlocution at once veiling and suggesting the mystery of his person," p. 198). It is this titular though nonapocalyptic use of Son of Man as a self-designation that is opposed by Vielhauer ("Jesus und der Menschensohn," 114-37). See also Schweizer's English summary and adaptation, "The Son of Man," *JBL* 79 (1960) 119-29.

22. G. Bornkamm, *Jesus von Nazareth* (Stuttgart: Kohlhammer, 1956), Exkurs 3, "Zur Frage der messianischen Hoheitsnamen in den Selbstaussagen Jesu" (pp. 206-10); Eng. trans., *Jesus of Nazareth,* trans. I. and E. McLuskey with J. M. Robinson (London: Hodder & Stoughton; New York: Harper, 1960), Appendix 3, "The Messianic Titles in Jesus' References to Himself" (pp. 226-31). This is in substance the same, with but minor variations, as the presentation by Rudolf Bultmann, *Theologie des Neuen Testaments* (Tübingen: Mohr-Siebeck, first fascicle 1948) 29-31; Eng. trans., *Theology of the New Testament,* trans. K. Grobel (2 vols.; New York: Scribner, 1951, 1955) 1:28-31.

23. Bornkamm's position was carried out by his pupils in their dissertations: Heinz Eduard Tödt, "Hoheits- und Niedrigkeitsvorstellungen in den synoptischen Menschensohnsprüchen" (1956), published as *Der Menschensohn in der synoptischen Überlieferung* (Gütersloh: Mohn, 1959); Eng. trans., *The Son of Man in the Synoptic Tradition* (London: SCM; Philadelphia: Westminster, 1965). Tödt argued for the authenticity of most of the futuristic Son of Man sayings in Q: 11:30; 12:8, 9, 40; 17:24, 26, 30 (not 17:28-29) (*Son of Man,* 60). The cohesiveness of the Heidelberg school on the Son of Man is evident from the fourth and fifth editions of Bornkamm's *Jesus von Nazareth* (1960 [not in the Eng. trans.] 195-96 n. 6a), where he rejected Vielhauer's original essay by appeal to Tödt, and where Tödt's book is praised as "the best investigation of the Son of Man sayings" (p. 209). See Vielhauer, "Jesus und der Menschensohn," in *Aufsätze zum Neuen Testament,* 92-140. Another dissertation under Bornkamm by Ferdinand Hahn, entitled "Anfänge christologischer Traditionen" (1961), was published as *Christologische Hoheitstitel: Ihre Geschichte im frühen Christentum* (FRLANT 83; Göttingen: Vandenhoeck & Ruprecht,

GÜNTHER BORNKAMM'S REVIVAL OF Q STUDIES

The revival of Q studies over the past generation took place in large part within the strand of the Bultmannian movement led by Günther Bornkamm. It is documented in the work of his pupils Heinz Eduard Tödt, Odil Hannes Steck, and Dieter Lührmann.

Tödt located the dominant trend in Q as the identification of Jesus with the apocalyptic Son of Man about whom Jesus himself had spoken, but only in the third person. Given the presence of the resurrected Jesus, the Q community experienced already the acquittal awaited at the judgment from the Son of Man, and thus came to identify Jesus with that figure and ascribe to him proleptically that title and authority[24]. Thus the basic orientation of Q itself is to Jesus as future Son of Man:

> The saying source, more strongly than any other collection of material within the Synoptic tradition, preserved the eschatological character of the proclamation of Jesus. ... Thus the eschatological sayings are now brought together in a substantive thematic group [Q 17:23-30]. In this group all sayings of the coming Son of Man appear, except for Luke 12:8-9 par. and Luke 11:30 par. ... An important position in the structure of the whole is accorded to the Son of Man sayings[25].

This eschatological christological definition of Q is basically different from the traditional view of Q as a parenetic supplement to the kerygma of cross and resurrection. Q now has a kerygma in its own right, thus suggesting that Q comes from an independent strand of primitive Christian tradition: "... the continued transmission of Jesus' teaching, in view

---

1963); Eng. trans., *The Titles of Jesus in Christology: Their History in Early Christianity* (London: Lutterworth; New York/Cleveland: World, 1969). See Vielhauer, "Ein Weg," in *Aufsätze zum Neuen Testament,* 141-98. Vielhauer had already added a refutation of Hahn in a "Nachtrag" to "Jesus und der Menschensohn" (pp. 138-40), beginning with a recognition of the togetherness of Tödt and Hahn's positions: "Hahn takes over Tödt's overall concept of the problem of the Synoptic Son of Man with unimportant modifications in detail" (13-53 [English translation, 15-53]). In the already-mentioned debate he defends the togetherness of 'kingdom of God' and 'Son of Man' in the proclamation of Jesus (27-32 [Eng. trans., 24-28]). The unpublished Heidelberg dissertation of 1953 by C. Iber, "Überlieferungsgeschichtliche Untersuchungen zum Begriff des Menschensohnes im Neuen Testament," was nonetheless appealed to by Vielhauer ("Jesus und der Menschensohn," 106 n. 22 [133-35 as Vielhauer's own view]): The distinction of Jesus from the Son of Man in Q 12:8-9 need not be taken as supporting the authenticity of sayings where this distinction is made (on the grounds that Jesus, but not the church, would have distinguished Jesus from the Son of Man), for it merely defines them as an early layer of the church's thinking when it had not yet come to describe the earthly status of Jesus in the language of his future apocalyptic status.

24. Tödt, *Der Menschensohn,* 248-49 (Eng. trans., 273).

25. Ibid., 246-47 (Eng. trans., 270).

of the divine authorization of the teacher, does not appear from the same source and with the same meaning as the passion kerygma, but has a source and a meaning by itself."[26] This is the origin of the current idea of a distinctive Q community or movement.

Odil Hannes Steck traced the history of the deuteronomistic view of history, to the effect that both exiles had been due to the disobedience of Israel producing "the violent fate of the prophets." His point of departure, however, is a detailed reconstruction of three Q texts, 6:22-23; 11:47-51; and 13:34-35 (though he doubts that the last belongs to Q), each of which presupposes that deuteronomistic tradition. Indeed he considers the deuteronomistic view of history as "the presupposed comprehensive conceptual framework" of Q[27].

Dieter Lührmann's study had its focus in the redaction of Q. He defined redaction narrowly as "a conscious formation under theological points of view, to be distinguished from 'collecting' according to catchword or topical arrangement."[28] He located Q's redactional focus in the apocalyptic judgment pronounced on Israel ("this generation") for having irrevocably rejected the Q movement. While arguing against Tödt that the identification of Jesus with the Son of Man had taken place in the Q community prior to the redaction and hence was not itself first introduced by the redaction[29], Lührmann does see in the apocalyptic judgment by the Son of Man a decisive redactional trait of Q:

> Even if this [apocalyptic] expectation of judgment goes back to Jesus himself, it is at least onesidedly emphasized in Q and has become in the

26. Ibid., 267 (Eng. trans., 296). This view is summarized by Bornkamm ("Evangelien, synoptische," *RGG³* 2 [1958] 753-66, "Spruchquelle" cols. 758-60, esp. col. 759). Bornkamm's *Jesus von Nazareth* (pp. 198-99 [Eng. trans., 217]) makes no such claim for Q. It may be that *Jesus von Nazareth*, which appeared in the same year as the submission (in May 1956) of Tödt's dissertation, was completed prior to that submission and that Tödt perhaps more than Bornkamm is responsible for the emphasis on the independence of the Q tradition, which Bornkamm then took up into his article that appeared two years later.

27. Odil Hannes Steck, *Israel and das gewaltsame Geschick der Propheten: Untersuchungen zur Überlieferung des deuteronomistischen Geschichtsbildes im Alten Testament, Spätjudentum und Urchristentum* (WMANT 23; Neukirchen-Vluyn: Neukirchener Verlag, 1967) 288. (His doubt about ascribing 13:34-35 to Q [p. 283 n. 1] is not shared by D. Lührmann [*Die Redaktion der Logienquelle* (WMANT 33; Neukirchen-Vluyn: Neukirchener Verlag, 1969) 44 n. 5].) According to the preface, this is a dissertation of 1965 under Bornkamm (p. 13). Ferdinand Hahn listed Steck as an assistant who helped him with proofreading and indexing (*Christologische Hoheitstitel*, preface 6).

28. D. Lührmann, *Die Redaktion der Logienquelle*, 84; see also 8, 16. The book was dedicated to Bornkamm. The preface reported that it was a 1968 *Habilitationsschrift* in Heidelberg, where Lührmann was assistant from 1965 to 1968 (p. 7).

29. Lührmann, *Die Redaktion der Logienquelle*, 41 n. 6; see also 85.

redaction the decisive interpretive tool for Jesus' proclamation of the basileia. One can hence even speak of a "re-apocalypticizing" of the proclamation of Jesus in Q[30].

Similarly with regard to Steck's thesis Lührmann argued that the deuteronomistic view of history is one ingredient, but only one ingredient, in the redactional focus of Q[31]. It is especially the Sophia orientation of Q 11:49-51; 13:34-35, which are two of Steck's three primary texts (along with 6:23c), as well as other Sophia texts in Q (7:35; 10:21-22; 11:31-32) and the sapiential genre of Q in general[32], that led Lührmann to bring wisdom motifs into new focus for defining the redaction of Q: "That means first of all that, in terms of the history of religions, the taking up of Jesus' proclamation of the basileia into the apocalyptic announcement of judgment is rooted in motifs derived from wisdom."[33] The redaction of Q would thus seem to be a history-of-religions hodgepodge without profile or directionality.

HELMUT KOESTER'S EARLY SAPIENTIAL LAYER IN Q

It is at this juncture that Lührmann quoted in an extended footnote a just-published essay ("now") by Helmut Koester as "an interesting thesis" where "new paths are indicated for the further work on the *Gospel of Thomas*":

30. Ibid., 94. Here (n. 4) Lührmann referred to Kümmel's essay "Eschatological Expectation in the Proclamation of Jesus" for the "status of the discussion" about the Son of Man, thereby implicitly reaffirming the position of Bultmann and Bornkamm over against Vielhauer. However, Lührmann seemed (*Die Redaktion der Logienquelle*, 41 n. 6) to be moving toward Vielhauer's position: Lührmann considered Q 12:8-9 decisive as to whether Jesus referred to a future Son of Man, and he was inclined to think that the language of confessing and denying with its courtroom overtones was more likely to be a creation of the community. Similarly (p. 75) Q 17:24, 26-27 are considered inauthentic, though (in the comments appended when reading proofs, p. 8) he conceded that R. A. Edwards ("The Eschatological Correlative as a Gattung in the New Testament," *ZNW* 60 [1969] 9-20) "contests more strongly than do I that these comparisons are original sayings of Jesus."

31. Lührmann, *Die Redaktion der Logienquelle*, 88.

32. Ibid., 91, 102; Lührmann appropriated my genre definition, λόγοι σοφῶν.

33. Lührmann, *Die Redaktion der Logienquelle*, 100; see also 97-98: "As the latest, and hence temporally (even if not necessarily tradition-historically) nearest layer to the redaction of Q there has emerged a series of logia that are clearly shaped by late Jewish wisdom. At first glance this may not seem surprising, for the influence of just this stream already on Jesus' proclamation is after all recognizable on all sides in the Synoptic tradition. Yet the frequency and special shape of these sayings, and the formation of the logia source as a whole in terms of a genre coming from wisdom literature, speak for the view that precisely this influence had significant weight in the transmission of the logia source."

The basis of the *Gospel of Thomas* is a Sayings collection which is more primitive than the canonical Gospels, even though its basic principle is not related to the creed of the passion and resurrection.

It must have been a version of Q in which the apocalyptic expectation of the Son of Man was missing and in which Jesus' radicalized eschatology of the Kingdom and his revelation of divine wisdom in his own words were the dominant motives[34].

It is clear that Lührmann himself did not follow up this "interesting thesis" in his own work on Q. It required that one be prepared to build upon Vielhauer's thesis of the secondary role of the futuristic sayings about the Son of Man to an extent that Lührmann, given his Heidelberg context, was not yet fully prepared to do. It also presupposed that the *Gospel of Thomas* is not built primarily upon the Synoptic Gospels – as was assumed by most European scholars at the time, following Wolfgang Schrage's *Habilitationsschrift* at Kiel[35] – but rather on oral tradition, as most American scholarship has tended to assume, following the prompt refutation of Schrage in the unpublished Claremont dissertation of John Sieber[36]. Thus Lührmann, though obviously attracted to Koester's thesis, did not in fact introduce it in a meaningful way into Q research.

If thus the Heidelberg branch of the Bultmannian movement did not investigate further a preapocalyptic, sapiential collection of sayings behind Q, such a possibility was envisaged in Dieter Zeller's 1976 *Habilitationsschrift* at nearby Freiburg im Breisgau, though rather isolated from the developments within the Bultmannian movement but at home in the somewhat different context of emergent Roman Catholic Q scholarship. "One can in any case also go about disengaging complexes of logia that precede Q, which possibly had their own 'Sitz im Leben.' Among them are six rather large groups of sayings that may have grown up around a kernel of admonitions."[37] The six complexes of sayings that Zeller listed are as follows:

1. Conduct toward enemies: Q 6:(20-23), 27-33, 35b-37a, 38b, 41-42, (43-49)

34. Ibid., 92-93 n. 4. He quoted Koester, "One Jesus and Four Primitive Gospels," *HTR* 61 (1968) 229-30, now reprinted in Robinson–Koester, *Trajectories,* 186. Lührmann's rejection of attempts to "distinguish in terms of *literary criticism* younger and older sources in Q" (*Die Redaktion der Logienquelle,* 89 n. 2) was directed against older, unrelated views.

35. W. Schrage, *Das Verhältnis des Thomas-Evangeliums zur synoptischen Tradition und zu den koptischen Evangelienübersetzungen: Zugleich ein Beitrag zur gnostischen Synoptikerdeutung* (BZNW 29; Berlin: Töpelmann, 1964).

36. J. Sieber, "A Redactional Analysis of the Synoptic Gospels with Regard to the Question of the Sources of the Gospel of Thomas" (Ph.D. diss., Claremont Graduate School, 1964).

37. D. Zeller, *Die weisheitlichen Mahnsprüche bei den Synoptikern* (Forschung zur Bibel 17; Würzburg: Echter Verlag, 1977) 191. Zeller adds with somewhat less assurance

2. Conduct of the messengers: Q 10:2-8a, 9-11a, 12 (+ 16?)
3. Prayer: Q 11:(2-4?), 9-13
4. Conduct under persecution: Q [11:33-36?]; 12:(2-3), 4-9, (10)
5. Attitude toward material things: Q 12:22-31, 33-34
6. Watchfulness: Q 12:(35-37?), 39-40, 42b-46

Zeller's complexes 1-5 are, with but minor variations, the first five sapiential speeches ascribed by John S. Kloppenborg, in his comprehensive analysis of the literary layering of Q, to the first edition of Q[38].

Only somewhat less striking is the list of six pre-Q collections of aphoristic sayings, each displaying a similar structure, presented by Ronald A. Piper[39]: Q 6:27-36 (in Matthew's order); 6:37-42; 6:43-45; 11:9-13; 12:2-9; 12:22-31. The first three of Piper's six collections are parts of the first cluster on Zeller and Kloppenborg's list, while the other three in Piper's list comprise major parts of items 3 through 5 of Zeller and Kloppenborg's list.

Whereas Kloppenborg, at the conclusion of his analysis of the sapiential speeches, does refer in passing in a note to Zeller's list, Piper, though making use in general of Zeller's work, nowhere refers to this listing of sapiential complexes; Kloppenborg's book appeared too late for Piper to include it[40]. Thus his conclusions are relatively independent.

Another striking aspect of these converging lists of sapiential collections is their focus on the Sermon on the Mount: The first collection listed by Zeller and Kloppenborg is the Sermon in Q, from which

---

that one might consider as a seventh complex the Q apocalypse, 17:23-24, 26-27, 30, 34-35, 37b.

38. J. S. Kloppenborg, *The Formation of Q: Trajectories in Ancient Wisdom Collections* (SAC; Philadelphia: Fortress Press, 1987). Kloppenborg ascribed apocalypticism, and hence Zeller's sixth and seventh complexes (and 12:8-9), to the second edition of Q, while himself disengaging a sixth sapiential speech in the first edition of Q scattered through Luke 13–17. Kloppenborg, in a paper prepared for the Q Seminar of SBL in 1988, "Redactional Strata and Social History in the Sayings Gospel Q," 5, n. 1, presented a slightly revised list of materials assigned to the two editions of Q: "To the instructional layer I assign: (1a) Q 6:20b-23b, 27-35, 36-45, 46-49; (1b) 9:57-62; 10:2-11, 16; (1c) 11:2-4, 9-13; (1d) 12:2-7, 11-12; (1e) 12:22b-31, 33-34; (1f) 13:24; 14:26-27; 17:33; 14:34-35 and probably also 15:4-7, (8-10?); 16:13; 17:1-2, 3b-4, 5-6 [probably verse 5 is not meant to be included, see Kloppenborg, Q *Parallels: Synopsis, Critical Notes and Concordance* (Sonoma, CA: Polebridge, 1988), 186-87]. The second layer consists of five large blocks of sayings, (2a) Q 3:7-9, 16-17; (2b) 7:1-10, 18-28, 31-35; 16:16 [presumably meant to precede 31-35, see Q *Parallels*, 56-57]; (2c) 11:14-26, (27-28?), 29-32, 33-36, 39b-42b, 43-44, 46-52; (2d) 12:39-40, 42-46, 49, 51-59; (2e) 17:23-24, 26-30, 34-35; 19:12-27; 22:28-30, and various interpolations: 6:23c; 10:12, 13-15; 12:8-9, 10; 13:25-27, 28-30, 34-35; 14:16-24. At a third level, Q 4:1-13; 11:42e and 16:17 were added."

39. R. A. Piper, *Wisdom in the Q-Tradition: The Aphoristic Teaching of Jesus* (SNTSMS 61; Cambridge/New York/New Rochelle/Melbourne/Sydney: Cambridge University Press, 1989).

40. Ibid., 209 n. 61.

three of the six Q collections of Piper also come. The enlargement of
Q's Sermon into the Sermon on the Mount (Matthew 5–7) adds collections 3 and 5 from the list of Zeller and Kloppenborg, and two of the
remaining three collections of Piper. Thus the disengaging of sapiential collections behind Q arrives at a position somewhat analogous to,
though quite independent of, Hans Dieter Betz's claim that the Sermon
on the Mount goes back behind Matthew to about 50 CE, that is, prior
to Q[41]. Thus Betz in his way supports those seeing a sapiential layer
behind Q.

To be sure, the independent existence of the Q Sermon prior to Q is
hardly provable[42], much less that of the Sermon on the Mount. But, just
as the existence of Zeller's collections 1, 3, and 5 is not dependent
on their initial collection into the Sermon on the Mount, so the existence
of three of Piper's six collections is not dependent on their initial collection in a Q Sermon prior to the composition of Q. The important thing is
the detection of some clustering activity at the early, formative stage of
Q. Rather than having to do merely with a number of sapiential sayings,
one has to do with a structuring of such sayings into clusters, a process
reflecting some intentional activity on the part of some person or persons
largely restricted to the Q community[43].

When one turns from the question of literary layering to that of the
history of traditions, the distinction drawn by Siegfried Schulz between
two stages in the tradition, "the kerygma of the Jewish-Christian Q community" and "the kerygma of the younger Q community of Syria," presented as the first layer a surprisingly high degree of overlap with the
sapiential collections, which is all the more surprising given Schulz's
orientation to an apocalyptic point of departure for the Q community[44].

41. H. D. Betz, *Essays on the Sermon on the Mount,* trans. L. L.Welborn (Philadelphia:
Fortress Press, 1985); see also H. D. Betz, "The Sermon on the Mount in Matthew's Inter-
pretation," in *The Future of Early Christianity: Essays in Honor of Helmut Koester,* ed.
B. A. Pearson, in collaboration with A. T. Kraabel et al. (Minneapolis: Fortress Press,
1991) 258-75; reprinted in idem, *Synoptische Studien: Gesammelte Aufsätze II* (Tübingen:
Mohr, 1992) 270-90.

42. Leif E. Vaage, "Composite Texts and Oral Myths: The Case of the 'Sermon'
(6:20b-49)," in *Society of Biblical Literature 1989 Seminar Papers,* ed. D. J. Lull (Atlanta:
Scholars Press, 1989) 424-39.

43. Piper, *Wisdom,* 161: "The distinctiveness of structure and argument which has
been found to characterize several aphoristic sayings-collections of the double tradition
leads one to infer the existence of a unique circle of people who formulated these collections. ..." This relatively restricted source-critical range within which the collections are
found strengthens the theory of a unique sapiential circle behind the collections.

44. S. Schulz, *Q: Die Spruchquelle der Evanglisten* (Zürich: Evangelischer Verlag,
1972).

He listed as the older layer Q 6:20b-21, 27-38, 41-42; 11:1-4, 9-13, 39, 42-44, 46-48, 52; 12:4-9, 22-31, 33-34; 16:17-18. Again it is striking how much of this is in the Q Sermon (6:20b-21, 27-38, 41-42) or in additions included in the Sermon on the Mount (Q 11:1-4, 9-13; 16:17-18; 12:22-31, 33-34). Actually in Schulz's oldest layer of tradition only a very few passages (Q 11:39, 42-44, 46-48, 52; 12:4-9) are not in the Sermon on the Mount. And only a few passages (11:39, 42-44, 46-48, 52; 16:17-18) are not in the sapiential collections of Zeller and Kloppenborg (who also left out 12:8-9).

Of the three monographs by Zeller, Kloppenborg, and Piper oriented to sapiential collections imbedded in Q, only that of Kloppenborg built consciously on the initiative of Koester, carrying through its implications in terms of redaction criticism.

> Koester observes that the forms most typical of the wisdom gospel or *logoi sophon* are wisdom sayings, legal pronouncements, prophetic sayings ("I"-words, blessings and woes) and parables. Least typical of this genre are apocalyptic sayings, especially apocalyptic Son of Man sayings. Therefore, as far as *Gattungsgeschichte* is concerned, the *Gos. Thom.* reflects a stage antecedent to the final form of Q. By including Son of Man sayings, Q produced a secondary version of a "wisdom-gospel." Koester conjectures that the introduction of apocalyptic eschatology was a means to attenuate the radicalized eschatology and gnosticizing tendencies at work in earlier forms of Q. ...
>
> His conclusions regarding the formative elements of Q are based on two assumptions: that Q belongs to the genre of "wisdom gospel" and that only certain kinds of sayings and theological tendencies are typical of the genre. According to Koester, apocalyptic Son of Man sayings and sayings which evince a strongly future-oriented eschatology run counter to the tendencies of the genre, and for that reason are to be judged secondary. In practice, Koester's method is comparative and the *Gos. Thom.* serves as a criterion for deciding what was formative in Q. *Gos. Thom.* lacks an apocalyptic thrust and has only one (non-apocalyptic) Son of Man saying (saying 86)[45].

Kloppenborg himself saw it as his task to carry through the redactional analysis that shows the Son of Man apocalyptic layer to be later than the sapiential instructional layer:

> It must be shown on redactional grounds that certain elements (e.g., apocalyptic Son of Man sayings) belong to a secondary compositional level and that compositionally and literarily the wisdom sayings, and the wisdom-gospel format, are foundational and formative for the document. Such a conclusion can be obtained in the first place only from an analysis of Q itself, not by comparative analysis[46].

45. Kloppenborg, *Formation of Q*, 32-33, 38.
46. Ibid., 38-39.

Thus Kloppenborg implemented Koester's working hypothesis of an early sapiential layer in Q in a way that Lührmann has not. For Lührmann, the sapiential layer responsible for the genre λόγοι σοφῶν was the latest layer, for here Sophia Christology is presupposed (Q 7:35; 10:21-22; 11:31-32, 49-51; 13:34-35). The result is that for Lührmann it would be at the redactional stage that sapiential influences would have been introduced, even though he recognized that sapiential sayings going back to Jesus himself should lead one to expect a sapiential orientation even earlier[47].

Yet the emergence of Sophia Christology not at the oldest layer of Q but only at the redactional level should not in itself be surprising, once one notes that Christology as such really only emerges at this secondary level. In the first edition of Q "sons ‹of God›" are all those who are god-like in loving their enemies (Q 6:35c-d), and it is only in the second edition of Q that sonship becomes an exclusive christological title of Jesus (Q 10:22; 4:3 and 9 may be even later). In the first edition of Q, the term Son of Man in Q 9:58 apparently goes back to a generic meaning "human" (*Gos. Thom.* 86), though it has become a reference to Jesus here and in 6:22 (lacking in Matt 5:11); however, in the second edition of Q it becomes, in addition to a reference to the earthly Jesus (7:34; 12:10; and perhaps 11:30), the christological title for Jesus as an apocalyptic figure who functions at the last judgment as character witness (12:8) or even as judge (12:40; 17:24, 26, 30). In the first edition of Q κύριος can refer to God (10:2; 16:13, both metaphorically), whereas for Jesus it is a form of address just meaning "Sir" (9:59). It develops into a title for Jesus in the first edition of Q only as teacher (6:46) and here is used only by persons who are criticized for their lack of conformity to the teaching. Only in Matt 7:22 does κύριος develop beyond Q into a title for the character witness at the last judgment, building there upon the metaphorical use of the secular meaning "Sir" (Q 13:25; Matt 25:11).

---

47. Lührmann, *Die Redaktion der Logienquelle,* 97-98, 100. The situation is similar in this regard with the 1984/85 Bern dissertation of Migaku Sato, *Q und Prophetie* (WUNT 2.29; Tübingen: Mohr, 1988) 161: "A few 'functional elements' of personified Wisdom have flowed into the sayings of the Exalted. ... This tendency of Q sayings is then picked up in a certain way by one of the Q redactions – no doubt C [the latest]." The dissertation is designed to replace the definition of the genre of Q in terms of sapiential literature with a genre definition in terms of OT prophecy. To this end a number of Q sayings are reconstructed and their genre defined as prophetic. Since Kloppenborg's thesis was not available to Sato, the fact that these "prophetic" sayings are practically all from what Kloppenborg has classified as the apocalyptic second edition of Q, in distinction from the sapiential first edition, is not taken into consideration. Rather the genre of the sapiential sayings is passed over in silence, as of necessity is that of the first edition of Q itself, where the designation λόγοι σοφῶν would be most appropriate.

Thus the relative absence of Christology from the first edition of Q and the relative prominence of Christology in the second edition of Q is striking. It is hence not surprising that the first edition of Q, though its genre and sayings are largely sapiential, does not present a Sophia Christology, but that this christological development can be sensed first among the christological developments of the second edition of Q. Thus in spite of the Sophia Christology emerging first in the second edition of Q, it is the first edition that is primarily a sapiential collection of λόγοι σοφῶν; in the second edition the literary genre moves in a narrative, chreia-like direction.

A NEW TRAJECTORY

The recognition of a pre-apocalyptic layer lying behind Q, which Koester first identified and which has subsequently come to expression in such a variety of ways, poses a new alternative for tracing the movement from Jesus to the church.

In modern scholarship Jesus had usually been placed historically between John the Baptist, into whose movement he was baptized, and Paul, whose letters are the first documentation of the religion venerating Jesus. Since both John and Paul were apocalypticists, the easiest working hypothesis has been to bridge the gulf of two decades between them with a straight-line development: Jesus too was an apocalypticist.

The idea of Jesus as apocalypticist had originally commended itself in the same way as did the Copernican revolution: As an organizing principle, the theory that the earth rotates around the sun left less by way of unresolved problems than did the previous geocentric model. Apocalypticism won on the aesthetic criterion of providing a cleaner, less-cluttered model. And so it became the working hypothesis for the quest of the historical Jesus in the twentieth century.

Now, almost a century later, though Schweitzer's apocalyptic derivation of Jesus has become the establishment view, it no longer plays that liberating role. As the old model it is now frayed, blemished by broken parts, no longer a heuristic tool drawing attention to new insights on all sides, but rather a Procrustean bed in which the discipline squirms, ill at ease. Today's growing edges are no longer edges of that given model but rather dangle off in space on their own, in a largely disintegrated discipline.

Emergent layering in Q may well provide the possibility to replace the apocalyptic model from John to Paul with a Q trajectory between John

and Matthew, on which a major sapiential deviation and a re-apocalypticizing may be plotted. There may be no other name significant enough
to associate with such a sapiential deviation than Jesus (especially since
Q names by name only John and Jesus), though academic rigor may make
us prefer "John Doe."

Such a rethinking should not, in an excess of exuberance, seek to deny
the apocalyptic nature of the two poles, John and Paul. John in Q 3:7-9,
16-17 is presented in a way that can be characterized as apocalyptic – that
is, forewarning of judgment imagined like natural disasters such as hur-
ricane and lighting, what in modern legal parlance are still called "acts
of God." There is a "impending rage" (3:7); "already" an ax is poised
to "chop down and throw on the fire" trees not bearing good fruit (3:9);
"the One to Come ... more powerful than I" – some divine agent – will
baptize with "[wind and] fire" (3:16); "the pitchfork" is poised to separate the "wheat" into the "granary" from the "chaff" to be cast into the
"fire that can never be put out" (3:17). These heavy metaphors tend to
point to some superhuman final resolution to the human dilemma, such
as the term apocalypticism tends to evoke. Rather than appealing behind
this apocalyptic portrayal of John to the standard Cynic critique of the
"soft" life of "finery" reflected in Q 7:25 as distinguishing the historical John as having been a Cynic[48], we need to cope with the probability
that Jesus underwent John's baptism and thus entered an apocalyptic
movement[49] and hence must have begun by believing its apocalyptic
message with considerable fervor.

Jesus, though initially such a fervent convert of John, would seem
not to have continued in a straight-line way the program or life-style of
John. He seems not to have continued John's symbolic act of baptism.

---

48. Leif Vaage documented quite fully the pejorative use of μαλακός ("soft") as Cynic
("Q: The Ethos and Ethics of an Itinerant Intelligence" [Ph.D. diss., Claremont Graduate
School, 1987] Appendix 3, "Matt 11:8 / Luke 7:25 – Clarifying a Characterization,"
[pp. 485-502]). Vaage has published a revised version of the appendix in his book *Galilean
Upstarts: Jesus' First Followers According to Q* (Valley Forge, Penn: Trinity Press Inter-
national, 1994) 96-102.

49. Kloppenborg has summarized the discussion, concluding that Jesus' baptism was
not in Q *(Formation of Q,* 84-85; and *Q Parallels,* 16). Yet it is not fully satisfactory to
assume that "the title 'Son of God' in Q 4 does not require an explanatory narrative any
more than does the title 'Son of man,' which is by far the more common title for Q" (*Q
Parallels,* 16). For the temptation narrative would be the first place in *Q* where Jesus is
presented as saying or doing anything, if his baptism were not mentioned. Yet the title Son
of God occurs in the temptation not as a familiar and unchallenged title, as is usual with
christological titles (e.g. Son of Man, or Son ‹of God› in Q 10:22), but rather is challenged
and made the issue. This seems to presuppose some provocative identification of Jesus with
that title, which the devil then contests. Thus to assume the inclusion of the baptism of
Jesus in Q seems relatively prudent.

Though both ate and dressed very simply, John seems not to have depended on civilization, but to have had an uncooked diet and an unwoven garb (Mark 1:6) typical of the bedouin[50], and to have frequented uninhabited places like an anchorite – the people had to come out and hunt him up (Q 7:24: in Mark 1:4 the wilderness may be derived from Isa 40:3 quoted in Mark 1:3). Jesus, on the other hand, seems to have depended on civilization, to have lived in Capernaum (Q 7:1 // John 2:12 and 4:46; Q 10:15; Mark 1:21; 2:1). though at times to have been a mendicant itinerant (Q 9:58; 10:2-11). Jesus' (lack of) gear is not that of John, but apparently clothes of the day of human-made cloth (though on the other hand not the garb of the Cynic, but even more rigorous [Q 10:4], though perhaps with a similar symbolic meaning). Thus John's and Jesus' life-styles could only be contrasted, even when caricatured (Q 7:34). We might use the contrast between the raw and the cooked. Given these divergences, which are all the more remarkable in view of Jesus' beginning with John's baptism, there is no strong reason to assume that Jesus continued John's ideology. The apocalypticism of the second edition of Q may in fact be a re-apocalypticizing of the Jesus tradition.

The early efforts by Karl Barth to argue that Paul, though occasionally borrowing categories from Jewish apocalypticism, was himself not an apocalypticist, were shown to be tendentious by Rudolf Bultmann: In such a text as 1 Cor 15:22-28 Paul did reason apocalyptically[51]. This is not just an unintelligible lapse on the part of Paul, but is

50. Philipp Vielhauer concluded: "As surely as John awaited no political Messiah 'in the desert,' just as certainly his eschatological message connected up with the old desert typology. From this the unusualness of his clothing and nourishment is to he explained in a better and more unified way than on the basis of asceticism or hostility to culture. His clothing and nourishment have their meaning as eschatological demonstration" ("Tracht und Speise Johannes des Täufers," in *Aufsätze zum Neuen Testament*, 54).

51. Karl Barth distinguished between "Schlussgeschichte," apocalypticism's series of final events in time and space, and "Endgeschichte," the ultimate substantive reality behind such language, that is, ultimately God (*Die Auferstehung der Toten: Eine akademische Vorlesung über 1. Kor. 15* [München: Kaiser, 1924] esp. 56-62, 94-99). So as to limit Paul to the latter, Barth twisted illegitimately the exegesis of 1 Cor 15:22-28 so as to eliminate from the text a series of final events. (The Eng. trans., *The Resurrection of the Dead* [London, 1933] is so inadequate that it might best be ignored.) Rudolf Bultmann had full appreciation for Barth's identification of the Pauline point behind the language, but insisted that Paul's language was sometimes inadequate to that point – e.g., when Paul himself became distracted into laying out a series of final things, as in 1 Cor 15:22-28 ("Karl Barth, Die Auferstehung der Toten," *Theologische Blätter* 5 [1926] 1-14; reprinted in *Glauben und Verstehen*, 1 [Tübingen: Mohr, 1933]; Eng. trans., "Karl Barth, The Resurrection of the Dead," *Faith and Understanding* [London: SCM; New York: Harper & Row, 1969; reprint, Philadelphia: Fortress Press, 1987] 66-94, esp. 84-86).

a built-in proclivity of finite human experience seeking to express inef-
fable ultimacy in its finite language that again and again gets the upper
hand[52].

Paul's theology is not derived in a significant way from that of Jesus,
and therefore Paul's apocalypticism might not weigh heavily in defining
Jesus' ideology. Only if that were all one had from the first generation
might one by default be obliged to follow the apocalyptic interpretation
of Jesus. But there is in fact Q, whose layers span the first generation, the
only other surviving "apostolic" text in a chronological sense – the noun
"apostle" is hardly in Q's vocabulary (Q 11:49?), though the verb
"send" is present (Q 7:27; 10:3, 16; 11:49; 14:17; the substantivized
aorist passive participle 13:34). Q is the extant text that reflects most
nearly, though not exclusively, Jesus' own thought. The question of Jesus'
apocalypticism is basically a question of the interpretation of Q.

If the earlier layer of Q would seem to be oriented heavily to sapiential traditions (though not without apocalyptic flickers or interpolations),
there are in the later layer strong indications of apocalyptic indulgences
and indeed of a re-apocalypticizing of the tradition. Those responsible
for the eschatological[53] or prophetic[54] correlatives were closely related to
the Q movement, in that four correlatives are in the second edition of Q
(Q 11:30; 17:24, 26-27, 30), and only one elsewhere in the Synoptic
Gospels (Matt 13:40-41). These correlatives are closely related to the
introduction of the future Son of Man into Q, in that at least half the
instances occur in correlatives: Q 17:24, 26-27, 30 (whether Q 11:30
refers to the Son of Man as future is unclear), whereas only two occur
elsewhere in Q (12:8, 40). The apocalyptic title John used to refer
to the future judge, "the One to Come," which the Q movement identi-

---

52. Hans Jonas, *Augustin und das paulinische Freiheitsproblem: Eine philosophische
Studie zum pelagianischen Streit* (ed. Rudolf Bultmann, FRLANT, 44; Göttingen: Vandenhoeck & Ruprecht, 1930; 2nd ed. 1965) 82: "All this derives from an unavoidable fun-
damental structure of the spirit as such. That it interprets itself in objective formulae and
symbols, that it is "symbolistic," is the innermost nature of the spirit – and at the same
time most dangerous! In order to come to itself, it necessarily takes this detour via the symbol, in whose enticing jungle of problems it tends to lose itself, far from the origin preserved symbolically in it, taking the substitute as ultimate. Only in a long procedure of
working back, after an exhausting completion of that detour, is a demythologized con-
sciousness able terminologically to approach directly the original phenomena hidden in this
camouflage (cf. the long path of the dogma of original sin up to Kierkegaard!)."

53. Edwards, "Eschatological Correlative," 9-20, esp. 11. This essay recurs with minor
alterations in his dissertation, *The Sign of Jonah in the Theology of the Evangelists and Q*
(SBT 2.18; London: SCM, 1971).

54. Daryl Schmidt, "The LXX *Gattung* 'Prophetic Correlative'," *JBL* 96 (1977) 517-
22, esp. 521-22.

fied with Jesus, is also limited to the second edition of Q: 3:16; 7:19; 13:35 (though Ps 118:26 is quoted at the triumphal entry in all four Gospels). The broadly attested polemic against those who cry out "Here!" or "There!" is indicative of such trends: Luke (Q?) 17:20-21, 23; Mark 13:21; *Gos. Thom.* 3 (// Matt 24:26) and 113; *Gospel of Mary (PBerol.* 8502, 8, 15-19)[55].

Kloppenborg has argued that even after the second edition of Q there was a final redaction that introduced Q 4:1-13; 11:42c; 16:17, with an emphasis on Jesus as advocate of strict Torah observance, perhaps as a last desperate effort to gain acceptance in Jewish circles. From here it is not far to the emphatically particularistic sayings in Matt 10:5-6, 23 (cf. Rom 15:8), which hardly reflect that evangelist's own view (Matt 28:18-20), but either some otherwise unknown strand of tradition, further attestation for the final redaction of Q which Luke might readily have omitted, or an addition to Q by the Matthean community after the Lukan copy of Q had been made.

If thus a clear distinction between a third edition of Q, a QMt and even a kind of Ur-Matthew cannot be drawn, since all these entities are themselves obscure, it would seem clear that the Q movement – at least a significant part of it – merged into the Matthean community, bringing into Matthew and the Gentile church, and thus into the canon and the modern world, the traditions of Jesus that Q had transmitted:

> Therefore we support the thesis that the Gospel of Matthew comes from a community which was founded by the wandering messengers and prophets of the Son of man of the Sayings Source and remains in close contact with them. The traditions of Q thus reflect, for the community, experiences from its own history. They are "its own" traditions[56].

Thus the model of an unbroken apocalypticism from John to Paul is to be replaced by a trajectory of the Q movement between John's apocalypticism and that of Matthew, but with a more nuanced, since better documented, course from one to the other. Here the early sapiential

---

55. James M. Robinson, "The Study of the Historical Jesus after Nag Hammadi," *Semeia* 44: *The Historical Jesus and the Rejected Gospels* (1988) 45-55, esp. 50-53 [*The Sayings Gospel Q,* pp. 275-84, esp. pp. 281]; James G. Williams, "Neither Here Nor There: Between Wisdom and Apocalyptic in Jesus' Kingdom Sayings," *Forum* 5.2: *The Jesus of Q* (1989) 7-30; Risto Uro, *Neither Here nor There: Lk 17:20-2 and Related Sayings in Thomas, Mark and Q* (Occasional Papers 20; Claremont, Calif.: Institute for Antiquity and Christianity, 1990).

56. Ulrich Luz, *Das Evangelium nach Matthäus (Mt 1–7)* (EKKNT 1.1; Zürich/Einsiedeln/Cologne: Benziger; Neukirchen-Vluyn: Neukirchener Verlag, 1985) 66; Eng. trans., *Matthew 1–7: A Commentary* (Minneapolis: Augsburg, 1989) 50.

layer, which may well involve a "paradigm shift" in our understanding of Jesus[57], is the most important discovery of the current phase of Q research, for which we are primarily indebted to Helmut Koester.

57. Hans Küng has popularized for theology this concept presented by Thomas S. Kuhn, *The Structure of Scientific Revolutions* (International Encyclopedia of Unified Science 2.2; Chicago: University of Chicago Press, 1962; 2nd ed. enlarged, 1970). F. Gerald Downing calls for "a 'paradigm shift'" with reference particularly to his emphasis on Cynic parallels to Jesus (*Jesus and the Threat of Freedom* [London: SCM, 1987] 149); see his n. 48.

CHAPTER 11

Theological Autobiography

My childhood was the very sheltered existence of faculty housing on the campus of a Presbyterian seminary in a suburb of Atlanta, where my father was Professor of Church History and Polity for over 40 years.

My father was an orthodox Calvinist. I recall him reporting at the dinner table that the Chairman of the Board of Trustees and the President of the Seminary had called him in to tell him to desist from writing, in church magazines, articles opposing the published positions of our next-door neighbor, who chaired a committee of our denomination to update the standards of the church, such as the Westminster Confession of Faith. My father replied that he had taken an ordination vow to defend these standards and would not desist from honoring his commitment – they would have to fire him (which of course they did not do). I was thoroughly impressed by his courage and integrity, without really being aware of or interested in the issues themselves.

When later I was a student at this same seminary, I was conscientious in making a good grade in the required course in Calvinist doctrine (Bavinck), but did not really get involved in specific doctrines. Walter Lowrie was just then translating Kierkegaard, and I avidly read what had been published by then. Kierkegaard seemed to have a more relevant way to come to grips with the human dilemma. Though I did not realize it at the time, a pattern was already being pre-formed.

Before going on to graduate studies, I taught for a year at my college (Davidson) ... a quite literal Old Testament. My students were mostly returning veterans, who must have experienced me as hopelessly naive. Whether or not they actually believed anything I said, by the end of the year I no longer did. I had tried to make sense of my childhood theology to myself, and had failed. But that year was decisive, in that I had become at least open to the strange new world of reality.

My brother (himself a returning veteran) and I went together for a year to study at the University of Basel, where our father had spent a brief sabbatical just before the war. For Basel had assembled perhaps the most distinguished theological faculty of the day, having become during the 1930s and 1940s a haven of refuge for distinguished German and Swiss theologians who had lost their professorships in Germany because of their resistance to Nazism.

During two periods of study at Basel, Barth happened to be lecturing once on supralapsarianism/infralapsarianism, once on angels. My only lasting impression was that Barth talked about certain valid values protected by one side of the debate, and other valid values protected by the other side of the debate. It later occurred to me that he did not really believe in the doctrine itself (whichever side he came down on), but only in those values expressed in that arcane language. I became convinced (only in retrospect) that he had demythologized dogmatics (and what about the angels?), without actually realizing it – no doubt he would not have accepted this interpretation.

This soon after the war, German students were not yet allowed to live in Basel, but were permitted to live just across the border (Lörrach) and come over each day for classes (with a free midday meal in kind Christian homes). Whatever else they may or may not have smuggled across the border, they did import demythologizing. Our father had told us of the Barth–Brunner debate (he of course was on Barth's side), but had not known what he would be exposing us to in the post-war debate. When another American studying at Basel (Paul Meyer) explained to me what it all meant, my first reaction was that, formulate it as one might in sophisticated Heideggerian German, what they were saying was not the resurrection. (It had not yet occurred to me that Barth's doctrines of the fall and of angels were not really seriously affirming these as facts either.)

Barth's debate with his Swiss co-founder of dialectic theology, Emil Brunner (whom I commuted to Zürich to hear), had stayed, so to speak, within doctrinal confines: the old problem of synergism vs. salvation as wholly an unearned and undeserved gift of God. Since Brunner's view that people have a certain capacity for receiving God's revelation seemed to Barth to open the door for a synergistic aberration, Barth had stoutly replied: Nein! But this pre-war sparring had been completely forgotten by the post-war generation, for whom theology, if it had anything at all to say, must mean something about people's actual existence.

After the year in Basel, I returned to Princeton, where I had all along planned to get my doctorate in New Testament. But I found that a boring field of study, and after a year returned to Basel, with Barth as my Doktorvater. I told him I would like to have a topic tracing the transition from Protestant Liberalism to the two alternative outgrowths of Dialectic Theology, his own Theology of the Word and Rudolf Bultmann's Existentialistic Interpretation. He said I should read Ernst Troeltsch, Rudolf Otto, and Wilhelm Herrmann, and then we would talk about settling on one as the focus of the dissertation. By the end of the nineteenth century the metaphysical theology that had been ended once for all (one would have thought) by Kant, and the deification of the historical process by Hegel, had given way to the neo-Kantian ethical definition of God as the good. I proposed for my dissertation area Herrmann, whose focus on the path to faith seemed to have brought Schleiermacher's interest in the religious person's experience into this ethical religiosity, for it was in one's ethical experience in interpersonal relations that God, or at least religion, is inescapable and indispensable.

Actually the end of the First World War had brought (German) Christendom to an end. Rather than Christian culture being the progressive revelation of God through (Western) history, German culture had in fact collapsed – just think of the million-Mark German postage stamps! But, paradoxically, this had cleared the ideological air of the cultural pride that practically deified the state (which 'established' the church). Hence it would seem that God, rather than man, could for a change be heard, a unique chance to hear God 'between the times', before a new culture emerged of which Germans could be 'justifiably proud'. Friedrich Gogarten interpreted the German collapse as just such a brief moment uncluttered by human self-assertion. Thus it was in the negation of Christian culture that the positive revelation of God was – dialectically – to be heard. (Heidegger: One becomes aware of the basic but forgotten insight that there is anything at all –'being' – precisely when one realizes that there could equally well not be anything at all – 'nothingness'.)

It was of course the very antithesis of this emerging 'dialectic theology' of the 1920s when, in the 1930s, the German *ressentiment* over the French revenge-taking in the Versailles Treaty provided a bed of ideological discontent that triggered the nationalism-with-a-vengeance that Hitler exploited – precisely what Woodrow Wilson had feared. The mainline 'German Church' became a tool of this self-assertive nationalism, while the seceding 'Confessing Church' followed Barth in the direction of resistance.

Barth had told me he could speak out publicly in Germany during the Third Reich on behalf of Jews only by deriving what he wanted to say from a biblical text, since the Confessing Church had paid the price for maintaining its freedom to proclaim the word of God. This inevitably modulated Dialectic Theology, as culture criticism, into the Theology of the Word of God.

This of course needed decoding, for something very basic was being said: The inalienable core of the humanity of humankind is the right and freedom to blurt out the truth, even when unwelcome and painful, as sometimes the last form of resistance to evil. I heard Karl Jaspers lecture on the difference, during the Inquisition, between the appropriateness of recanting a 'heresy' that was irrelevant to one's very being, and on the other hand dying for a cause upon which one's own understanding of existence, constitutive of one's being, stood or fell. My father's refusal to be silenced, Herrmann's encounter with the good as God in interpersonal responsibility, the Confessing Church's 'word of God', Bultmann's 'authentic existence', the new hermeneutic's 'word event', though all buried somewhere back in my past, have nonetheless left their mark on what still today seems to me decent.

Given the retreat into traditional dogmatic language when called upon to speak out, it is no coincidence that Rudolf Bultmann, who had been convinced by Barth's *Römerbrief* that dialectic theology was in fact the best modern translation of Pauline, and hence Lutheran, theology, presented his demythologizing essay in 1941, just when the Confessing Church (of which he was part) was rigidifying into Neo-Orthodoxy. Whereas Barth had been a product of Ritschlian Liberalism (what we call the 'social gospel'), Bultmann had been trained in the even more radical history-of-religions school. Here the competing mythologies of the mystery religions had all become open to relevant interpretation as mythological objectifications of solutions to the human dilemma, languaged in terms of dying and rising gods – including the dying and rising Christ the Lord (what later was restated as the 'kerygma'). Whereas the New Testament's message was so enshrouded in such mythological jargon as to be offensive to modern people's better judgment (and thus to justify the widespread ignoring of whatever the church had to say), Bultmann argued that the kerygma as understood by Paul and John did have a strikingly compelling and intelligible meaning when put into the 'scientific' language of existentialism. For Bultmann's philosophical colleague at the University of Marburg, Martin Heidegger, had in fact produced a table of categories for interpreting human existence scientifically, worthy of being put alongside Aristotle's table of categories for understanding natural phenomena, upon which natural science had been so successfully built. When thus reformulated in modern scholarly terms, the Christian message turned out to be the most convincing presentation of authentic existence. Or so it seemed at the time.

Since Herrmann had taught at Marburg, and hence the library there would have what I needed to flesh out the context of his career, I proposed to Barth that I go for a time to study there – of course, to hear Bultmann. When I talked to Bultmann later about my dissertation topic ('Das Problem des Heiligen Geistes bei Wilhelm Herrmann'), he commented with some surprise that, after all, Herrmann had had very little to say about the Holy Spirit. When I explained that this was of course the doctrinal category where religious experience comes up for discussion, he no doubt forgave my Church Dogmatics lingo[1].

I asked Marburg classmates where things were moving in the Bultmannian stream, and they said the most exciting Bultmannian, Ernst Käsemann, had just begun his teaching career at Mainz. I wrote him requesting an interview in passing through Mainz on my way out of Germany. We met for an hour in the train station. This was in 1951, two years before he proposed what I later called a new quest of the historical Jesus[2]. I thus became a 'post-Bultmannian' (to use a term I coined to express the defections among Bultmann's pupils) before I actually became a Bultmannian. In effect, my theological trajectory over half a century has moved step by step from right to left. Käsemann provided a crucial early transition, once it had become clear to me that Oscar Cullmann, my house-father at the Alumneum in Basel, was hopelessly out of it. For my future lay not in dogmatics but in New Testament studies, which I taught first at Emory University (during which time I belatedly completed a second doctorate in this field at Princeton after all[3]).

I had, by this time, become Professor of New Testament and Theology at the School of Theology at Claremont, and then, as an inducement not to accept a professorship at Harvard, Professor of Religion at Claremont Graduate School. Here I founded the Institute for Antiquity and Christianity of which I became Director.

It was clear to me at the time that the main centers of theological scholarship, where the basic tools of the discipline were created in massive tomes, were in Europe and the Ivy League (plus Chicago), whereas the West Coast was at best involved in popularizing at the retail level. My intention was to create a center of basic research in the roots of Western civilization, out of which the medieval synthesis of Christendom and then the modern world have emerged. The approach, more culturally than theologically based, had been launched in Germany by Franz Dölger at the University of Bonn, out of which emerged the massive many-volumed *Reallexikon für Antike und Christentum*. For his approach had been to trace antiquity through to its medieval and modern transformations as 'Christentum'. After his death an institute was founded to carry on his

1. James M. Robinson, *Das Problem des Heiligen Geistes bei Wilhelm Herrmann*, Marburg an der Lahn: Karl Gleiser, Inhaber der R. Friedrichs Universitäts-Buchdruckerei, 1952.

2. James M. Robinson, *A New Quest of the Historical Jesus* (Studies in Biblical Theology 25), London: SCM; Naperville, IL: Alec R. Allenson, 1959.

3. James M. Robinson, *The Problem of History in Mark* (Studies in Biblical Theology 21), London: SCM; Naperville, IL: Alec R. Allenson, 1957.

legacy, and hence named the Franz-Dölger-Institut. This left the technical term he had made famous, *Antike und Christentum*, available as the most suitable name for the institute I had in view at the secular institution Claremont Graduate School: The Institute for Antiquity and Christianity[4].

Since I had taught a semester as a visiting professor at Göttingen in the chair of the retired New Testament lexicographer Walter Bauer, I negotiated after his death the purchase of his library for Claremont. Among the pamphlets that were part of his holdings were three editions of the statutes of the Göttingen Academy of Sciences – before Hitler, during Hitler, and after Hitler. I studied these to get a grasp of how such a research center could function. Our crucial point of departure in Claremont was a small cluster of young Turks ('Project Directors') in the biblical and patristic fields who shared my vision.

What we lacked (and still do) was funding. Normally such enterprises are not authorized by a university unless there is some assurance that funding will be available. I wrote an application to the newly created National Endowment for the Humanities to launch the six initial Projects (each directed by a different professor) with which the Institute began. Only my Nag Hammadi project was successful in obtaining modest funding (for three years, for a total of about $50,000), but that was enough for the well-wishing and (soft-hearted) president of the Graduate School to let us come into existence.

Actually, he never sought approval from the Board of Fellows of Claremont University Center to launch such a venture, since he knew they would not approve. Instead, he invited them, in a printed invitation stating the invitation was from the Board itself, to a gala opening ceremony at the newly created Music Center in Los Angeles.

My mentor, Ernest Cadman Colwell, who had been President of the University of Chicago before moving to Emory, and then assumed the presidency of the School of Theology at Claremont (taking me along with him), had reported the following anecdote about Chicago's pioneering Orientalist James Henry Breasted: He had interested the McCormick family in building and endowing the Oriental Institute, by bringing a huge stone winged bull from Babylon and storing it in a dark, dank, cramped basement room. Mr McCormick agreed it was so magnificent it should be in better accommodations! – I did in fact succeed in flying over from France, to put on display at that opening banquet, a (much smaller) bronze bull from Dan (infamous in the Old Testament for

4. James M. Robinson, 'The Institute for Antiquity and Christianity', *New Testament Studies* 16 (1970) 178-95.

erecting just such an idol). But the $35,000 for which we could have acquired it was not forthcoming.

Yet, in spite of the Achilles' heel of hardly any research funds, the Institute has published in its first 30 years of existence some 50 massive tomes. At first, projects were published at distinguished European publishing houses where the public was already accustomed to finding serious publications in that specialty, such as E. J. Brill, the Pontifical Biblical Institute, Oxford University Press, and Patristische Texte und Studien. But such scattering made the publication achievements of the Institute, as such, less visible, and newer projects have tended not to continue European publishing traditions. Hence our own monograph series, Studies in Antiquity and Christianity, has been publishing about a volume a year from various of our Projects for over a decade[5].

I taught modern theology only to a limited extent: A course on 'The Beginnings of Dialectic Theology' traced through the 1920s my own trajectory a generation later from Barth to Bultmann (with the help of Jürgen Moltmann's two-volumes of collected essays under that title, whose English translation I edited in 1968). A course on 'The New Hermeneutic' traced the development within the Bultmannian school from the 'existentialism' of Being and Time, to the language philosophy of the later Heidegger[6] as theologized by Gerhard Ebeling and Ernst Fuchs[7].

The sayings of Jesus played the central role of the 'language event' (= the word of God) in the new hermeneutic. Thus the Bultmannian school's focus on kerygmatic texts, such as the confessions and hymns imbedded in the New Testament[8], gave way to a revival of interest in the Sayings Gospel Q[9]. For, by this time, the new hermeneutic had in effect gone behind the kerygma's coded mythological language, which had made Jesus's decisive significance intelligible back then, but unintelligible today (Ebeling). It found a new basis in the word of Jesus as the language event constitutive of Christianity. It was Ernst Fuchs who, in his

---

5. Jon Ma. Asgeirsson, *The Institute for Antiquity and Christianity: Publications of the First Quarter-Century* (Occasional Papers 29), Claremont: Institute for Antiquity and Christianity, 1994.

6. James M. Robinson and John B. Cobb: *The Later Heidegger and Theology* (New Frontiers in Theology: Discussions among German and American Theologians, vol. 1), New York: Harper & Row, 1963 3-76.

7. James M. Robinson and John B. Cobb: *The New Hermeneutic* (New Frontiers in Theology: Discussions among Continental and American Theologians, vol. 2), New York: Harper & Row, 1964 1-77.

8. James M. Robinson, 'A Formal Analysis of Col. 1,15-20', *Journal of Biblical Literature* 76 (1957) 270-87.

9. James M. Robinson, 'Basic Shifts in German Theology', *Interpretation* 16 (1962) 76-97.

garbled pious jargon that few went to the trouble to try to understand, spoke of Jesus's sayings as gifts God lays on the table before us. Bultmann's famous or notorious oneliner to the effect that Jesus rose into the kerygma needed to be updated to read that Jesus 'rose' into the continuing validity of his own word.

Bultmann's own existential interpretation of Jesus, his *Jesus and the Word*, published in 1924 for a popular audience, had painted a humanly very authentic picture of ... a Jew. As Bultmann moved via Barth into his kerygmatic theology, this Jesus came to have a rather awkward position in his system as a whole – not part of New Testament theology, but only a presupposition of it, whatever that means. For he had sought to maintain that only through the Christian kerygma does one reach authentic existence ... like the pre-kerygmatic Jesus the Jew?

Käsemann's proposal to revive the theological relevance of the historical Jesus did not, in fact, face up to this problem. Rather Käsemann argued, via the threat of modern docetism, that neglecting as irrelevant what can be known through historiography about Jesus, that is to say, neglecting what in our modern world has the ring of reality about it, is tantamount to the early church's heretical denial of real humanity to Jesus. But the avoidance of docetism turned out not to be a major concern in the modern world, since that orientation was still grappling with validating the history of dogma rather than the historical Jesus.

It is only the relatively new ecumenical dialogue between Jews and Christians that makes Jesus the Jew not a theological liability, but rather the central meeting-ground for that dialogue. If Jesus was one of the greatest persons Judaism has produced, and yet was quite critical of the Judaism of which he was a part, the Jesus whom Christianity has exalted to high heaven would be at least as critical of what today is passed off in his name as Christian. Thus Jews and Christians share a valid claim to Jesus, but also share an awkward claim of Jesus upon both[10].

I had entered into the rehabilitation of Q by arguing it belonged to a literary genre in its own right, rather than just being a catechetical appendix to the kerygma[11]. My insight had been triggered by the discovery of another gospel of the same sayings genre among the Nag Hammadi codices, *The Gospel of Thomas*, which at first had often been dismissed

10. James M. Robinson, *The Sayings of Jesus: The Sayings Gospel in English* (Facets series), Minneapolis, Minn.: Fortress, 2001.

11. James M. Robinson, 'ΛΟΓΟΙ ΣΟΦΩΝ: Zur Gattung der Spruchquelle Q', in *Zeit und Geschichte, Dankesgabe an Rudolf Bultmann zum 80. Geburtstag*, edited by Erich Dinkler, Tübingen: J. C. B. Mohr [Paul Siebeck], 1964 77-96. [In *The Sayings Gospel Q. ΛΟΓΟΙ ΣΟΦΩΝ: On the Gattung of Q*, pp. 37-74.]

as no more than excerpts from narrative gospels long since available in the canon.

Yet this new access to Jesus was promptly sidetracked by my following up on another strand in the Bultmannian synthesis, his view that the Gnostic Redeemer myth was presupposed in and influential upon the New Testament. In order to ensure that the New Testament was free from such contamination, more conservative scholarship had all along argued that Gnosticism itself was a secondary product of post-apostolic Christianity, where system-building Gnosticism after all was first documented. No texts, no history! But then, the claim was made (Alexander Böhlig) that a Nag Hammadi text he published, the *Apocalypse of Adam*, documented pre-Christian Gnosticism! Though this claim itself later became controversial (as was inevitable), it was enough to send me to Cairo (while on a sabbatic, as Annual Professor at the American Schools of Oriental Research in Jerusalem), to see when the bulk of the new gnostic texts, still inaccessible to scholarship, might become available.

The answer was quite dismal: First a French, then a German monopoly had blocked access to the material for a generation. As long as a French Abbot headed the Department of Antiquities of Egypt and a Paris-trained Copt directed the Coptic Museum in Cairo, only French scholarship had access. Indeed the head of the Paris establishment literally gloated over his 'revenge' on the Germans, who had not been able, during the period of the two World Wars, to publish a Gnostic papyrus codex in Berlin to which he wanted access. Then when the Suez Crisis expelled the French, and a Berlin-trained Director took over the Coptic Museum, the Germans moved in, and assignments went only to Germans (even to the exclusion of East Germans). And all these impediments to the advancement of scholarship in favor of one or another first-world nation's hegemony over a third-world nation's culture, and one scholar's professional advancement at the expense of the rest of the scholarly community, were clothed in the loftiest terms. I entered the real world of scholarship quite abruptly.

The French had counterattacked by motivating UNESCO (which of course was based in Paris and hence used French scholars as consultants) to intervene. But when they learned that the Coptic Museum had assigned the plums to the Germans, indeed were told that many were already published (a claim which turned out to be false), the French, and hence UNESCO, lost interest. UNESCO's involvement was pruned down to the plan to photograph the material and publish it in a facsimile edition, thus making it available to all (which the French, now on the outside, had come to favor). But at UNESCO the whole undertaking got enmeshed in the bureaucracy, and was not moving forward. It only meant that no one had access, neither the French, nor the Germans, nor myself.

To speak of 'methodology' in connection with my frantic expedients to put the material in the public domain, enmeshed in the utter chaos of the Nag Hammadi situation, would seem to be quite an overstatement. Only if one recalls that, etymologically, method has to do with a path directed toward a goal, would it seem faintly appropriate to describe what I did as methodical. In any case, the first thing that would have to be said is that in such circumstances a method must be worked out ad hoc, from inside the situation, and would be largely inapplicable to other circumstances. It was only the basic commitment, the dogged determination, the willingness to do what it took, even to take risks, play a subservient role, have endless patience, be exploited by doing the chores no one else would do, seize every opportunity, go to any length, that made success in such a hopeless situation even remotely possible.

When I asked at the Coptic Museum to see the texts, I was told that they would of course have been glad to let me see them, had they not turned control over to UNESCO. I should address myself to the Center of Documentation in Cairo that administered the UNESCO photographic project. There I was told that UNESCO only controlled the photography, not the papyri themselves, which of course were under the control of the Coptic Museum. If I wanted to see the photographs, I should go to UNESCO in Paris.

Since I was at the moment not in Paris but in Cairo, I followed a lead from the pastor of the German church there, to ask about previously-made photographs at the German Institute in Cairo. I was indeed given access to a rather large number of photographs by the Acting Director, who told me I could study them while he was gone for three days to visit an archaeological excavation. I took the photographs to my inexpensive lodging in the Presbyterian Mission, and there transcribed the photographs 24 hours a day for three days and nights, finishing them all in time to return them before the Acting Director arrived back in town.

I attended on that same trip a congress of the International Association for the History of Religions in Messina, Sicily, on the origins of Gnosticism. Here I was suddenly hailed as an authority on the photographic project in Cairo, from which I had just come. Hence I was assigned to a committee to draw up a telegram that the congress officially endorsed and sent to UNESCO, urging the completion of the photography and the publication of a facsimile edition. I went to Paris to inquire at UNESCO how the telegram I had composed had been received. I was assured the photography had indeed been completed and the publication of a facsimile edition was imminent. In retrospect, when it became clear that nothing was happening, I realized that this good news was merely a convenient maneuver to get me out of the functionary's office.

I then visited the German university where the leading German Nag Hammadi specialist I had met in Sicily taught Coptology. For, on learning that I had plans to visit his university, he had acceded to my request to let me copy when in Germany his transcription of a short Nag Hammadi tractate (after I had sat up all night in Messina producing a translation of a sample page, to accredit myself as qualified – which I actually was not).

On arrival in Germany I was told by my host (the textual critic Kurt Aland of the Theological Faculty) that, unknown to myself, I was to be the guest speaker the next day at a joint meeting of the university's Theological Faculty with a nearby Theological Seminary. In order to give me a chance to prepare something to say, once it became clear I had never received the written invitation to speak, he made the kind offer to xerox the transcription I had planned to re-transcribe all that evening. But, since the notebook containing that transcription contained other transcriptions as well, I sat up all night transcribing those texts that had not been xeroxed. The next day I gave as my German lecture an introduction I had written for the German paperback edition of Albert Schweitzer's *Quest of the Historical Jesus*[12], which, after all, was (I thought) in the area of my ongoing scholarship.

My innocent inquiries in Cairo had thus enticed me bit by bit into the whole morass, ending in my investing almost 20 years (in my case the prime of life) in breaking the monopoly.

After returning home, I was alerted to the problem that the UNESCO photographs were probably not usable for a facsimile edition, since presumably the many fragments had not been reassembled into legible pages. I wrote UNESCO to inquire if that was the case. On getting no reply, I had to return to Paris to ask in person. When I made a mild complaint to the functionary's superior that he did not answer letters, I was informed that I was not a citizen of the country (in UNESCO jargon: 'member state') whose cultural heritage was in question, and, besides, the functionary in charge of the photographic project was from an oral culture (Afghanistan). But when I went to his office, he graciously received me, listened to my problem, and suggested I spend a weekend working in an adjacent office finding for myself the answer to my question. He was kind enough to put at my disposal the negatives of about half the texts,

12. Albert Schweitzer, *Die Geschichte der Leben-Jesu-Forschung* (Taschenbuch-Ausgabe), München and Hamburg: Siebenstern Taschenbuch, 1966 7-24.

and enlarged glossy prints of the other half (presumably, so that I would not have a complete file of either, and hence would not be tempted to abscond with them).

I returned Saturday morning to my new office, got the negatives, and took them to a suburb of Paris, where I knew a photography shop, and paid dearly to have them make two enlargements of more than 500 negatives by Sunday evening. I then hurried back to Paris and, with a simple tripod and tourist's 35 mm camera, photographed the glossy prints one by one as I laid them on the floor beneath the tripod. UNESCO was of course completely empty on the weekend. I had finished just in time to return to the Paris suburb, pick up the enlarged prints, and return the negatives to the UNESCO office before the leisurely tempo of a bureaucracy's Monday morning began. Thus I was finally in possession of good photographs of all the Nag Hammadi codices, and to this extent was in a position to break the monopoly. But I still had no publication rights! On my return home I studied the photographs enough to write up and send to UNESCO a report answering my question: The leaves would indeed have to be reassembled from fragments before a facsimile edition (that would finally break the monopoly) could be published.

The facsimile edition planned by UNESCO envisaged an international committee of Nag Hammadi experts that would organize the publication. But the committee had never been convened. I wrote repeatedly to inquire when that would take place, and, after my patience had worn out, arranged to live during a sabbatic year at the American Church in Paris, as scholar in residence, within walking distance of UNESCO. Although I had gone to the trouble to attend a follow-up meeting of the International Association for the History of Religions in Sweden, and persuaded them to authorize its Secretary to write UNESCO on my behalf, I discovered on presenting myself again at UNESCO that the letter had never been sent. I was nonetheless provided with an office, where I spent all autumn labeling the photographs at UNESCO with the identification of fragments and page sequences that the team of young American scholars I had organized had established. We had in fact prepared draft transcriptions and translations of all the material. Hence when, in November, I had persuaded my superior at UNESCO to name a committee (including myself as the American delegate) and schedule a meeting in Cairo for December, I was able to send to each member of the committee, in advance of the meeting, this rough draft of everything. The net effect of that gesture was that I was later elected Permanent Secretary of the International Committee for the Nag Hammadi Codices (1970-1984), which meant I was authorized to do all the work for the committee.

The publishing house E. J. Brill in The Netherlands had had the good fortune some years earlier to publish The *Gospel of Thomas* in an inexpensive 'preliminary edition' that sold over 40 000 copies in the Christmas rush. Hence the head of the firm, F. C. Wieder, Jr., was eager to publish the whole, and had become my decisive, trustworthy, and effective partner. We had an unspoken agreement that, come hell or high water, we would publish the texts. And we had made the following concrete plan: Brill would hire a photographer and make for him a plane reservation to Cairo for the day after the UNESCO meeting convened, so as to photograph everything while the papyri was available to the UNESCO committee. For, since Egypt was technically at war with Israel, all the papyri, conserved each between panes of plexiglass, was in safe keeping. Bringing it to the Coptic Museum for the meeting was the one condition I had been able to have honored – I pointed out that otherwise we might meet less expensively and more conveniently in Paris rather than in Cairo, which of course Egyptian officialdom did not want to do for reasons of national prestige.

What I had not counted on was that the first day of the Cairo meeting of the UNESCO committee was filled with pomp and ceremony, such as newspaper reporters photographing the Minister of Culture with officials of the Coptic Museum (not with world-famous European scholars). He was then given a guided tour of the Museum to impress upon him that next year's budget should include funds for renovating the Museum (a very worthy cause, unfortunately not honored). But I had to get the committee down to business at least long enough to choose Brill (rather than some Egyptian publisher) to do the facsimile edition! For a delay of even a day would frustrate our best-laid plans, since by now the tourism just before Christmas had booked up all plane seats to Cairo. I appealed (while we were cooling our heels during the pomp and ceremony) to the very distinguished Swedish delegate, one of the committee's several honorary Presidents, to shift that item to the top of the agenda, and to call upon the committee to come to order long enough to handle at least one item on the agenda.

Once this was thus achieved, all I had to do was telegraph Brill to put the photographer on the plane the next morning. Only then did I learn that one could not normally send telegrams to addresses outside of Egypt. The Nile Hilton Hotel had its own telegraphic service, for persons staying there (but we were of course in a different hotel, one owned by the Egyptian government), except in dire cases of emergency. I conjured up a big enough emergency that my telegram was accepted. The photographer arrived the next day and photographed steadily while the committee met. I proposed a 'Technical Sub-Committee' stay to work on assembling fragments (on the basis of the lists of placements the American team had provided), along with the photographer, once the official meeting adjourned, which did take place. Then we broke for Christmas, but returned again in early January for another ten days of work. By the time the Technical Sub-Committee adjourned, a complete updated file of photographs was at Brill – and at Claremont. But we were far from completing placing all the fragments.

The Technical Sub-Committee returned each year for a couple of weeks to work further on the fragments. Since UNESCO paid for the trips by issuing the plane tickets, we had to have its approval, which in turn meant the functionary there had to have the approval of the President of the Egyptian Antiquities Organization. When I received no replies to my letters to Paris and Cairo, I went to Cairo and made arrangements with the official there, even getting him to initial a draft contract with Brill that Mr Wieder and I had worked out.

In a subsequent year I had to fly to Paris, to handle a last-minute snag: The Egyptian official was to be out of the country (receiving an honorary doctorate in France, part of the French counter-attack), and hence the planned time for Cairo did not suit. The UNESCO official explained he had talked by phone with the Cairo official, who had requested that the time should be changed if that was not an undue inconvenience to the Technical Sub-Committee. I explained that indeed it was quite inconvenient for us, since we had each made arrangements for absenting ourselves from our classes, and I was already in Paris, with the others on alert awaiting momentarily their plane tickets. I insisted he phone Cairo again for clearance, and sat in his office several hours until he did in fact get through by phone to Cairo and got its approval for the trip to proceed.

In Cairo things were equally chaotic. Once the wrong crate had been brought from 'security' (the unlighted basement of the Egyptian Museum, a state secret we were not supposed to know until it became necessary for us to produce a truck to return the wrong crate and bring the right one). We also found the lights had gone out at the Coptic Museum, and so had to wait until the official, now *Dr.* Gamal Mokhtar, returned from France, to authorize bringing in a generator and stringing electric wires all over the floor and tables in our work area.

We imported from London rat poison to cope with the uninvited guest that prevented the Museum staff from walking into one half of our work area. The resultant odor which over the years only gradually went away was hardly an improvement.

Each year I brought with me members of the American team to assist the Technical Sub-Committee in the placing of fragments and the establishment of page sequences. When the UNESCO money ran out and of course the Technical Sub-Committee stopped working on its unfinished assignment, I brought some of the American team for seven months non-stop to get the job completed. Our pressure on the Museum staff to arrive when the Museum officially opened and stay until the official closing time led them finally to move us into a room by ourselves and give me the key.

When it comes to reconstructing a papyrus codex, one can with more justification speak of scholarly method. On the basis of photographs, we had initially been dependent on the lettering, placing fragments where the resultant text made sense. Sometimes, as in a jigsaw puzzle, the broken edges fit exactly, but often the fragment did not actually touch the leaf to which it belonged, but stood off by itself, in what we called an 'island placement'. When in Cairo we finally had access to the papyrus itself, each such placement had to be verified by the fiber patterns (as distinctive for a trained eye as fingerprints), horizontal on one side and vertical on the other. Most of the 'easy' placements based on the text had already been done on the basis of the photographs by the time we began, but with painstaking and prolonged effort (one team member stayed over a couple of years more), all fragments larger than a fingernail were ultimately placed.

The sequence of leaves in several codices was completely unknown, due to the disorder in which the material had been conserved. We discovered that the horizontal fibers not only aided in placing a fragment on a leaf, but also made it possible to identify which leaf in the other half of the quire had joined it, at the (now broken) fold at the spine. This double-leaf had then horizontal fiber continuity with the next double-leaves above and below it in the quire, since in effect these double leaves had been cut in sequence one after the other from a papyrus scroll and laid one on top of the other in a stack that, when folded down the center, had produced the quire.

The roll itself had been manufactured by pasting end to end long strips of papyrus – when the horizontal fiber continuity on our leaves ended, we found a half-inch wide overlap where one papyrus strip had been pasted to another. When there was no such pasted overlap, we knew we had reached the end of a roll. Thus we had to reconstruct the rolls from which the codex had been manufactured to be sure we had established the correct sequence of leaves, especially in fragmentary codices where the text itself no longer made the sequence clear.[13]

13. James M. Robinson, 'The Construction of the Nag Hammadi Codices', in *Essays on the Nag Hammadi Texts in Honour of Pahor Labib* (edited by Martin Krause; Nag Hammadi Studies 6), Leiden: E.J. Brill, 1975 170-90; James M. Robinson, 'On the Codicology of the Nag Hammadi Codices', in *Les textes de Nag Hammadi: Colloque du Centre d'histoire des religions (Strasbourg, 23-25 octobre 1974)* (edited by Jacques-E.

Ultraviolet lamps, which we had brought from California, aided in transcribing the text (once we produced a dark setting under a blanket in the sweltering heat), since the ink had included iron and hence showed up as purple stain even when the ink itself had flaked off.

The monopoly was completely broken by the end of 1977, when the last of the 13 codices was published by E. J. Brill for UNESCO in *The Facsimile Edition of the Nag Hammadi Codices,* just seven years after I had first seen the originals in Cairo. At the same time we published a one-volume English translation, which has subsequently sold over 100 000 copies[14]; the 14-volume critical edition was completed and the last volume published by E. J. Brill in 1995.

Part of the broader responsibility put on me by the UNESCO committee had been to verify the site of the discovery. I had once already (on my way to Sicily) made a hurried trip to Nag Hammadi, where my procedure was to turn myself promptly in to the police, and ask them to engage for me a taxi and translator, to help me visit the presumed site of the discovery. It was my good fortune that the translator was a godly Copt (he refused a generous tip, but did take me to church), who taught math at the local Boys Preparatory School. He mentioned that his father had been offered one of the books, but had not bought it, since he owned a Bible and that was all he needed.

Once the law was lifted that had subsequently made Upper Egypt (except for tourist traps like Luxor) inaccessible to foreigners (while the Soviets built the High Dam), I immediately returned to Nag Hammadi on behalf of my assignment from the UNESCO committee to investigate the site of the find. I found agreeable lodging at the Guest House of the nineteenth-century Belgian Sugar Factory. I first inquired at the Boys Preparatory School for my interpreter, since he was also connected, via his father, with the marketing of the codices. The Principal told me he had moved to Cairo, and wrote down the Cairo address for me.

I then tracked down that address, but no one there had ever heard of the person I sought. In desperation I came up with a wild hunch: Since in Arabic one writes in the opposite direction from English, except for numerals, perhaps the Principal had reversed the numbers of the street address, unfamiliar as he was with writing for an English reader. So I asked my driver to turn around and drive to the other end of the street,

Ménard; Nag Hammadi Studies 7), Leiden: E.J. Brill, 1975 15-31; James M. Robinson, *The Facsimile Edition of the Nag Hammadi Codices: Introduction,* Leiden: E.J. Brill, 1984.

14. James M. Robinson (ed.), *The Nag Hammadi Library in English,* Leiden: E.J. Brill; San Francisco: Harper & Row, 1977.

where the reversed number would be located. There we found not only my former translator, but his friend the Principal, on a visit from Nag Hammadi. Sometimes a wild hunch does pay off! But you also have to earn your luck.

The Principal said his teacher of English at the Boys Preparatory School lived in the same village as did the discoverer of the Nag Hammadi Codices, and knew not only who the discoverer was, but would be willing to put me in contact with him when I went to Nag Hammadi the following week. I also mentioned the previously unnoticed name I had found in the Registry of Acquisitions of the Coptic Museum, as having sold the first codex to the Museum. The Principal said of course he, and any other Copt of the region, knew that name, since the person had taught English and History, on a circuit of Coptic parochial schools, before Nasser closed Coptic schools to replace them with public schools. Thus I was put on the track of both the discoverer and first middleman, leads which I did in fact follow up year after year, drinking tea endlessly in villages of the Nag Hammadi region, until I had interviewed repeatedly each person still alive who had been involved in the discovery and trafficking. This is, I think, the first time that the details of an important illicit manuscript discovery have been tracked down with such patience and care that the story could be accurately recorded, from the illiterate Muslim camel driver who made the discovery, through villagers who acquired for cigarettes or oranges one or more codex, to the final conservation of the material in the Coptic Museum[15]. There was of course a less scientific, more dramatic side of the story, having to do with the discoverer, Muhammad Ali, having been involved in a blood feud at the time of the discovery.

One night his father, a night watchman for valuable irrigation machinery that had been imported from Germany, killed a marauder from the nearby village Hamra Dum, a village that had an ongoing blood feud with

15. For further details, see James M. Robinson, 'The Discovery of the Nag Hammadi Codices', *Biblical Archeologist* 42 (Fall 1979) 206-24; James M. Robinson, 'From the Cliff to Cairo: The Story of the Discoverers and the Middlemen of the Nag Hammadi Codices', in *Colloque international sur les textes de Nag Hammadi (Québec, 22-25 août 1978)* (Bibliothèque copte de Nag Hammadi, Section 'Etudes' 1), Québec: Les presses de l'Université Laval; Louvain: Peeters, 1981 [1982] 21-58; James M. Robinson, 'Nag Hammadi: The First Fifty Years', in *The Nag Hammadi Library after Fifty Years: Proceedings of the 1995 Society of Biblical Literature Commemoration* (edited by John D. Turner and Anne McGuire; Nag Hammadi and Manichean Studies 44), Leiden, New York, and Cologne: Brill, 1997 3-33. Abridged reprint in *The Fifth Gospel: The Gospel of Thomas Comes of Age*, edited by Steven J. Patterson and James M. Robinson, with a New English Translation by Hans-Gebhard Bethge et al., Harrisburg, Pa.: Trinity Press International, 1998 77-110.

Muhammad Ali's own village al-Qasr. The next day that murder was avenged, in that Muhammad Ali's father was found shot through the head, lying beside the remains of the man from Hamra Dum he had killed. Muhammad Ali's mother, beside herself, told her seven sons to keep their mattocks sharp so as to be ready when an occasion for revenge presented itself.

Some six months later someone ran to the house of Muhammad Ali to tell the family that the murderer, Ahmad Ismail, was asleep in the heat of the day on a dirt road nearby, with a jug of sugar cane molasses, the local product, by his side. The sons grabbed their mattocks, fell on the hapless person before he could flee, hacked him up, cut open his heart, and, dividing it among them, ate it raw, the ultimate act of blood vengeance.

The story of the blood feud came out in connection with Muhammad Ali explaining why he would not accompany me to the cliff to show me the site of the discovery: The hamlet of the opposing clan lay just at the foot of the cliff, and controlled it as its turf. He had avenged his father's murder just about a month after the discovery, and hence had been afraid ever since to return to the site. So I had to go to Hamra Dum myself, find the son of Ahmad Ismail, the man Muhammad Ali had butchered, and get his assurance that, since he had long since shot up a funeral *cortège* of Muhammad Ali's family, wounding Muhammad Ali and killing a number of his clan, he considered the score settled. Hence he would not feel honor-bound to attack Muhammad Ali if he returned to the foot of the cliff. I took this good news back to Muhammad Ali, who opened his shirt, showed me his scar, bragged that he had been shot but not killed, yet emphasized that if he ever laid eyes on Ahmad Ismail again, he would kill him on the spot. As a result of this display of a braggadocio's fearlessness, I called his hand and thus persuaded him to go to the cliff, camouflaged in my clothes, in a government jeep, with me sitting on the bullets side facing the village and him on the safer cliff side, at dusk in Ramadan, when all Muslims are at home gorging themselves after fasting throughout the daylight hours.

One false lead from a local priest was that the papyri had for a time been in the nearby city of Dishna, in the possession of a deceased priest he had known. In tracking down that lead, a representative of the Department of Agriculture (who was interested in what came out of the ground, and not just the local crop of sugar cane) told me the name of the antiquities dealer in Alexandria to whom some of the papyri had been sold (presumably by this person himself).

I went to Alexandria and found the shop, but the original owner had died. I visited his son in his sumptuous home (dealing in antiquities paid off). He showed me a stack of photographs of objects his father had sold. In thumbing through them, I found two photographs of manuscript pages, and asked if I might borrow them. I had them photographed in America and then mailed them back to him.

One that contained the Psalms in Greek was identified as a Bodmer Papyrus by a specialist in the Septuagint whom I knew (John Wevers of Toronto). The other, a page from the Song of Songs in Coptic, is a text that had been reported to be also in the Bibliothèque Bodmer, but not yet published. I asked a German Coptologist at the Pontifical Biblical Institute in Rome (Hans Quecke), on his way back to Germany for summer vacation, to pass by Geneva and verify whether this picture belonged to that codex, which it did.

Thus I had by mistake floundered upon the story of the discovery and marketing of the Bodmer Papyri, among which the best papyrus manuscripts of Luke and John are found, which I pursued with similar energy, until the site of the discovery and the middlemen had all come to light[16]. As a result, I was able to show that the Bodmer Papyri are the remains of the library of the Pachomian Monastic Order.

In the case of the discoverer, my trusted Principal of the Boys Preparatory School of Nag Hammadi later wrote me that he had been sent to examine students applying for graduation from the High School of a small hamlet near the cliff behind Dishna, and had tracked down the discoverer, whom we had heard lived in that hamlet. I made an extra trip to Egypt to follow up that lead.

The hamlet had its first electric light bulb, functional and obviously on display, in a large public room – the High Dam had just generated enough electricity to permit rural electrification! The room was crowded full of curious (male) villagers. The discoverer had just finished telling us his story, when someone from the back of the room spoke up to the effect that he too had been involved in the story, since he had once had one of the books. I asked (through the Principal, functioning as my translator) for his name. He gave me, in standard Arab style, his name and that of his father. I immediately recognized the

16. For further details see James M. Robinson, 'The Discovering and Marketing of Coptic Manuscripts: The Nag Hammadi Codices and the Bodmer Papyri', in *The Roots of Egyptian Christianity*, edited by Birger A. Pearson and James E. Goehring, Philadelphia: Fortress, 1986 1-25; James M. Robinson, 'The First Christian Monastic Library', in *Coptic Studies: Acts of the Third International Congress of Coptic Studies, Warsaw, 20-25 August 1984*, Warsaw: PWN—Panstwowe Wydawnictwo Naukowe, 1990 371-78; James M. Robinson, 'The Pachomian Monastic Library at the Chester Beatty Library and the Bibliothèque Bodmer', in *The Role of the Book in the Civilisations of the Near East* (Manuscripts of the Middle East 5, 1990-1991 [1993]) 26-40.

name as one that had been repeatedly mentioned to me as that of a middleman. Often Arabic names include in third place the name of the grandfather. This had been the case when, in previous interviews, persons had narrated this person's role in the story. So when he gave me two names, I, without waiting for the translator, immediately threw in the name of his grandfather. There was dead silence in the overcrowded room. How could an American, who could not even speak Arabic, and who, for the first time, was in their hamlet, know the name of this unknown peasant's grandfather? Obviously I must have all the facts, in an almost magic way! (The discoverer had just reported that he thought the books had been written by monsters – no doubt his sense of alienation, at seeing a script that did not look like Arabic, was objectified in mythological terms.) I was, to put it mildly, in a pre-Enlightenment setting.

Since my involvement had escalated far beyond my initial intentions, and had necessitated acquiring such competencies as Coptology, Papyrology and Codicology (not to speak of Archaeology as a cover for espionage), for which I had no previous preparation, it became an all-consuming investment of time that meant an almost total hiatus in my previous scholarly career. But this kind of scholarship was not really where my heart lay.

I did in fact subsequently get involved in publishing a two-volume facsimile edition of the unpublished fragments from Cave 4 of the Dead Sea Scrolls discovery[17], in order to break that monopoly, but that involved only a minor investment of energy, a project on the side, once I happened to get access to the photographs and felt morally bound to publish them[18].

When at the age of 60 I had completed the bulk of my Nag Hammadi responsibilities, the question arose as to what next, since neither I nor my field were the same. The quite distinguished New Testament scholar Ernest Cadman Colwell, in many ways my academic mentor, had, after investing a generation in academic administration, sought to re-enter New Testament scholarship, but was forced to the painful conclusion that it was no longer possible in his case, and so retired to his favorite fishing

17. Robert H. Eisenman and James M. Robinson, *A Facsimile Edition of the Dead Sea Scrolls*, 2 volumes, Washington, DC: Biblical Archaeology Society, 1991, second revised impression 1992.

18. James M. Robinson, 'Manuscript Discoveries of the Future', *Zeitschrift für Papyrologie und Epigraphik* 92 (1992) 281-96; James M. Robinson, 'Ethics in Publishing Manuscript Discoveries: Panel Discussion', in *Methods of Investigation of the Dead Sea Scrolls and the Khirbet Qumran Site: Present Realities and Future Prospects* (edited by M. O. Wise et al.; Annals of the New York Academy of Sciences 722), New York: New York Academy of Sciences, 1994 468-71.

pier in Florida. Was there anything that I could actually do in my field that was also worth doing?

The change in myself consisted not just in new scholarly methods and skills I had to acquire, but in the basic shift out of the ivory tower and into the feuding villages of Upper Egypt, where my excavations of the site of the Nag Hammadi discovery put me year after year all too literally into the line of fire, but also into the intrigues, selfishness and phoniness of distinguished European colleagues. To give but one example: The last holdout in the monopoly had been the Jung Codex (Nag Hammadi Codex I), since it was in a bank vault in Zürich, accessible only to its lethargic editors, but not available to the UNESCO Committee in Cairo. I was told by the Swiss representative on the Committee that the long-standing agreement to return the Codex to Egypt when the editors had completed their transcription had not been honored, because the heirs of Jung knew of its high financial value. I contacted the spokesperson for the heirs, who said they were ready to return it to Egypt as soon as the editors would give their approval. He even agreed to write them requesting their permission to return it. But then he had to write me back that one editor had blocked their good intentions: The Swiss representative on the UNESCO Committee![19]

Such scholars looked down condescendingly on the Egyptians as natives one could never trust; yet they themselves, once their own behind-the-scenes machinations had become clear to me, turned out to have absolutely no high ground from which to pontificate such (in any case outdated) colonialist views. The awe with which I had automatically held European scholars turned into disdain for some for whom I could no longer have respect. All this coincided with the Watergate scandal that toppled an American president for just such behind-the-scenes machinations. I found myself mired in what I gradually had to concede was the prevalent reality. Reporting on what great European scholars were doing could no longer be my thing. I had to strike out on my own.

The Gospel of John has always been associated most closely, among New Testament texts, with Gnosticism, and hence the question had been in my mind for some time as to whether I should not seek to write the Hermeneia Commentary on John. But I could not convince myself that the progress in Johannine scholarship, which my working the Nag Hammadi texts into the scholarly literature would effect, was ultimately worth

19. James M. Robinson, 'The Jung Codex: The Rise and Fall of a Monopoly', *Religious Studies Review* 3 (January 1977) 17-30.

the effort on my part (quite apart from the fact that my competence was really not in the History of Religions and Gnosticism). Instead, I decided to return to my new beginning that had been aborted with the Nag Hammadi intrusion, the Sayings Gospel Q.

The nineteenth century's quest of the historical Jesus had been a driving force behind Liberalism in German theology. The outcome had been, by the opening of our century, the Two Document Hypothesis: Matthew and Luke were so similar, so 'synoptic', because where they agreed they were copying out Mark, or, when the material on which they agreed was not in Mark to be copied, they must have been following a hypothetical second source nicknamed Q, the acronym of the German word *Quelle,* meaning 'source'. It was thought (Adolf von Harnack) to be early enough not yet to have been corrupted by (Pauline) theology, and hence a reliable source for Jesus's teachings, just as Mark was for Jesus's biography.

Albert Schweitzer attacked all this, not because he did not share Liberalism's trust in the reliability of the sources, but rather because he thought that the sources presented Jesus not as a modern social reformer, but as a hopelessly obsessed apocalypticist. Schweitzer was the last to take the Gospels as chronologically accurate literal historical narration. In this regard, and hence in his picture of Jesus, he was as wrong as those he so eloquently criticized.[20]

Then all this had changed after the opening of the century. It became clear (William Wrede) that Mark was obsessed by the dogma of the 'Messianic secret', and hence was narrating anything other than objective history or biography. The form critics (Martin Dibelius and Rudolf Bultmann) next argued that Jesus's sayings were first of all products of the transmitting church, whose use of such traditions had led to their reformulation and even in many cases their creation, so that what Jesus actually said is hardly more than a faint echo or whisper behind what the church said he said. It is impossible to write a biography of Jesus, since all the traditions about him were 'kerygmatized', and one cannot really get behind that prism to the objective facts themselves.

Q's relevance had earlier been played down, as merely the ethical, catechetical instruction for newly baptized converts to the kerygma, no more than its 'application'. But then it became clear that Q did not build on the kerygma of Jesus's death and resurrection at all, but had its own

20. See my Introduction to Albert Schweitzer, *The Quest of the Historical Jesus,* New York: Macmillan, 1968 xi-xxxiii; reprinted in *A New Quest of the Historical Jesus and Other Essays,* Philadelphia: Fortress, 1983 172-95.

'kerygma' ('something more than Jonah'). It was the document of a distinct branch of primitive Christianity (Heinz Eduard Tödt), for which 'the' kerygma was not the all-inclusive 'unity' with which Christianity was supposed to have begun. Form criticism's 'history of the synoptic tradition' (the title of Bultmann's book), with its focus on oral tradition, had in fact not written the history of the Q tradition. But Q's layering can after all be traced back to a core of authentic sayings of Jesus (roughly comparable to the Sermon on the Mount). The oldest layer in Q is the nearest to Jesus that one can get, and hence may well prove to have pay dirt![21]

Of course it can always be said that the oldest layer of tradition is after all a layer of the church's (or: the Q community's) transmission, which may or may not consist of actual quotations of Jesus. But as one works back from Matthew and Luke's editing to the final redactional level of Q itself, and from that back to preredactional smaller clusters and collections, and then to the individual saying, one can see a directionality in which the tradition was moving:

When looking forward in time, the tradition is moving toward a more moralizing, spiritualizing, christologizing, domesticating way of imagining Jesus, an amazingly successful enterprise that produced the image of Jesus most Christians still have today. But then those interpretive stages can be traced in the reverse direction, pointing back toward Jesus, the point of departure of this whole procedure. These arrows back through the layers of tradition do point to a convergence point, even if that point itself remains, so to speak, enclosed in a black box of uncertain authenticity. Such arrows do make it possible to know, not quite Jesus's *ipsissima verba* (Joachim Jeremias), but at least what he was up to, what he proposed, and what made such a dramatic impact on those who heard him.

There is then really no cogent reason not to ascribe to him such striking sayings that crop up rather densely in this oldest material. Its basic authenticity is all the more probable in view of the fact that the editing by Matthew and Luke was moving away from resolving the desperate

---

21. James M. Robinson, 'History of Q Research', in *The Critical Edition of Q: Synopsis including the Gospels of Matthew and Luke, Mark and Thomas with English, German, and French Translations of Q and Thomas*, edited by James M. Robinson, Paul Hoffmann, and John S. Kloppenborg, Minneapolis: Fortress; Leuven: Peeters, 2000 xix-lxxi; slightly abbreviated as 'Introduction' in *The Sayings Gospel Q in Greek and English with Parallels from the Gospels of Mark and Thomas* (edited by James M. Robinson, Paul Hoffmann, and John S. Kloppenborg; Contributions to Biblical Exegesis and Theology 30), Leuven, Paris, Sterling, Va.: Peeters, 2001; Minneapolis: Fortress, 2002 xiii-cvii.

plight of the needy, into an endorsement of the disciples, and a clearly discernible spiritualizing rather than concretizing[22]. Hence, in view of the directionality of the flow, the point of departure in Jesus shows a remarkable consistency with the material in the oldest layer of Q itself.

Jesus really is not a shadowy founding figure beyond our reach, comparable to Qumran's 'teacher of righteousness', but rather is someone who can be encountered as an historical figure. The problem the historical Jesus poses is really not that we do not know what he had to say, but rather that, when we get wind of it, we do not know how to handle it. Rather bear those ills we have than fly to others we know not of! And so the church prefers to whistle in the dark.

In my case, this working hypothesis of pursuing Q back to Jesus seemed quite worth pursuing. After all, some sayings seem to pick up just where I had left off: 'Why do you call me Master, Master, and do not do what I say?' 'Do not be afraid of those who kill the body, but cannot kill the soul.'

My return to New Testament scholarship thus took the form of organizing in 1985 the International Q Project (consisting of a new team of some 40 younger scholars) to establish a critical text of the Sayings Gospel Q. For this written Greek collection of a couple of hundred sayings ascribed to Jesus had been used by the authors of the Gospels of Matthew and Luke, who in the process had 'improved' the wording of Q to make it more clearly reflect their own understanding of Jesus's sayings. It was this damage that needed to be repaired.

Our method for reconstituting the wording of Q has been to get deeply enough into the vocabulary, grammar, style, and slant of those two Evangelists to be able to detect, in the many small divergences of the Matthean and Lukan text from each other, which Evangelist is responsible for the 'improvement', and then to undo that good work by restoring the way the text of Q originally read.

Previous scholarship's studies of Matthew and Luke's editing of Mark had already provided detailed information about their vocabulary, syntax, theological tendencies, and the like, so that there was already available a vast amount of information to apply to our task. When Matthew and Luke disagreed in the wording or word order of Q sayings, the 'fingerprints' of one Evangelist or the other made clear that this Evangelist had changed the text. This did not automatically mean that the reading of the other

---

22. James M. Robinson, 'The Jesus of Q as Liberation Theologian', in *The Gospel Behind the Gospels: Current Studies on Q* (edited by Ronald A. Piper; Supplements to Novum Testamentum 75), Leiden: E.J. Brill, 1995 259-74. [In this volume, pp. 147-61.]

Evangelist was that of Q, since both Evangelists could have, and in fact often did, 'improve' what both sensed to be 'deficient'.

Since I was coming at the task directly from manuscript study, I applied to the reconstruction of this text, though no manuscripts survived, methods familiar to the textual criticism of the New Testament text itself: When a scribe makes a scribal error (in our case read: 'improvement'), the error often consists not just in a single word, but includes whatever consequences in rewriting the one change may have made. A different preposition requires often a different case ending. Sometimes the consequences are more subtle and far-reaching. Indeed we have found the task of delimiting precisely the 'variation units' within each saying to be a very time-consuming enterprise, requiring that one get to the bottom of each of the Matthean and Lukan reformulations.

Each saying in Matthew and Luke had to be coded with numbered sigla, making each variation unit discrete, so that the documentation for precisely that variation unit, on which our decision as to how it read Q at that precise place was based, could be amassed in a voluminous database. The database itself went *seriatim* through the numeration of the discrete variation units, each of which was divided into four subdivisions: Luke = Q, Pro; Luke = Q, Con; Matthew = Q, Pro; Matthew = Q, Con. Then German, French and English scholarly literature over the past century and a half was gleaned for opinions as to how Q read for each variation unit. The verbatim quotations in all three languages were printed in chronological order in these four sequences. Then the person who had collected all this data presented a written Evaluation of the data, stating how that person thought the Q text actually read for each variation unit of one's assignment. Then two other members of our team read this database and Evaluation and wrote their own agreeing or disagreeing Evaluations. All this was then distributed by mail, sometimes in rather massive mailings, to all the members. Each variation unit on which the three Evaluators did not agree was then discussed at our next semi-annual meeting, and a vote was taken. The resultant text of Q, for the sayings treated the previous year, was published each October in the *Journal of Biblical Literature*. It has taken eight years (1989-1996) to work through the whole Q text in this way.

We then revised our procedure, in view of a one-volume second edition of the critical text of Q. In addition to Claremont, two subsidiary centers had been created in Toronto, Canada, and Bamberg, Germany. The leaders of those two centers and myself had become General Editors, who go through the previous results and re-vote to establish an improved critical text. Meanwhile younger Managing Editors are revising the databases into publishable form.

The outcome of this new phase of the project is a one-volume synopsis of the critical text of Q flanked by the Matthean and Lukan texts, formatted so that users can see for themselves each divergence between Matthew and Luke and the degree of certainty, in our judgment (graded A to D) with which the Q text has at each such juncture been reconstructed[23]. It should become a standard tool in the discipline, much as the Nestle-Aland *Novum Testamentum Graece*, or Aland's *Synopsis Quattuor Evangeliorum*, or Bauer's *Greek-English Lexicon*, are assumed to be on the desk of anyone involved in serious work in our discipline. As a back-up to the critical edition, the database of citations from scholarly literature of the past hundred or more years, on the basis of which the final decisions for each variation unit have been determined, is being published in a series estimated to comprise 31 volumes[24].

It now appears to be the case that the final editing of Q took place at about the time of the fall of Jerusalem, but that it contained not only isolated sayings ascribed to Jesus, but even small clusters of his sayings that had previously been brought together. For there is rather general agreement that this final redaction was preceded by some layering procedure in which smaller collections were already involved, although no specific proposal has received general acceptance. Yet enough such pre-redactional layering has become apparent to make it possible to trace the broad lines of the Jesus movement, as it has come to be called, from Jesus, through Q, to the Gospel of Matthew, and thus into the main stream of the Christianity of which we are heirs.

It has usually been overlooked, what gaping holes there have traditionally been in our knowledge of primitive church history. For in our mind's eye, we have normally moved from Jesus via Easter to the church history of Acts (to whatever extent reliable historical sources can be presupposed there): the Jerusalem church and its expansion to Antioch, then the Pauline mission as also reflected in Acts, with the Pauline and Deutero-Pauline Epistles providing a parallel and, as needed, a corrective source of such information, until the Paulinist Ignatius of Antioch brings us to the second century, where the church historian can take over.

23. James M. Robinson, Paul Hoffmann, and John S. Kloppenborg (eds.), *The Critical Edition of Q: Synopsis Including the Gospels of Matthew and Luke, Mark and Thomas with English, German and French Translations of Q and Thomas*, Leuven: Peeters; Minneapolis: Fortress, 2000.

24. James M. Robinson, Paul Hoffmann, and John S. Kloppenborg (eds.), *Documenta Q: Reconstructions of Q Through Two Centuries of Gospel Research Excerpted, Sorted, and Evaluated*, Leuven: Peeters, 1996 ff.

What is overlooked in this overly reassuring projection is the fate of Jesus's disciples who stayed in or returned to Galilee – there is only a single passing reference in all of Acts to a church in Galilee! Unwritten is the history of a Jesus movement whose variety of religious experience was primarily the reproclamation of the sayings of Jesus (which is not a variety attested in Acts), until ultimately the Galilean Q movement became the Matthean community of Antioch. Indeed, what happened in Antioch between Paul's crisis there in mid-century and the composition of the Gospel of Matthew a generation or so later?

Actually, there would appear to be imbedded in Matthew, discernible from a rather clear seam between chapters 11 and 12, an echo of a transition from a primarily Jewish Christian community based on Q to a Gentile Christian community based on Mark. Thus we can begin to mock up, in the layering of Q and Matthew, the course of Jewish Christianity from its first beginnings, recorded in early chapters of Acts and in Paul, to its absorption into mainline Christianity, no doubt at the expense of losing some of its membership to emergent normative Judaism and what we have come to consider heresies, such as the Ebionites and Nazarenes. But yet it is also here that the historical connection between Jesus himself and all subsequent Christianity has for the first time become discernible in the Q trajectory.

The predominance of Matthew in the early church is well attested statistically by the number of surviving manuscripts of Matthew, the quantity of quotations from Matthew in early Christian literature, and the assimilations by scribes copying Mark, Luke and John to the more familiar readings of Matthew. Paul and John provided the main line of development for the intelligentsia, be they orthodox or Gnostic. But Matthew provided the substance for the Christian living of most Christians, and therein survived the Judaism of Jesus and his earliest followers[25].

The problem of relating Jesus to the church used to be posed in terms of how Jesus's only-implicit Christology became explicit in the church, or how his indirect Christology became direct, or how the proclaimer became the Proclaimed (Bultmann). All such ways of posing the problem (for which no really satisfactory answer emerged) had in view, when speaking of the church, the kerygmatically-oriented church attested in Paul and Acts, which built not on Jesus but on Easter. But when one realizes that the Matthean church is really the precursor of the bulk of Christian believers, the problem is posed differently, and is subject to a different resolution: The miracle ('Easter') is that, with Jesus's awful death,

25. James M. Robinson, 'The Real Jesus of the Sayings Gospel Q', *Princeton Seminary Bulletin*, n.s. 18,2 (1997) 135-51. [In this volume, chap. 3.]

his talk of a loving, caring God who supplies our every need was not simply dumped as tragically misinformed, but instead continued to be proclaimed, believed, and put into practice.

The best-known early collection imbedded in Q, and no doubt its most important, is the Sermon, which seems to have held pride of place from the very beginning as representing the epitome of Jesus's teaching (though not an actual sermon he ever held on a given occasion on a Mount or Plain). It is here that one finds the blessing of the poor and hungry, the love of enemies, turning the other cheek, giving the shirt off one's back, hearing and doing rather than just talking high Christology. When one associates other equally early collections, which have much the same gist, such as the Lord's Prayer, the Caring Human Father who gives bread and fish, not stones and snakes, and the Ravens and Lilies whom God takes care of so splendidly (whose affinity Matthew still sensed strongly enough to move them all into his Sermon on the Mount), one catches sight of what Jesus meant.

The basic problem for focusing in on the center of what Jesus had to say, even for critical historical scholarship, has been that Christian research has been too much determined by an apologetic interest, somehow to root one's own Christology in Jesus himself. Now that there is general agreement that most christological titles do not go back to Jesus, a last-ditch stand has been taking place about his use of the Aramaic idiom for 'human', literally 'the son of man'. On Jesus's tongue, was this a non-titular generic reference to a human, who, for instance, in distinction from birds and foxes has no place to lay his head, or was it already for Jesus a titular understanding of the (originally non-titular) use in Daniel, hence referring to Jesus as a heavenly figure, the final Judge, such as is the case in Mark and even more explicitly in Matthew?

In the oldest layer of Q Jesus claimed no title, and seemed not to have been involved in our christological reflections at all. (The Gospel of John has misled us into thinking he was obsessed with his own status, which is almost all Jesus talks about there.) He exorcised not through some distinctive role he played, but by *God's* finger, as evidence of *God's* kingdom, much as he thought other exorcists functioned (a completely overlooked/avoided saying in Q). Faith for him was not belief in certain beliefs, but trust in God to be there when needed. One would be acquitted in the judgment not on the basis of certain beliefs, but for actually doing what Jesus said one should do. However, even the rationale for this does not come to expression through a christological title, but apparently, at first, through imagining Jesus functioning at the judgment as a character witness. Even this function ascribed to Jesus may not go back to Jesus himself, but might be a subsequent mythological objectification based on Jesus's conviction that doing what he said would acquit in the judgment. For him, this was really enough.

The problem with this position advocated by Jesus is not just that it does not satisfy one's interest to find roots for one's Christology, but, perhaps still more basically, that people do not have the slightest intention of doing what Jesus said one must do to be acquitted. Rather we prefer to exalt Christ as our savior. Thus Paul provided the core of our Christian faith, not Jesus. Even such a Pauline concession as his comment that we will all stand before the judgment seat of God to give account of ourselves is easily passed over. The church at any given time tends to hear only what it wants to hear.

I am often asked by Christians who are not academics the leading question as to how a lifetime of critical biblical scholarship has affected my faith as a Christian. The implied answer is that such 'higher criticism' obviously destroyed it. Hence my standard reply has been that, if I had entered upon a quite unrelated profession, I would no doubt have abandoned Christianity completely as hopelessly outdated and irrelevant. After all, the godly Christianity in which I grew up did not catch sight of racial segregation, militarism, or the plight of share-croppers, as problems to be addressed.

It is of course true, as has already become abundantly evident in what I have said thus far, that my objective scholarship has not been disinterested, and that my personal convictions have evolved not independently of the intellectual trajectory sketched above. I surely have reached my seventies with a different faith from what I had when I began. Let me therefore conclude this theological autobiography with a summary of where my scholarship and my faith now tend to converge:

What Jesus had to say centered around the ideal of God's rule ('the kingdom of God'), the main 'theological' category Jesus engendered. Calling the ideal God's rule puts it in an antithetical relation both to other political and social systems, and to individual self-interest, 'looking out for number one'. The wild birds and flowers prosper without working to secure their needs. God cares about every sparrow sold a dime a dozen. For God will not give a stone when asked for bread, or a snake when asked for fish, but can be counted on to give what one really needs. Indeed, people should trust God to know what they need even before they ask. This 'utopian' vision was the core of what Jesus had to say. It was both good news, reassurance that the good would happen to undo one's plight in actual experience, and the call upon people to do that good in actual practice.

For the Jesus people this was their gospel – what they called evangelizing the poor, a kerygma greater than that of Jonah. But since Paul anathematized any other gospel than his own, even if proclaimed by angels, and said that persons who had known the human Jesus (as Paul had not) need know him that way no longer, the acknowledgment that Jesus's gospel should be accorded at least equal status with the gospel has only slowly gained ground among Christians (Francis of Assisi, Tolstoy, Mahatma Gandhi, Martin Luther King, Jr., ...).

Jesus was, after all, a real idealist, a committed radical, in any case a profound person who had come up with a solution to the human dilemma that is at least worth listening to[26].

The human dilemma is in large part that we are each other's fate, the tool of evil that ruins the other person, as we look out for number one, having wised up with regard to any youthful idealism we might once have cherished. But if I would basically cease and desist from pushing you down to keep myself up, and you for your part would do the same, then the vicious circle would be broken. Society would become mutually supportive, rather than self-destructive. Count on God to look out for you, to provide people that will care for you, and listen to him when he calls on you to provide for them. This radical trust in and responsiveness to God is what makes society function (as God's society). This is what, for Jesus, faith and discipleship were all about. Nothing else has a right to claim any functional relationship to him.

Put in language derived from his sayings: I am hungry because you hoard food. You are cold because I hoard clothing. So we are all to get rid of our backpacks and wallets! Such 'security' is to be replaced by 'God's rule', which means both what we trust God to do (to motivate the other person to share food with me), and what we hear God telling us to do (to share clothing with the other person). One does not carry money while bypassing the poor (literally: 'the beggars'), or a backpack full of extra clothes and food, while the cold and hungry lie in the gutter ignored. This is why the beggars, the hungry, the depressed, are actually fortunate ('blessed'). God, that is to say, those who hearken to God, those in whom God rules, will care for them. They are called upon to trust in God's rule as being there for them ('theirs is the kingdom of God'). One does not even carry a club for self-protection, but rather returns good for evil even with regard to one's enemies. One turns the other cheek. God is the kind of person who provides sunshine and rain even to those who oppose him. So it is those who care for ('love') even their enemies who are sons (and daughters) of God.

---

26. James M. Robinson, *The Gospel of Jesus. In Search of the Original Good News*, San Francisco: HarperSanFrancisco, 2005, paperback 2006.

In the original form of the Lord's Prayer, what followed directly upon 'Let your reign come', as its concrete meaning, was: 'Our day's bread give us today' (Q 11:2b-4). People should ask for no more than a day's ration of food, trusting God to provide for today, and then tomorrow trusting for tomorrow.

God's rule was interpreted by Matthew's community to mean: 'Thy will be done on earth as it is in heaven'. This petition added to the Lord's Prayer is, technically speaking, not a call for action, but, like 'Let your reign come' which it interprets, an appeal to God. When one prays, one trusts in God to answer. But God answers through motivating people to turn the other cheek; to give the shirt off one's back; to lend, expecting nothing in return. The person who prays to God for help is the same person whom God motivates to help: 'Cancel our debts for us *as we too have cancelled for those in debt to us*!'

Part of God ruling in one's life was helping the disabled with whatever the primitive psychosomatic medicine of the day could provide. One went from door to door, and, if admitted for bed and breakfast (the answer to the prayer for a day's bread), one placed God's *Shalom* on the house, which meant one healed as best one could, as God ruling, the infirm there: 'Cure the sick there, and say to them: God's reign has reached unto you' (Q 10:9).

Just as the sharing of food and clothing, the canceling of debts, the non-retaliation against enemies, were not seen as human virtues, but rather as God acting through those who trust him, just so healings were not attributed to some witch-doctor's or magician's individual technique or skill, but to God's finger that made use not only of Jesus's fingers, but of the hands of others as well. Clearly, all this that one could not oneself do, from renunciation of self-interest to healing disease, took place because God was doing it. God was ruling in this unusual human society – this was in fact the 'coming' of 'the kingdom of God'! For Jesus was a 'faith healer' in the sense that he trusted God to interject his 'finger' into the human dilemma, to overcome the plight of the disadvantaged.

But not everything had been done: Not all people lived such trust in God, not all the helpless had been helped, not all the disabled were healed. Of course, one trusted God to follow through to completion ('eschatology'). But Jesus's 'eschatological' message was not to distract from grim reality by means of the utopian ideal of 'pie in the sky by-and-by', but rather to focus attention on trusting God for today's ration of life, and on hearing God's call to give life now to one's neighbor.

All this is as far from mainline Christianity as it was from the Judaism practiced in Jesus's day. The 'hardest' saying of Jesus is: 'Why do you call me: Master, Master, and do not do what I say?' One laments the absence of a 'high Christology' in the sayings of Jesus. But what could be 'higher' than maintaining that doing Jesus's word is what acquits in the day of judgment? A Neo-Platonic metaphysical speculation secondarily Christianized? Christological creeds may be no more than pious dodges to avoid this unavoidable condition of discipleship: Actually do what he said to do!

People do not do what he said, not simply because of the shift in cultural conditions, for which an adequate hermeneutic might provide a solution, but, ultimately, because people do not trust God as Jesus did (though of course one claims to have Christian 'faith', that is to say, a traditional ideology). This is what should be unsettling about finding out what Jesus had to say.

All this of course sounds incredibly naive. Once Jesus launched himself into this lifestyle, practicing what he preached, he did not last long. A reality check is called for! Yet the bottom line is not necessarily so cynical. In concentration camps, cells of a few who can really trust each other, due to a shared ethnic, religious, or political commitment, and who are hence willing to give an extra portion of their meager food and other necessities of life to the feeblest, have turned out to have a higher chance of survival than do individuals looking out only for number one. Selfishness may ultimately turn out to be a luxury we can ill afford. There is a paradoxical saying to the effect that when one saves one's life one loses it, but when one loses it one saves it. To be sure, this has in view less longevity than integrity. It is all the more worthy of serious consideration.

APPENDIX

The Sayings Gospel Q in English

WHAT IS THE SAYINGS GOSPEL Q?

A Sayings Gospel, in distinction from a Narrative Gospel, contains mainly sayings ascribed to Jesus, with hardly any of the stories so familiar to us from the four Narrative Gospels of the New Testament.

The Sayings Gospel Q is even older than the Gospels in the New Testament. In fact, it is the oldest Gospel known! Yet it is not in the New Testament itself—rather, it was known to, and used by, the authors of the Gospels of Matthew and Luke in the eighties and nineties of the first century when they composed their Gospels. But then it was lost from sight and only rediscovered in 1838, embedded in Matthew and Luke. It was nicknamed "Q," the first letter of the German word for "source" (*Quelle*), to refer to the second "source" used by Matthew and Luke, whose first source was Mark. Since Q usually (though not always) follows the Lukan sequence, we have adopted the habit of using Lukan chapter and verse numbers to cite Q. Hence, "Q 6:22" refers to the Q verses used in Luke 6:22 (and in Matthew 5:11).

After all, Q is a product of the Jewish Jesus movement that continued to proclaim his message in Galilee and Syria for years to come, but from which practically no first-century texts have survived. The New Testament is mainly a Gentile collection, and hence only preserves the sources of Gentile churches.

This is clearest in the case of Matthew, the canonical Gospel that grew out of the Q movement, marking the point when it finally merged into the Gentile churches. Matthew 3-11 is primarily oriented to vindicating the Jewish Gospel Q, whereupon Matthew 12-28 simply edits and copies out the oldest Gentile Gospel, Mark. The Great Commission with which Matthew concludes (Matthew 28:18-20) makes this Gospel an ecumenical text: It not only authorizes the Gentile church's mission ("make disciples of all nations"), but also the Jewish church's focus on the sayings of Jesus found in Q ("teaching them to observe all that I have commanded you").

Conversely, the Gentile Gospel that most fully represents the final triumph of Gentile churches, Luke, has simply imbedded Q into the Markan Gentile Gospel. And Luke continued with a second volume, the Acts of the Apostles, where the history of the Gentile churches very soon tends to become the history of the churches as a whole.

One can identify Q sayings in Matthew and Luke by a rule of thumb: Sayings (and a few stories) that occur in Matthew and Luke but not in

Mark, or in Matthew and Luke in a very different form from that in Mark (for example, the temptation story in Matt. 4:1-11, parallel Luke 4:1-13; see Mark 1:12-13), probably come from Q.

THE GREEK COMPOSITION OF Q

Although Jesus' mother tongue was Aramaic, his sayings had been largely translated into Greek for missionary purposes. Then they were collected into small clusters, which were eventually brought together into the Sayings Gospel Q. The sometimes very high degree of verbal identity in the Q sayings of Matthew and Luke makes it apparent that they were working from a shared Greek text. For each could not have translated from Aramaic into such highly similar, often identical, Greek, if they had translated independently of one another (for example, Matt. 3:7-10, parallel Luke 3:7-9).

At another place (citing Q by reference to Luke's chapter and verse numbers: Q 12:27), the fact of a written Greek text of Q is strikingly attested by the presence of a Greek scribal error. Both Matthew and Luke (Matt. 6:25-33, parallel Luke 12:22b-31), and therefore Q, list in quite parallel form three tasks that ravens and lilies, free of anxiety, do not perform, as role models for humans to imitate, indicating that they too are free of anxiety: Ravens do now sow, or reap, or gather into barns. But in the case of the lilies, Q reads: "how they grow: They do not work nor do they spin." Here the first of the three tasks anxiety-free lilies do not perform is neither a negative statement, nor a verb naming a task involved in making cloth. But a very slight change in the Greek lettering produces the meaning: "They do not card, nor do they work, nor do they spin." The formulation "not card" is not just a convincing conjecture, but is faintly attested, as an erased original reading, in an ancient manuscript of Matthew (6:28b), preserved down through the centuries in the Monastery of St. Catherine at Mount Sinai (now in the British Library in London), and in a Greek fragment of saying 36 of the *Gospel of Thomas,* in Papyrus Oxyrhynchus 655, preserved in the dry sands of Egypt near the town of Nag Hammadi (and now in the Houghton Library of Harvard University).

THE DISAPPEARANCE OF Q

The loss of much of what may have been written in the earliest churches should now surprise us, since no New Testament manuscripts of the first century survive (and only a very few small fragments from the second). In 1 Corinthians 5:9 and 2 Corinthians 2:3-4, 9, Paul refers to other letters he wrote to Corinth, which are either completely lost or incorporated into the two canonical Corinthian letters. (The is analogous to Q surviving only as incorporated into Matthew and Luke.)

The disappearance of Q may have been facilitated by scribes not making new copies during the second century. For the canonizing process that was going on at the time involved choosing what should, and what should not, be used for community purposes. In Matthew and Luke, the Q sayings had been rephrased to avoid misunderstandings, and updated so as to fit their new situations and understanding of what Jesus had really meant. For this very practical reason, churches would have commissioned scribes to make copies of Matthew and Luke, rather than copying Q, which had fallen into disuse.

Such creeds as the Apostles' Creed, which developed out of the second-century baptismal liturgy of Rome, bypassed completely the sayings of Jesus ("born of the virgin Mary, suffered under Pontius Pilate"). This provided no basis for canonizing Sayings Gospels, such as Q and the *Gospel of Thomas* (the latter was lost for more than 1,500 years and only discovered in 1945). But the creeds did validate as canonical the narrative Gospels Matthew, Mark, Luke, and John, because of their emphasis on the cross and resurrection.

MEMORABLE SAYINGS OF JESUS IN Q

The Sayings Gospel Q contains some of the most memorable of Jesus' sayings. To mention only a few: The most familiar Q text is the Lord's Prayer (Q 11:2b-4). Q presents it in a more original form that what we use in our liturgy today. For what we know by heart is Matthew's enlargement of the Q Prayer: Matthew 6:9-13.

Q also preserves for us most of the Sermon on the Mount: The beatitudes (Q 6:20-23); the love of enemies (Q 6:27-28, 35c-d); turning the other cheek, giving the shirt off one's back, going the second mile, giving, expecting nothing in return (Q 6:29-30); the Golden Rule (Q 6:31); the tree known by its fruit (Q 6:43-45). This is all in Q's early draft of the Sermon (Q 6:20-49), to which Matthew has added even more of the oldest Q clusters of sayings to produce his considerable enlarged Sermon on the Mount with which we are familiar (Matthew 5–7): Not only the Lord's Prayer, but also the certainty of the answer to prayer (ask, seek, knock, for a caring Father does provide, Q 11:9-13); storing up treasures in heaven (Q 12:33-34); being free from anxiety like ravens and lilies (Q 12:22b-31); the sound eye rather than the evil eye (Q 11:33-35).

Q has many other important and familiar sayings, such as taking up one's cross (Q 14:27), and losing one's life to save it (Q 17:33). Q also preserves a number of well-known parables, such as the mustard seed (Q 13:18-19); the yeast (Q 13:20-21); the invited dinner guests (Q 14:16-23); the lost sheep (Q 15:4-7); the lost coin (Q 15:8-10); and the talents (Q used the much smaller coin, "minas": Q 19:12-26). All such sayings and parables are familiar to us, since they are found in Matthew and Luke. But we know them only because Matthew and Luke found them in Q, and thus handed them down to us in the New Testament.

THE IMAGE OF JESUS IN Q

The image of Jesus one gets from the Sayings Gospel Q is primarily that of the authoritative speaker of his sayings. Doing what he says is really all that counts: "Why do you call me: Master, Master, and do not do what I say?" (Q 6:46). For it is only the person who hears his sayings and acts on them who will stand in the judgment (Q 6:47-49).

Jesus refers to himself in Q largely by means of a Semitic idiom for "human," literally "son of man," or, more accurately, "son of humanity" (Q 6:22; 7:34; 9:58; 11:30; 12:8, 10). Toward the end of Q, the sayings tend to focus increasingly on Jesus returning from heaven, and then the idiom is used more as a title to refer to him as a heavenly figure (Q 12:40; 17:24, 26, 30): "Son of Humanity." But Jesus' own focus was on God reigning ("the kingdom of God"), not on himself.

John had predicted "One to Come," as the final arrival of God for judgment (Q 3:16b-17). The first part of Q (Q 3-7) is carefully structured to prove that it is Jesus who fulfills this prophecy, even though on the surface he hardly fits John's description. For in Q 7:18-23 John sends a delegation to ask if Jesus is indeed that "One to Come." Jesus answers in the affirmative and lists as evidence his healings (Q 7:22), for which reason the healing of the centurion's boy immediately precedes (Q 7:1-10). This list is climaxed by reference to Jesus giving good news to the poor, which is a reference back to Q's early draft of the Sermon on the Mount (Q 6:20-49). For it had begun: "Blessed are you poor."

Other titles are also used of Jesus, such as "Son of God" (Q 3:22; 4:3, 9; 10:22). This title was initially used of any "son of God," a God-like person who loves even one's enemies (Q 6:27-28). For Jesus' remarkable view of God was that he gives sunshine and rain equally to bad and good persons (Q 6:35). Those who act similarly show that God is their Father and they his children.

"Lord" is the standard epithet for God in the Greek translation of the Hebrew Bible, and so is of course used of God in Q (Q 4:12, 8; 10:2, 21; 13:35; 16:13). But the same word is also used in its secular meaning of a human "master" (Q 12:42, 43, 46; 13:25; 14:21; 19:16, 18, 20) or "teacher" (Q 6:46; 9:59). Of course such human designations acquired progressively a higher implication, when referring to or even just implying Jesus.

Perhaps the most striking thing about epithets for Jesus in Q is the complete absence of the title "Christ." This fits the absence of a birth narrative in Bethlehem, the prophesied birthplace of the Messiah.

THE DEATH OF JESUS IN Q

The oldest theology addressed to Gentile believers to have survived is the collection of letters of Paul, which date from the fifties. But for

Paul, the center of the gospel message was Jesus' cross and resurrection, not his sayings, which Paul himself had not heard. Since Paul's mission was to "Gentile sinners" (Gal 2:15), he focused on Jesus' death as compensation for human sin. So, for us as modern Gentile Christians, Paul's message has tended to obscure Jesus' own message, though Jesus' sayings had, after all, been preferred by his own disciples.

Of course the Q people knew of Jesus' death. But they saw it more as the inevitable culmination of the activity of God's Wisdom, who had sent messengers to Israel down through the course of biblical history, prophets who had often been required to give their lives for God's cause (Q 11:47-51; 12:4-5; 13:34-35). In spite of Jesus' terrible death, his message of complete trust in God was resumed by his disciples in the Q movement, as being as true as ever—their way of bringing to expression what we express as Easter faith.

JESUS' JEWISH DISCIPLES IN Q

The Sayings Gospel Q, though on the surface only reporting about Jesus, also reveals almost all we know about Jesus' Jewish followers of the first generation in Galilee. For since the New Testament, as we have it, is a collection almost exclusively of Gentile texts, it contains only occasional passing references to Jewish churches.

There is something of a biographical cast in the early part of Q (baptism, temptation, inaugural sermon, healing of the centurion's boy, delegation from John). On the other hand, the sayings of Jesus also mirror something like the sequence of the Q community's own experience. This begins with what may well be the oldest cluster of Jesus' sayings in the inaugural sermon, then the Jewish mission, its very limited success, the resultant alienation from the Jewish community, and finally the expectation of final vindication at the last judgment.

Paul gained acceptance for his Gentile mission from the "pillars" of the church in Jerusalem (James, Cephas, and John: Gal 2:1-10), though this amicable division of labor soon broke down (Gal 2:11-21), when Peter and the disciples from Jerusalem tried to "judaize" Gentile disciples (Gal 2:14) by subjecting them to Jewish cultic law, such as circumcision and segregated table fellowship. Paul withstood the claims of any other "gospel" than his own (Gal 1:6-12), which served to cast a shadow over the divergent message and practice of those from Jerusalem.

Actually, the disciples of the Q movement do not seem to have been these leaders stationed in Jerusalem. For the "apostles" and the "twelve" are not mentioned in Q, either by title or by name, nor does Q make any reference to the problems that were central issues in the debate with Paul. The Q people would seem to have been the disciples of Jesus who had stayed behind in Galilee. Some were originally itinerant (like the "workers" mentioned in Q 10:2 and 7), wandering from door to door with Jesus' message, as is evident from the mission instructions in Q 10:2-16.

Yet the lack of success in winning over appreciable numbers of Jewish converts led to disillusionment, over against an invidious awareness of the success of the Gentile mission (Q 13:29-30; 14:11-23). The tone became judgmental toward Israel (Q 3:7-9; 10:10-15; 11:23, 42-51; 13:24-28, 34-35; 22:28, 30). Indeed, the destruction of Jerusalem and its temple was interpreted (Q 13:34-35) as divine punishment on "this generation" (Q 7:31; 11:29 twice, 30, 31, 32, 50, 51), and especially on its leaders, upon whom "woes" were pronounced (Q 11:42-48). The breaking of family ties (Q 12:49-53; 14:26), the rigors of the primitive lifestyle (Q 12:4-7; 14:27; 17:33), even persecution (Q 6:22-23; 12:8-12), surely made quitting the Jesus movement a live option (Q 14:34-35). The dominant lifestyle was probably becoming less itinerant and more sedentary (like the "son of peace" mentioned in Q 10:6) as time went on.

The "final" Greek text of Q, that is to say, the text shared by Matthew and Luke, probably dates from around the time of the war with Rome (since Q 13:34-35 seems to envisage the destruction of Jerusalem in 70 C.E.). Under such desperate circumstances, the Matthean merger into the more successful Gentile church was a rather inevitable outcome.

Thus is may be understandable that by Luke's time these remaining Galilean disciples could be largely overlooked in the Acts of the Apostles. For the description of the mission there, "from Jerusalem and in all Judea and Samaria and to the end of the earth" (Acts 1:8), simply bypassed Galilee, with only one reference later in Acts (9:31) to a church in Galilee being built up. Nor can one find in Acts any attestation for disciples still proclaiming Jesus' sayings. The Sayings Gospel Q thus supplements Acts in a very central way concerning what we know about the first generation of the Jesus movement.

THE JEWISH-CHRISTIAN DIALOGUE

In the contemporary Jewish-Christian dialogue, it is very important to recognize this unbreakable bond between Jews and Christians: Jesus was a Jew, as were his first disciples. What Jesus and they proclaimed was a message by and for the Jews. It was such an idealized message that it presents a real challenge for modern Jews and Christians alike. Yet it is a message that we all can join in seeking to live up to. Its basis is trust in the same God.

* * * * *

THE SAYINGS GOSPEL Q IN ENGLISH

The translation of Q that is supplied here is intended to be readable by the general public. For this reason the text is not cluttered with marks indicating the various kinds and degrees of certainty or uncertainty. Those wishing such detailed information may find it in *The Critical Edition of Q* (2000), or in the somewhat simplified and abbreviated form in *The Sayings Gospel Q in Greek and English* (2001, 2002). Therefore the translation presented here is encumbered only rarely, with markings of three kinds: If there is a high degree of uncertainty about a particular word or phrase, no text is provided, but the place is marked with three dots . . . indicating that there was some text here. Two dots . . indicate that it is even uncertain whether anything at all was here. Parentheses ( ) are used where the text had to be emended, or where only the gist or train of thought, but not the actual language, could be provided. The chapter and verse numbers of Q follow the Gospel of Luke. For example, the reference to Q 6:22 indicates the Q version of the saying found in Luke 6:22 (and in its Matthean parallel, Matt 5:11). Where there is an apparent jump in sequence, this indicates a scholarly judgment that Matthew has preserved the order of Q better than Luke for that saying.

* * * * *

Opening Line
(. . . Jesus . . .)

Q 3:0

The Introduction of John
²ᵇ(. . .) John ³ᵃ (. . .) all the region of the Jordan (. . .).

Q 3:2b-3a = Matt. 3:1, 5

John's Announcement of Judgment
⁷He said to the crowds coming to be baptized: Snakes' litter! Who warned you to run from the impending rage? ⁸So bear fruit worthy of repentance, and do not presume to tell yourselves: We have as forefather Abraham! For I tell you: God can produce children for Abraham right out of these rocks! ⁹And the ax already lies at the root of the trees. So every tree not bearing healthy fruit is to be chopped down and thrown on the fire.

Q 3:7-9 = Matt. 3:7-10

John and the One to Come
¹⁶ᵇI baptize you in water, but the one to come after me is more powerful than I, whose sandals I am not fit to take off. He will baptize you in holy Spirit and fire. ¹⁷His pitchfork is in his hand, and he will clear his threshing floor and gather the wheat into his granary, but the chaff he will burn on a fire that can never be put out.

Q 3:16b-17 = Matt. 3:11-12

The Baptism of Jesus

[21] . . Jesus . . . baptized, heaven opened . . ., [22] and . . the Spirit . . . upon him . . . Son . . . .

Q 3:21-22 = Matt. 3:16-17

The Temptations of Jesus

[1] And Jesus was led into the wilderness by the Spirit [2] to be tempted by the devil. And he ate nothing for forty days: . . he became hungry. [3] And the devil told him: If you are God's Son, order that these stones become loaves. [4] And Jesus answered him: It is written: A person is not to live only from bread.

[9] The devil took him along to Jerusalem and put him on the tip of the temple and told him: [10] For it is written: He will command his angels about you, [11] and on their hands they will bear you, so that you do not strike your foot against a stone. [12] And Jesus in reply told him: It is written: Do not put to the test the Lord your God.

[5] And the devil took him along to a very high mountain and showed him all the kingdoms of the world and their splendor, [6] and told him: All these I will give you, [7] if you bow down before me. [8] And in reply Jesus told him: It is written: Bow down to the Lord your God, and serve only him.

[13] And the devil left him.

Q 4:1-4, 9-12, 5-8, 13 = Matt. 4:1-11

Nazara

[16] (. . .) Nazara (. . .).

Q 4:16 = Matt. 4:13

Beatitudes for the Poor, Hungry, and Mourning

[20] (. . .) And raising his eyes to his disciples he said: Blessed are you poor, for God's reign is for you. [21] Blessed are you who hunger, for you will eat your fill. Blessed are you who mourn, for you will be consoled.

Q 6:20-21 = Matt. 5:1-4, 6; cf. *Thomas* 54; 69.2

The Beatitude for the Persecuted

[22] Blessed are you when they insult and persecute you, and say every kind of evil against you because of the son of humanity. [23] Be glad and exult, for vast is your reward in heaven. For this is how they persecuted the prophets who were before you.

Q 6:22-23 = Matt. 5:11-12; cf. *Thomas* 69.1a; 68.1

Love Your Enemies

[27] Love your enemies [28] and pray for those persecuting you, [35c-d] so that you may become sons of your Father, for he raises his sun on bad and good and rains on the just and the unjust.

Q 6:27-28, 35c-d = Matt. 5:44-45

Renouncing One's Own Rights

[29] The one who slaps you on the cheek, offer him the other as well; and to the person wanting to take you to court and get your shirt, turn over to him the coat as well. [Matt. 5:41] And the one who conscripts you for one mile, go with him a second. [30] To the one who asks of you, give; and from the one who borrows, do not ask back what is yours.

Q 6:29, 30 = Matt. 5:39-42; cf. *Thomas* 95

The Golden Rule

[31] And the way you want people to treat you, that is how you treat them.

Q 6:31 = Matt. 7:12; cf. *Thomas* 6.3

Impartial Love

[32] . . If you love those loving you, what reward do you have? Do not even tax collectors do the same? [34] And if you lend to those from whom you hope to receive, what (reward do) you (have)? Do not even the Gentiles do the same?

Q 6:32, 34 = Matt. 5:46, 47; cf. *Thomas* 95

Being Full of Pity like Your Father

[36] Be full of pity, just as your Father . . is full of pity.

Q 6:36 = Matt. 5:48

Not Judging

[37] . . Do not pass judgment, so you are not judged. For with what judgment you pass judgment, you will be judged. [38] And with the measurement you use to measure out, it will be measured out to you.

Q 6:37-38 = Matt. 7:1-2

The Blind Leading the Blind

[39] Can a blind person show the way to a blind person? Will not both fall into a pit?

Q 6:39 = Matt. 15:14; cf. *Thomas* 34

The Disciple and the Teacher

[40] A disciple is not superior to the teacher. It is enough for the disciple that he become like his teacher.

Q 6:40 = Matt. 10:24-25a

The Speck and the Beam

[41] And why do you see the speck in your brother's eye, but the beam in your own eye you overlook? [42] How can you say to your brother: Let me throw out the speck from your eye, and just look at the beam in your own eye? Hypocrite, first throw out from your own eye the beam, and then you will see clearly to throw out the speck in your brother's eye.

Q 6:41-42 = Matt. 7:3-5; cf. *Thomas* 26

The Tree Is Known by Its Fruit

[43] . . No healthy tree bears rotten fruit, nor on the other hand does a decayed tree bear healthy fruit. [44] For from the fruit the tree is known. Are figs picked from thorns, or grapes from thistles? [45] The good person from one's good treasure casts up good things, and the evil person from the evil treasure casts up evil things. For from exuberance of heart one's mouth speaks.

Q 6:43-45 = Matt. 7:16b, 18; 12:33b, 34-35; cf. *Thomas* 45

Not Just Saying Master, Master

[46] . . Why do you call me: Master, Master, and do not do what I say?

Q 6:46 = Matt. 7:21

Houses Built on Rock or Sand

⁴⁷ Everyone hearing my sayings and acting on them ⁴⁸ is like a person who built one's house on bedrock; and the rain poured down and the flash-floods came, and the winds blew and pounded that house, and it did not collapse, for it was founded on bedrock. ⁴⁹ And everyone who hears my sayings and does not act on them is like a person who built one's house on the sand; and the rain poured down and the flash-floods came, and the winds blew and battered that house, and promptly it collapsed, and its fall was devastating.

Q 6:47-49 = Matt. 7:24-27

The Centurion's Faith in Jesus' Word

¹ And it came to pass when he . . ended these sayings, he entered Capernaum. ³ There came to him a centurion exhorting him and saying: My boy (is) doing badly. And he said to him: Am I, by coming, to heal him? ^{6b-c} And in reply the centurion said: Master, I am not worthy for you to come under my roof; ⁷ but say a word, and let my boy be healed. ⁸ For I too am a person under authority, with soldiers under me, and I say to one: Go, and he goes, and to another: Come, and he comes, and to my slave: Do this, and he does it. ⁹ But Jesus, on hearing, was amazed, and said to those who followed: I tell you, not even in Israel have I found such faith. ¹⁰ (. .)

Q 7:1, 3, 6b-9, 10 = Matt. 7:28a; 8:5-10, 13

John's Inquiry about the One to Come

¹⁸ And John, on hearing about all these things, sending through his disciples, ¹⁹ said to him: Are you the one to come, or are we to expect someone else? ²² And in reply he said to them: Go report to John what you hear and see: The blind regain their sight and the lame walk around, the skin-diseased are cleansed and the deaf hear, and the dead are raised, and the poor evangelized. ²³ And blessed is whoever is not offended by me.

Q 7:18-19, 22-23 = Matt. 11:2-6

John—More Than a Prophet

²⁴ And when they had left, he began to talk to the crowds about John: What did you go out into the wilderness to look at? A reed shaken by the wind? ²⁵ If not, what did you go out to see? A person arrayed in finery? Look, those wearing finery are in kings' houses. ²⁶ But then what did you go out to see? A prophet? Yes, I can tell you, even more than a prophet! ²⁷ This is the one about whom it has been written: Look, I am sending my messenger ahead of you, who will prepare your path in front of you. ²⁸ I tell you: There has not arisen among women's offspring anyone who surpasses John. Yet the least significant in God's kingdom is more than he.

Q 7:24-28 = Matt. 11:7-11; cf. *Thomas* 78; 46

For and Against John

²⁹ For John came to you . . the tax collectors and . . . (responded positively) ³⁰ but the (religious authorities rejected) him.

Q 7:29-30 = Matt. 21:32

This Generation and the Children of Wisdom

[31] . . To what am I to compare this generation and what is it like? [32] It is like children seated in the market-places, who, addressing the others, say: We fluted for you, but you would not dance; we wailed, but you would not cry. [33] For John came, neither eating nor drinking, and you say: He has a demon! [34] The son of humanity came, eating and drinking, and you say: Look! A person who is a glutton and a drunkard, a chum of tax collectors and sinners! [35] But Wisdom was vindicated by her children.

Q 7:31-35 = Matt. 11:16-19

Confronting Potential Followers

[57] And someone said to him: I will follow you wherever you go. [58] And Jesus said to him: Foxes have holes, and birds of the sky have nests; but the son of humanity does not have anywhere he can lay his head. [59] But another said to him: Master, permit me first to go and bury my father. [60] But he said to him: Follow me, and leave the dead to bury their own dead.

Q 9:57-60 = Matt. 8:19-22; cf. *Thomas* 86

Workers for the Harvest

[2] He said to his disciples: The harvest is plentiful, but the workers are few. So ask the Lord of the harvest to dispatch workers into his harvest.

Q 10:2 = Matt. 9:37-38; cf. *Thomas* 73

Sheep among Wolves

[3] Be on your way! Look, I send you like sheep in the midst of wolves.

Q 10:3 = Matt. 10:16

No Provisions

[4] Carry no purse, nor knapsack, nor shoes, nor stick, and greet no one on the road.

Q 10:4 = Matt. 10:9-10a

What to Do in Houses and Towns

[5] Into whatever house you enter, first say: Peace to this house! [6] And if a son of peace be there, let your peace come upon him: but if not, let your peace return upon you. [7] And at that house remain, eating and drinking whatever they provide, for the worker is worthy of one's reward. Do not move around from house to house. [8] And whatever town you enter and they take you in, eat what is set before you. [9] And cure the sick there, and say to them: God's reign has reached unto you.

Q 10:5-9 = Matt. 10:7-8, 10b-13; cf. *Thomas* 14.4

Response to a Town's Rejection

[10] But into whatever town you enter and they do not take you in, on going out from that town, [11] shake off the dust from your feet. [12] I tell you: For Sodom, it shall be more bearable on that day than for that town.

Q 10:10-12 = Matt. 10:14-15

Woes against Galilean Towns

[13] Woe to you, Chorazin! Woe to you, Bethsaida! For if the wonders performed in you had taken place in Tyre and Sidon, they would have repented long ago, in

sackcloth and ashes. [14] Yet for Tyre and Sidon it shall be more bearable at the judgment than for you. [15] And you, Capernaum, up to heaven will you be exalted? Into Hades shall you come down!

Q 10:13-15 = Matt. 11:21-24

Whoever Takes You in Takes Me In

16 Whoever takes you in takes me in, and whoever takes me in takes in the one who sent me.

Q 10:16 = Matt. 10:40

Thanksgiving that God Reveals Only to Children

[21] At (that time) he said: I praise you, Father, Lord of heaven and earth, for you hid these things from sages and the learned, and disclosed them to children. Yes, Father, for that is what it has pleased you to do.

Q 10:21 = Matt. 11:25-26

Knowing the Father through the Son

[22] Everything has been entrusted to me by my Father, and no one knows the Son except the Father, nor does anyone know the Father except the Son, and to whomever the Son chooses to reveal him.

Q 10:22 = Matt. 11:27; cf. *Thomas* 61.3b

The Beatitude for the Eyes that See

[23] Blessed are the eyes that see what you see . . . [24] For I tell you: Many prophets and kings wanted to see what you see, but never saw it, and to hear what you hear, but never heard it.

Q 10:23b-24 = Matt. 13:16-17

The Lord's Prayer

[2b] When you pray, say: Father—may your name be kept holy!—let your reign come: [3] Our day's bread give us today; [4] and cancel our debts for us, as we too have cancelled for those in debt to us; and do not put us to the test!

Q11:2b-4 = Matt. 6:9-13a

The Certainty of the Answer to Prayer

[9] I tell you: Ask and it will be given to you, search and you will find, knock and it will be opened to you. [10] For everyone who asks receives, and the one who searches finds, and to the one who knocks will it be opened. [11] . . What person of you, whose child asks for bread, will give him a stone? [12] Or again when he asks for a fish, will give him a snake? [13] So if you, though evil, know how to give good gifts to your children, by how much more will the Father from heaven give good things to those who ask him!

Q 11:9-13 = Matt. 7:7-11; cf. *Thomas* 92.1; 94

Refuting the Beelzebul Accusation

[14] And he cast out a demon which made a person mute. And once the demon was cast out, the mute person spoke. And the crowds were amazed. [15] But some said: By Beelzebul, the ruler of demons, he casts out demons! [17] But, knowing their thoughts, he said to them: Every kingdom divided against itself is left barren, and every household divided against itself will not stand. [18] And if Satan is divided

against himself, how will his kingdom stand? ¹⁹ And if I by Beelzebul cast out demons, your sons, by whom do they cast them out? This is why they will be your judges. ²⁰ But if it is by the finger of God that I cast out demons, then there has come upon you God's reign.

Q 11:14-15, 17-20 = Matt. 9:32-34; 12:25-28

Looting a Strong Person
²¹ (A strong person's house cannot be looted, ²² but if someone still stronger overpowers him, he does get looted.)

Q 11:21-22 = Matt. 12:29; cf. *Thomas* 35

The One Not with Me
²³ The one not with me is against me, and the one not gathering with me scatters.

Q 11:23 = Matt. 12:30

The Return of the Unclean Spirit
²⁴ When the defiling spirit has left the person, it wanders through waterless regions looking for a resting-place, and finds none. Then it says: I will return to my house from which I came. ²⁵ And on arrival it finds it swept and tidied up. ²⁶ Then it goes and brings with it seven other spirits more evil than itself, and moving in, they settle there. And the last circumstances of that person become worse than the first.

Q 11:24-26 = Matt. 12:43-45

Hearing and Keeping God's Word
²⁷⁻²⁸ . .

Q 11:27-28; cf. *Thomas* 79.1-2

The Sign of Jonah for This Generation
¹⁶ But some . . were demanding from him a sign. ²⁹ But . . he said . . : This generation is an evil . . generation; it demands a sign, but a sign will not be given to it—except the sign of Jonah! ³⁰ For as Jonah became to the Ninevites a sign, so also will the son of humanity be to this generation.

Q 11:16, 29-30 = Matt. 12:38-40

Something More than Solomon and Jonah
³¹ The queen of the South will be raised at the judgment with this generation and condemn it, for she came from the ends of the earth to listen to the wisdom of Solomon, and look, something more than Solomon is here! ³² Ninevite men will arise at the judgment with this generation and condemn it. For they repented at the announcement of Jonah, and look, something more than Jonah is here!

Q 11:31-32 = Matt. 12:41-42

The Light on the Lampstand
³³ No one lights a lamp and puts it in a hidden place, but on the lampstand, and it gives light for everyone in the house.

Q 11:33 = Matt. 5:15; cf. *Thomas* 33.2-3

The Jaundiced Eye Darkens the Body's Radiance

[34] The lamp of the body is the eye. If your eye is generous, your whole body is radiant; but if your eye is jaundiced, your who body is dark. [35] So if the light within you is dark, how great must the darkness be!

Q 11:34-35 = Matt. 6:22-23; cf. *Thomas* 24.3

Woes against the Pharisees

[39a] . . [42] Woe to you, Pharisees, for you tithe mint and dill and cumin, and give up justice and mercy and faithfulness. But these one had to do, without giving up those. [39b] Woe to you, Pharisees, for you purify the outside of the cup and dish, but inside they are full of plunder and dissipation. [41] Purify . . the inside of the cup, . . . its outside . . . pure. [43] Woe to you, Pharisees, for you love the place of honor at banquets and the front seat in the synagogues and accolades in the markets. [44] Woe to you, Pharisees, for you are like indistinct tombs and people walking on top are unaware.

Q 11:39a, 42, 39b, 41, 43-44 = Matt. 23:1-2a, 6-7, 23, 25, 26b-27; cf. *Thomas* 89.1

Woes against the Exegetes of the Law

[46b] And woe to you, exegetes of the Law, for you bind . . . burdens, and load on the backs of people, but you yourselves do not want to lift your finger to move them. [52] Woe to you, exegetes of the Law, for you shut the kingdom of (God) from people; you did not go in, nor let in those trying to get in. [47] Woe to you, for you built the tombs of the prophets, but your forefathers killed them. [48] Thus you witness against yourselves that you are the sons of your forefathers.

Q 11:46b, 52, 47-48 = Matt. 23:4, 13, 29-32; cf. *Thomas* 39.1-2

Wisdom's Judgment on This Generation

[49] Therefore also . . Wisdom said: I will send them prophets and sages, and some of them they will kill and persecute, [50] so that a settling of accounts for the blood of all the prophets poured out from the founding of the world may be required of this generation, [51] from the blood of Abel to the blood of Zechariah, murdered between the sacrificial altar and the House. Yes, I tell you: An accounting will be required of this generation!

Q 11:49-51 = Matt. 23:34-36

Proclaiming What Was Whispered

[2] Nothing is covered up that will not be exposed, and hidden that will not be know. [3] What I say to you in the dark, speak in the light; and what you hear whispered in the ear, proclaim on the housetops.

Q 12:2-3 = Matt. 10:26-27; cf. *Thomas* 5.2-6.5; 33.1

Not Fearing the Body's Death

[4] And do not be afraid of those who kill the body, but cannot kill the soul. [5] But fear . . the one who is able to destroy both the soul and body in Gehenna.

Q 12:4-5 = Matt. 10:28

More Precious than Many Sparrows

[6] Are not five sparrows sold for two cents? And yet not one of them will fall to earth without your Father's consent. [7] But even the hairs of your head all are numbered. Do not be afraid, you are worth more than many sparrows.

Q 12:6-7 = Matt. 10:29-31

Confessing or Denying

⁸ Anyone who may speak out for me in public, the son of humanity will also speak out for him before the angels . . . . ⁹ But whoever may deny me in public will be denied before the angels . . .

Q 12:8-9 = Matt. 10:32-33

Speaking against the Holy Spirit

¹⁰ And whoever says a word against the son of humanity, it will be forgiven him; but whoever speaks against the holy Spirit, it will not be forgiven him.

Q 12:10 = Matt. 12:32a-b; cf. Thomas 44

Hearings before Synagogues

¹¹ When they bring you before synagogues, do not be anxious about how or what you are to say; ¹² for the holy Spirit will teach you in that . . hour what you are to say.

Q 12:11-12 = Matt. 10:19

Storing up Treasures in Heaven

³³ Do not treasure for yourselves treasures on earth, where moth and gnawing deface and where robbers dig through and rob, but treasure for yourselves treasures in heaven, where neither moth nor gnawing defaces and where robbers do not dig through nor rob. ³⁴ For where your treasure is, there will also be your heart.

Q 12:33-34 = Matt. 6:19-21; cf. Thomas 76.3

Free from Anxiety like Ravens and Lilies

²²ᵇ Therefore I tell you, do not be anxious about your life, what you are to eat, nor about your body, with what you are to clothe yourself. ²³ Is not life more than food, and the body than clothing? ²⁴ Consider the ravens: They neither sow nor reap nor gather into barns, and yet God feeds them. Are you not better than the birds? ²⁵ And who of you by being anxious is able to add to one's stature a . . cubit? ²⁶ And why are you anxious about clothing? ²⁷ Observe the lilies, how they grow: They do not work nor do they spin. Yet I tell you: Not even Solomon in all his glory was arrayed like one of these. ²⁸ But if in the field the grass, there today and tomorrow thrown into the over, God clothes thus, will he not much more clothe you, persons of petty faith! ²⁹ So do not be anxious, saying: What are we to eat? Or: What are we to drink? Or: What are we to wear? ³⁰ For all these the Gentiles seek; for your Father knows that you need them all. ³¹ But seek his kingdom, and all these shall be granted to you.

Q 12:22b-31 = Matt. 6:25-33; cf. Thomas 36.1, 4, 2-3

The Son of Humanity Comes as a Robber

³⁹ But know this: If the householder had known in which watch the robber was coming, he would not have let his house be dug into. ⁴⁰ You also must be ready, for the Son of Humanity is coming at an hour you do not expect.

Q 12:39-40 = Matt. 24:42-44; cf. Thomas 21.5; 103

The Faithful or Unfaithful Slave

⁴² Who then is the faithful and wise slave whom the master put over his household to give them food on time? ⁴³ Blessed is that slave whose master, on coming, will find so doing. ⁴⁴ Amen, I tell you, he will appoint him over all his possessions. ⁴⁵ But if that slave says in his heart: My master is delayed, and begins to

beat his fellow slaves, and eats and drinks with the drunkards, [46] the master of that slave will come on a day he does not expect and at an hour he does not know, and will cut him to pieces and give him an inheritance with the faithless.

Q 12:42-46 = Matt. 24:45-51

Children against Parents

[49] Fire have I come to hurl on the earth, and how I wish it had already blazed up! [51] Do you think that I have come to hurl peace on earth? I did not come to hurl peace, but a sword! [53] For I have come to divide son against father, and daughter against her mother, and daughter-in-law against her mother-in-law.

Q 12:49, 51, 53 = Matt. 10:34-35; cf. *Thomas* 10, 16.1-2, 3b

Judging the Time

[54] But he said to them: When evening has come, you say: Good weather! For the sky is flame red. [55] And at dawn: Today it's wintry! For the lowering sky is flame red. [56] The face of the sky you know to interpret, but the time you are not able to?

Q 12:54-56 = Matt. 16:2-3; cf. *Thomas* 91.2

Settling out of Court

[58] While you go along with your opponent on the way, make an effort to get loose from him, lest the opponent hand you over to the judge, and the judge to the assistant, and the (assistant) throw you into prison. [59] I say to you: You will not get out of there until you pay the last penny!

Q 12:58-59 = Matt. 5:25-26

The Mustard Seed

[18] What is the kingdom of God like, and with what am I to compare it? [19] It is like a seed of mustard, which a person took and threw into his garden. And it grew and developed into a tree, and the birds of the sky nested in its branches.

Q 13:18-19 = Matt. 13:31-32; cf *Thomas* 20

The Yeast

[20] And again: With what am I to compare the kingdom of God? [21] It is like yeast, which a woman took and hid in three measures of flour until it was fully fermented.

Q 13:20-21 = Matt. 13:33; cf. *Thomas* 96.1-2

I Do Not Know You

[24] Enter through the narrow door, for many will seek to enter and few are those who (enter through) it. [25] When the householder has arisen and locked the door, and you begin to stand outside and knock on the door, saying: Master, open for us, and he will answer you: I do not know you, [26] then you will begin saying: We ate in your presence and drank, and it was in our streets you taught. [27] And he will say to you: I do not know you! Get away from me, you who do lawlessness!

Q 13:24-27 = Matt. 7:13-14; 25:10-12; 7:22-23

Many Shall Come from Sunrise and Sunset

[29] And many shall come from Sunrise and Sunset and recline [28] with Abraham and Isaac and Jacob in the kingdom of God, but you will be thrown out into the outer darkness, where there will be wailing and grinding of teeth.

Q 13:29, 28 = Matt. 8:11-12

The Reversal of the Last and First

³⁰ . . The last will be first, and the first last.

Q 13:30 = Matt. 20:16; cf. *Thomas* 4.2

Judgment over Jerusalem

³⁴ O Jerusalem, Jerusalem, who kills the prophets and stones those sent to her! How often I wanted to gather your children together, as a hen gathers her nestlings under her wings, and you were not willing! ³⁵ Look, your house is forsaken! . . I tell you: You will not see me until (the time) comes when you say: Blessed is the one who comes in the name of the Lord!

Q 13:34-35 = Matt. 23:37-39

The Exalted Humbled and the Humble Exalted

¹¹ Everyone exalting oneself will be humbled, and the one humbling oneself will be exalted.

Q 14:11 = Matt. 23:12

The Invited Dinner Guests

¹⁶ A certain person prepared a large dinner, and invited many. ¹⁷ And he sent his slave at the time of the dinner to say to the invited: Come, for it is now ready. ¹⁸ (One declined because of his) farm. ¹⁹ (Another declined because of his business.) ²⁰ . . ²¹ (And the slave, on coming, said) these things to his master. Then the householder, enraged, said to his slave: ²³ Go out on the roads, and whomever you find, invite, so that my house may be filled.

Q 14:16-18, 19-20?, 21, 23 = Matt. 22:2-5, 6?, 7-10; cf. *Thomas* 64

Hating One's Family

²⁶ (The one who) does not hate father and mother (can)not (be) my (disciple); and (the one who does not hate) son and daughter cannot be my disciple.

Q 14:26 = Matt. 10:37; cf. *Thomas* 55; 101.1-2

Taking One's Cross

²⁷ . . The one who does not take one's cross and follow after me cannot be my disciple.

Q 14:27 = Matt. 10:38; cf. *Thomas* 55.2

Finding or Losing One's Life

³³ The one who finds one's life will lose it, and the one who loses one's life for my sake will find it.

Q 17:33 = Matt. 10:39

Insipid Salt

³⁴ Salt is good; but if salt becomes insipid, with what will it be seasoned? ³⁵ Neither for the earth nor for the dunghills is it fit—it gets thrown out.

Q 14:34-35 = Matt. 5:13

God or Mammon

¹³ Nobody can serve two masters; for a person will either hate the one and love the other, or be devoted to the one and despise the other. You cannot serve God and Mammon.

Q 16:13 = Matt. 6:24; cf. *Thomas* 47.2

Since John the Kingdom of God

[16] . . The law and the prophets were until John. From then on the kingdom of God is violated and the violent plunder it.

Q 16:16 = Matt. 11:12-13

No Serif of the Law to Fall

[17] But it is easier for heaven and earth to pass away than for one iota or one serif of the law to fall.

Q 16:17 = Matt. 5:18; 24:35

Divorce Leading to Adultery

[18] Everyone who divorces his wife and marries another commits adultery, and the one who marries a divorcée commits adultery.

Q 16:18 = Matt. 5:32

Against Enticing Little Ones

[1] It is necessary for enticements to come, but woe to the one through whom they come! [2] It is better for him if a millstone is put around his neck and he is thrown into the sea, than that he should entice one of these little ones.

Q 17:1-2 = Matt. 18:7, 6

The Lost Sheep

[4] Which person is there among you who has a hundred sheep, on losing one of them, will not leave the ninety-nine in the mountains and go hunt for the lost one? [5a] And if it should happen that he finds it, [7] I say to you that he rejoices over it more than over the ninety-nine that did not go astray.

Q 15:4-5a, 7 = Matt. 18:12-13; cf. *Thomas* 107

The Lost Coin

[8] Or what woman who has ten coins, if she were to lose one coin, would not light a lamp and sweep the house and hunt until she finds? [9] And on finding she calls the friends and neighbors, saying: Rejoice with me, for I found the coin which I had lost. [10] Just so, I tell you, there is joy before the angels over one repenting sinner.

Q 15:8-10, not in Matthew

Forgiving a Sinning Brother Repeatedly

[3] If your brother sins against you, rebuke him; and if he repents, forgive him. [4] And if seven times a day he sins against you, also seven times shall you forgive him.

Q 17:3-4 = Matt. 18:15, 21

Faith like a Mustard Seed

[6] If you have faith like a mustard seed, you might say to this mulberry tree: Be uprooted and planted in the sea! And it would obey you.

Q 17:6 = Matt. 17:20b; cf. *Thomas* 48

The Kingdom of God within You

[20] But on being asked when the kingdom of God is coming, he answered them and said: The kingdom of God is not coming visibly. [21] Nor will one say: Look, here! or: There! For, look, the kingdom of God is within you!

Q 17:20-21 = Matt. 24:23; cf. *Thomas* 3.1-3; 113

The Son of Humanity like Lightning

²³ If they say to you: Look, he is in the wilderness, do not go out; look, he is indoors, do not follow. ²⁴ For as the lightning streaks out from Sunrise and flashes as far as Sunset, so will the Son of Humanity be on his day.

Q 17:23-24 = Matt. 24:26-27; cf. *Thomas* 3.1-2

Vultures around a Corpse

³⁷ Wherever the corpse, there the vultures will gather.

Q 17:37 = Matt. 24:28

As in the Days of Noah

²⁶ . . As it took place in the days of Noah, so will it be in the day of the Son of Humanity. ²⁷ For as in those days they were eating and drinking, marrying and giving in marriage, until the day Noah entered the ark and the flood came and took them all, ²⁸⁻²⁹ . . ³⁰ so will it also be on the day the Son of Humanity is revealed.

Q 17:26-27, 28-29, 30 = Matt. 24:37-39

One Taken, One Left

³⁴ I tell you: There will be two men in the field; one is taken and one is left. ³⁵ Two women will be grinding at the mill; one is taken and one is left.

Q 17:34-35 = Matt. 24:40-41; cf. *Thomas* 61.1

The Entrusted Money

¹² . . A certain person, on taking a trip, ¹³ called ten of his slaves and gave them ten minas and said to them: Do business until I come. ¹⁵ . . After a long time the master of those slaves comes and settles accounts with them. ¹⁶ And the first came saying: Master, your mina has produced ten more minas. ¹⁷ And he said to him: Well done, good slave, you have been faithful over a little, I will set you over much. ¹⁸ And the second came saying: Master, your mina has earned five minas. ¹⁹ He said to him: Well done, good slave, you have been faithful over a little, I will set you over much. ²⁰ And the other came saying: Master, ²¹ I knew you, that you are a hard person, reaping where you did not sow and gathering up from where you did not winnow; and, scared, I went and hid your (mina) in the ground. Here, you have what belongs to you. ²² He said to him: Wicked slave! You know that I reap where I have not sown, and gather up from where I have not winnowed? ²³ Then you had to invest my money with the money changers! And at my coming I would have received what belongs to me plus interest. ²⁴ So take from him the mina and give it to the one who has the ten minas. ²⁶ For to everyone who has will be given; but from the one who does not have, even what he has will be taken from him.

Q 19:12-13, 15-24, 26 = Matt. 25:14-15b, 19-29; cf. *Thomas* 41

You Will Judge the Twelve Tribes of Israel

²⁸ . . You who have followed me ³⁰ will sit . . on thrones judging the twelve tribes of Israel.

Q 22:28, 30 = Matt. 19:28

* * * * *

Further Reading

There is an extensive bibliography in other languages, especially German, which is omitted here, and only a small selection of English literature is included. For a complete bibliography one may consult F. Neirynck, J. Verheyden, and R. Corstjens, *The Gospel of Matthew and the Gospel Source Q: A Cumulative Bibliography 1950-1995* (2 vols., BETL 140; Leuven: Leuven University Press and Peeters, 1998); or David M. Scholer, *Q Bibliography, Twentieth Century* (Documenta Q: Supplementum; Leuven: Peeters, 2001).

For the text of Q in Greek and English, and in the context of a synopsis of the Gospels, see James M. Robinson, Paul Hoffmann, and John S. Kloppenborg, general editors, Milton C. Moreland, managing editor, *The Critical Edition of Q: Synopsis, including the Gospels of Matthew and Luke, Mark and Thomas, with English, German, and French Translations of Q and Thomas* (Minneapolis: Fortress Press; and Leuven: Peeters, 2000), and in shortened form in *The Sayings Gospel Q in Greek and English with Parallels from the Gospels of Mark and Thomas.* Leuven: Peeters, 2001; and Minneapolis: Fortress Press, 2002.

Kloppenborg, John S. 1987. *The Formation of Q: Trajectories in Ancient Wisdom Collections.* Studies in Antiquity and Christianity. Philadelphia: Fortress Press. (Reprint: Harrisburg, Penn.: Trinity Press International, 2000.)

———. 1988. *Q Parallels: Synopsis, Critical Notes, and Concordance.* Foundations and Facets: New Testament. Sonoma, Calif.: Polebridge.

———, ed. 1994. *The Shape of Q: Signal Essays on the Sayings Gospel.* Minneapolis: Fortress Press.

———, ed. 1995. *Conflict and Invention: Literary, Rhetorical, and Social Studies on the Sayings Gospel Q.* Valley Forge, Penn.: Trinity Press International.

Kloppenborg Verbin, John S. 2000. *Excavating Q: The History and Setting of the Sayings Gospel.* Minneapolis: Fortress Press; and Edinburgh: T & T Clark.

Lindemann, Andreas, ed. 2001. *The Sayings Source Q and the Historical Jesus.* Bibiotheca ephemeridum theologicarum lovaniensium 158. Leuven: Leuven University Press and Peeters.

Piper, Ronald A., ed. 1995. *The Gospel behind the Gospels: Current Studies on Q.* Supplements to Novum Testamentum 75. Leiden: Brill.

Robinson, James M., *The Sayings Gospel Q: Collected Essays.* Christoph Heil and Joseph Verheyden, eds. Bibliotheca Ephemeridum Theologicarum Lovaniensium 189. Leuven: University Press; and Leuven and Dudley, Mass.: Uitgeverij Peeters, 2005.

Robinson, James M. and Helmut Koester. 1971, paperback 1979. *Trajectories through Early Christianity.* Philadelphia: Fortress Press. Reprint Eugene, Oregon: Wipf & Stock, 2006.

Theissen, Gerd. 1992, 1993. *Social Reality and the Early Christians: Theology, Ethics, and the World of the New Testament.* Translated by Margaret Kohl. Minneapolis: Fortress Press; and Edinburgh: T. & T. Clark.

Tuckett, Christopher M. 1996. *Q and the History of Early Christianity: Studies on Q.* Edinburgh: T. & T. Clark; and Peabody, Mass.: Hendrickson.

Uro, Risto, ed. 1996. *Symbols and Strata: Essays on the Sayings Gospel Q.* Suomen Eksegeettisen Seuran Julkaisuja. Publications of the Finnish Exegetical Society 65; Helsinki: Finnish Exegetical Society; and Göttingen: Vandenhoeck & Ruprecht.

INDEX OF AUTHORS